BEHAVIORAL SCIENCE
and the
MANAGER'S ROLE

Second Edition,
Revised and Enlarged

Edited by

William B. Eddy
W. Warner Burke

University Associates
8517 Production Avenue
San Diego, California 92121

Contents

Preface

Ten years ago, along with our colleagues Vladimir Dupre and Oron South, we compiled a group of our favorite articles on management and published them as the first edition of this book. We believed that there was a need for a collection of both standard and "leading edge" readings in applied behavioral science—readings addressed to practicing managers and management aspirants, particularly those involved in educational and training programs. In reading the preface to that earlier edition today, we are struck with the sense of newness we attached to the application of behavioral science in management. We knew the idea of the book made sense to us as behavioral scientists, but we were not sure whether it would appeal to managers. The success of the book, which paralleled the growth of the field, demonstrated managers' interest in keeping abreast of new thrusts.

The earlier edition is now outdated. For that reason, we have again attempted to select a group of representative, significant, and readable articles directed at various aspects of behavioral science and management. Although we are both intimately involved in the academic and applied sides of management, we were taken by surprise as we surveyed the significant advances that have taken place in a decade. The field has gained momentum, the amount of research has increased, and organizations have shown their continued interest by increasing their commitment to training and development programs, especially those that emphasize applied behavioral science. On the basis of the manuscripts we selected, as well as the larger number of equally deserving articles we were not able to use, we conclude that our earlier predictions about the potential contribution of behavioral science were well founded.

In 1969, organization development (OD) was a new and promising field but had been tried in relatively few organizations. Now OD is widely accepted, widely researched, and has been structurally built into many organizations. In 1969, the new wave of studies on adult learning and adult education had not significantly affected management development, except in a few isolated situations. We now find it a significant enough development to warrant inclusion as the first section in the revised edition—along with another new thrust: the field of career development. The list of new topics can hardly be recounted without listing each one of the new articles that encompass 70 percent of the material in the book. Some of the highlights include McClelland's important work on power, an analysis of managerial stress, more comprehensive views of leadership, and the expectancy theory of employee motivation.

We have retained about one third of the original readings—mostly material that was then or has now become "classic," if such a label is legitimate in this embryonic field. We felt that new readers should have the opportunity to read, for example, Carl Rogers' thoughts about personal growth, Douglas McGregor's original statements of the Theory X versus Theory Y dilemma, and Sheldon Davis' account of the pioneering OD program in TRW Systems.

In considering the chapters of this revised edition, we come to the inescapable conclusion that although knowledge in the behavioral sciences is accumulating at a geometric rate and we are learning more and more about the nature of the human being, this additional knowledge has led to greater complexity, not to simplicity. Human behavior is not simple, managers' roles are not simple, group processes and organizational dynamics are not simple. All are composed of a myriad of multiple causes and interacting variables. Thus the reader will find no simple formulas for success. There are, however, some interesting and challenging ideas, some findings that go considerably beyond common sense and folklore, and some frameworks for analyzing managerial situations to make them more understandable.

We are pleased to give the major credit for this book to the authors of the original articles and are grateful for their permission and that of their publishers to reprint the material. Also, we are grateful for the suggestions of our colleagues—those with whom we have been associated over the years in the NTL Institute of Applied Behavioral Science and those newer ones, at least for us, with University Associates.

We want to express our appreciation to Jane Gallagher, who helped considerably with the literature search while she was an MBA student at Clark University, and to Louise Janhunen and Sibyl Storm who assisted us administratively and with the inevitable typing job.

William B. Eddy
W. Warner Burke

Part 1. The Manager as Learner

There may have been a time in less dynamic days when intentional learning was something managers could afford to leave to chance. After their formal schooling and the orientation programs they experienced early in their careers, training and education were not a priority for most managers. But today, a manager who is not actively engaged in his or her own development runs the risk of falling behind. Because organizational and societal changes are occurring at an increasingly rapid rate, new information and new techniques quickly replace the old. This means that the knowledge required for effective performance in complex organizations becomes outdated and new skills are needed to solve new problems. Learning—or development, renewal, human growth, upgrading—is a necessary part of the managerial experience.

The rising popularity of the fields of management development and organizational development testifies to the recognition by most organizations of the need to provide ongoing learning opportunities and techniques for the planning of change.

A relatively new development is the focus on the *process* of adult learning and development. Knowles (1970) drew educators' attention to the very different considerations that exist when one moves from traditional school classrooms to the adult-development setting. For example, adults bring more information with them into the learning situation, are able to take more responsibility for their own learning, and are more committed to applying what they learn for immediate impact. The articles in this section are examples of the new focus on managerial learning. They are intended to help the manager to understand more about learning and to begin diagnosing his or her own learning needs. A strong case can be made for the notion that the best place to begin a program of learning and development is with the self.

The first article in part 1, Kolb's "Management and the Learning Process," reports the results of several years of research in the field of management education. A four-stage learning model emphasizes the important part that experience plays in organizational learning. It also demonstrates the role played in the ongoing learning process by such contrasting modes of learning as concreteness versus abstraction and active involvement versus reflective observation. These modes, taken together, describe the cycle of effective learning and problem solving.

Kolb moves from his descriptive learning model to an analysis of different learning styles. For a variety of reasons, most of us utilize some phases of the learning process more than we do others. These different learning orientations have allowed Kolb to categorize managers according to their distinct styles of learning. Each style carries with it attendant interests, problem-solving approaches, and ways of dealing with people. When a manager's learning style is not in harmony with the styles of colleagues, then conflict or enrichment are potential outcomes, depending on how the differences are handled.

The fact that styles of learning differ from one individual to another has significant implications for management-education programs. In order to integrate scholarly and practical learning, a program must be designed to deal with differences in learning style. The experiential learning model can be used to help managers to learn how to learn and to take into account their own strengths and weaknesses as learners.

Kolb's article concludes with a challenging discussion of the organization as a learning system. Organizations do learn, and different organizational subsystems may develop distinctive learning styles. Compatibility among the subsystems of an organization can be examined by using the learning-styles model. The establishment of explicit learning goals marks the beginning of management of the learning processes within the system.

In the second article, "The Process of Building an Agenda for Adult Learning," Frank P. Sherwood continues the discussion of goal setting as it applies to one aspect of adult learning—career development. As managers' careers evolve, they pass through a succession of roles—each demanding somewhat different competencies. As an individual moves up the organization hierarchy, the requirements at each level from individual worker to executive are somewhat predictable. Sherwood presents a model to help the reader assess his or her progress in developing the competencies required.

Role theory is a useful approach to career planning. Each time we move into a new role, a different set of behaviors is expected by the social system around us (company or agency, family, church, etc.). Our understanding of these expected behaviors, our ease in moving from one role to another, and the competencies we acquire to perform the role are important. Career development challenges the manager to predict what the requirements of future roles are likely to be.

Thinking into the future is such a difficult assignment that many people are skeptical about predictions. Yet some degree of anticipation of future directions is necessary if career planning is to take place. One way of avoiding the pitfalls of prediction involves the identification of competencies associated with the roles an individual is most likely to acquire. These competencies are then compared with the individual's present strengths and an agenda of necessary learnings can be developed.

In the last article in part 1, "Distortions of Behavioral Science," James V. Clark sounds a note of caution to those who would apply behavioral science to management. Managers participating in educational and training programs may evaluate behavioral scientists' ideas as unrealistic or, conversely, may accept tentative or limited findings too quickly. The findings and methods of the applied social sciences are frequently distorted and misunderstood. For example, there is good evidence that there are nonlogical aspects to human behavior. However, it is a distortion of these findings to assert that they only apply to therapy groups or sensitivity training. It is also a distortion to believe that the nonlogical, emotional side of people is more important than the logical, rational side.

Clark traces one cause of these distortions to the fact that, historically, behavioral scientists and managers have focused on different aspects of human behavior. Scientists have, in Clark's view, tended to study those aspects of behavior that emphasize stability and reaction, while managers have emphasized change and proactivity. Since Clark's article first appeared in 1963, some behavioral scientists have shifted their interest toward processes of growth and change. However, there is still a problem in communication between the two groups. Each is influenced by its own value system when it perceives the activities of the other. Clark challenges both managers and behavioral scientists to examine their motives as well as their perceptions.

It is hoped that the articles in this section will stimulate the reader to think about his or her development as a manager and to begin to assemble a learning plan. Some of the necessary characteristics of such a plan should be evident. It should be based on clear self-understanding, be consonant with one's style of learning, include a realistic appraisal of the requirements of present and future roles, and avoid simplistic or superficial concepts. The articles in part 2 discuss some of the significant substantive ideas that may form the content of a learning program.

Reference

1. Knowles, M. S. *The modern practice of education: Andragogy versus pedagogy.* New York: Association Press, 1970.

1

Management and the Learning Process

by David A. Kolb

Today's highly successful manager or administrator is distinguished not so much by any single set of knowledge or skills but by his ability to adapt to and master the changing demands of his job and career—by his ability to learn. The same is true for successful organizations. Continuing success in a changing world requires an ability to explore new opportunities and learn from past successes and failures. These ideas are neither new nor particularly controversial. Yet it is surprising that this ability to learn, which is so widely regarded as important, receives so little explicit attention from managers and their organizations. There is a kind of fatalism about learning. One either learns or he doesn't. The ability to consciously control and manage the learning process is usually limited to such schoolboy maxims as "Study hard" and "Do your homework."

Part of the reason for this fatalism lies, I believe, in a lack of understanding about the learning process itself. If managers and administrators had a model about how individuals and organizations learn, they would better be able to enhance their own and their organizations' ability to learn. This article describes such a model and attempts to show some of the ways in which the learning process and individual learning styles affect management education, managerial decision making and problem solving, and organizational learning.

The Experiential Learning Model

Let us begin with a model of how people learn, which I call the experiential learning model. The model is labeled "experiential" for two reasons.

David A. Kolb is professor, Department of Organizational Behavior, School of Management, Case-Western Reserve University.

©1976 by the Regents of the University of California. Extracted from *California Management Review*, vol. XVIII, no. 3, pp. 21 to 31 by permission of the Regents.

The first is historical, tying it to its intellectual origins in the social psychology of Kurt Lewin in the 1940s and the sensitivity training and laboratory education work of the 1950s and 1960s. The second reason is to emphasize the important role that experience plays in the learning process, an emphasis that differentiates this approach from other cognitive theories of the learning process. The core of the model is a simple description of the learning cycle—how experience is translated into concepts, which in turn are used as guides in the choice of new experiences (Figure 1).

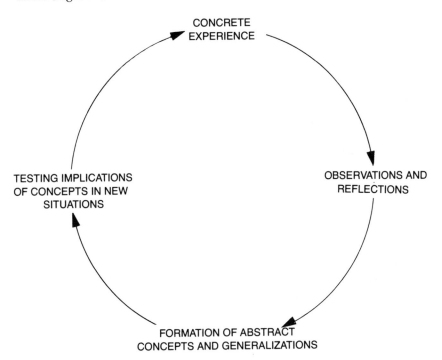

Figure 1. The experiential learning model

Learning is conceived of as a four-stage cycle. Immediate concrete experience is the basis for observation and reflection. These observations are assimilated into a theory from which new implications for action can be deduced. These implications or hypotheses then serve as guides in acting to create new experiences. The learner, if he is to be effective, needs four different kinds of abilities—*concrete experience* (CE), *reflective observation* (RO), *abstract conceptualization* (AC), and *active experimentation* (AE). That is, he must be able to involve himself fully, openly, and without bias in new experiences (CE); he must be able to reflect on and observe these experiences from many perspectives (RO); he must be able to create concepts that integrate his observations into logically sound theories (AC); and he must be able to use these theories to make decisions and solve problems (AE).

Yet how difficult this ideal is to achieve! Can anyone become highly skilled in all of these abilities, or are they necessarily in conflict? How can one act and reflect at the same time? How can one be concrete and immediate and still be theoretical? Indeed, a closer examination of the four-stage learning model reveals that learning requires abilities that are polar opposites and that the learner, as a result, must continually choose which set of learning abilities he will bring to bear in any specific learning situation.

More specifically, there are two primary dimensions to the learning process. The first dimension represents the concrete experiencing of events at one end and abstract conceptualization at the other. The other dimension has active experimentation at one extreme and reflective observation at the other. Thus, in the process of learning one moves in varying degrees from actor to observer, from specific involvement to general analytic detachment.

Most cognitive psychologists see the concrete/abstract dimension as a primary dimension on which cognitive growth and learning occurs.[1-4] Goldstein and Scheerer suggest that greater abstractness results in the development of the following abilities: to detach our ego from the outer world or from inner experience; to assume a mental set; to account for acts to oneself, to verbalize the account; to shift reflectively from one aspect of the situation to another; to hold in mind simultaneously various aspects; to grasp the essential of a given whole—to break up a given into parts to isolate and synthesize them; to abstract common properties reflectively, to form hierarchic concepts; to plan ahead ideationally, to assume an attitude toward the more possible, and to think or perform symbolically.[5] Concreteness, on the other hand, represents the absence of these abilities, the immersion in and domination by one's immediate experiences.

Yet as the circular model of the learning process would imply, abstractness is not exclusively good and concreteness exclusively bad. To be creative requires that one be able to experience anew, freed somewhat from the constraints of previous abstract concepts. In psychoanalytic theory this need for a concrete, childlike perspective in the creative process is referred to as regression in service of the ego.[6] In his essay on the conditions for creativity, Bruner further emphasizes the dialectic tension between abstract detachment and concrete involvement.[2] For him the creative act is a product of detachment and commitment, of passion and decorum, and of a freedom to be dominated by the object of one's inquiry.

The active/reflective dimension is the other major dimension of cognitive growth and learning. As growth occurs, thought becomes more reflective and internalized, based more on the manipulation of symbols and images than covert actions. The modes of active experimentation and reflection, like abstractness/concreteness, stand in opposition to one another. Reflection tends to inhibit action and vice versa. For example, Singer has found that children who have active internal fantasy lives are more capable of inhibiting action for long periods of time than are children with little internal fantasy life.[7] Kagan has found, on the other hand, that very active orientations toward learning situations inhibit reflection and thereby preclude the development of analytic concepts.[8] Herein lies the second major dialectic in the learning process — the tension between actively testing the implications of one's hypothesis and reflectively interpreting data already collected.

Individual Learning Styles

As a result of our hereditary equipment, our particular past life experience, and the demands of our present environment most people develop learning styles that emphasize some learning abilities over others. We come to resolve the conflicts between being alive and reflective and between being immediate and analytical in characteristic ways. Some people develop minds that excel at assimilating disparate facts into coherent theories, yet these same people are incapable of or uninterested in deducing hypotheses from their theories. Others are logical geniuses but find it impossible to involve and surrender themselves to an experience, and so on. A mathematician may come to place great emphasis on abstract concepts, while a poet may value concrete experience more highly. A manager may be primarily concerned with the active application of ideas, while a naturalist may develop his observational skills highly. Each of us in a unique way develops a learning style that has some weak and some strong points.

For some time now I have been involved in a program of research studies aimed at identifying different kinds of learning styles and their consequences. The purpose of this research is to better understand the different ways that people learn and solve problems so that we can both make individuals aware of the consequences of their own learning style and of the alternative learning modes available to them, and improve the design of learning experiences to take into account these learning-style differences. In this work we have developed a simple self-description inventory, the Learning Style Inventory (LSI), which is designed to measure an individual's strengths and weaknesses as a learner. The LSI measures an individual's relative emphasis on the four learning abilities described earlier, concrete experience (CE), reflective observation (RO), abstract conceptualization (AC) and active experimentation (AE) by asking him, several different times, to rank in order four words that describe these different abilities. For example, one set of four words is "feeling" (CE), "watching" (RO), "thinking" (AC), and "doing" (AE). The inventory yields six scores, CE, RO, AC, and AE plus two combination scores that indicate the extent to which the individual emphasizes abstractness over concreteness (AC-CE) and active experimentation over reflection (AE-RO).

The LSI was administered to 800 practicing managers and graduate students in management to obtain a norm for the management population. In general these managers tended to emphasize active experimentation over reflective observation. In addition, managers with graduate degrees tended to rate their abstract learning skills higher.[9,10] While the managers we tested showed many different patterns of scores on the LSI, we have identified four dominant types of learning styles that occur most frequently. We have called these four styles the converger, the diverger, assimilator, and accommodator. (The reason that there are four dominant styles is that AC and CE are highly negatively correlated as are RO and AE. Thus individuals who score highly on both AC and CE or on both AE and RO occur with less frequency than do the other four combinations of LSI scores.)

The converger's dominant learning abilities are AC and AE. His greatest strength lies in the practical application of ideas. We have called this learning style the converger because a person with this style seems to do best in situations such as conventional intelligence tests, where there is a single correct answer or solution to a question or problem.[11] His knowledge is organized in such a way that, through hypothetical-deductive reasoning, he can focus it on specific problems. Hudson's research on this style of learning shows that convergers are relatively unemotional, preferring to deal with things rather than people.[12] They tend to have narrow technical interests and choose to specialize in the physical sciences. Our research shows that this learning style is characterisic of many engineers.

The diverger has the opposite learning strengths of the converger. He is best at CE and RO. His greatest strength lies in his imaginative ability. He excels in the ability to view concrete situations from many perspectives. We have labeled this style diverger because a person with this style performs better in situations that call for generation of ideas such as a "brainstorming" session. Hudson's work on this learning style shows that divergers are interested in people and tend to be imaginative and emotional.[12] They have broad cultural interests and tend to specialize in the arts. Our research shows that this style is characteristic of managers from humanities and liberal arts backgrounds. Personnel managers tend to be characterized by this learning style.

The assimilator's dominant learning abilities are AC and RO. His greatest strength lies in his ability to create theoretical models. He excels in inductive reasoning—in assimilating disparate observations into an integrated explanation. He, like the converger, is less interested in people and more concerned for abstract concepts, but he is less concerned with the practical use of theories. For him it is more important that the theory be logically sound and precise. As a result, this learning style is more characteristic of the basic sciences rather than the applied sciences. In organizations this learning style is found most often in the research and planning departments.

The accommodator has the opposite learning strengths of the assimilator. He is best at CE and AE. His greatest strength lies in doing things, in carrying out plans and experiments and involving himself in new experiences. He tends to be more of a risk taker than people with the other three learning styles. We have labeled this style accommodator because he tends to excel in situations where he must adapt himself to specific immediate circumstances. In situations where the theory or plans do not fit the facts, he will most likely discard the plan or theory. (His opposite style type, the assimilator, would be more likely to disregard or reexamine the facts.) The accommodator is at ease with people but is sometimes seen as impatient and "pushy." His educational background is often in technical or practical fields such as business. In organizations people with this learning style are found in action-oriented jobs, often in marketing or sales . . .

Learning Styles and Management Education

Differences in learning style create similar problems for management education. The manager who comes to the university for mid-career education experiences something of a culture shock. Fresh from a world of time deadlines and concrete, specific problems that he must solve, he is suddenly immersed in a strange, slow-paced world of generalities where the elegant solution to problems is sought even when workable solutions have been found. One gets rewarded here for reflection and analysis rather than concrete, goal-directed action. The manager who "acts before he thinks—if he ever thinks" meets the scientist who "thinks before he acts—if he ever acts."

Our research on learning styles has shown that managers on the whole are distinguished by very strong active experimentation skills and are very weak on reflective observation skills. Business school faculty members usually have the reverse profile. To bridge this gap in learning styles the management educator must somehow respond to pragmatic demands for relevance and the application of knowledge while encouraging the reflective examination of experience that is necessary to refine old theories and to build new ones. In encouraging reflective observation the teacher often is seen as an interrupter of action—as a passive, "ivory tower" thinker. Indeed, this is a critical role to be played in the learning process. Yet if the reflective observer role is not internalized by the students themselves, the learning process can degenerate into a value conflict between teacher and student, each maintaining that his is the right perspective for learning.

Neither the faculty nor student perspective alone is valid, in my view. Managerial education will not be improved by eliminating theoretical analysis or relevant case problems. Improvement will come through *integration of the scholarly and practical learning styles*. My approach to achieving this integration has been to apply directly the experiential learning model in the classroom.[10] To do this we created a workbook providing games, role plays, and exercises (concrete experiences) that focus on fifteen central concepts in organizational psychology. These simulations provide a common experiential starting point for managers and faculty to explore the relevance of psychological concepts for their work. In traditional management education methods the conflict between scholar and practitioner learning styles is exaggerated because the material to be taught is filtered through the learning style of the faculty member in his lectures or his presentation and analysis of cases. The student is "one down" in his own analysis because his data are second-hand and already biased.

In the experiential learning approach this filtering process does not take place because both teacher and student are observers of immediate experiences, which they both interpret according to their own learning styles. In this approach the teacher's role is that of a facilitator of a learning process that is basically self-directed. He helps students to experience in a personal and immediate way the phenomena in his field of specialization. He provides observational schemes and perspectives from which to observe these experiences. He stands ready with alternative theories and concepts as the student attempts to assimilate his observations into his own conception of reality. He assists in deducing the implications of the student's concepts and in designing new experiments to test the implications through practical, "real world" experience.

There are two goals in the experiential learning process. One is to learn the specifics of a particular subject. The other goal is to learn about one's own strengths and weaknesses as a learner—learning how to learn from experience. When the process works well, managers finish their educational experience not only with new intellectual insights, but also with an understanding of their own learning style. This understanding of learning strengths and weaknesses helps in the application of what has been learned and provides a framework for continuing learning on the job. Day-to-day experience becomes a focus for testing and exploring new ideas. Learning is no longer a special activity reserved for the classroom; it becomes an integral and explicit part of work itself.

Learning Styles and Managerial Problem Solving

We have been able to identify relationships between a manager's learning style and his educational experiences, but how about his current behavior on the job? Do managers with different learning styles approach problem solving and decision making differently? Theoretically, the answer to this question should be yes, since learning and problem solving are not different processes but the same basic process of adaptation viewed from different perspectives. To illustrate this point I have overlaid in Figure 2 a typical model of the problem-solving process on the experiential learning model.[13] In this figure we can see that the stages in a problem-solving sequence generally correspond to the learning-style strengths of the four major learning styles described previously. The accommodator's problem-solving strengths lie in executing solutions and initiating problem finding based on some goal or model about how things should be. The diverger's problem-solving strengths lie in identifying the multitude of possible problems and opportunities that exist in reality ("compare model with reality and identify differences"). The assimilator excels in the abstract model building that is necessary to choose a priority problem and alternative solutions. The converger's strengths lie in the evaluation of solution consequences and solution selection. . . .

The Organization as a Learning System

Like individuals, organizations learn and develop distinctive learning styles. They do so through their transactions with the environment and through their choice of how to relate to that environment. This has come to be known as the "open systems" view of organizations. Since many organizations are large and complex, the environment they relate to becomes highly differentiated and diverse. The way the organization adapts to this external environment is to differentiate itself into units, each of which deals with just one part of the firm's external conditions. Marketing and sales face problems associated with the market, customers, and competitors. Research deals with the academic and technological worlds. Production deals with production equipment and raw materials sources. Personnel and labor relations deal with the labor market, and so on.

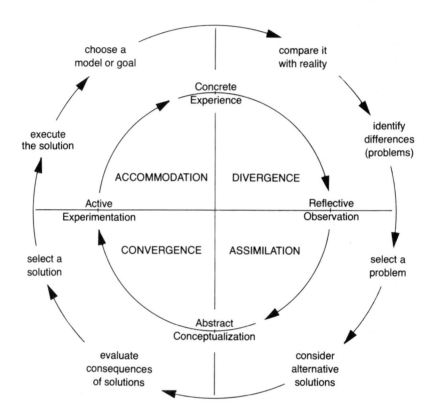

Figure 2. Comparison of the experiential learning model with a typical model of the problem-solving process (after Pounds 1965)

Because of this need to relate to different aspects of the environment, the different units of the firm develop characteristic ways of thinking and working together, different styles of decision making and problem solving. These units select and shape managers to solve problems and make decisions in the way their environment demands. In fact, Lawrence and Lorsch define organizational differentiation as "the difference in cognitive and emotional orientation among managers in different functional departments."[14]

If the organization is thought of as a learning system, then each of the differentiated units that is charged with adapting to the challenges of one segment of the environment can be thought of as having a characteristic learning style that is best suited to meet those environmental demands. . . .

Managing the Learning Process

To conclude, let us return to the problem we began with—how managers and organizations can explicitly manage their learning process. We have seen that the experiential learning model is useful not only for examining the educational process but also for understanding managerial problem solving and organizational adaptation. But how can an awareness of the experiential learning model and our own individual learning style help improve individual and organizational learning? Two recommendations seem important.

First, learning should be an explicit objective that is pursued as consciously and deliberately as profit or productivity. Managers and organizations should budget time to specifically learn from their experiences. When important meetings are held or important decisions made, time should be set aside to critique and learn from these events. In my experience all too few organizations have a climate that allows for free exploration of such questions as, What have we learned from this venture? Usually active experimentation norms dictate—We don't have time; let's move on.

Which leads to the second recommendation. The nature of the learning process is such that opposing perspectives, action and reflection, concrete involvement and analytical detachment, are all essential for optimal learning. When one perspective comes to dominate others, learning effectiveness is reduced in the long run. From this we can conclude that the most effective learning systems are those that can tolerate differences in perspective.

This point can be illustrated by the case of an electronics firm that I have worked with over the years. The firm was started by a group of engineers with a unique product. For several years they had no competitors and when some competition entered the market they continued to dominate and do well because of their superior engineering quality. Today is a different story. They are now faced with stiff competition in their original product area. In addition, their very success has caused new problems. They are no longer a small, intimate company but a large organization with several plants in the U.S. and Europe. The company has had great difficulty in responding to these changes because it still responds to problems primarily from an engineering point of view. Most of the top executives in the company are former engineers with no formal management training. Many of the specialists in marketing, finance, and personnel who have been brought in to help the organization solve its new problems feel like second-class citizens. Their ideas just don't seem to carry much weight. What was once the organization's strength—its engineering expertise—has become to some extent its weakness. Because engineering has flourished at the expense of the development of other organizational functions, such as marketing and the management of human resources, the firm is today struggling with rather than mastering its environment.

References

1. John Flavell, *The Developmental Psychology of Jean Piaget* (New York: Van Nostrand Reinhold Co., 1963).

2. J. S. Bruner, *Essays for the Left Hand* (New York: Atheneum, 1966).

3. J. S. Bruner, *The Process of Education* (New York: Vintage Books, 1960).

4. O. J. Harvey, David Hunt and Harold Schroder, *Conceptual Systems and Personality Organization* (New York: John Wiley, 1961).

5. K. Goldstein and M. Scheerer, "Abstract and Concrete Behavior: An Experimental Study with Special Tests," *Psychological Monographs* (1941), p. 4.

6. Ernst Kris, *Psychoanalytic Explorations in Art*, (New York: International Universities Press, 1952).

7. J. Singer, "The Importance of Daydreaming," *Psychology Today* (1968), pp. 18-26.

8. Jerome Kagan, Bernice L. Rosman, Deborah Day, Joseph Alpert, and William Phillips, "Information Processing in the Child: Significance of Analytic and Reflective Attitudes," *Psychological Monographs* (1964).

9. David A. Kolb, "Individual Learning Styles and the Learning Process," MIT Sloan School Working Paper No. 535-71, 1971.

10. David Kolb, Irwin Rubin and James McIntyre, *Organizational Psychology: An Experiential Approach* (Englewood Cliffs, N.J.: Prentice-Hall, 1971).

11. David Torrealba, "Convergent and Divergent Learning Styles," MS thesis, MIT Sloan School, 1972.

12. L. Hudson, *Contrary Imaginations* (Middlesex, England: Penguin Books Ltd., 1966).

13. William Pounds, "On Problem Finding," Sloan School Working Paper No. 145-65, 1965.

14. Paul Lawrence and Jay Lorsch, *Organization and Environment* (Boston: Division of Research, Graduate School of Business Administration, 1967), p. 11.

The Process of Building an Agenda for Adult Learning

by Frank P. Sherwood

There is increasing recognition of the need to be proactive toward one's career and its development. Such awareness is undoubtedly a product of a mobile and highly changing society, and it also reflects a greater sophistication in thinking about work and its relationship to overall life satisfaction. We have become mindful that a great many of our most valuable hours are spent at the workplace and that rewards, both psychic and monetary, derive in major degree from such activity. Inevitably, the work role in which we participate must be a matter of great concern.

As individuals, we meet the expectations embodied in a role with varying degrees of success. Sometimes we are superbly suited for a role, in others not so well suited. Whether or not we are prepared for the obligations we have shouldered has a great deal to do with the rewards we ultimately experience. Individuals always match up with roles, and the trick is to contrive as good a fit as possible.

We can influence our prospects for success in substantial degree, and that comes largely from the care with which we have thought about our possibilities and then have gone systematically at the process of personal development. From the career standpoint, continuing learning is the principal vehicle by which we ready ourselves for change and new promises of rewards. This is an adult undertaking—we must take charge of our own learning. Toward that end, this essay advances a framework for developing an agenda for personal learning.

Frank P. Sherwood is professor, Federal Executive Institute, and professor of public administration, University of Southern California.

DEVELOPING A SENSE OF ROLE

An important part of the process of personal planning and goal setting in career development is the use of some targets or models as points of comparison. Ideally, we aspire to roles that are more consequential and more demanding than we presently occupy. But in what ways are these roles different? Do they require intrinsic competencies that diverge from the requirements of present roles? Do they simply demand greater competencies along the lines of current responsibility? Or is the mix and emphasis different?

The requirements placed on us by the roles we occupy may vary considerably as we move through life. For example, it has been commonly assumed that there is a *vital shift* as one moves from specialist-technical responsibilities in an organization to generalist-managerial ones. Henry Fayol (1916/1949), whose work on industrial management in France is a classic, argued strongly that the competencies required of the managerial leader are qualitatively different from those associated with lesser roles in the organizational hierarchy.

Corson and Paul (1962) advanced a somewhat different theory. they argued that as individuals move higher in an organization, instead of experiencing a vital shift, they are required to have a broader repertoire of competencies. At the very bottom, where individuals are accountable only for their own work, the competencies required are basically individual-technical. At the supervisory level, an ability to work with and influence others in face-to-face situations must be added to the individual-technical competencies. At the middle-management level, a new ingredient involves a mastery of all the institutional-impersonal processes and procedures that leaders must use in influencing organizations at the non-face-to-face level. And, finally, the executive must learn how to live both inside his organization and as a representative of it outside.

The essential point of the Corson and Paul notion of evolving competencies is that everything builds on everything else. A fully functioning executive is one who has not forgotten what he learned at the individual-specialist level; and clearly no one can forget about the need for interpersonal skills in working in all kinds of face-to-face situations, no matter what the level of responsibility may be.

In career planning, therefore, it is important to be insightful about one's past. Those who find the Corson and Paul concept of evolving competencies attractive should be particularly sensitive to four steps in a career:

1. Development as an individual worker;
2. Development as a supervisor;
3. Development as a middle manager;
4. Development as an executive.

It is possible to take a reading on one's present position in terms of these four stages. For example, a person who is now defined as a middle manager might ask two basic questions:

1. Did my previous life experience permit me full growth and development as an individual worker? As a supervisor?
2. In my present position am I securing (and seeking) the growth and development opportunities that will enable me to acquire the full range of competencies expected of a middle manager?

In making these kinds of assessments, it is necessary to think in terms of role. We do not normally think of an individual when we hear the word supervisor; instead, the word typically conjures a set of behaviors in which any number of people might engage. *Supervisor* conveys an image of *role*. To test understanding of the concept of role as a tool of career analysis, list the kinds of behaviors that attach to each of the roles in the Corson and Paul approach (see Figure 1): the individual worker, the supervisor, the middle manager, the executive. The degree of success you have in specifying the behaviors that attach to these four roles indicates the degree to which they have meaning and analytical significance.

THE PROCESS OF ROLE TAKING

Individuals, of course, take many roles, in terms of both time and space. At essentially the same time, the space in which an individual moves may include that person's roles as leader, family member, community participant, religious follower, and sports activist. Although we may have some choices concerning which roles we will play and the way in which they will be handled, the broad outlines of the roles are socially mandated. They are niches in space to which we are directed, either by chance or by design.

There is also a temporal dimension to role taking. At an early point in the life cycle, we assume the role of child in relation to the parent. At a later point in the cycle, a role reversal typically occurs, and we as parents contend with another child. The different ways in which the parent-child relationship is enacted show substantial possibilities for individualism in role taking; but it is dramatically apparent that roles and relationships are socially induced. How often do we express a new awareness of the problems of our fathers and mothers as we confront the role of parent? And is it not striking how often we re-enact the behaviors of parents in the rearing of our own children?

Our development as individuals is substantially shaped by our role-taking experience. Since the expectations directed toward a role may vary greatly from one situation to another, one child may have a totally different development experience from another. The way in which a role was structured and enacted has profound implications for personality development, and the amount, variety, and range of roles enacted contribute significantly to such growth. In a rural community, for example, there often are more opportunities to play a variety of roles than in the highly specialized milieu of the city. Consequently, some people may be comfortable but not highly skilled in the performance of a great many roles; others may demonstrate high skill in a limited number of roles and be acutely uncomfortable outside these accustomed areas.

Personal flexibility seems to be related to experiences in role taking, which is why mobility is such an important idea in leadership development. Not only do varied kinds of experience expand the repertoire of capabilities, but, more importantly, they build personal confidence. The environment is perceived less as an aggregation of threats and more as a web of opportunities. And the more successes we enjoy in confronting a new circumstance, the more likely it is that we will seek out and embrace change.

To summarize, it is important to think in terms of role taking. An analysis of role taking should include a summary of past role engagements; but it should be more than a listing of assignments. The individual should ask herself or himself the following questions:

- What kinds of behaviors did each role require?
- How well were they mastered?
- What kinds of strengths can now be identified as a result of these experiences?
- From the standpoint of leadership development along the Corson and Paul continuum, where do I stand now?
- Has the experience allowed me to develop a sense of confidence in my ability to move on through the positions of middle manager and executive?

In this kind of analysis, it is obviously important to take a careful reading of the present situation. Does it provide a vehicle for continued growth and development? Or is it time that other possibilities should be pursued? Are there other factors that either dictate a move or suggest that stability in the work role is required? There can easily be times when imperatives generated by other roles will require stability (defined here as a development plateau) in the professional work. Such a review should do much to build a time frame for thinking in terms of the future.

THINKING ABOUT THE FUTURE

Whether it is easy to accept or not, we are consistently in the process of negotiating new terms for the roles we enact. In some cases, the shifts will be dramatic enough to occasion new titles and social symbolism; in others, the changes will be less observable. Many of these role shifts are obviously related to the stages in human life. In the early, exploratory period there is a particular need to experience broadly and to grow into new roles. Later, as competencies and strengths begin to accumulate and become identified, the range and type of role taking may lessen and formal changes in role will be approached with great care and consideration. Such is the likely mood for people in their thirties whose career lines and interests have rather clearly emerged. At a later period, in the fifties and sixties, differing types of roles begin to appear. For the individual, these later shifts are no less important; but they are generally less consequential for organizations.

In any case, the future continues to unfold, and we must confront change continually. Despite this reality, people often have a marked aversion to thinking about, and planning for, the things that are yet to occur. Much of that resistance seems to arise from two sources: (a) a tendency to see future planning wholly in predictive terms and (b) a feeling that planning leads to individual "freezing" and inhibits independence and opportunity for maximum growth and development.

The Predictable Future

Most people have a healthy skepticism about predictions, and they are right. Logically, the future is impossible to predict because every one of our current acts shapes the future we will experience. However, that problem can be avoided by taking an *a-temporal* view of the future. Within this context, we do not attempt to speculate how we will live in the future. Instead, we seek to anticipate consequences of processes and events that we can see right now and to ask ourselves what skills and competences are needed to deal with these anticipations. Furthermore, there is no reason to think in terms of a single scenario. There might be several for which preparations might be made.

In career planning, this perspective is particularly important because it is true that many good things (and some bad) can unexpectedly happen in the course of a career. Although the future-forecasting orientation is often construed to require exact predictions of what will happen,

ORGANIZATIONAL LEVEL OF LEADER	KNOWLEDGE REQUIRED OF AN EFFECTIVE LEADER			
	The substantive field in which the organization is involved	Interpersonal skills—to lead small groups in face-to-face situations	Institutional dynamics and processes—in order to provide leadership at the impersonal, non-face-to-face level	The environment and interdependencies of the organization—to identify goals and strategies and be able to communicate throughout the organization
EXECUTIVE				
MIDDLE MANAGER				
SUPERVISOR				
INDIVIDUAL WORKER				

Figure 1. Competencies (knowledge, skills, understanding) required of a leader at four organizational levels (This chart was developed by Frank Sherwood, based on a model in John J. Corson and R. Shale Paul, *Men Near the Top.* Baltimore: Johns Hopkins Press, 1966, p. 135.)

the a-temporal view suggests that we take a look at our present situation and try to anticipate the directions that are likely to open up to us. Among other things, such an approach provides some help in knowing when a good opportunity has presented itself.

In short, career planning does not rest heavily on a set of accurate predictions of the future. Rather, the task is to sketch out possibilities, to make some judgments about their attractiveness, to ask personal questions to discover what is needed in order to experience success in new roles, and to develop strategies that might help to smooth the way toward a role that has a particular attraction.

Planning as Freezing

The comment is frequently made that career success results from taking advantage of unanticipated opportunities. The very act of trying to plan may in itself set up boundaries and limitations on a zestful search for new directions and possibilities. If the point of departure is prediction and the plan is conceived as a means by which a specified and chosen goal is to be achieved, such freezing can undoubtedly occur.

If, on the other hand, planning is seen in more personal terms as a process of preparing for an uncertain future, then freezing is less likely. The individual engages the role; generally speaking, the terms of the role are socially defined. Therefore, the variable over which the individual has some possibility of control is himself or herself. Planning in this context consists of consciously preparing for a constellation of roles that seems within reach. The planning involves knowing one's competencies and motivations well enough to recognize "fit"—that a role being offered is well-suited to one's individual performance potential.

Clearly, the more one has an interest in developing a conscious plan for learning, the more these considerations will have relevance.

THE PROCESS OF PLANNING FOR LEARNING

Knowles (1975) provides considerable specificity about ways in which individuals can take responsibility for their own learning. Because adults bring their own experience to learning situations, it is not reasonable to assume that someone else can dictate what an individual's needs are. As suggested earlier, individual personalities, competencies, and widely varied experiences in role taking make it mandatory that the process of adult learning be a highly personal one.

This requirement to take charge is particularly important in the case of persons who aspire to leadership roles. In fact, the capacity to construct and implement an individual learning agenda is a good indicator of leadership potential. The person who cannot set individual goals and therefore feels subordinate to someone else's judgments is not likely to behave differently in initiating structures and directions within the organization.

As Knowles emphasizes, it is important to recognize that planning for learning is not a randomized process. It deserves great care and rigorous thought. These steps in the planning process can be identified:

1. A systematic canvass and identification of the types of roles in which the individual would like to engage in the future.

2. A detailed analysis of a role (or set of roles) with particular appeal.

3. The development of a model role encompassing the behavior expectations empirically identified in step 2.

4. The extrapolation of the competencies required of an individual in order to behave successfully in the model role.

5. The construction of a model of the competencies that appear necessary for the discharge of the role or roles in which the individual seeks to participate.

   Although there are several ways in which such a model can be developed, the process that has been suggested emphasizes task analysis. Review of literature, consultation with experts, and working with others can be helpful mechanisms for gathering information, but the construction of the role on which the model of competence is based should be a highly individual effort.

6. The assessment of current strength levels.

   Here the issue involves the extent to which the individual's present competencies are consistent with those of the model. In order to gain further data for such an assessment, feedback from others should be sought. In most cases this involves the preparation of an instrument in which current evaluations of competencies are made. It is important to emphasize that the concern is not with a random set of competencies but rather with those that are directly tied to the desired role(s) in which the individual seeks further participation. Logically, the feedback sought by one individual will differ markedly from that needed by another.

7. The development of a profile of competence levels (see Knowles, p. 90, for an example of a profile of competence levels).

   It should be possible to introduce some quantification into the analysis of current levels of competence; to the extent that is done, areas for priority attention should be apparent.

8. The preparation of the individual learning plan, based on the priorities identified in step 7.

SUMMARY

Basic to the idea of adult education is the assumption of responsibility and control of the process by the learner. This crucial shift in power is considered imperative because the adult, unlike the child, has generated a unique set of experiences, looks at the future in terms of those experiences, and now needs to concentrate on learnings that will have maximum payoff for a particular set of goals and needs.

That is the theory. But its implementation can be very difficult. Frequently, we do not think of experiences as pathways to learning, have not been very specific about the things we want out of life, and tend to be crippled by our previous learning as a child. We are not accustomed to taking charge and asking hard questions about costs and benefits.

As a consequence, it is highly important to pursue the development of a learning agenda as an adult in a conscious and systematic way. The suggestion of such a process has been the main purpose of this essay, and the following dimensions have been emphasized.

1. The concept of role is very important, and it forms the framework within which models of competence are developed.
2. Planning is a significant part of taking charge of learning as an adult. However, it does not require that an individual engage in predictions or become frozen by the planning done.
3. An essential requirement is the development of a competence profile for the individual, which should involve not only personal perceptions but feedback from others.
4. The adult learning plan should be a direct outcome of the comparison of the model of competence for the role and the individual's competence profile.

References

Corson, J., & Shale, P. R. *Men near the top.* Baltimore: Johns Hopkins Press, 1962.

Fayol, H. [*General and industrial management*]. London: Pitman and Sons, 1949. (Originally published, 1916.)

Knowles, M. *Self-directed learning: A guide for learners and teachers.* New York: Association Press, 1975.

Distortions of
Behavioral Science

by James V. Clark

Schools of business administration and in-company training programs are spending more and more money and time on education in the behavioral sciences. Carnegie Tech, Chicago, Harvard, MIT, Stanford, UCLA, and Yale, to name only a few, all have substantial organizational behavior, human relations, anthropology, psychology, and sociology course offerings in their business schools—at the undergraduate, graduate, and executive program levels. Away from the ivory towers, the American Management Association, Alcan, ESSO, Pacific Finance, and many other firms and industrial organizations have major residential training programs devoted exclusively to theory and practice in the behavioral sciences.

As a teacher and student of behavior in formal organizations, I spend much of my time in these programs. I view my task there as bringing to students some of the findings and methods of the behavioral sciences which have been found relevant to their practice as administrators. Briefly, these findings and methods highlight aspects of the administrator's "territory" which he typically overlooks, due to his background and/or the pressures under which he operates. Given this modest aim, however, the most extraordinary things generally happen in these programs. I very early learned, for example, that it was next to impossible for me to say, "Here is something you are overlooking" without being heard

James V. Clark is vice chairman, Graduate School of Business Administration, University of California, Los Angeles.

©1963 by the Regents of the University of California. Reprinted from *California Management Review*, vol. VI, no. 2, pp. 55-60 by permission of the Regents.

as saying, "Behavioral science knows everything—the average administrator knows nothing."

First in astonishment, then in anger, and lately from scientific curiosity (or more accurately from a mixture of all three), I have become intrigued by this kind of misunderstanding. Again and again, simple findings and basic methods of scientific investigators become shockingly distorted by intelligent listeners. And most training programs are set up for such short periods of time that the teacher can scarcely hope to deal with more than a few of these confusions. Consequently, they spread.

As my experience in this educational adventure extended, I began to notice a consistency in the distortions. The same mistaken impressions were turning up again and again, whether I was teaching in a university or an industry and whether I was teaching twenty-, forty-, or sixty-year-olds, top management or first line foreman, management, or union personnel. And conversations with colleagues convinced me these particular misunderstandings were not encountered only in my classes—they were endemic.

As I informally collected and sorted these confusions, I thought I saw a pattern in them and a plausible explanation for their prevalence. In the hope that it might contribute to an improved understanding of some of the communication problems between businessmen and social and psychological investigators of business, I will list some of the more frequently heard distortions and advance a few ideas about what might be behind them.

Black or White Magic?

The misunderstanding of what teachers of behavioral science, human relations, organizational behavior, or call it what you will, are trying to say takes two major forms. People either believe that the behavioral scientists believe a distortion, or they themselves believe it. That is, people take a tentative or partial statement of ours, magnify it out of all proportion, and then conclude either that we are fools or that we are wizards who have the answers to everything. Fritz Roethlisberger once said in a classroom lecture that businessmen take behavioral scientists for either black magicians or white magicians. As his remark suggests, and as I shall try to show, these superficially different perceptions are variations on the same viewing dynamic.

But first, let us look at some of the distortions themselves. Here is a list of assertions commonly advanced by many business-oriented behavioral scientists, followed by oversimplified representations of the distortions which often crop up in their presence. Recall that a distortion can take two forms: the listener either thinks behavioral scientists believe it, or he believes it.

Since these confusions arise around different topics, I have grouped them accordingly.

Organizational Behavior

Statement: Knowledge exists about organizational behavior.

Distortion: If you know enough, you can solve any administrative problem.

Statement: Much data has been collected on social and nonlogical behavior at the work group level, but little concerning top management groups.

Distortion: People on the bottom of a formal organizational chart are illogical. People above the bottom are logical.

Statement: There are nonlogical aspects to people's behavior.

Distortion: Nobody is logical.

Individual Behavior

Statement: Psychological determinants of behavior are important.

Distortion: One's behavior is entirely determined by his psychological makeup.

Small Workgroup Behavior

Statement: Social determinants of behavior are important.

Distortion: One's behavior is determined by his membership in social groups.

Statement: It is helpful to realize that people's aspirations at work have many aspects; they seek membership, self-esteem, economic security, prestige, and so on.

Distortion: Pay—even incentive pay—isn't of much importance anymore.

Statement: Social behavior and individual need satisfaction are related in some significant fashion to productivity.

Distortion: You ought to give workers whatever they want. If they're happy, they'll produce more.

Statement: Social subsystems in organizations exert much control over their members. Consequently, an administrator's control is limited.

Distortion: Nobody can really be a boss, only a follower. We should all be soft and tender-minded.

Intergroup Behavior

Statement: It is helpful if an administrator has a way of thinking that helps him account for conflict between groups.

Distortion: You should always get along with everybody and not have conflicts.

Statement: Shared goals are important for collaboration between groups.

Distortion: Everybody should think alike so they can work together as a group.

Administration

Statement: It is helpful for an administrator to have a way of thinking about collecting information and learning about problems in organizational behavior.

Distortion: Administrators should be research types, studying things but not acting on them.

Statement: Thinking about organizational behavior as occurring in a sociotechnical system helps in dealing with specific administrative problems.

Distortion: You ought to be a social scientist if you're going to be an administrator.

Statement: Sometimes the interactive process involved in understanding an administrative problem alleviates the problem.

Distortion: If you're a nondirective leader all your problems take care of themselves.

Statement: Appropriate and useful administrative behavior often involves an administrator in responding flexibly to different situations.

Distortion: Consistency of values is neither desirable nor useful.

Statement: Top management often exerts considerable influence on the social system of an organization.

Distortion: Unless you're top management, you're stymied and can't change anything.

Statement: It is important for an administrator to pay attention to the internal processes of his organization.

Distortion: If you pay attention to human relations, you don't need to know anything about the business.

Statement: Some of the methods and findings of psychotherapy have relevance to the administrator's understanding and skill in communication.

Distortion: An administrator has to practically be a psychiatrist in order to communicate.

Statement: An administrator should know his own limits.

Distortion: Administrators should put others ahead of themselves.

Statement: Administrators should be able to accept feelings of inadequacy.

Distortion: Administrators should be introspective all the time.

In my experience, most businessmen and many professors of business agree with a dozen or more of the distortions. Anyone agreeing with only eight or nine of them has probably done considerable reading in the area. If one agrees with five or less, he may well have spent the equivalent of a full-time year studying and discussing these matters. It takes between two and five years of full-time work before people believe none of the distortions and know that very few behavioral scientists believe them either.

Why are these distortions so prevalent? Clearly, this is a complicated question, and no small part of its answer is suggested by the old adage that when the pupil hasn't learned, the teacher hasn't taught. But these misunderstandings are encountered by such a variety of teachers and in such a range of teaching contexts that some more general force seems likely to be an underlying contributing factor.

Progressive or Stubborn?

I believe that much of the problem stems from the fact that, for the most part, behavioral scientists and businessmen have recently been concerned with different aspects of human behavior. The great discoveries of the behavioral scientists over the last fifty to seventy-five years, for example, have been around the stubborn, recalcitrant nature of human personality, alone or in groups. Of course, man has known for thousands of years that behavior does not change easily, but not with the depth of understanding of contemporary social science. The extent to which the human organism reacts so as to maintain equilibrium and resist change, therefore, has occupied perhaps the most prominent part of social science inquiry since it began in earnest around the latter part of the nineteenth century.

Businessmen, on the other hand, have experienced the last sixty-odd years as the golden age of economic expansion, development, change, and progress. They have created vast organizations in which great technological and distributive inventions have produced economic developments beyond anyone's dreams. And still today, ten new horizons open up for every one crossed. The fruits of these labors are obvious; we do have a different economic situation today than we had sixty years ago, and the businessman has been spending his time working to bring it about.

It is important here to note that both groups may be in a stage of reacting against what they are beginning to feel are excesses. Behavioral scientists, for example, are becoming increasingly interested in rationality and growth. At the very root of the postwar existential school of psychoanalysis now being regarded so seriously by American psychotherapists, for instance, lies the exercise of will, choice, and commitment. Meanwhile, business is beginning to rediscover the complexity of human needs. Sheer technological or economic improvement is wearing thin for many, and a worried discussion of national goals is replacing the breast-beating which has characterized the American businessman during much of this century. Moreover, he is reading books, taking courses in behavioral science and human relations, and hiring Ph.D.'s at an ever-increasing rate and with an ever-increasing seriousness.

Regardless of the historical antecedents or future possibilities for reconciliation, however, a different orientation toward human behavior has existed for the past sixty years between social scientists and most businessmen. During this period, these two groups seem to have picked out and focused on different aspects of human behavior. I say these two *groups* because there have been individuals in each whose interest was wider than that of his co-workers. Many behavioral scientists (and particularly many who have been based in schools of business administration) have been interested in the growthful, willful, "open-ended" aspects of human personality and groups. And many businessmen have been profoundly aware—in theory and in practice—that their organization's members had more needs than economic theory alone might suggest.

Nevertheless, a number of social and psychological investigators have appeared to focus on one side of human behavior, while the businessmen centered their attention on the other. It appears to some observers, however, that human behavior in fact always includes *both* the aspect in which the behavioral scientists have been interested *and* the facet on which the businessmen have concentrated. It is possible we have been struggling with a choice when none was logically necessary. Many writers now think that all individuals and groups exhibit, on the one hand, a tendency and capacity to *maintain* themselves in something like a steady state and, on the other hand, a tendency and capacity to *differentiate* and elaborate themselves internally and externally.

The psychologist Gordon Allport believes that both these tendencies are requirements for open, mature personalities. But, he observes, "Most current theories of personality ... emphasize stability rather than growth, permanence rather than change, 'uncertainty reduction' (information theory) and 'coding' (cognitive theory) rather than creativity. In short, they emphasize *being* rather than *becoming*."[1]

Allport conducted an informal investigation to reveal the underlying preference of his psychologist colleagues as to whether they conceived the human personality to be essentially equilibrium-seeking or forward-pushing. His findings are interesting. Studying *Psychological Abstracts* issues over the past thirty years, and randomly sampling five-page excerpts in current journals, Allport discovered the ratio of the former to the latter to be five-to-one. As he put it, the psychologist's vocabulary is five times richer in terms like *reaction, response, reinforcement, reflex, respondent, retroaction, recognition, regression, repression, reminiscence* than in terms like *production, proceeding, proficiency, problem-solving, probiate,* and *programming*."[2] To an outsider, these terms of—let us call them for shorthand purposes "reaction" and "pro-action"—seem innocuous enough, being almost sheer description. But there is considerable debate brewing here in psychological circles. Many writers are contending that behavioral science needs to take fuller account of growth, will, and the forward-thrusting aspects of people. Their critics maintain that such tendencies are not observable in the strict sense.

The Reactive—Pro-active Dimension

Well, isn't this a problem we should leave to the psychologists to iron out? Maybe so, but we haven't. The psychologists are just one group among many in this discussion. Profound feelings are evoked around it far beyond the confines of the psychology department. This can be seen if we let our mind's eye roam over the images called up by the following set of terms, each of which has been used in place of "reactive" and "pro-active" to point to similar phenomena. Think of "reactionary—liberal," or "passive—active," and "maintenance oriented—task oriented," "equilibrium—growth," "realism—mysticism," "nonlogical—logical," "emotion—will," "intellectual—anti-intellectual," "tough-minded—tender-minded," "devil—angel," "masculine—feminine." And there are others.

Even whole cultures line up on either side of these hyphens. For example, the Hindus, anticipating certain modern psychologists by two or three millennia, stated that man's needs were, in ascendant order, for pleasure, success, duty, and to search for meaning or to know. Clearly, our Western value system tends to emphasize the lower levels of this

1. Allport, Gordon, "The Open System in Personality Theory." *Personality and Social Encounter*, Beacon Press, Boston, 1960.

2. *Ibid.*

need hierarchy. We do not venerate our philosophers; we idolize our movie stars, sports heroes, "wheelers and dealers," and political leaders.

At any rate, I hope our list has been sufficient to underscore the fact that feelings run deep around this reactive-pro-active business. This is an area where people's taste is very much a matter of dispute.

It shouldn't surprise us, therefore, that social scientists and businessmen align themselves on one side or the other of this discussion. While Allport's study shows where the choices of many of his colleagues lie, no one has done a similar study in journals of business, but I believe it would show the opposite. I am almost certain that in business publications *progress, problem solving, production, proficiency,* and the like squeeze out *resistance to change, reaction, regression,* and so forth, by at least the five-to-one Allport found for the opposite direction among psychologists. Another indication of the same preference is the high percentage of "How to" books and articles published for businessmen. All carry the same implication and feed the same underlying preference: The world can—and should—be improved rationally, fixed up.

It is possible that this difference between business and management writers on the one hand and social and psychological writers on the other may help us understand some of the problems they have had in communication with each other. Each, defending and justifying the work and progress of themselves and their fellows, often confuses an aspect of reality with reality itself. It seems to me, for example, that the famous critic of behavioral science education, Malcolm McNair, Professor of Retailing at Harvard, shows a strong preference for the pro-active side of reality which he does not realize is a preference. He writes incisively as he asks "What Price Human Relations?",[3] but he writes with the incision of one who is defending a position against onslaught. Professor McNair and other pioneers in business education were dedicated to the value of improving business practice rationally. They were—and remain— vigorous pro-actives. But in their efforts to resist, or at least to contain, the advances of the social scientists who point to the existence of reactive behaviors, they appear to be fighting a battle of values which has some meaning for them above and beyond trying to understand behavior from the scientific point of view. It's as if they would be letting their side down by admitting any truth for the "opposition." In their defense, however, let us not forget that this works two ways: the social science invasion into schools of management often appears to be flying a banner which reads, "Give me nonlogical, emotional behavior or give me death!" Of course, the final and almost impenetrable confusion in this continuing debate is

---

3. McNair, Malcolm, "Thinking Ahead: What Price Human Relations?"*Harvard Business Review,* XXXV (2).

that the pro-actives often find themselves defending against the attacking reactives. And does not this somewhat absurd situation, with its reactive pro-actives paired off against the pro-active reactives, suggest to us that a false dichotomy is producing more heat than light?

Keeping the World Safe for Progress

In the shadow of this discussion, turn back briefly to the distortions listed earlier. Notice that all except one or two caricature the image of the pro-active's opposite. Think of everything the typical vigorous, progress-ive businessman does not believe himself to think or be, and you have the list of distortions we saw there. That is, businessmen many times think behavioral scientists believe that knowledge is everything, people are completely nonlogical, pay isn't important, executives ought to make workers happy, ought never to have conflict, never pay attention to the business of the business, and act like nondirective therapists. Clearly, none of these describes the image of the firm, tough, pro-active busi-nessman dutifully and powerfully improving his business (and hence the world) through the use of rationality and consciousness.

Of course, what a businessman can get out of manufacturing these distorted statements—statements which he can resist in such good conscience—is the comforting belief that he is keeping the world safe for progress. Notice that he can thus actually defend himself against new knowledge (much of which points to realistic aspects of organizational behavior which in fact limits his control as executive) by using words of offense. He thus uses pro-active-sounding *talk* in order to *behave* reac-tively.

So much for the resisting kind of distortions. The other type of listeners, you will remember, themselves believe the distortions we looked at earlier. Thus, a student sitting in a classroom or an executive listening to a consultant's report, suddenly believes that enough scien-tific knowledge will solve all labor problems, workers can be influenced if enough is known of their illogicality, other enticements can always be extended instead of pay, workers will produce more if they are made happy, and communication problems will dissolve if all managers are taught how to be "nondirective." Clearly, what is involved in these distor-tions is that the listener has so convinced himself that the end of science is to improve technology that he grasps at the behavioral scientist's assertions as new and powerful tools of manipulation. Unfortunately, many of the commercial motivation research organizations, executive selection firms, and similar concerns have cruelly played on this over-simplified hope and given it some credence.

In summary, then, these distortions come from those people who share the culturally supported value that an executive's duty is to firmly and toughly improve the world technologically, through science and business. Given this deep-seated belief, then, most listeners find the partial, limited statements of the behavioral scientists—as often as not pointing to reactive aspects of behavior—as either antimanagement or supermanagement. Thus, behavioral science, to many businessmen, is either against him or a secret weapon on his side. Either way, of course, the basic misunderstandings remain.

An issue buried this deep cannot, of course, be cured easily. But it seems to me that some understanding of its nature can be helpful. Having seen the distortions listed here, for example, businessmen, students, administrators of training programs and the like can perhaps spot them better next time—in themselves and in others. Then, too, they can see that behavioral science should not be evaluated on its popularity alone. Given this analysis, any good educational program in this area will predictably encounter—and produce—resistances. Teachers of this material need special training and much experience before they can begin to help people clarify some of these distortions. Teaching psychology or sociology to liberal arts students with one set of values and to present or future businessmen with another set are very different experiences. Also, much time needs to be given to such education. High expectations for short-term programs must be tempered by some insight into the vast nature of the undertaking.

Then, too, behavioral scientists reading these remarks can ask themselves whether they favor stable, closed theories and disregard the forward-pushing, growing aspects of behavior. If the answer is "yes," they might further ask themselves what they are getting out of such a preference? What does it protect them from?

I find these implications easy to write, since they all involve other people. The implication which emerges for us teachers I pass on humbly, for I have firsthand knowledge of how profoundly hard it is: to be patient. We spend much time showing our businessmen, students, or clients how little control they often have over the behavior of their subordinates and what this fact means for themselves and for their administrative practice. Is not this good medicine for us? How much of what happens in our classrooms have we control over? How much control do we have, for example, over such beliefs as the basic cultural value discussed in this article that the duty of man is to improve the world rationally? Are not the implications of this fact for ourselves and our teaching practice at least as profound as those we pass on to our students? I think so, but this is another subject, and one which awaits an essay similar to this, but on the misunderstanding of businessmen by behavioral scientists, and preferably written by a businessman and former student!

Part 2. The Manager as a Person

Traditional management theory prescribed a set of impersonal *principles of management* as the keys to effectiveness. Those who aspired to the upper echelons of organizations were advised to master the principles of planning, organizing, controlling, etc. Today, management theory emphasizes an additional aspect of managerial knowledge—self-knowledge. No manager has a completely operational theory of management unless that theory contains a component subtheory about himself or herself. In order to function effectively, the manager needs to understand his or her strengths, weaknesses, motives, blind spots, behavioral styles, fears, and aspirations.

Part 1 contained a series of readings about the process whereby some of these aspects of oneself might be discovered. In part 2, more substantive issues regarding self-insight are examined in readings that provide a sampling of pertinent information about managers as people. The purpose here is to provide the reader with several viewpoints for assessing what he or she as a manager needs to learn.

The first article is by leading humanistic psychologist Carl Rogers. In "Toward Becoming a Fully Functioning Person," he shares some of the insights he has gained in helping individuals chart directions for their lives. The avenues for growth and development that Rogers discusses are not the typical concrete goals we often identify—oriented to outcomes such as earning a degree, receiving a promotion, etc. Rogers describes trends or patterns of behavior that lead to psychological maturity and enrichment of our experiences and provide some interesting benchmarks for evaluating the way we live our lives.

According to Rogers, "becoming more fully functioning" implies that the individual achieves greater integration, creativity, and ability to experience more fully the many facets of life. Such experiences are preferable to simply seeking enjoyment or contentment.

The McClelland and Burnham reading shifts the focus to look at some of the personality attributes of successful managers. In "Power Is the Great Motivator," McClelland continues a long and significant series of studies of motivation. His research techniques involve using projective tests to measure managers' levels of motivation for power, achievement, and affiliation. The findings provide a profile that is surprising at first, but after closer examination it seems to be compatible with other current views of effective managerial behavior.

Through the use of case studies of managers' styles, McClelland and Burnham illustrate how a power orientation can be acted out in productive ways. The style shown to be most successful in creating an effective work climate is characterized as having strong but well-controlled power needs. The data indicate how managers may successfully use their power for institutional gain and enhancement of subordinates' power, rather than for personal aggrandizement.

In his article on "Interpersonal Communication," Warner Burke discusses two personal-skill areas important to managers: the abilities to speak and to listen. One of the problems in communicating among people is that barriers to understanding may be set up within each of the communicating individuals or between them. Burke identifies some of the important barriers and suggests ways of coping with them.

Listening skills are often given inadequate coverage in discussions of communication. It is the more observable speaking or "output" side of communication that is the subject of a variety of training approaches. However, effective listening requires both an understanding of one's own barriers and the acquisition of specific skills. The responsibility for successful communication cannot be placed on one participant, but must be assumed by both.

One of the consequences of disequilibrium between the manager's personal qualities and the demands of the situation is *stress*. The physiological and psychological damage caused by stress is serious and the monetary cost in lost productivity is immense. In "On Consuming Human Resources: Perspectives on the Management of Stress," John Adams reviews some of the causes of stress and develops a typology of *stressors* (stress-producing factors). Stress stems from numerous ongoing work and life events and conditions, often related to changes and demands, in interaction with the particular characteristics of the individual.

A set of recommendations for reducing stress in work situations was derived from a research effort with an organization. These suggestions, as well as a listing of personal stress-management techniques, are provided by Adams. The article concludes with a discussion of some things a manager can do for persons in the organization who are overstressed.

One of the twentieth-century rediscoveries of applied psychology is that adults go through a series of fairly predictable stages of development. This is a departure from the common assumption that after adolescence, the social-emotional development of most individuals is complete and unchanging. Research evidence that describes and illustrates the phases of adult growth and development is reviewed by Robert T. Golembiewski in "Mid-Life Transition and Mid-Career Crisis: A Special Case for Individual Development."

He describes three distinct phases of development that adults pass through in their progression to old age. The ending of the first phase is the middle-years transition, which for some individuals becomes mid-life crisis. This is a pivotal time for many managers, who at the height of their careers find themselves confused about their priorities and in doubt about choices that once seemed clear-cut. Organizations can help ease the impact of the mid-life transition on their members and thus perhaps prevent some of the accompanying loss of productivity. The author suggests several measures that may be possible in a partnership between the individual, his or her employing organization, and professional association.

In "The Androgynous Blend: Best of Both Worlds," Alice G. Sargent clarifies one of the important issues in contemporary organizations. Both men and women managers may be entrapped in traditional and narrow views of how each sex should behave. These sex-role stereotypes define the appropriate modes of male and female behavior as polar opposites—women are expected to be nurturing, expressive, and oriented toward the development of other people, while men should be cool, tough, and competitive. Since these male behaviors are often seen as synonymous with desirable managerial style, management is often a new and difficult role for women.

Sargent reports evidence that views of appropriate managerial behavior are changing to encompass aspects of both the masculine and feminine styles. The androgynous manager is an individual who is not limited to one style or the other, but can combine the most useful elements of both. Such a blend is both more effective in many organizational situations and healthier for the manager.

Sargent's ideas should be useful to those male managers who, although exhorted by modern leadership theories to be more supportive, humanistic, and democratic, may hesitate because such behavior seems weak and unmasculine. Sargent's article also has implications for those female managers who may feel they should stick with traditional "womanly wiles" to get their way, rather than acquire the male styles of directness, assertiveness, and independence.

The articles in this section amply illustrate the many facets of the human being who moves into a managerial role. The manager, as a person, has the capacity to grow, to achieve, and to form richer and more effective relationships. But there are also some pitfalls along the way—including the narrowing of one's repertoire because of sex-role stereotyping, stress, and crisis in mid-life transition. The purpose of these readings is to help the manager capitalize on the development opportunities while avoiding some of the pitfalls.

Toward Becoming a Fully Functioning Person

by Carl R. Rogers

I am sure that each of us has puzzled from time to time as to his own goals, and the goals which he believes would be desirable for others. "What is my purpose in life?" "What am I striving for?" "What do I want to be?" These are questions which every individual asks himself at one time or another, sometimes calmly and meditatively, sometimes in agonizing uncertainty or despair. They are old, old questions which have been asked and answered in every century of history. Yet they are also questions which every individual must ask and answer for himself, in his own way. They are questions which I, as a therapist, hear expressed in many differing ways as men and women in personal distress try to learn, or understand, or choose the directions which their lives are taking.

THE PROBLEM

As I have worked for many years with troubled individuals, I believe that I can discern a pattern, a trend, a direction, an orderliness, a commonality, in the tentative answers to these questions which these people have found for themselves. And so I would like to share with the reader the picture of the optimum human person, as I have formed this picture from my experience with my clients. It is my perception of what human beings appear to be striving for, when they feel free to choose their own direction. It is also my picture of what constitutes personal or psychological health.

Carl R. Rogers is resident fellow, Center for Studies of the Person, La Jolla, California.

From *Perceiving, Behaving, Becoming: A New Focus for Education*. 1962 yearbook, Washington, DC: Association for Supervision and Curriculum Development, 1962, pp. 21-33. Reprinted with permission of the Association for Supervision and Curriculum Development and Carl R. Rogers. Copyright © 1962 by the Association for Supervision and Curriculum Development. All rights reserved.

The Background From Which the Problem Is Approached

I shall have to make it clear at the outset that my observations are made from a background of client-centered therapy. Quite possibly all successful psychotherapy has a similar personality outcome, but I am less sure of that than formerly, and hence wish it to be clear that I speak from a particular perspective. The trends I have observed have occurred in a relationship which, when it is at its best, partakes of these characteristics. The therapist has been willing to *be* his real feelings, has been willing to be genuine, in the relationship with the client. He has been able to enter into an intensely personal and subjective relationship with the client— relating not as a scientist to an object of study, not as a physician expecting to diagnose and cure, but as a person to a person.

The therapist feels this client to be a person of unconditional self-worth; of value no matter what his condition, his behavior, or his feelings. The therapist is able to let himself go in understanding this person; no inner barriers keep him from sensing what it feels like to be the client at each moment of the relationshp, and he has been able to convey to the client something of this empathic understanding. It means that the therapist has been comfortable in entering this relationship fully, without knowing cognitively where it will lead, satisfied with providing a climate which will free the client to become himself.

For the client, this optimal therapy has meant an exploration of increasingly strange and unknown and dangerous feelings in himself; the exploration proving possible only because he is gradually realizing that he is accepted unconditionally. Thus, he becomes acquainted with elements of his experience which have in the past been denied to awareness as too threatening, too damaging to the structure of the self. He finds himself experiencing these feelings fully, completely, in the relationship, so that for the moment he *is* his fear, or his anger, or his tenderness, or his strength. And as he lives and accepts these widely varied feelings, in all their degrees of intensity, he discovers that he has experienced *himself*, that he *is* all these feelings. He finds his behavior changing in constructive fashion in accordance with his newly experienced and newly accepted self. He approaches the realization that he no longer needs to fear what experience may hold, but can welcome it freely as a part of his changing and developing self.

This is a thumbnail sketch of what client-centered therapy might be at its optimum. I give it here to suggest the kind of situation in which I have observed certain trends occurring in clients who have participated in such therapy. I would like now to proceed to my main concern: what are these directions, and what personality characteristics appear to develop in the client as a result of this kind of experience?

CHARACTERISTIC DIRECTIONS

What follows is based both upon clinical observation and upon research. It tries to present the trends I have seen in our clients, but it also pushes these trends to the limit, as it were, in order better to see the kind of person who would emerge if therapy were optimal, the kind of person who might be said to be the goal which individuals discover they are aiming toward.

An Increasing Openness to Experience

A major observation is that the individual moves toward being open to his experience. This is a phrase which has come to have increasily definite meaning for me. It is the polar opposite of defensiveness. Defensiveness I have described in the past as being the organism's response to experiences which are perceived or anticipated as incongruent with the structure of the self. In order to maintain the self-structure, such experiences are given a distorted symbolization in awareness, which reduces the incongruity. Thus, the individual defends himself against any threat of alteration in the concept of self by not perceiving those meanings in his experience which contradict his present self-picture.

In the person who is open to his experience, however, every stimulus, whether originating within the organism or in the environment, would be freely relayed through the nervous system without being distorted by a defensive mechanism. There would be no need of the mechanism of "subception"[1] whereby the organism is forewarned of any experience threatening to the self. On the contrary, whether the stimulus was the impact of a configuration of form, color or sound in the environment on the sensory nerves, or a memory trace from the past, or a visceral sensation of fear or pleasure or disgust, the person would be "living it," would have it completely available to awareness.

Perhaps I can give this concept a more vivid meaning if I illustrate it from a recorded interview. A young professional man reports in the forty-eighth interview the way in which he has become more open to some of his bodily sensations, as well as other feelings.

> *Client:* It doesn't seem to me that it would be possible for anybody to relate all the changes that you feel. But I certainly have felt recently that I have more respect for, more objectivity toward, my physical make-up. I mean I don't expect too much of myself. This is how it works out: It feels to me that in the past I used to fight a certain tiredness that I felt after supper. Well now I feel

---

1. A term used by R. S. Lazarus and R. A. McCleary in "Autonomic Discrimination without Awareness: A Study of Subception." *Psychological Review* 58: 113-22, 1951.

pretty sure that I really am *tired*—that I am not making myself tired—that I am just physiologically lower. It seemed that I was just constantly criticizing my tiredness.

Therapist: So you can let yourself *be* tired, instead of feeling along with it a kind of criticism of it.

Client: Yes, that I shouldn't be tired or something. And it seems in a way to be pretty profound that I can just not fight this tiredness, and along with it goes a real feeling of *I've* got to slow down, too, so that being tired isn't such an awful thing. I think I can also kind of pick up a thread here of why I should be that way in the way my father is and the way he looks at some of these things. For instance, say that I was sick, and I would report this, and it would seem that overtly he would want to do something about it, but he would also communicate "Oh, my gosh, more trouble." You know, something like that.

Therapist: As though there were something quite annoying really about being physically ill.

Client: Yeah, I am sure that my father has the same disrespect for his own physiology that I have had. Now last summer I twisted my back; I wrenched it; I heard it snap and everything. There was real pain there all the time at first, real sharp. And I had the doctor look at it and he said it wasn't serious; it should heal by itself as long as I didn't bend too much. Well this was months ago—and I have been noticing recently that—hell, this is a real pain and it's still there—and it's not my fault, I mean it's—

Therapist: It doesn't prove something bad about you—

Client: No—and one of the reasons I seem to get more tired than I should maybe is because of this constant strain and so on. I have already made an appointment with one of the doctors at the hospital that he would look at it and take an X-ray or something. In a way I guess you could say that I am just more accurately sensitive—or objectively sensitive to this kind of thing. I can say with certainty that this has also spread to what I eat and how much I eat. And this is really a profound change, as I say, and of course my relationship with my wife and the two children is—well you just wouldn't recognize it if you could see me inside—as you have—I mean—there just doesn't seem to be anything more wonderful than really and genuinely—really *feeling* love for your own children and at the same time *receiving* it. I don't know how to put this. We have such an increased respect—both of us—for Judy, and we've noticed just—as we participated in this—we have noticed such a tremendous change in her—it seems to be a pretty deep kind of thing.

Therapist: It seems to me you are saying that you can listen more accurately to yourself. If your body says it's tired, you listen to it and believe it, instead of criticizing it, if it's in pain you can listen to that, if the feeling is really loving your wife or children, you can *feel* that, and it seems to show up in the differences in them, too.

Here, in a relatively minor by symbolically important excerpt, can be seen much of what I have been trying to say about openness to experience. Formerly he could not freely feel pain or illness, because being ill meant being unacceptable. Neither could he feel tenderness and love for his child, because such feelings meant being weak, and he had to maintain his facade of being strong. But now he can be genuinely open to the experience of his organism—he can be tired when he is tired, he can feel pain when his organism is in pain, he can freely experience the love he feels for his daughter, and he can also feel and express annoyance toward her, as he goes on to say in the next portion of the interview. He can fully live the experience of his total organism, rather than shutting them out of awareness.

I have used this concept of availability to awareness to try to make clear what I mean by openness to experience. This might be misunderstood. I do not mean that this individual would be self-consciously aware of all that was going on within himself, like the centipede who became aware of all his legs. On the contrary, he would be free to live a feeling subjectively, as well as be aware of it. He might experience love, or pain, or fear, living in this attitude subjectively. Or he might abstract himself from this subjectivity and realize in awareness, "I am in pain"; "I am afraid"; "I do love." The crucial point is that there would be no barriers, no inhibitions, which would prevent the full experiencing of whatever was organismically present, and availability to awareness is a good measure of this absence of barriers.

Openness to experience is not a construct which is easy to measure with our present instruments, but such research as exists tends to support the notion that it is characteristic of those who are coping effectively with life. Chodorkoff (1954), for example, found in a very careful study that the better adjusted subjects perceived themselves more accurately. They were, that is, more open to the facts of their experience and thus perceived themselves in much the same way as they were seen by a group of competent and unbiased observers. Even more interestingly, they tended accurately to recognize threatening experiences (in this case tachistoscopically presented threatening words) more quickly than they recognized neutral experiences. They thus seemed very open even to stimuli which were threatening. The poorly adjusted group showed the reverse trend, and seemed to have a set toward keeping threatening experiences inadequately differentiated and inadequately symbolized.

Toward Becoming a Process

A second major trend which I have observed is that the individual moves toward more acceptantly being a process, a fluidity, a changing. He lives in a more existential fashion, living fully in each moment. Let me see if I can explain what I mean.

I believe it would be evident that for the person who was fully open to his experience, completely without defensiveness, each moment would be new. The complex configuration of inner and outer stimuli which exists in this moment has never existed before in just this fashion. Consequently, such a hypothetical person would realize that, "What I will be in the next moment, and what I will do, grow out of that moment, and cannot be predicted in advance either by me or by others." Not infrequently we find clients expressing this sort of feeling. Thus one, at the end of therapy, says in rather puzzled fashion, "I haven't finished the job of integrating and reorganizing myself, but that's only confusing, not discouraging, now that I realize this is a continuing process. ... It is exciting, sometimes upsetting, but deeply encouraging to feel yourself in action and apparently knowing where you are going even though you don't always consciously know where that is."

One way of expressing the fluidity which is present in such existential living is to say that the self and personality emerge *from* experience, rather than experience being translated or twisted to fit a preconceived self-structure. It means that one becomes a participant in and an observer of the ongoing process of organismic experience, rather than being in control of it. As one client put it: "I have a feeling that what I have to do is to take more the position of passenger, rather than driver. See how things go when they're left alone. It's awful kind of scary—feeling that nobody's at the wheel. Of course it's a tremendously challenging feeling, too. Perhaps *this* is the key to freedom."

Or again, the same client, a bit later: "I'm not changing from *me* into something else. I'm changing from *me* to *me*. More like being an amoeba than a caterpillar-butterfly. The amoeba changes shape, but it's still an amoeba. In a way that's sort of a relief. I can keep the parts of me I really like. I don't have to chuck the whole thing, and start all over again."

Such living in the moment, then, means an absence of rigidity, of tight organization, of the imposition of structure on experience. It means instead a maximum of adaptability, a discovery of structure *in* experience, a flowing, changing organization of self and personality.

It is this tendency toward existential living which appears to me very evident in people who are involved in the process of psychological health. It means discovering the structure of experience in the process of living the experience. Most of us, on the other hand, bring a preformed structure and evaluation to our experience and never relinquish it, but cram and twist the experience to fit our preconceptions, annoyed at the fluid qualities which make it so unruly in fitting our carefully constructed pigeonholes. To open one's self to what is going on *now*, and to discover in that present process whatever structure it appears to have—this to me is one of the qualities of the healthy life, the mature life, as I see clients approach it.

An Increasing Trust in His Organism

Still another characteristic of the person who is living the process of health appears to be an increasing trust in his organism as a means of arriving at the most satisfying behavior in each existential situation. Again let me try to explain what I mean.

In choosing what course of action to take in any situation, many people rely upon guiding principles, upon a code of action laid down by some group or institution, upon the judgment of others (from wife and friends to Emily Post), or upon the way they behaved in some similar past situation. Yet as I observe the clients whose experiences in living have taught me so much, I find that increasingly such individuals are able to trust their total organismic reaction to a new situation because they discover to an ever-increasing degree that if they are open to their experience, doing what "feels right" proves to be a competent and trustworthy guide to behavior which is truly satisfying.

As I try to understand the reason for this, I find myself following this line of thought: The hypothetical person who is fully open to his experience would have access to all of the available data in the situation, on which to base his behavior—the social demands; his own complex and possibly conflicting needs; his memories of similar situations; his perception of the uniqueness of this situation. The data would be very complex indeed. But he could permit his total organism, his consciousness participating, to consider each stimulus, need and demand, its relative intensity and importance, and out of this complex weighing and balancing, discover that course of action which would come closest to satisfying all his needs in the situation.

An analogy which might come close to a description would be to compare this person to a giant electronic computing machine. Since he is open to his experience, all of the data from his sense impressions, from his memory, from previous learning, from his visceral and internal states, are fed into the machine. The machine takes all of these multitudinous pulls and forces which are fed in as data, and quickly computes the course of action which would be the most economical vector of need satisfaction in this existential situation. This is the behavior of our hypothetical person.

The defects which in most of us make this process untrustworthy are the inclusion of information which does *not* belong to this present situation, or the exclusion of information which *does*. It is when memories and previous learnings are fed into the computations as if they were *this* reality, and not memories and learnings, that erroneous behavioral answers arise. Or when certain threatening experiences are inhibited from awareness, and hence are withheld from the computation or fed into it in distorted form, this too produces error. But our hypothetical person would find his organism thoroughly trustworthy, because all of the available data would be used, and it would be present in accurate rather than distorted form. Hence his behavior would come as close as possible to satisfying all his needs—for enhancement, for affiliation with others, and the like.

In this weighing, balancing and computation, his organism would not by any means be infallible. It would always give the best possible answer for the available data, but sometimes data would be missing. Because of the element of openness to experience, however, any errors, any following of behavior which was not satisfying, would be quickly corrected. The computations, as it were, would always be in process of being corrected, because they would be continually checked against their consequences.

Perhaps the reader will not like my analogy of an electronic computing machine. Let me put it in more human terms. The client I previously quoted found himself expressing annoyance to his daughter, as well as affection, when he "felt like it." Yet he found himself doing it in a way which not only released the tension in himself, but which freed this small girl to voice her annoyances. He describes the differences between communicating his annoyance and directing his feeling of anger at, or imposing it on, her: "'Cause it just doesn't feel like I'm imposing my feelings on her, and it seems to me I must show it on my face. Maybe she sees it as 'Yes, daddy is angry, but I don't have to cower.' Because she never *does* cower. This in itself is a topic for a novel, it just feels that good." In this instance, being open to his experience, he selects, with astonishing intuitive skill, a subtly guided course of behavior which meets his need for release of angry tension, but also satisfies his need to be a good father and his need to find satisfaction in his daughter's healthy development. Yet he achieves all this by simply doing the thing that feels right to him.

Another way of saying this is that the individual guides his behavior by the meanings which he discovers in the immediate feeling process which is going on within him. Gendlin (1961) terms this immediately present feeling process "experiencing," and shows how the individual can turn again and again to his experiencing to discover further meanings in it. The experiencing is thus a referent by which the individual may guide his behavior.

Observation has shown that clients who appear to have gained the most from therapy come to trust their experiencing. They accept the realization that the meanings implicit in their experiencing of a situation constitute the wisest and most satisfying indication of appropriate behavior. I think of one client who, toward the close of therapy, when puzzled about an issue, would put his head in his hands and say, "Now what *is* it I'm feeling? I want to get next to it. I want to learn what it is." Then he would wait, quietly and patiently, until he could discern the exact flavor of the feelings occurring in him. Often I sense that the client is trying to listen to himself, is trying to hear the messages and meanings which are being communicated by his own physiological reactions. No longer is he so fearful of what he may find. He comes to realize that his own inner reactions and experiences, the messages of his senses and his viscera, are friendly. He comes to want to be close to his inner sources of information rather than closing them off.

Again there is a bit of research evidence to indicate that this trust of one's own experiencing is associated with the healthy personality. Crutchfield (1955), in a most interesting study, presented potential military leaders with a situation in which the individual's clear perception and experience of a given situation appeared to be at variance with the judgment of all the other members of the group. Should he now rely on the evidence of his own senses or defer to the judgment of the group? The evidence shows that those who trusted their own experiencing were better adjusted individuals, more mature, with greater leadership ability. Those who distrusted their own sensing of the situation and adopted the group judgment were the less mature, less well adjusted persons.

It seems to be this trust of his own experiencing which guided the scientific behavior of Einstein, holding him toward a given direction, long before he could give any completely conscious and rational basis for it. During this initial period he simply trusted his total organismic reaction. He says, "During all those years there was a feeling of direction, of going straight toward something concrete. It is, of course, very hard to express that feeling in words, but it was decidedly the case, and clearly to be distinguished from later considerations about the rational form of the solution."[2] This is the type of behavior which is also, I believe, characteristic of the person who has gained greatly from therapy.

SOME IMPLICATIONS

The three trends I have tried to describe—toward openness to experience, living as a process, and trust of one's own experiencing—add up to the fact that the person in whom they are observed is becoming a more fully functioning person. This picture of a more fully functioning individual has many implications, but I will restrict myself to pointing out three which I believe have special importance.

---

2. Wertheimer, Max. *Productive Thinking*. New York, Harper & Brothers: 1945, pp. 183-84.

Integration

The trends I have presented describe an individual who is becoming integrated. He is unified within himself from the surface level to the level of depth. He is becoming "all of one piece." The distinctions between "role self" and "real self," between defensive facade and real feelings, between conscious and unconscious, are all growing less the further these trends continue. All that the individual experiences and is, within the envelope of his organism, is increasingly available to his conscious self, to himself as a person. There is a continuing growth of good communication between all the different aspects and facets of himself.

Creativity

Watching my clients, I have come to a much better understanding of creative people. El Greco, for example, must have realized, as he looked at some of his early work, that "good artists do not paint like that." But somehow he trusted sufficiently his own experiencing of life, the process of himself, so that he could go on expressing his own unique perceptions. It was as though he could say, "Good artists do not paint like this, but *I* paint like this." Or, to move to another field, Ernest Hemingway was surely aware that "good writers do not write like this." But fortunately he moved toward being Hemingway, being himself, rather than toward someone else's conception of a good writer.

Einstein seems to have been unusually oblivious to the fact that good physicists did not think his kind of thoughts. Rather than drawing back because of his inadequate academic preparation in physics, he simply moved toward being Einstein, toward thinking his own thoughts, toward being as truly and deeply himself as he could. This is not a phenomenon which occurs only in the artist or genius. Time and again in my clients, I have seen simple people become significant and creative in their own spheres, as they have developed more trust of the processes going on within themselves, and have dared to feel their own feelings, live by values which they discover within, and express themselves in their own unique ways.

Such a person would, I believe, be recognized by the student of evolution as the type most likely to adapt and survive under changing environmental conditions. He would be able creatively to make sound adjustments to new as well as old conditions. He would be a fit vanguard of human evolution.

Trustworthiness of Human Nature

It will have been evident that one implication of the view presented here is that the basic nature of the human being, when functioning freely, is constructive and trustworthy. For me this is an inescapable conclusion from a quarter century of experience in psychotherapy. When we are able to free the individual from defensiveness, so that he is open to the wide range of his own needs, as well as to the wide range of environmental and social demands, his reactions may be trusted to be positive, forward-moving, constructive. We do not need to ask who will socialize him, for one of his own deepest needs is for affiliation and communication with others. When he is fully himself, he cannot help but be realistically socialized. We do not need to ask who will control his aggressive impulses, for when he is open to all of his impulses, his need to be liked by others and his tendency to give affection are as strong as his impulses to strike out or to seize for himself. He will be aggressive in situations in which aggression is realistically appropriate, but there will be no runaway need for aggression. His total behavior, in these and other areas, when he is open to all his experience, is balanced and realistic—behavior which is appropriate to the survival and enhancement of a highly social animal.

I have little sympathy with the rather prevalent concept that man is basically irrational, and that his impulses, if not controlled, would lead to destruction of others and self. Man's behavior is exquisitely rational, moving with subtle and ordered complexity toward the goals his organism is endeavoring to achieve. The tragedy for most of us is that our defenses keep us from being aware of this rationality, so that consciously we are moving in one direction, while organismically we are moving in another. But in our hypothetical person there would be no such barriers, and he would be a participant in the rationality of his organism. The only control of impulses which would exist or which would prove necessary is the natural and internal balancing of one need against another and the discovery of behaviors which follow the vector most closely approximating the satisfaction of all needs. The experience of extreme satisfaction of one need (for aggression, sex, etc.) in such a way as to do violence to the satisfaction of other needs (for companionship, tender relationship, etc.)—an experience very common in the defensively organized person—would simply be unknown in our hypothetical individual. He would participate in the vastly complex self-regulatory activities of his organism—the psychological as well as physiological thermostatic controls—in such a fashion as to live harmoniously, with himself and with others.

Becoming a Fully Functioning Person

Let me conclude by drawing together these observational threads into a more unified strand. As I have observed individuals who appear to have made important strides toward psychological health, I believe they may be thought of as moving toward an implicit goal—that of becoming a fully functioning person.

I find such a person to be a human being in flow, in process, rather than having achieved some state. Fluid change is central in the picture.

I find such a person to be sensitively open to all of his experience— sensitive to what is going on in his environment, sensitive to other individuals with whom he is in relationship, and sensitive perhaps most of all to the feelings, reactions, and emergent meanings which he discovers in himself. The fear of some aspects of his own experience continues to diminish, so that more and more of his life is available to him.

Such a person experiences in the present, with immediacy. He is able to live in his feelings and reactions of the moment. He is not bound by the structure of his past learnings, but these are a present resource for him, insofar as they relate to the experience of the moment. He lives freely, subjectively, in an existential confrontation of this moment of life.

Such a person is trustingly able to permit his total organism to function freely in all its complexity in selecting, from the multitude of possibilities, that behavior which in this moment of time will be most generally and genuinely satisfying. He thus is making use of all of the data his nervous system can supply, using this data in awareness, but recognizing that his total organism may be, and often is, wiser than his awareness.

Such a person is a creative person. With his sensitive openness to his world, and his trust of his own ability to form new relationships with his environment, he is the type of person from whom creative products and creative living emerge.

Finally, such a person lives a life which involves a wider range, a greater richness, than the constricted living in which most of us find ourselves. It seems to me that clients who have moved significantly in therapy live more intimately with their feelings of pain, but also more vividly with their feelings of ecstasy; that anger is more clearly felt, but so also is love; that fear is an experience they know more deeply, but so is courage; and the reason they can thus live fully in a wider range is that they have this underlying confidence in themselves as trustworthy instruments for encountering life.

I believe it will have become evident why, for me, adjectives such as happy, contented, enjoyable, do not seem quite appropriate to any general description of this process I have called psychological health, even though the person in this process would experience each one of these feelings at appropriate times. But the adjectives which seem more generally fitting are adjectives such as enriching, exciting, rewarding, challenging, meaningful. This process of healthy living is not, I am convinced, a life for the fainthearted. It involves the stretching and growing of becoming more and more of one's potentialities. It involves the courage to be. It means launching oneself fully into the stream of life. Yet the deeply exciting thing about human beings is that when the individual is inwardly free, he chooses this process of becoming.

References

Chodorkoff, B., "Self-Perception, Perceptual Defense, and Adjustment." *Journal of Abnormal and Social Psychology* (1954) 49: 508-12.

Crutchfield, R. S., "Conformity and Character," *American Psychologist* (1955) 10: 191-98.

Gendlin, E., "Experiencing: A Variable in the Process of Therapeutic Change," *American Journal of Psychotherapy* (1961) 15: 233-45.

Power Is the
Great Motivator

by David C. McClelland and David H. Burnham

What makes or motivates a good manager? The question is so enormous in scope that anyone trying to answer it has difficulty knowing where to begin. Some people might say that a good manager is one who is successful; and by now most business researchers and businessmen themselves know what motivates people who successfully run their own small businesses. The key to their success has turned out to be what psychologists call "the need for achievement," the desire to do something better or more efficiently than it has been done before. Any number of books and articles summarize research studies explaining how the achievement motive is necessary for a person to attain success on his own.[1]

But what has achievement motivation got to do with good management? There is no reason on theoretical grounds why a person who has a strong need to be more efficient should make a good manager. While it sounds as if everyone ought to have the need to achieve, in fact, as psychologists define and measure achievement motivation, it leads people to behave in very special ways that do not necessarily lead to good management.

For one thing, because they focus on personal improvement, on doing things better by themselves, achievement-motivated people want to do things themselves. For another, they want concrete short-term feedback on their performance so that they can tell how well they are doing. Yet a

Author's note: All the case material in this article is disguised.

1. For instance, see my books *The Achieving Society* (New York: Van Nostrand, 1961) and (with David Winter) *Motivating Economic Achievement* (New York: Free Press, 1969).

David C. McClelland is professor of psychology at Harvard University. David H. Burnham is president and chief executive officer of McBer and Company, a behavioral science consulting firm in Boston.

manager, particularly one of or in a large complex organization, cannot perform all the tasks necessary for success by himself or herself. He must manage others so that they will do things for the organization. Also, feedback on his subordinate's performance may be a lot vaguer and more delayed than it would be if he were doing everything himself.

The manager's job seems to call more for someone who can influence people than for someone who does things better on his own. In motivational terms, then, we might expect the successful manager to have a greater "need for power" than need to achieve. But there must be other qualities beside the need for power that go into the makeup of a good manager. Just what these qualities are and how they interrelate is the subject of this article.

To measure the motivations of managers, good and bad, we studied a number of individual managers from different large U.S. corporations who were participating in management workshops designed to improve their managerial effectiveness. (The workshop techniques and research methods and terms used are described in the ruled insert on page 54.)

The general conclusion of these studies is that the top manager of a company must possess a high need for power, that is, a concern for influencing people. However, this need must be disciplined and controlled so that it is directed toward the benefit of the institution as a whole and not toward the the manager's personal aggrandizement. Moreover, the top manager's need for power ought to be greater than his need for being liked by people.

Now let us look at what these ideas mean in the context of real individuals in real situations and see what comprises the profile of the good manager. Finally, we will look at the workshops themselves to determine how they go about changing behavior.

MEASURING MANAGERIAL EFFECTIVENESS

First off, what does it mean when we say that a good manager has a greater need for "power" than for "achievement"? To get a more concrete idea, let us consider the case of Ken Briggs, a sales manager in a large U.S. corporation who joined one of our managerial workshops (see the ruled insert). Some six or seven years ago, Ken Briggs was promoted to a managerial position at corporate headquarters, where he had responsibility for salesmen who service his company's largest accounts.

In filling out his questionnaire at the workshop, Ken showed that he correctly perceived what his job required of him, namely, that he should influence others' success more than achieve new goals himself or socialize with his subordinates. However, when asked with other members of the workshop to write a story depicting a managerial situation, Ken unwittingly revealed through his fiction that he did not share those concerns. Indeed, he discovered that his need for achievement was very high—in fact over the 90th percentile—and his need for power was very low, in about the 15th percentile. Ken's high need to achieve was no surprise—after all, he had been a very successful salesman—but obviously his motivation to influence others was much less than his job required. Ken was a little disturbed but thought that perhaps the measuring instruments were not too accurate and that the gap between the ideal and his score was not as great as it seemed.

Then came the real shocker. Ken's subordinates confirmed what his stories revealed: he was a poor manager, having little positive impact on those who worked for him. Ken's subordinates felt that they had little responsibility delegated to them, that he never rewarded but only criticized them, and that the office was not well organized, but confused and chaotic. On all three of these scales, his office rated in the 10th to 15th percentile relative to national norms.

As Ken talked the results over privately with a workshop leader, he became more and more upset. He finally agreed, however, that the results of the survey confirmed feelings he had been afraid to admit to himself or others. For years, he had been miserable in his managerial role. He now knew the reason: he simply did not want to nor had he been able to influence or manage others. As he thought back, he realized that he had failed every time he had tried to influence his staff, and he felt worse than ever.

Ken had responded to failure by setting very high standards—his office scored in the 98th percentile on this scale—and by trying to do most things himself, which was close to impossible; his own activity and lack of delegation consequently left his staff demoralized. Ken's experience is typical of those who have a strong need to achieve but low power motivation. They may become very successful salesmen and, as a consequence, may be promoted into managerial jobs for which they, ironically, are unsuited.

If achievement motivation does not make a good manager, what motive does? It is not enough to suspect that power motivation may be important; one needs hard evidence that people who are better managers than Ken Briggs do in fact possess stronger power motivation and perhaps score higher in other characteristics as well. But how does one decide who is the better manager?

Real-world performance measures are hard to come by if one is trying to rate managerial effectiveness in production, marketing, finance, or research and development. In trying to determine who the better managers were in Ken Brigg's company, we did not want to rely only on the

Workshop Techniques

The case studies and data on companies used in this article were derived from a number of workshops we conducted where executives came to learn about their managerial styles and abilities as well as how to change them. The workshops had a dual purpose, however. They provided an opportunity for us to study which motivation pattern, whether it be a concern for achievement, power, people, or a combination thereof, makes the best managers.

When the managers first arrived at the workshops, they were asked to fill out a questionnaire about their job. Each participant analyzed his job, explaining what he or she thought it required of him. The managers were asked to write a number of stories to pictures of various work situations. The stories were coded for the extent to which an individual was concerned about achievement, affiliation, or power, as well as for the amount of inhibition or self-control they revealed. The results were then matched against national norms. The differences between a person's job requirements and his or her motivational patterns can often help assess whether the person is in the right job, whether he is a candidate for promotion to another job, or whether he is likely to be able to adjust to fit his present position.

At the workshops and in this article, we use the technical terms "need for achievement," "need for power," and "need for affiliation" as defined in the books *The Achieving Society* and *Power: The Inner Experience*. The terms refer to measurable factors in groups and individuals. Briefly, these characteristics are measured by coding an individual's spontaneous thoughts for the frequency with which he thinks about doing something better or more efficiently than before (need for achievement), about establishing or maintaining friendly relations with others (need for affiliation), or about having impact on others (need for power). (When we talk about power, we are not talking about dictatorial power, but about the need to be strong and influential.) As used here, therefore, the motive labels are precise terms, referring to a particular method of defining and measuring, much as "gravity" is used in physics, or "gross national product" is used in economics.

To find out what kind of managerial style the participants had, we gave them a questionnaire in which they had to choose how they would handle various realistic work situations in office settings. Their answers were coded for six different

---

Workshop Techniques (continued)

management styles or ways of dealing with work situations. The styles depicted were democratic, affiliative, pacesetting, coaching, coercive, and authoritarian. The managers were asked to comment on the effectiveness of each style and to name the style that they prefer.

One way to determine how effective managers are is to ask the people who work for them. Thus, to isolate the characteristics that good managers have, we surveyed at least three subordinates of each manager at the workshop to see how they answered questions about their work situations that revealed characteristics of their supervisors along several dimensions, namely: (1) the amount of conformity to rules required, (2) the responsibility they feel they are given, (3) the emphasis the department places on standards of performance, (4) the degree to which they feel rewards are given for good work as opposed to punishment for something that goes wrong, (5) the degree of organizational clarity in the office, and (6) its team spirit.[1] The managers who received the highest morale scores (organizational clarity plus team spirit) from their subordinates were determined to be the best managers, possessing the most desirable motive patterns.

The subordinates were also surveyed six months after the managers returned to their offices to see if the morale scores rose after the workshop.

One other measure was obtained from the participants to find out which managers had another characteristic deemed important for good management: maturity. Scores were obtained for four stages in the progress toward maturity by coding the stories which the managers wrote for such matters as their attitudes toward authority and the kinds of emotions displayed over specific issues.

People in Stage I are dependent on others for guidance and strength. Those in Stage II are interested primarily in autonomy, in controlling themselves. In Stage III, people want to manipulate others; in Stage IV, they lose their egotistic desires and wish to selflessly serve others.[2]

The conclusions presented in this article are based on workshops attended by over 500 managers from over 25 different U.S. corporations. However, the data in the exhibits are drawn from just one of these companies for illustrative purposes.

---

[1] Based on G.H. Litwin and R.A. Stringer's *Motivation and Organizational Climate* (Boston: Division of Research, Harvard Business School, 1966).

[2] Based on work by Abigail Stewart reported in David C. McClelland's *Power: The Inner Experience* (New York: Irvington Publishers, 1975).

opinions of their superiors. For a variety of reasons, superiors' judgments of their subordinates' real-world performance may be inaccurate. In the absence of some standard measure of performance, we decided that the next best index of a manager's effectiveness would be the climate he or she creates in the office, reflected in the morale of subordinates.

Almost by definition, a good manager is one who, among other things, helps subordinates feel strong and responsible, who rewards them properly for good performance, and who sees that things are organized in such a way that subordinates feel they know what they should be doing. Above all, managers should foster among subordinates a strong sense of team spirit, of pride in working as part of a particular team. If a manager creates and encourages this spirit, his subordinates certainly should perform better.

In the company Ken Briggs works for, we have direct evidence of a connection between morale and performance in the one area where performance measures are easy to come by — namely, sales. In April 1973, at least three employees from this company's 16 sales districts filled out questionnaires that rated their office for organizational clarity and team spirit (see the ruled insert). Their scores were averaged and totaled to give an overall morale score for each office. The percentage gains or losses in sales for each district in 1973 were compared with those for 1972. The difference in sales figures by district ranged from a gain of nearly 30% to a loss of 8%, with a median gain of around 14%. *Exhibit I* shows the average gain in sales performance plotted against the increasing averages in morale scores.

In *Exhibit I* we can see that the relationship between sales and morale is surprisingly close. The six districts with the lowest morale early in the year showed an average sales gain of only around 7% by years' end (although there was wide variation within this group), whereas the two districts with the highest morale showed an average gain of 28%. When morale scores rise above the 50th percentile in terms of national norms, they seem to lead to better sales performance. In Ken Briggs' company, at least, high morale at the beginning is a good index of how well the sales division actually performed in the coming year.

And it seems very likely that the manager who can create high morale among salesmen can also do the same for employees in other areas (production, design, and so on), leading to better performance. Given that high morale in an office indicates that there is a good manager present, what general characteristics does he possess?

A Need for Power

In examining the motive scores of over 50 managers of both high and low morale units in all sections of the same large company, we found that

Average percent gain in sales by district from 1972 to 1973

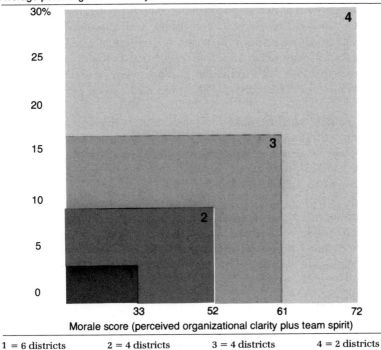

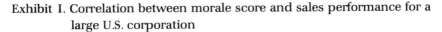

1 = 6 districts   2 = 4 districts   3 = 4 districts   4 = 2 districts

Exhibit I. Correlation between morale score and sales performance for a
    large U.S. corporation

most of the managers—over 70%—were high in power motivation compared with men in general. This finding confirms the fact that power
motivation is important for management. (Remember that as we use the
term "power motivation," it refers not to dictatorial behavior, but to a
desire to have impact, to be strong and influential.) The better managers,
as judged by the morale of those working for them, tended to score even
higher in power motivation. But the most important determining factor of
high morale turned out not to be how their power motivation compared
to their need to achieve but whether it was higher than their need to be
liked. This relationship existed for 80% of the better sales managers as
compared with only 10% of the poorer managers. And the same held true
for other managers in nearly all parts of the company.

   In the research, product development, and operations divisions, 73%
of the better managers had a stronger need for power than a need to be
liked (or what we term "affiliation motive") as compared with only 22% of
the poorer managers. Why should this be so? Sociologists have long
argued that, for a bureaucracy to function effectively, those who manage
it must be universalistic in applying rules. That is, if they make exceptions

for the particular needs of individuals, the whole system will break down.

The manager with a high need for being liked is precisely the one who wants to stay on good terms with everybody, and, therefore, is the one most likely to make exceptions in terms of particular needs. If a male employee asks for time off to stay home with his sick wife to help look after her and the kids, the affiliative manager agrees almost without thinking, because he feels sorry for the man and agrees that his family needs him.

When President Ford remarked in pardoning ex-President Nixon that he had "suffered enough," he was responding as an affiliative manager would, because he was empathizing primarily with Nixon's needs and feelings. Sociological theory and our data both argue, however, that the person whose need for affiliation is high does not make a good manager. This kind of person creates poor morale because he or she does not understand that other people in the office will tend to regard exceptions to the rules as unfair to themselves, just as many U.S. citizens felt it was unfair to let Richard Nixon off and punish others less involved than he was in the Watergate scandal.

Socialized Power

But so far our findings are a little alarming. Do they suggest that the good manager is one who cares for power and is not at all concerned about the needs of other people? Not quite, for the good manager has other characteristics which must still be taken into account.

Above all, the good manager's power motivation is not oriented toward personal aggrandizement but toward the institution which he or she serves. In another major research study, we found that the signs of controlled action or inhibition that appear when a person exercises his or her imagination in writing stories tell a great deal about he kind of power that person needs.[2] We discovered that, if a high power motive score is balanced by high inhibition, stories about power tend to be altruistic. That is, the heroes in the story exercise power on behalf of someone else. This is the "socialized" face of power as distinguished from the concern for personal power, which is characteristic of individuals whose stories are loaded with power imagery but which show no sign of inhibition or self-control. In our earlier study, we found ample evidence that these latter individuals exercise their power impulsively. They are more rude to other people, they drink too much, they try to exploit others sexually, and they collect symbols of personal prestige such as fancy cars or big offices.

---

2. David C. McClelland, William N. Davis, Rudolf Kalin, and Erie Warner, *The Drinking Man* (New York: The Free Press, 1972).

Individuals high in power and in control, on the other hand, are more institution minded; they tend to get elected to more offices, to control their drinking, and to want to serve others. Not surprisingly, we found in the workshops that the better managers in the corporation also tend to score high on both power and inhibition.

PROFILE OF A GOOD MANAGER

Let us recapitulate what we have discussed so far and have illustrated with data from one company. The better managers we studied are high in power motivation, low in affiliation motivation, and high in inhibition. They care about institutional power and use it to stimulate their employees to be more productive. Now let us compare them with affiliative managers — those in whom the need for affiliation is higher than the need for power—and with the personal power managers—those in whom the need for power is higher than for affiliation but whose inhibition score is low.

In the sales division of our illustrative company, there were managers who matched the three types fairly closely. *Exhibit II* shows how their subordinates rated the offices they worked in on responsibility, organizational clarity, and team spirit. There are scores from at least three subordinates for each manager, and several managers are represented for each type, so that the averages shown in the exhibit are quite stable. Note that the manager who is concerned about being liked by people tends to have subordinates who feel that they have very little personal responsibility, that organizational procedures are not clear, and that they have little pride in their work group.

In short, as we expected, affiliative managers make so many ad hominem and ad hoc decisions that they almost totally abandon orderly procedures. Their disregard for procedure leaves employees feeling weak, irresponsible, and without a sense of what might happen next, of where they stand in relation to their manager, or even of what they ought to be doing. In this company, the group of affiliative managers portrayed in *Exhibit II* were below the 30th percentile in morale scores.

The managers who are motivated by a need for personal power are somewhat more effective. They are able to create a greater sense of responsibility in their divisions and, above all, a greater team spirit. They can be thought of as managerial equivalents of successful tank commanders such as General Patton, whose own daring inspired admiration in his troops. But notice how in *Exhibit II* these men are still only in the 40th percentile in the amount of organizational clarity they create, as compared to the high power, low affiliation, high inhibition managers, whom we shall term "institutional."

Managers motivated by personal power are not disciplined enough to be good institution builders, and often their subordinates are loyal to them as individuals rather than to the institution they both serve. When a personal power manager leaves, disorganization often follows. His subordinates' strong group spirit, which the manager has personally inspired, deflates. The subordinates do not know what to do for themselves.

Of the managerial types, the "institutional" manager is the most successful in creating an effective work climate. *Exhibit II* shows that his subordinates feel that they have more responsibility. Also, this kind of manager creates high morale because he produces the greatest sense of organizational clarity and team spirit. If such a manager leaves, he or she can be more readily replaced by another manager, because the employees have been encouraged to be loyal to the institution rather than to a particular person.

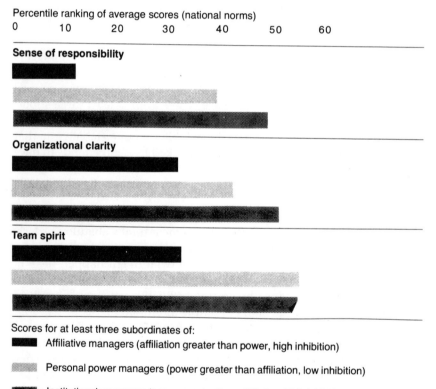

Percentile ranking of average scores (national norms)

0   10   20   30   40   50   60

Sense of responsibility

Organizational clarity

Team spirit

Scores for at least three subordinates of:

Affiliative managers (affiliation greater than power, high inhibition)

Personal power managers (power greater than affiliation, low inhibition)

Institutional managers (power greater than affiliation, high inhibition)

Exhibit II. Average scores on selected climate dimensions by subordinates of managers with different motive profiles.

Managerial Styles

Since it seems undeniable from *Exhibit II* that either kind of power orientation creates better morale in subordinates than a "people" orientation, we must consider that a concern for power is essential to good management. Our findings seem to fly in the face of a long and influential tradition or organizational psychology, which insists that authoritarian management is what is wrong with most businesses in this country. Let us say frankly that we think the bogeyman of authoritarianism has in fact been wrongly used to downplay the importance of power in management. After all, management is an influence game. Some proponents of democratic management seem to have forgotten this fact, urging managers to be primarily concerned with people's human needs rather than with helping them to get things done.

But a good deal of the apparent conflict between our findings and those of other behavioral scientists in this area arises from the fact that we are talking about *motives*, and behaviorists are often talking about *actions*. What we are saying is that managers must be interested in playing the influence game in a controlled way. That does not necessarily mean that they are or should be authoritarian in action. On the contrary, it appears that power motivated managers make their subordinates feel strong rather than weak. The true authoritarian in action would have the reverse effect, making people feel weak and powerless.

Thus another important ingredient in the profile of a manager is his or her managerial style. In the illustrative company, 63% of the better managers (those whose subordinates had higher morale) scored higher on the democratic or coaching styles of management as compared with only 22% of the poorer managers, a statistically significant difference. By contrast, the latter scored higher on authoritarian or coercive management styles. Since the better managers were also higher in power motivation, it seems that, in action, they express their power motivation in a democratic way, which is more likely to be effective.

To see how motivation and style interact, let us consider the case of George Prentice, a manager in the sales division of another company. George had exactly the right motive combination to be an institutional manager. He was high in the need for power, low in the need for affiliation, and high in inhibition. He exercised his power in a controlled, organized way. His stories reflected this fact. In one, for instance, he wrote, "The men sitting around the table were feeling pretty good; they had just finished plans for reorganizing the company; the company has been beset with a number of organizational problems. This group, headed by a hard-driving, brilliant young executive, has completely reorganized the company structurally with new jobs and responsibilities...."

This described how George himself was perceived by the company, and shortly after the workshop he was promoted to vice president in charge of all sales. But George was also known to his colleagues as a monster, a tough guy who would "walk over his grandmother" if she stood in the way of his advancement. He had the right motive combination and, in fact, was more interested in institutional growth than in personal power, but his managerial style was all wrong. Taking his cue from some of the top executives in the corporation, he told people what they had to do and threatened them with dire consequences if they didn't do it.

When George was confronted with his authoritarianism in a workshop, he recognized that this style was counterproductive—in fact, in another part of the study we found that it was associated with low morale—and he subsequently changed to acting more like a coach, which was the scale on which he scored the lowest initially. George saw more clearly that his job was not to force other people to do things but to help them to figure out ways of getting their job done better for the company.

The Institutional Manager

One reason it was easy for George Prentice to change his managerial style was that in his imaginative stories he was already having thoughts about helping others, characteristic of men with the institution-building motivational pattern. In further examining institution builders' thoughts and actions, we found they have four major characteristics:

1

They are more organization-minded; that is, they tend to join more organizations and to feel responsible for building up these organizations. Furthermore, they believe strongly in the importance of centralized authority.

2

They report that they like to work. This finding is particularly interesting, because our research on achievement motivation has led many commentators to argue that achievement motivation promotes the "Protestant work ethic." Almost the precise opposite is true. People who have a high need to achieve like to get out of work by becoming more efficient. They would like to see the same result obtained in less time or with less effort. But managers who have a need for institutional power actually seem to like the discipline of work. It satisfies their need for getting things done in an orderly way.

3

They seem quite willing to sacrifice some of their own self-interest for the welfare of the organization they serve. For example, they are more willing to make contributions to charities.

4

They have a keen sense of justice. It is almost as if they feel that if a person works hard and sacrifices for the good of the organization, he should and will get a just reward for his effort.

It is easy to see how each of these four concerns helps a person become a good manager, concerned about what the institution can achieve.

Maturity

Before we go on to look at how the workshops can help managers to improve their managerial style and recognize their own motivations, let us consider one more fact we discovered in studying the better managers at George Prentice's company. They were more mature (see ruled insert, p. 54). Mature people can be most simply described as less egotistic. Somehow their positive self-image is not at stake in what they are doing. They are less defensive, more willing to seek advice from experts, and have a longer range view. They accumulate fewer personal possessions and seem older and wiser. It is as if they have awakened to the fact that they are not going to live forever and have lost some of the feeling that their own personal future is all that important.

Many U.S. businessmen fear this kind of maturity. They suspect that it will make them less hard driving, less expansion-minded, and less committed to organizational effectiveness. Our data do not support their fears. These fears are exactly the ones George Prentice had before he went to the workshop. Afterward he was a more effective manager, not despite his loss of some of the sense of his own importance, but because of it. The reason is simple: his subordinates believed afterward that he genuinely was more concerned about the company than about himself. Where once they respected his confidence but feared him, they now trust him. Once he supported their image of him as a "big man" by talking about the new Porsche and the new Honda he had bought; when we saw him recently he said, almost as an aside, "I don't buy things anymore."

CHANGING MANAGERIAL STYLE

George Prentice was able to change his managerial style after learning more about himself in a workshop. But does self-knowledge generally improve managerial behavior?

Some people might ask, "What good does it do to know, if I am a manager, that I should have a strong power motive, not too great a concern about being liked, a sense of discipline, a high level of maturity, and a coaching managerial style? What can I do about it?" The answer is that workshops for managers that give information to them in a supportive setting enable them to change.

Consider the results shown in *Exhibit III*, where "before" and "after" scores are compared. Once again we use the responses of subordinates to give some measure of the effectiveness of managers. To judge by their subordinates' responses, the managers were clearly more effective afterward. The subordinates felt that they were given more responsibility, that they received more rewards, that the organizational procedures were clearer, and that morale was higher. These differences are all statistically significant.

But what do these differences mean in human terms? How did the managers change? Sometimes they decided they should get into another line of work. This happened to Ken Briggs, for example, who found that the reason he was doing so poorly as a manager was because he had almost no interest in influencing others. He understood how he would have to change if he were to do well in his present job, but in the end decided, with the help of management, that he would prefer to work back into his first love, sales.

Ken Briggs moved into "remaindering," to help retail outlets for his company's products get rid of last year's stock so that they could take on each year's new styles. He is very successful in his new role; he has cut costs, increased dollar volume, and in time has worked himself into an independent role selling some of the old stock on his own in a way that is quite satisfactory to the business. And he does not have to manage anybody anymore.

In George Prentice's case, less change was needed. He was obviously a very competent person with the right motive profile for a top managerial position. When he was promoted, he performed even more successfully than before because he realized the need to become more positive in his approach and less coercive in his managerial style.

But what about a person who does not want to change his job and discovers that he does not have the right motive profile to be a manager?

The case of Charlie Blake is instructive. Charlie was as low in power motivation as Ken Briggs, his need to achieve was about average, and his affiliation motivation was above average. Thus he had the affiliative manager profile, and, as expected, the morale among his subordinates was very low. When Charlie learned that his subordinates' sense of responsibility and perception of a reward system were in the 10th percentile and that team spirit was in the 30th, he was shocked. When shown a film depicting three managerial climates. Charlie said he preferred what

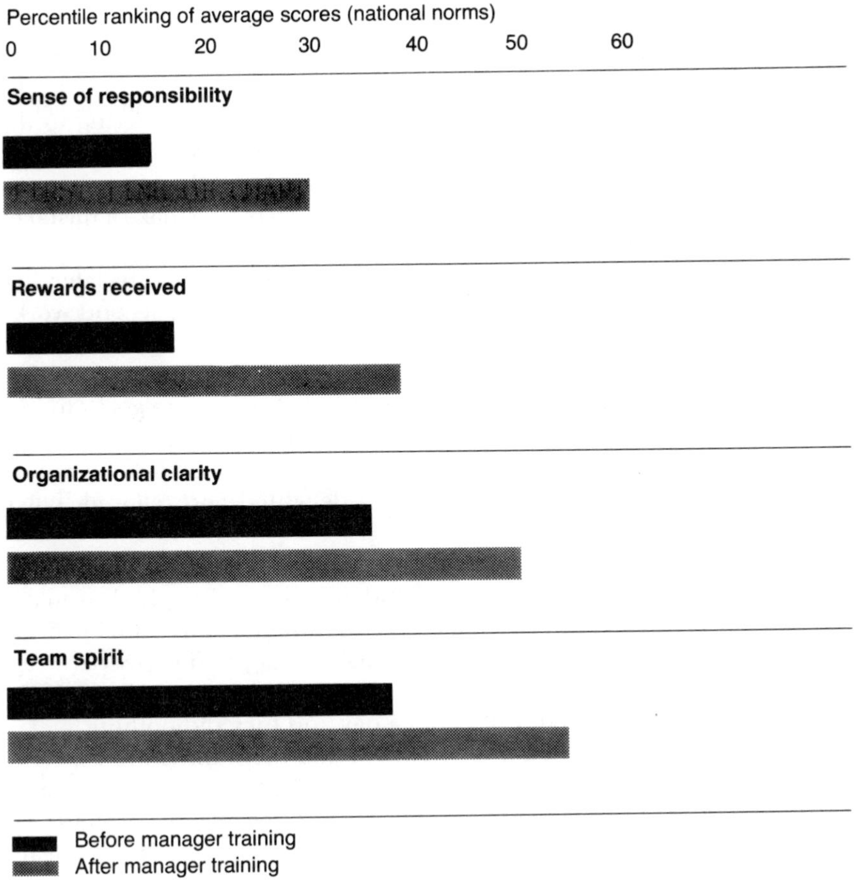

Percentile ranking of average scores (national norms)

Exhibit III. Average scores on selected climate dimensions by over 50 salesmen before and after their managers were trained

turned out to be the authoritarian climate. He became angry when the workshop trainer and other members in the group pointed out the limitations of this managerial style. He became obstructive in the group process and objected strenuously to what was being taught.

In an interview conducted much later, Charlie said, "I blew my cool. When I started yelling at you for being all wrong, I got even madder when you pointed out that, according to my style questionnaire, you bet that that was just what I did to my salesmen. Down underneath I knew something must be wrong. The sales performance for my division wasn't so good. Most of it was due to me anyway and not to my salesmen.

Obviously their reports that they felt very little responsibility was delegated to them and that I didn't reward them at all had to mean something. So I finally decided to sit down and try to figure what I could do about it. I knew I had to start being a manager instead of trying to do everything myself and blowing my cool at others because they didn't do what I thought they should. In the end, after I calmed down on the way back from the workshop, I realized that it is not so bad to make a mistake; it's bad not to learn from it."

After the course, Charlie put his plans into effect. Six months later, his subordinates were asked to rate him again. He attended a second workshop to study these results and reported, "On the way home I was very nervous. I knew I had been working with those guys and not selling so much myself, but I was very much afraid of what they were going to say about how things were going in the office. When I found out that the team spirit and some of those other low scores had jumped from around the 30th to the 55th percentile, I was so delighted and relieved that I couldn't say anything all day long."

When he was asked how he acted differently from before, he said, "In previous years when the corporate headquarters said we had to make 110% of our original goal, I had called the salesmen in and said, in effect, 'This is ridiculous; we are not going to make it, but you know perfectly well what will happen if we don't. So get out there and work your tail off.' The result was that I worked 20 hours a day and they did nothing.

"This time I approached it differently. I told them three things. First, they were going to have to do some sacrificing for the company. Second, working harder is not going to do much good because we are already working about as hard as we can. What will be required are special deals and promotions. You are going to have to figure out some new angles if we are going to make it. Third, I'm going to back you up. I'm going to set a realistic goal with each of you. If you make that goal but don't make the company goal, I'll see to it that you are not punished. But if you do make the company goal, I'll see to it that you will get some kind of special rewards."

When the salesmen challenged Charlie saying he did not have enough influence to give them rewards, rather than becoming angry Charlie promised rewards that were in his power to give—such as longer vacations.

Note that Charlie has now begun to behave in a number of ways that we found to be characteristic of the good institutional manager. He is, above all, higher in power motivation, the desire to influence his salesmen, and lower in his tendency to try to do everything himself. He asks the men to sacrifice for the company. He does not defensively chew them out when they challenge him but tries to figure out what their needs are so that he can influence them. He realizes that his job is more one of strengthening and supporting his subordinates than of criticizing them. And he is keenly interested in giving them just rewards for their efforts.

The changes in his approach to his job have certainly paid off. The sales figures for his office in 1973 were up more than 16% over 1972 and up still further in 1974 over 1973. In 1973 his gain over the previous year ranked seventh in the nation; in 1974 it ranked third. And he wasn't the only one in his company to change managerial styles. Overall sales at his company were up substantially in 1973 as compared with 1972, an increase which played a large part in turning the overall company performance around from a $15 million loss in 1972 to a $3 million profit in 1973. The company continued to improve its performance in 1974 with an 11% further gain in sales and a 38% increase in profits.

Of course not everyone can be reached by a workshop. Henry Carter managed a sales office for a company which had a very low morale (around the 20th percentile) before he went for training. When morale was checked some six months late, it had not improved. Overall sales gain subsequently reflected this fact since it was only 2% above the previous year's figures.

Oddly enough, Henry's problem was that he was so well liked by everybody that he felt little pressure to change. Always the life of the party, he is particularly popular because he supplies other managers with special hard-to-get brands of cigars and wines at a discount. He uses his close ties with everyone to bolster his position in the company, even though it is known that his office does not perform well compared with others.

His great interpersonal skills became evident at the workshop when he did very poorly at one of the business games. When the discussion turned to why he had done so badly and whether he acted that way on the job, two prestigious participants immediately sprang to his defense, explaining away Henry's failure by arguing that the way he did things was often a real help to others and the company. As a result, Henry did not have to cope with such questions at all. He had so successfully developed his role as a likeable, helpful friend to everyone in management that, even though his salesmen performed badly, he did not feel under any pressure to change.

CHECKS AND BALANCES

What have we learned from Ken Briggs, George Prentice, Charlie Blake, and Henry Carter? Principally, we have discovered what motive combination makes an effective manager. We have also seen that change is possible if a person has the right combination of qualities.

Oddly enough, the good manager in a large company does not have a high need for achievement, as we define and measure that motive, although there must be plenty of that motive somewhere in his organization. The top managers shown here have a high need for power and an interest in influencing others, both greater than their interest in being liked by people. The manager's concern for power should be socialized—controlled so that the institution as a whole, not only the individual, benefits. Men and nations with this motive profile are empire builders; they tend to create high morale and to expand the organizations they head.

But there is also danger in this motive profile; empire building can lead to imperialism and authoritarianism in companies and in countries.

The same motive pattern which produces good power management can also lead a company or a country to try to dominate others, ostensibly in the interests of organizational expansion. Thus it is not surprising that big business has had to be regulated from time to time by federal agencies. And it is most likely that international agencies will perform the same regulative function for empire-building countries.

For an individual, the regulative function is performed by two characteristics that are part of the profile of the very best managers—a greater emotional maturity, where there is little egotism, and a democratic, coaching managerial style. If an institutional power motivation is checked by maturity, it does not lead to an aggressive, egotistic expansiveness.

For countries, this checking means that they can control their destinies beyond their borders without being aggressive and hostile. For individuals, it means they can control their subordinates and influence others around them without resorting to coercion or to an authoritarian management style. Real disinterested statesmanship has a vital role to play at the top of both countries and companies.

Summarized in this way, what we have found out through empirical and statistical investigations may just sound like good common sense. But the improvement over common sense is that now the characteristics of the good manager are objectively known. Managers of corporations can select those who are likely to be good managers and train those already in managerial positions to be more effective with more confidence.

Interpersonal Communication

by W. Warner Burke

Communication, by definition, involves at least two individuals, the sender and the receiver. Consider yourself, first of all, as the sender of some message. There are certain filters or barriers (internal) which determine whether or not the message is actually transmitted. These barriers may be categorized as follows: (1) Assumptions about yourself—Do I really have something to offer? Am I safe to offer suggestions? Do I really want to share the information? Will others really understand? How will the communication affect my self-esteem? (2) Attitudes about the message itself—Is the information valuable? Do I see the information correctly, or understand it well enough to describe it to others? (3) Sensing the receiver's reaction—Do I become aware of whether or not the receiver is actually understanding? Or in other words, can I "sense" from certain cues or reactions by the receiver whether or not we are communicating?

Now consider yourself as the receiver. As a receiver you may filter or not hear certain aspects (or any aspect for that matter) of a message. Why? Because the message may seem unimportant or too difficult. Moreover, you may be selective in your attention. For example, you may feel that the sender is being redundant, so you quit listening after the first few words. You may be preoccupied with something else. Or your filtering or lack of attention may be due to your past experience with the sender. You may feel that "this guy has never made a point in his life and never will!"

Many times the receiver never makes use of his "third ear." That is, trying to be sensitive to nonverbal communication. The sender's eyes, gestures, and sometimes his overall posture communicate messages that the insensitive listener never receives.

W. Warner Burke is professor of psychology and education, Department of Educational Psychology, Teachers College, Columbia University.

There may be barriers that exist *between* the sender and the receiver, e.g., cultural differences. Environmental conditions may also cause barriers, e.g., poor acoustics. More common, however, are the differences in frames of reference. For example, there may not be a common understanding of purpose in a certain communication. You may ask me how I'm feeling today. To you the phrase, "How ya doing?" is nothing more than a greeting. However, I may think that you really want to know and I may tell you—possibly at some length.

Now that some of the problems in interpersonal communication have been mentioned, let us delve somewhat deeper into this process of transferring a message from the brain and emotion of one person to the brain and emotion of another human being.

Sending the Message

In communicating a message effectively to another person, there are several obvious factors which are beneficial. Such things as correct pronunciation, lack of distracting brogue, dialect, or accent, or a pleasant resonance in one's voice usually facilitate the sending of a message.

Assuming the sender of a message really has a desire to be heard and understood and not just speak for the sake of speaking, he wants some assurance that he has communicated. The key to effective communication on the part of the speaker, then, is to obtain some feedback, of one form or another, from his listener(s). Some bright persons who really have something to say are ineffective speakers, be it lecturing or speaking to someone at a cocktail party, because they are unable to tell or care whether their listener(s) is understanding, or they do not make any effort to check on their effectiveness as a communicator. For example, many lecturers in a classroom situation are often unaware of when a listener is sound asleep. Unless there is interaction of some type between the speaker and his listener, the speaker is susceptible to "losing" his listener. Often the speaker must take the initiative in order to receive any feedback regarding the effectiveness of his communication. When speaking before a large group, I often resort to the simple act of requesting my audience to shake their head "yes" they understand what I have just said, or "no" they did not understand. Even though this technique is simple, I usually get considerable feedback quickly and I know immediately what I must do at that point to make my speech more effective or whether to continue on with my next point.

Even when talking to just one other person the speaker must often take the initiative, in an interactive sense, to determine whether his message is being understood. Even though I sometimes take the risk of "bugging" my listener, I often stop and ask him if he understands what I mean, or I occasionally ask him to tell me what he thinks I meant in my message.

There is a fairly small percentage of people who speak articulately and clearly enough to be understood most of the time. Most of us have to work at it, especially when we are attempting to communicate a message which is fairly abstract or when we want to tell something which is quite personal or highly emotional. In sending the message effectively, we must do two things simultaneously, (1) work at finding the appropriate words and emotion to express what we want to say, and (2) continually look for cues from the listener to get some feedback even if we must *ask* our listener for some.

Receiving the Message

In considering interpersonal communication, we might, at first thought, think that listening is the easier of the two functions in the process. If we assume, however, that the listener really wants to understand what the speaker is saying, then the process is not all that easy. The basic problem that the listener faces is that he is capable of thinking faster than the speaker can talk. In their *Harvard Business Review* article, Nichols and Stevens state that the average rate of speech for most Americans is about 125 words per minute. Most of our thinking processes involve words, and our brains can handle many more words per minute than 125. As Nichols and Stevens point out, what this means is that, when we listen, our brains receive words at a very slow rate compared with the brain's capabilities.

As you have experienced many times, you know that you can listen to what someone is saying and think about something else at the same time. As the "cocktail party" phenomenon illustrates, the human brain is truly remarkable in its ability to process a considerable amount of input simultaneously. Sometimes, at a cocktail party, I want to hear not only what the person in my small gathering is saying, but also what that lovely creature is talking about in the group about six feet away. If the overall noise level is not too loud, I can hear and understand both conversations.

The problem with listening, then, is that we have "spare" time in our thinking processes. How we use that spare time determines the extent of our listening effectiveness. It is easy for us to be distracted in listening, especially if the speaker talks slowly or haltingly or if he says something that stimulates another thought. For example, suppose you are listening to a friend who is telling you about a problem he is having in his department. In the process of describing the problem, he mentions a person whom you know, whereupon you start thinking about the person at length. Later, when your friend asks you what you would do about his problem, you're apt to respond, "what problem?"

Thus, a fundamental problem the listener must consider in the communicative process is the fact that his brain is capable of responding to a speaker at several different levels simultaneously. Naturally, this can be an asset to the listener rather than a problem. For example, the listener can attend to nonverbal cues the speaker gives, e.g., facial expression, gesture, or tone of voice, as well as listen to the words themselves.

Besides a highly active brain, an effective listener has another factor to consider in the communication process. This factor involves the process of trying to perceive what the speaker is saying from his point of view.

A Barrier and a Gateway

According to Carl Rogers, a leading psychotherapist and psychotherapy researcher, the major barrier to effective communication is the tendency to evaluate. That is, the barrier to mutual interpersonal communication is our very natural tendency to judge, to evaluate, to approve or disapprove the statement or opinion of the other person or group. Suppose someone says to you, "I didn't like what the lecturer had to say." Your typical response will be either agreement or disagreement. In other words, your primary reaction is to evaluate the statement from your point of view, from your own frame of reference.

Although the inclination to make evaluations is common, it is usually heightened in those situations where feelings and emotions are deeply involved. Thus, the stronger our feelings, the more likely it is that there will be no mutual element in the communication. There will be only two ideas, two feelings, two judgements, missing each other in the heat of the psychological battle.

If having a tendency to evaluate is the major barrier to communication, then the logical gateway to communication is to become an active listener, to listen with understanding. Don't let this simple statement fool you. Listening with understanding means to see the expressed idea and attitude from the other person's point of view, to see how it feels to him, to achieve his frame of reference concerning his subject. One word that summarizes this process of listening with understanding is "empathy."

In psychotherapy, for example, Carl Rogers and his associates have found from research that empathetic understanding—understanding *with* a person not about him—is such an effective approach that it can bring about major changes in personality.

Suppose that in your next committee meeting you were to conduct an experiment which would test the quality of each committee member's understanding. Institute this rule: "Each person can speak up for himself only after he has first related the ideas and feelings of the previous speaker accurately and to that speaker's satisfaction." This would mean that before presenting your own point of view, it would be necessary for you to achieve the other speaker's frame of reference — to understand his thoughts and feelings so well that you could summarize them for him.

Can you imagine what this kind of approach might mean if it were projected into larger areas, such as congressional debates or labor-management disputes? What would happen if labor, without necessarily agreeing, could accurately state management's point of view in a way that management could accept; and management, without necessarily approving labor's stand, could state labor's case in a way that labor agreed was accurate? It would mean that real communication was established, and conditions would be more conducive for reaching a workable solution.

Toward More Effective Listening

Some steps the listener can take to improve interpersonal communication have been stated. To summarize and be more explicit, let us consider these steps.

1. Effective listening must be an active process. To make certain that you are understanding what the speaker is saying, you, as the listener must interact with him. One way to do this is to paraphrase or summarize for the speaker what you think he has said.

2. Attending to nonverbal behavior that the speaker is communicating along with his verbal expression usually helps to understand the oral message more clearly. Often a facial expression or gesture will "tell" you that the speaker feels more strongly about his subject than his words would communicate.

3. The effective listener does not try to memorize every word or fact the speaker communicates, but, rather, he listens for the main thought or idea. Since your brain is such a highly effective processor of information, spending your listening time in more than just hearing the words of the speaker can lead to more effective listening. That is, while listening to the words, you can also be searching for the main idea of the message. Furthermore, you can attempt to find the frame of reference for the speaker's message as well as look at what he is saying from his perspective. This empathetic process also includes your attempting to experience the same feeling about the subject as the speaker.

These three steps toward more effective listening seem fairly simple and obvious. But the fact remains that we don't practice these steps very often. Why don't we?

According to Carl Rogers, it takes courage. If you really understand another person in this way, if you are willing to enter his private world and see the way life appears to him without any attempt to make evaluative judgements, you run the risk of being changed yourself. This risk of being changed is one of the most frightening prospects many of us face.

Moreover, when we need to utilize these steps the most, we are likely to use them the least, that is, when the situation involves a considerable amount of emotion. For example, when we listen to a message that contradicts your most deeply held prejudices, opinions, or convictions, our brain becomes stimulated by many factors other than what the speaker is telling us. When we are arguing with someone, especially about something that is "near and dear" to us, what are we typically doing when the other person is making his point? It's certainly not listening empathetically! We're probably planning a rebuttal to what he is saying, or we're formulating a question which will embarrass the speaker. We may, of course, simply be "tuning him out." How often have you been arguing with someone for 30 minutes or so, and you make what you consider to be a major point for your point of view, and your "opponent" responds by saying, "But that's what I said 30 minutes ago!"

When emotions are strongest, then, it is most difficult to achieve the frame of reference of the other person or group. Yet it is then that empathy is most needed if communication is to be established. A third party, for example, who is able to lay aside his own feelings and evaluation, can assist greatly by listening with understanding to each person or group and clarifying the views and attitudes each holds.

When the parties to a dispute realize that they are being understood, that someone sees how the situation seems to them, the statements grow less exaggerated and less defensive, and it is no longer necessary to maintain the attitude, "I am 100% right and you are 100% wrong."

Summary

Effective communication, at least among human beings, is not a one-way street. It involves an interaction between the speaker and the listener. The responsibility for this interaction is assumed by both parties. You as the speaker can solicit feedback and adjust your message accordingly. As a listener, you can summarize for the speaker what you think he has said and continually practice the empathetic process.

One of the joys of life, at least for me, is to know that I have been heard and understood correctly and to know that someone cares enough to try to understand what I have said. I also get a great deal of satisfaction from seeing the same enjoyment on the face of a speaker when he knows I have understood him.

7

On Consuming Human Resources: Perspectives on the Management of Stress

by John D. Adams

Most of us like to assume that we can bounce back completely from a period of heavy stress at work by taking a day off or getting a good night's sleep. Evidence to the contrary is mounting, however, and it appears that we must pay some price for our stressful experiences, a cost that is difficult, at best, to recover. In other words, the human resources in our organizations (the way we operate them) are nonrenewable resources, much like fuels and mineral ores. Once consumed, they do not renew themselves.

Chronically stressful situations, especially those in which episodic or surprise stressors also are frequent, exert a wear-and-tear influence on the body, mind, and spirit of those who live or work in them. Eventually, an overload of stressful experiences can cause a person's resistances to drop, making individuals vulnerable to illnesses, chronic conditions (such as hypertension), depression, and feelings of apathy and alienation. Most organizations today give little or no attention to these outcomes—many actively deny them—because it is difficult to establish direct cause-and-effect linkages. The focus is most often on short-term objectives, such as "productivity today" and "quarterly goals," as opposed to and at the expense of the longer-term objective of human well-being. Those who "burn-out," "rust out," or become less productive in other ways are transferred, shelved, or dismissed with little awareness on anyone's part of the reasons for the drop in productivity. It is still a "survival-of-the-fittest" world in which not everyone is expected to make it. This chapter explores some options to this viewpoint as they apply to managers at all levels.

John Adams has an international practice as a consultant to organizations. He specializes in exploring the interrelationships among organizational stress, health, and organization development. He resides in Arlington, Virginia.

STRESS IS UNAVOIDABLE

The first basic contention here is that life at all levels of management is excessively stressful due to factors that are inherent in the normal ways organizations choose to operate. An example is the result obtained when people are asked to review the following sets of descriptions and select the set that most typifies successful managers they know.

I	II
High achiever	Relaxed, easy going
Competitive	Seldom lacks time
Aggressive	Speaks slowly
Fast worker	Steady worker
Pressure performer	Not preoccupied with achievement
Deadline oriented	Even tempered

Most people select Column I, or at least most of the terms in Column I. These two columns are from lists of Type-A and Type-B behavior traits identified by Friedman and Rosenman (1974). They and others have found that individuals whose behavior is characterized by Type-A traits (Column I) are two to three times as likely to experience a heart attack as those whose behavior is characterized by Type-B traits (Column II). Type-A behavior is now considered by doctors to be one of the major risk factors in coronary heart disease. Taken together, heart attacks and strokes account for nearly one-half of the deaths in this country, and a large proportion of them are related to prolonged experiences of stress.

The following statement from a senior manager in a large organization illustrates a commonly accepted point of view.

> The managers in the training department don't work until 7:30 every night like I do. I worry about that; I really do. No one can become president of this organization without extending himself!

Most organizations also exhibit very strong norms about how hard people work. Being forever in a position of rushing to keep even with the demands of one's job frequently is seen as desirable. I have done stress-management consulting with many organizations in which managers complain a lot about having "too much to do and too little time to do it." They actually desire this state of affairs. Usually, I say it is doubtful that any of them will use whatever time- or stress-management techniques I teach them to change this norm. After the protests die down, I ask them how they would describe a peer who states that she has her job under control and is not bothered continually by work overload, interruptions, surprise changes, and so on. The responses most often expressed include: "lazy," "goof-off," "doesn't have enough to do," and "must be missing something." In other words, if someone actually applies good time- or stress-management principles and thereby gets on top of her job, she is going to be seen as a deviant from this basic, although highly stress-provoking, norm of contemporary organizational life.

Once again, the first basic contention of this chapter is that excessive levels of stress are an inherent part of the manager's daily environment.

STRESS IS COSTLY

The second basic contention of this chapter is that the costs associated with these high levels of stress are immense and largely hidden. Therefore, they are denied or ignored. In how many organizations is there direct acknowledgment that a heart attack suffered on the job was in large part caused by the organization itself? And if the heart attack happens at home or on vacation? There will be some acknowledgment that "Joe has been under a lot of stress lately," but seldom, if ever,will anything be changed in the organization to reduce stress levels for other "Joes." Ulcers and less climactic chronic conditions (e.g., hypertension, depression, high cholesterol, nervous tics, etc.) usually receive even less attention by the powers that be.

The main reason for this damage is that each stressor has a generalized effect on the body. Regardless of the cause of the stress—for example, work load or criticism from the boss—one's body responds in a predictable way. The autonomic nervous system and endocrine gland system, ordinarily the governors of this equilibrium, go into action to prepare the individual to fight the stressor or "get out of its way." The entire body is affected: the cardiovascular and respiratory systems speed up; the gastrointestinal system slows down; the muscles get stronger; and the immunological process prepares for a possible infection.

Setting all this in motion too often over a period of time has an erosive effect, which eventually may lead to some kind of physical, mental, or spiritual breakdown. Since individuals have unique heredities, habits, personalities, and past histories, Tom may develop ulcers, while Mary "catches" every virus that passes through town, and Geoffrey flies off the handle at unexpected moments. Although cause-and-effect linkages have not been established between specific stressors and specific dysfunctions, there is no longer any doubt that excessive stress levels do induce physical illness, mental distress, and spiritual malaise.

In a recent study (Adams, 1978), I found amount of illness to be correlated positively with the number of stressful events experienced by managers on the job. Correlated inversely with the level of chronic daily stress experienced by managers on the job were health, level of satisfaction, and feelings of productivity.

In other studies, University of Michigan psychologists (French & Caplan, 1972) have made similar findings in investigating stress and illness among employees of the National Aeronautics and Space Administration (NASA). Put most briefly, they have found consistently that factors such as role conflict and ambiguity, work overload, poor relationships, too much responsibility, and too little participation are correlated with the primary risk factors associated with coronary heart disease.

Conservative estimates, looking at the population at large, indicate that 10 percent of the people in this country are hypertensive and 10 percent have "alcohol-related problems." In most of these cases, the origins of both these problems now are considered to be stress related.

Although no meaningful estimate can be established, it is necessary to conclude that the costs associated with stress, in terms of ill health alone, are immense. In view of the fact that Americans spend $120 billion per year on health care, the implications of the following quote become clear (Lazarus, 1977).

> It has become increasingly apparent that stress is important as a factor in illness in general and in chronic illness in particular. Many present-day illnesses cannot be explained in terms of a single "cause." Research suggests that a significant portion of the population seeking medical care is suffering from stress-based illness.

The costs of securing, training, and orientating new employees also can be considered, at least partially, to be stress-related costs. For example, one new corporation is hurrying to get its production plant on line while it still is wrestling with the new technologies with which it is involved. As a result of the stresses associated with this fast-paced new effort, the organization has been averaging a 34 percent turnover of its operations people each year. Top management estimates that it costs $4,000 to recruit, orient, and train a new person. During 1978, approximately 1,000 new people were needed in the organization at a cost of over $4 million to get them job-ready.

To summarize, the first basic contention of this chapter is that excessive levels of stress are an inherent part of the manager's daily environment. The second basic contention is that the costs associated with these high levels of stress are immense and largely hidden. So, what does this boil down to? It is this—there is a general lack of awareness or consciousness among contemporary managers about the dysfunctional nature of most organizations relative to stress.

By and large, the most debilitating sources of stress are rooted in the norms of an organization, as illustrated in the "too much to do with too little time to do it in" norm. Since norms are more difficult to change than policies or procedures, it is unlikely that stress will be removed by policy changes or organizational decision making. What is needed is an increase of awareness (consciousness raising) followed by behavioral changes on a large scale. In other words, the first step must be to create a critical mass of consciousness about stress and its possible effects.

After they become more aware of stress, managers should learn more about managing their stresses and those of their employees. They need techniques both for immediate response to specific stressors and for developing long-term protection or buffering against the cumulative effects of stress. Ultimately, someone should develop a systems approach to the management of human resources that takes stressors and stress-management factors into account along with presently considered task factors. Such a systems approach might be called "holistic management" to the extent that it includes a physical (illness to wellness), psychological (depression to excitement), and spiritual (alienation to integration) balance in its consideration of stress.

THE EXPERIENCE OF ORGANIZATIONAL STRESS

Most approaches to stress management spend little time identifying where the stress is coming from in an individual's environment. However, an understanding of the sources of stress in one's life is an important prelude to developing a plan for effective stress management. Furthermore, understanding the organizational sources of stress is basic to developing processes for reducing or removing unnecessary stress. Where most stress programs focus only on the individual and her or his ability to withstand stress better (e.g., through meditation or "body work"), a complete approach also must consider altering stressful organizational norms and management practices. Therefore, as a consultant, I ask clients to identify their primary stressors in each of four sectors, as illustrated in Figure 1.

Primary Stress Types (Stressors)

Types I and II are derived principally from the work of Holmes and Rahe (1967) and their colleagues at the University of Washington. They were instrumental in developing the now widely known social-readjustment rating scale, which predicts a growing likelihood of illness following periods of high change in an individual's life.

	On the Job	Away from Work
Recent Events	Type I	Type II
On-going Conditions	Type III	Type IV

Figure 1. Sources of stress

Stress Type I. Recent events on the job include changes for an individual, such as:

1. Major changes in instructions, policies, or procedures;
2. A requirement to work more hours per week than normal;
3. A sudden significant increase in the activity level or pace of work;
4. Major reorganization;
5. Etc.

A thirty-one-item list of such events has been developed by Naismith (1975). Each event has a point value reflecting the average amount of readjustment required for an individual to feel "back to normal" following the experience of that change event. In my research project (1978), I found the number of readjustment points accumulated by managers during a twelve-month period to be correlated significantly with the number of health conditions they were experiencing.

Stress Type II. Recent events away from work include changes for an individual, such as:

1. Restriction of social life;
2. Marriage;
3. Death of family member;
4. Serious illness;
5. Etc.

Following Holmes and Rahe, a list of change events such as this was developed by Cochrane and Robertson (1973). Here again, each change event has a certain number of points associated with it, reflecting the average amount of readjustment required to get back to normal. In my project (1978), the number of readjustment points accumulated by managers was again correlated with the numbers of health conditions they reported.

To summarize, events (both on and off the job) cause disruptions for us. Whether or not we are conscious of it, these events trigger a chain reaction intended to restore equilibrium, because a certain amount of readjustment is always necessary. The more often we trigger the stress response, the more likely it is that we will become ill. In most cases, specific kinds of stress cannot be linked to specific illnesses. However, with too much stress, our inherent tendencies to become ill or psychologically distressed, whatever they are, are more likely to come to the surface.

Types III and IV (Figure 1) are derived principally from the work of French and Caplan (1972) and their colleagues at the Institute for Social Research at the University of Michigan. This group of professionals has worked extensively with NASA in the study of day-to-day or chronic stress and its effect on health and well-being.

Stress Type III. On-the-job conditions include daily pressures on an individual, such as:

1. Too much work, too little time;
2. Feedback only when performance is unsatisfactory;
3. Conflicts between his unit and others it must work with;
4. Unclear standards and responsibilities;
5. Etc.

These kinds of stressors are similar to the primary sources of stress identified by French and his colleagues: work overload, role ambiguity and conflict, responsibility level, poor interpersonal relationships, and lack of participation. It is safe to say that most people in most large organizations today can readily identify with these conditions—and few are surprised that too much of them can be debilitating.

In my research study (1978), I found the frequency with which managers were experiencing these conditions to be correlated positively with the number of chronic health conditions they reported and correlated negatively with their felt work effectiveness and their felt satisfaction and growth. It has already been pointed out that this type of stressor is frequently normative in nature. Thus, changing negative norms, to the extent that is possible, can lead to lower levels of chronic stress at work.

Stress Type IV. Away-from-work conditions include pressure on an individual, such as:

1. Pollution;
2. Noise;

3. Concern over the economy;

4. Anxiety about children's activities;

5. Etc.

Here again, the frequency with which managers experience these and other conditions as stressful is correlated (though less strongly) with the number of chronic health conditions they report. This type of stress has had much less attention from researchers than the other three.

In summary, daily conditions cause pressures that, even after a person becomes accustomed to them, can cause illness and lower feelings of satisfaction, growth, and work effectiveness. When change events occur on the job in large numbers to people already working under highly stressful conditions, the incidence of sick leave, accidents, and inattention to work increases rapidly.

The overall format I have devised to guide my work on stress is portrayed by Figure 2. The types of stressors are listed at the top of the diagram.

Situational Givens

The context or the inherent givens of a situation may serve to diffuse or to intensify stress, depending on their nature. These givens include:

1. The personal characteristics and background of the individual;

2. Quality and amount of support; and

3. Organizational factors.

First, individuals inherit strengths and weaknesses or develop them through good or bad personal habits, accidents, or abuses. Furthermore, our behavioral orientations both predispose us to certain types of stress (e.g., needing close direction but working in an ambiguous role) and influence how we might break down (e.g., people who are more driven, competitive, deadline and achievement oriented—Type A behavior—are more likely to have heart attacks). With an awareness of one's orientations and idiosyncracies, one has more choices available relative to avoiding overly stressful situations.

Secondly, people who work in an environment lacking in social support are likely to have more health and emotional problems than people working in more supportive settings.

Thirdly, the nature of the organization one works in can either heighten or reduce stress levels. Factors such as the number of deadlines, manner of facing crises, and the frequency and nature of client demands all should be considered for their role in increasing or decreasing stress.

Usually we cannot change these three factors much (personality, quality of support, nature of organization), but the manager needs to

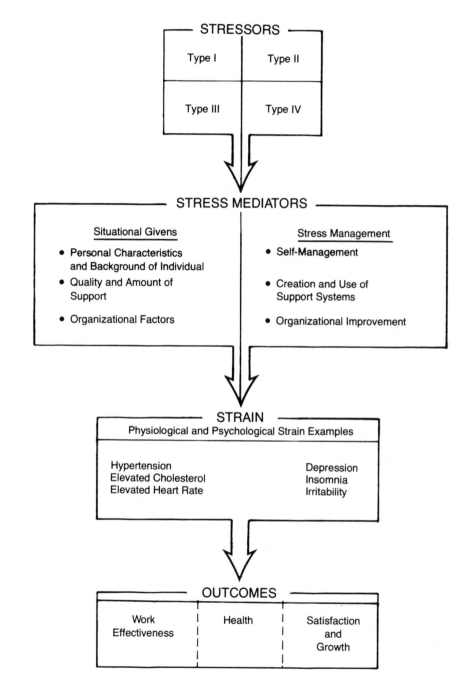

Figure 2. The experience of stress

develop an understanding of how they affect stress levels in order to promote effective stress management.

Stress Management

A different sort of mediating variable has to do with how well the individual manages his own stress in each of these same three areas: within himself, in relation to others, and within the organizational context. Training in this area, first in mixed groups of managers and then in face-to-face work groups, seems to be the most promising approach to managing the high levels of stress in contemporary organizations. Both long-term (preventive) and immediate (responsive) stress-management techniques are needed to protect an organization's human resources from the effects of stress. Although most stress-management training focuses on one basic technique (e.g., progressive relaxation or meditation), it is important to cover a variety of techniques in cafeteria style and encourage individuals to develop stress-management plans suited to their own situations and preferences.

SUGGESTIONS FOR STRESS MANAGEMENT

In addition to managing stress effectively for themselves, it is important for managers to understand the organizational stress process well enough to assist others with their experiences of stress. Some options for both of these facets of stress management are offered here.

Self-Management

The paragraphs that follow represent the broad range of techniques that may be used both for buffering oneself against the impact of stress in the long run and for responding directly to stressors in the short run.

First, every manager should be enhancing her or his self-awareness continually. Knowledge of our own idiosyncracies, preferences, and needs enables us to make more choices that avoid stressful situations. If, for example, an individual prefers to work alone, participative management can be a stressful experience. On the job, we can enhance our self-awareness with feedback from trusted colleagues and during performance reviews. Away from work, self-awareness can be developed by reading, introspection, feedback from family and friends, psychological tests, therapy, and participation in a variety of kinds of groups. Generally, we all are surrounded with information that could enhance our self-awareness, if we would only pay attention to it.

In a study involving a large number of managers, Burke (1971) identified ten of the most frequently used responses to job stress and tension; these are listed in Figure 3.

Rank by Use (%)	Rank by Symptoms	Coping Responses
1 (64)	6	Change to engrossing nonwork activity
2 (49)	4	Talk it through on the job with peers
3 (41)	9	Analyze situation and change strategy
4 (40)	2	Compartmentalize work life and home life
5 (35)	3	Engage in regular physical exercise
6 (26)	7	Talk it through with spouse
7 (25)	1	Build resistance through healthful life-style habits
8 (25)	5	Withdraw physically from the situation
9 (24)	8	Work harder
10 (15)	10	Change to a different work task

Figure 3. Managers' coping responses to job stress and tension

Howard (1975) has used these same coping responses in a separate study of differences among managers in their ability to protect their health when under stress. He listed the responses in rank order according to how frequently each is used, as shown in the first column of Figure 3. The reader might benefit from noting which of the ten items he or she uses. The second column shows rank order according to how many symptoms of chronic ill health were experienced by people who had practiced each of the responses.

In the "Rank by Use" column, the number one item is the most widely used response. In the "Rank by Symptoms" column, the number one item has the lowest average number of symptoms experienced by those who regulary use that response. The implication of this ranking of symptoms is that some of the coping responses are more likely to protect health in the face of stress than others.

It should be noted that the five most effective coping strategies (i.e., having the fewest symptoms associated with them) are of a "work smarter"type: (1) build resistance through healthful life style; (2) compartmentalize work life and home life; (3) engage in regular physical exercise; (4) talk it through on the job with peers; and (5) withdraw physically from the situation.

The five less effective strategies (i.e., having the most symptoms associated with them) are more of a "work harder" or "nose-to-the-grindstone" variety: (6) change to engrossing nonwork activity; (7) talk it through with spouse; (8) work harder; (9) analyze situation and change strategy; and (10) change to a different work task.

In Howard's study (1975), those coping strategies that involve taking care of oneself and dealing directly with stressors appear to lead to relatively fewer symptoms of illness than do strategies that involve attempts to overwhelm the stressors with higher energy outputs. The responses dealing with healthful life-style habits and exercise include some of the most important long-term health maintenance habits: *nutrition, exercise, relationships,* and *relaxation.*

Nutrition

A glance into the typical manager's "lunch box" is likely to reveal a deficient or marginally balanced diet. Most managers have little awareness of good nutritional principles; few of them get three sound meals a day, including a balance of meats, dairy products, fruits and vegetables, and cereals and grains. Although these four food groups are necessary to ensure that people get sufficient vitamins, minerals, protein and fiber, one or more of the groups often is overlooked.

On the other hand, there are marked tendencies for managers to: eat on the run; consume foods that are high in refined starch, fat, salt, sugar and chemical additives; drink too much alcohol and caffeine; and rely too often on overcooked, heavy, restaurant meals. Good nutritional habits are necessary in the long run to combat the effects of stress.

Exercise

Relatively few managers engage in any regular exercise program; although, happily, this situation does seem to be changing. Most management roles do not require anywhere near the physical exertion human bodies are designed for, or indeed require, to maintain full health. Therefore, the manager who does not have any regular nonwork activities requiring sustained exertion is at risk.

In order to improve cardiovascular fitness to the levels needed to combat stress, an individual's pulse should be elevated to around 130 beats per minute and that pace should be maintained for twenty to thirty minutes an average of three times each week. This creates what is referred to as the aerobic effect, which improves the efficiency of one's cardiovascular system and lowers the resting pulse rate. Some long distance runners, for example, have heart rates below fifty beats per minute. Activities that create this effect include: running, swimming, vigorous walking, rowing, bicycling, jumping rope, and sports that are not marked with pauses or time-outs (e.g., hockey, soccer, rugby).

Kenneth Cooper (1970) has developed tables for measuring an individual's progress in several different aerobic activities. He also suggests training programs and provides training tips for beginners. One of his most important points is that those who are planning to start jogging, for example, should have a complete physical, including the treadmill stress test, prior to beginning. This will give one additional assurance that a running or other heavy exercise program will not be dangerous—or it will rule out this exercise if some unknown heart problem is uncovered.

Relationships

Most managers give too little attention to maintaining high quality relationships. Numerous studies (e.g., Berkman, 1977; Cassel, 1976; French & Caplan, 1972) have emphasized that maintaining solid interpersonal relationships is important to continued good health in the face of prolonged high levels of stress. Often, managers who are working vigorously to advance their careers keep themselves so busy with work matters that they have little time or energy remaining for developing ongoing relationships with others, either on or off the job. In most organizations, there is little encouragement to do so and, frequently, the inherent nature of the system pits the manager against his peers and potential friends in a no-holds-barred competition for the next promotion.

We all need supportive relationships in order to feel connected, to be challenged, to gain access, to be respected, to exchange ideas, and so on. For reasons not yet clearly known, when we lack such relationships for too long, the risk of our developing stress-related physical and psychological conditions increases.

Relaxation

The final dimension of personal stress management to be included here is relaxation. It seldom is legitimate for one to take a half-hour test break on the job, even though such a practice would enhance performance considerably more than do coffee breaks. Tremendous progress has been made in understanding the effects and potential of relaxation techniques such as meditation (e.g., Benson, 1975). Such activities still are rather foreign to the American culture and definitely do not fit into the image of the American manager. As a consequence, very few managers practice one of these remarkable restorative and protective techniques.

The following is a superficial and yet revealing test of the potentials inherent in easily learned relaxation techniques:

> Simply close your eyes and take ten slow deep breaths. Each time you exhale, count silently—"one" after the first breath, "two" after the second breath, etc.—up to ten. If you lose count or find yourself "working" on thoughts as they pass through your mind, start your count over. When you are finished,

you should feel relaxed (your blood pressure will go down temporarily, too, if it tends to be high) and ready to concentrate fully on your next activity.

Twenty minutes of uninterrupted relaxation could have a tremendous impact on most managers' work effectiveness, as well as increasing their ability to withstand stress.

This section has looked at some ideas that managers can implement for themselves—self-management—to confront stressors directly and protect themselves from prolonged stress. The next step is to consider some things managers can do for others who are experiencing too much stress on the job.

Stress in Others

First of all, how can we recognize that another person may be experiencing too much stress, when we often do not even notice when we are getting overloaded ourselves? Sometimes it takes another person to point it out to us. The "signals of stress" list shown here, although not complete, provides some clues of behaviors displayed by a person who is experiencing high levels of stress. These behaviors are the ones most frequently identified by participants in several stress-management workshops as being signals of stress. They are similar both to behaviors identified in studies of burnout among human-service professionals and to characteristics of system overload.

Signals of Stress

1. Disregarding low (or high) priority tasks;
2. Giving reduced amount of time to each task;
3. Redrawing boundaries to shift or avoid responsibilities;
4. Blocking out new information;
5. Being superficially involved; appearing to give up;
6. Expressing negative or cynical attitudes about customers/clients;
7. Appearing depersonalized, detached;
8. "Going by the book";
9. Being overly precise; intellectualizing;
10. Displaying inappropriate humor;
11. Stealing or using other means of "ripping off" the organization;
12. Obviously wasting time; being "unavailable" much of the time;
13. Being late for work; frequently being absent.

When any of these signals appear as *new* behaviors, they are probably signs of excessive levels of stress. Learning to identify these symptoms is the first step toward helping others manage their stress more effectively.

The second step involves understanding what is involved in coping with Type I (episodic) and Type III (chronic) sources of stress.

Coping with Episodic Stressors

A Type I (episodic) stressor is experienced as stressful by individuals to the extent that it takes them by surprise. For example, in a department in which a major new policy is simply announced as an accomplished fact and imposed, more stress will be induced than in a department in which the manager has helped her people understand that the new policy is coming, why it has been developed, and how it will apply to them. When it arrives, the "low-stress manager" helps her people try out the policy and, if necessary, sound off about it. Although the aforementioned example is overly simplified, it does communicate the essence of reducing the impact of Type I stressors—full two-way communications. The more information we have about an event, the less we will be taken by surprise by it and, therefore, the less stress we will experience as a result.

Coping with Chronic Stressors

Type III (chronic) stressors, such as ambiguous work roles, are more pervasive in their impact than the Type I (episodic) stressors because they are there every day. Also, the chronic stressors are rooted most often in the norms of the organization rather than in its policies or procedures, and they are, therefore, more difficult for the manager to address and change.

It is possible, however, to remove some of the stressful norms in any organization. The first step is to identify them. Second, everyone in a given work unit should acknowledge that a particular norm ought to be changed. As an example, recall the "too much to do and too little time to do it" norm mentioned earlier. Even though this norm is identified and acknowledged to be a cause of stress in a unit, if some of the other members of that unit are unwilling to change their behaviors relative to this norm, then the unit's manager cannot afford to change her behavior and risk being seen as underemployed or lazy.

Many of these stressors require actions other than behavior change. For example, depending on the nature of the chronic stressors that have been identified, a work unit may need to engage in team building, role negotiation, conflict management, the establishment or revision of job descriptions, management by objectives, problem solving, and so on. As the reader who is familiar with intentional organizational change processes will recognize, organization-development techniques are particularly suited to dealing with Type III stressors.

Organization development, however, is not enough by itself. People ordinarily will not mobilize to face the stressors inherent in their organizations without an awareness of what stress is, where it comes from, and what it can do. Furthermore, they need to know what they can do about stress. This suggests that some form of education and training is needed. Whatever approach is taken, the objective must be to create a critical mass of consciousness about stress, without which changes are unlikely.

And finally, the organization, if it is to respond effectively, must build a holistic approach to its management of human resources — making sure that people are given encouragement and opportunities to replenish their physical, mental, and spiritual energies. Some examples of what this might mean include: management by objectives, plans that include personal-development objectives; quiet relaxation rooms; nutritional-awareness programs; exercise programs with changing areas; the hiring of a physical-exercise trainer; stress counseling associated with an annual physical examination; yoga instruction; availability of fruits and juices at meetings and seminars; and ongoing stress-education programs.

References

Adams, J. D. Improving stress management: An action-research-based OD intervention. In W. W. Burke (Ed.), *The cutting edge*. San Diego, CA: University Associates, 1978.

Benson, H. *The relaxation response*. New York: William Morrow and Co., 1975.

Burke, R. J. Are you fed up with work? *Personnel Administration*, 1971, January-February.

Cassel, J. The contribution of social environment to host resistance. *American Journal of Epidemiology*, 1976, *104*(2), 107-123.

Cochrane, R., & Robertson, A. The life events inventors. *The Journal of Psychosomatic Research*, 1973, *17*, 135-139.

Cooper, K. *The new aerobics*. New York: Bantam Books, 1970.

French, J. R. P., & Caplan, R. P. Organizational stress and individual strain. In A. Marrow (Ed.), *The failure of success*. New York: AMACOM, 1972.

Friedman, M., & Rosenman, R. H. *Type A behavior and your heart*. New York: Knopf, 1974.

Holmes, T. H., & Rahe, R. H. The social readjustment rating scale. *The Journal of Psychosomatic Research*, 1967, *11*, 213-218.

Howard, J. H., Rechnitzer, P. A., & Cunningham, D. A. Coping with job tension — effective and ineffective methods. *Public Personnel Management*, 1975, September-October, *4*(5), 317-326.

Lazarus, R. S. *Proceedings of the National Heart and Lung Institute* (now Heart, Lung and Blood Institute) *Working Conference on Health Behavior*, 1977 (DHEW NIH77-868). Washington, D.C.: U.S. Government Printing Office, 1977.

Naismith, D. *Stress among managers as a function of organizational change*. Unpublished doctoral dissertation. The George Washington University, Washington, DC, 1975.

Mid-Life Transition and Mid-Career Crisis: A Special Case for Individual Development

by Robert T. Golembiewski

Adult life is neither unpredictable nor of a single piece. The present article proposes to show why this is the case as well as to highlight some major organizational consequences. The focus is on the mid-life transition, through which we all must pass whether lightly or with much travail. For those in organizations, that transition often manifests itself as a mid-career crisis. The two effects are interactive, but it often will be the case that an individual will precipitate a mid-career crisis as a result of a panic reaction to a mid-life transition, with the individual precipitously changing professions, getting a divorce or following some other similar course of action.

Although there are still far more questions than answers, useful experiences and research are beginning to accumulate on this subject. Recent advances in knowledge at once reinforce the need for organizations and professional associations to provide facilitative experiences for mid-life transitionists, and they also suggest some specifics about the "when" and the "what" of these experiences. Specifically, the succeeding emphases will be upon:

- some general agreements about mid-life transition
- the location of mid-life transition in the broader flow of adulthood

Robert T. Golembiewski is research professor of political science and management at the University of Georgia.

Reprinted from *Public Administration Review*. Copyright © 1978 by The American Society for Public Administration, 1225 Connecticut Avenue, N.W. Washington, D.C. All rights reserved. Used by permission.

- some major issues in the mid-life transition
- how the mid-life transition has an especial nowness, a contemporary significance in mid-career choices
- what can be done in organizations to meet the challenges of mid-life transition and, more broadly, to make the worksite more responsive to human needs and cycles

General Agreements About Mid-Life Transition

Existing accumulated research and experience suggest six characteristics of the mid-life transition. First, the middle years have a subtle developmental texture. A real appreciation of the point rests on recent, even contemporary, research. As late as 1974, a distinguished group of behavioral scientists decried "the tremendous neglect of development and socialization in the main adult years, roughly 20-65, in psychology, psychiatry, sociology, and so on." They conclude: "We speak as though development goes on to age 6, or perhaps to age 18; then there is a long plateau in which random things occur; and then at around 60 or 65 'aging' begins.[1] Roger Gould colorfully paints the derivative and inadequate concept of these "main adult years." He observes:

> Like a butterfly, an adult is supposed to emerge fully formed and on cue, after a succession of developmental stages in childhood. Equipped with all the accounterments [sic], such as wisdom and rationality, the adult supposedly remains quiescent for another half century or so. While children change, adults only age.[2]

Second, the period of age 35-43 is most favored[3] as dating the mid-life transition. The time of onset, severity, and duration will vary from individual to individual, however. Some persons are hardly affected during this transitional period; some experience a great torment; and most people feel some pangs in the transition.

Third, the transition seems to affect both men and women, coming at roughly the same ages but with some significant differences between the sexes as to mode of onset and coping.[4] Jacques effectively makes both points:

> The transition is often obscured in women by the proximity of the onset of changes connected with the menopause. In the case of men, the change has from time been referred to as the climacteric, because of the reduction in the intensity of sexual behavior which often occurs at that time.[5]

Fourth, depression is the common toxic reaction to mid-life transition, and it seems to derive from a fact that is chronologically simple but psychologically momentous. "The individual has stopped growing up," Jacques observes, "and has begun to grow old." He concludes:

> The first phase of adult life has been lived. Family and occupation have become established (or ought to have become established unless the individual's adjustment has gone seriously awry); parents have grown old, and children are at the threshold of adulthood. Youth and childhood are past and gone, and demand to be mourned. The achievement of mature and independent adulthood presents itself as the main psychological task. The paradox is that of entering the prime of life, the stage of fulfillment, but at the same time prime and fulfillment are dated. Death lies beyond.[6]

The mid-life transition fishes in deep and dark waters, that is to say. Parts of the processes of aging are obvious; other parts may be largely unconscious, influencing the adaptive processes of life when the individual is unaware of them or even denies their influence.[7]

Fifth, evidence strongly implies the criticality of the mid-life transition. Among persons of great accomplishment, for example, many observers have noted that in their middle thirties the prominent often become "beset with misgivings, agonizing inquiries, and a loss of zest."[8] Jacques concludes that this common crisis can be resolved in three ways:

- the career of accomplishment may come to an end, as in a drying-up of creative work or even in death
- a decisive change in the kind and quality of the accomplishment may occur
- for a few, a successful mid-life transition may express itself in a release for the first time of major accomplishments

The transition also seems important for Everyman as well.[10] A failure to come to grips with the mid-life transition, Jacques notes, implies an "impoverishment of emotional life" and may even lead to "real character deterioration." Other observers chart an even more sorrowful catalog of the consequences of an ineffective transition. Commenting about professionals in their mid-30s, for example, Kaufman observes:

> During this period professionals perceive that what they have been doing is no longer fulfilling or important and they have not attained the success in their careers that they expected. ... It is during this period that careers, as well as marriages, go on the rocks and high rates of alcoholism, depression, suicides, and serious accidents occur. In fact, a peak in the death rate occurs between ages 35 and 40, and some have attributed it to the physical illness that is likely to accompany the emotional shock and severe depression that follow the individual's perception that he is on an irreversible downward path.[11]

To be sure, many professionals continue to be effective throughout the transition, and some go on to even greater achievements, but the rates are not known.

Sixth, evidence suggests that mid-life phenomena is not peculiar to western civilization. One study, for example, finds basic similarities in the psychology of later life between Lowland Mayans and urban Americans.[12]

Major Developmental Periods in Male Adulthood

How do the mid-life years fit into the context of full adulthood? Exhibit I provides one useful perspective on how the mid-life transition is the entry to the last half of life through which all must pass. Successfully negotiated, the transition can lead to a long period of fulfilling life that is both stable and productive. An unsuccessful effort, alternatively, can lead to a frustrating life of turmoil and despair.

Exhibit 1 must be interpreted with caution since it is derived from an intensive study of only forty persons. Moreover, the central tendencies reported there were often obscured by great variations in individual experiences. In addition, the persons studied were all males. Adult developmental phases for females may differ significantly from those abstracted in Exhibit 1. Finally, the research necessary deals with many issues still the subject of intense debate, e.g., the clinical judgment that a person is "stable and productive."

While suggestive, Exhibit 1 is best viewed as a set of working hypotheses about the texture of adult developmental phases. The sparse available evidence does suggest "relatively universal, genotypic, age-linked, adult developmental periods,"[12] but that conclusion might not stand up to closer scrutiny.

Major Issues in Mid-Life Transition

Exhibit 1 implies that there is reality to this common usage—the fearsome forties. The issues of the mid-life transition are powerful ones, centering as they do on the disparity between what has been achieved and what is desired, a disparity to which urgency and poignancy are added by the growing consciousness of the inexorable march of time. Not only are those issues awesome, but they often are exacerbated by needs of adolescent children and/or a spouse, each of whom may be contending with their own transitional concerns or traumas. In addition, the stakes are high, for success or failure in the transition probably will have a long time to influence all of us as we proceed toward our own rendezvous with death.

There are numerous ways to suggest the kinds of issues that may be encountered in mid-life transition. Perhaps the most convenient approach has been advanced by Roger Gould.[14] He studied 524 men and women, separated into seven age groups, one of which was 35-43. Each person was asked 124 questions, which referred to a broad sweep of life: relationships to parents, friends, children, and spouses; and feelings toward their own personality, job, time, and sexual behavior. Gould was able to track the significance of each of these questions for each of the age groups, thereby getting a sense of the ebb-and-flow of specific issues for persons at various chronologic ages. Gould acknowledges the defects of his research design which, for example was more convenient than—but not as elegant as—a longitudinal study of the same persons throughout their full life cycle.

Gould shows that persons in mid-life transition differ markedly from other age groups on only a few of the 124 questions. These differences provide useful clues about the concerns that are central to the transition. In summary, the frequency and significance of these statements *decreases* markedly during the mid-life years.[15]

- For me marriage has been a good thing.
- There's still plenty of time to do most of the things I want to do.
- I like a very active social life.

In summary, also, the salience of only eight statements *increases* during the same years. They are:

- I don't make enough money to do what I want.
- I regret my mistakes in raising my children.
- It's too late to make any major changes in my career.
- My personality is pretty well set.
- I try to be satisfied with what I have and not think so much about the things I probably won't be able to get.
- Life doesn't change much from year to year.
- My greatest concern is my health.
- My parents are the cause of many of my problems.

In sum, mid-life transitionists seem to be grappling with momentous issues, and even minor differences in the fine-tuning of adjustments might lead toward greater fulfillment or greater trouble. The latter implies chances lost, pessimism, an impending end before fulfillment in many critical areas of life, and the chances of a kind of spiritual withdrawal seem high. Thus, parents can be used as scapegoats for any developmental failure; the pressure of time can encourage lassitude as well as efficient effort; past mistakes can come to be seen as vexacious and irremediable; and pessimism about marriage and social life can deprive the individual of what he needs to cushion the transition as well as to extract value from it.

Exhibit 1
Important Stages of Adult Male Development
Centering on Mid-Life Transition.*

I. Early Adulthood (roughly, ages 20-40)

1. Leaving the Family

   A transition phase which begins at 16-18 and ends at perhaps 20-24, and sees the individual in the process of leaving the family of origin—a balance between "being in" and "moving out."

2. Getting into the Adult World

   Begins in the early 20's and typically extends to the early 30's, with the focus on building an adult life—"to explore the available possibilities of the adult world, to arrive at an initial definition of oneself as an adult, and *to fashion an initial life structure* that provides a viable link between the valued self and the wider adult world." (p. 247).

   A "dream" or vision of the future is a central feature of this period for many, often with an occupational focus. Early progress is checked against this dream or vision.

   Several patterns characterize this period of exploration and choice, including:

   a. for many males, a provisional commitment to an occupation and perhaps a marriage with, around 30, a transitional period focusing on whether or not to make a deeper commitment to the initial career and marriage choices

   b. for some males, a moderate or drastic change about 30 in initial occupation and life structure, which are seen as too constraining

   c. for some males, a transient and unsettled life in the 20's which leads around 30 to desperate attempts to "get more order and stability into . . . life" (p. 248).

3. Settling Down

   Begins in the early 30's for those who successfully make the transition. This typically occurs by the mid-30's, or not at all. Includes two central aspects:

   a. order, stability, security, control

   b. "making it"—planning, striving, moving onward and upward

   Overall, the individual "makes deeper commitments; invests more of himself in his work, family, and valued interests; and within the framework of this life structure, makes and pursues more long-range plans and goals" (p. 249).

---

*Based on Daniel J. Levinson, Charlotte M. Darrow, Edward B. Klein, Maria H. Levinson, and Braxton McKee, "The Psychosocial Development of Men in Early Adulthood and the Mid-Life Transition," pp. 243-68, in David Ricks, Alexander Thomas and Merrill Roff, (eds.), *Life History Research in Psychopathology*, Vol. 3 (Minneapolis, Minn.: University of Minnesota Press, 1974).

Exhibit 1 (continued)

4. Becoming One's Own Man

   This is a time of peaking and transition, often beginning in the middle or late 30's and lasting in cases until the 40's. The prime feature is a sense of constraint and oppression in work, marriage, and other relationships. Whatever the accomplishments, that is, the individual perceives self as insufficiently his own man. Central features of this striving for new autonomy typically include:

   a. a rejection or substantial modification of relationships with "mentors," older colleagues who have been supportive but parental ego-ideals, a process that usually has run its course by age 40

   b. The choice of some key event or achievement against which the individual will measure his affirmation or devaluation by society or relevant others—a promotion, new job, or some other achievement—which outcome may take 3-6 years to unfold.

5. Mid-Life Transition

   This is a pivotal time between two more stable periods, which period usually peaks in the early 40's. The transition can be smooth or turbulent.

   The central issue is the disparity between what has been achieved and what is desired. Related issues involve:

   a. bodily decline and the growing sense of mortality

   b. aging

   c. the emergence and the integration of the "more feminine" aspects of the self

II. Middle Adulthood (roughly, ages 40-60)

   1. Restabilization

      At around 45, the Mid-Life Transition is typically complete and men come to a time of great threat or major developmental advance.

      For those who succeed, this can be a period of great vitality built on the new life structure evolved in the Mid-Life Transition.

III. Late Adulthood (roughly, ages 60 +)

These dark possibilities seem to make a successful transition that much sweeter, however. This is implicit in Gould's description of what a successful adjustment seems to mean for those past the age of 50, for whom there is a "mellowing of feelings and relationships" even as death becomes a newly-real presence for them. Gould observes:

> People of this age seemed to focus on what they have accomplished in half a century, and they were unrushed by the sense of urgency that accompanied the achieving 30s. At the same time, they were more eager to have "human" experiences, such as sharing joys, sorrows, confusions and triumphs of everyday life rather than searching for the glamor, the glitter, the power or the abstract. Precious moments of contact and deep feeling define the value of being in touch.

Some Perspectives on the Nowness of the Mid-Life Transition

The mid-life transition is not merely with us; it is with us in significant senses for the first time, despite the fact that people patently have lived through their 40's for many generations past. No argument can be definitive, but four interacting features imply that the impact of the transition is, in crucial respects, unprecedented.

First, mid-life phenomena are being felt by increasing masses of people. The contrast with the past is something like that between scattered cases of a disease and an epidemic. As Longfellow observed,[17] we may really be seeing mass mid-life transitions for the first time, and not only because there are more people alive today. In addition, our life-spans have increased dramatically in just a few generations, and hence so have the proportion of live births that survive beyond their 40's. Moreover, far fewer people than ever before are preoccupied with bare physical survival. The quality of life can get correspondingly greater attention, even as "killing time" becomes more of a necessary skill for many.

Second, mid-life transition seems obviously easier when the changing individual can count on society and technology being relatively stable. Moreover, the essence of the mid-life transition is learning how to accept and deal with being out of control of some inexorable life-forces. The pace of social and technological change grotesquely exaggerates this sense of being out of control over central life-events, of being the acted-upon rather than the actor.

Third, to say somewhat the same thing, probably fewer people proportionately than ever before are role-bound or status-bound. This is consistent with high-velocity social change, of course; and it implies an increased freedom of opportunity to choose among alternative life-styles.

Danger is the other side of the coin of opportunity, however. Overabundance of choices can be as troublesome as paucity, and the latter at least has the superficial advantage of legitimating for many people the "OK-ness" of living lives of quiet desperation. Abundant choices can dramatically heighten the costs of failure to take adequate advantage of them; and it is at least the case that abundance can create major problems of choice as well as numerous opportunities to go wrong in seeking to select a life-style attuned to one's inner rhythms.

Fourth, probably greater proportions of people than ever before have substantially raised their expectations about what is acceptable — acceptable to them as persons and to the societies of which they are a part. The phenomenon may be world-wide; but it is at least pervasive in the western world. T. George Harris incisively captures the new rhythms to which so many dance. "It's as if some idiot raised the ante on what it takes to be a person," he explains, "and the rest of us accepted it without noticing." The result? An "aspiration gap. What we are as individuals and groups fall short of what we now consider normal. We feel sent for and can't get there."[18]

The impact of raising the ante for personhood clearly complicates the mid-life transition. For example, sex, race, class, and nation can lock people into roles that are unresponsive to individual qualities. Since they limit human potential, sexism and racism and class consciousness must be neutralized in the person and in the society. This is a far taller order for quality personhood than was current not so very long ago. Harris also suggests the multiple-binds inherent in raising the ante for effective personhood within the family, with increased and perhaps unreconcilable demands on its members. That is:

> Family members assume that they ought to love each other, understand one another, or at least get their hostilities up front. [Few] mothers and almost no fathers used to seek such emotional luxuries. A wife who once considered sex as a marital duty now expects to be an orgasmic playmate, intellectual companion, and growth partner, as well as an emotionally independent person, a cross between Mesdames Pompadour and Curie.[19]

It also appears that the ante for personhood has been raised in organizations, and especially by many of those who have been more successful. Thus one 1972 survey of managers indicated that nearly one-half were considering a complete change of career;[20] and popular management magazines have spotlighted dramatic cases of well-heeled successes who have chucked one blossoming career for a less-exalted but more satisfying alternative.[21] Some other equally disenchanted but less financially-cushioned individuals have taken greater risks in attempting shifts in careers and life-styles, perhaps most characterized by those leaving the priesthood or orders of nuns. Moreover, signs of mid-life transition seem unmistakable in the "blue-collar blues,"[22] a social ferment suggesting that even the organizationally humble are no longer content to lead lives of more or less quiet desperation, variously locked into unsatisfying roles that they cannot or will not leave. The period of mid-life transitions, the late 30's or early 40's, sees most such mid-career changes.

Some Organizational Challenges

Adult life is neither unpredictable nor of a single piece, then, and therein lay several major challenges for employing organizations and professional groups.

To be sure, what follows is vulnerable to the charge that it points with alarm more than it provides viable solutions. Moreover, adjustments in the public sector might be difficult or impossible, due to civil service practices and policies; but so be it. The answers are not conveniently at hand; and much consciousness-raising in organizations seems necessary before any concerted problem-solving can start.

At least five challenges seem involved in initial efforts to deal with mid-life transition. First, a greater awareness of the organizationally-relevant features of the transition is required, as it applies to all employees. However, few organizations have manifested an awareness of mid-life transition in specific informational or experiential programs. Some useful attention has been given to career planning,[23] but these newly-won beachheads require major expansion.

This neglect is especially troublesome because many organizations are characterized by waves of employment. Given recent hiring practices in colleges and universities that added numerous young and highly-trained teacher scholars, for example, large proportions of many faculties soon will be coming into the mid-life transition together. Organizationally-sponsored attention to transition phenomena thus could be important not only to faculty, but also to their employing organizations, students, and families.

Second, organizations should develop a more acute ethical and economic sense of the costs/benefits of aiding their members through a mid-life transition. The data do not exist, but there seem enormous costs—both psychic and economic—in awkward mid-life transitions. Blue-collar workers seem especially prone to the "blahs" during this period, with both attitudes and productivity subject to substantial declines.[24] Similarly, organizational folklore has long recounted the ravages common among salespeople who have been on the road 10-15 years. It seems no accident that mid-career crisis for professionals and managers—which "while hardly an epidemic, is no longer rare"[25]— tends to hit in the mid-30's. Transitions in personhood, that is, are reasonably linked to changes in career.

Looked at from another angle, enormous productive forces exist in the post-transition years. The point is sometimes too little appreciated. Recently-available longitudinal studies indicate that—although physical decline sets in and energy loss will occur—even the December of life can be a period of psychological growth.[26] Moreover, the common notion of a massive deterioration in psychological functioning in those beyond, say, seventy years of age, gets no support from newly-available studies.[27] In addition, many specific skills or attributes seem to have their own unique decay rates. Some steadily decline, beginning with the teens! Others hold steady or increase till the mid-40's or later.[28]

Perhaps the most dramatic devaluing of the productive energies of the post-transition years lies in the common belief that most outstanding creative work is done no later than the 30's, which many claim is a fact "as useless to bemoan . . . as to deny. . . ."[29] This understanding may rest on faulty methodology, however. In the case of contributions by philosophers, for example, one student concludes that the apparent peak of productivity by philosophers at around age 30 is "primarily due to the fact" that many more philosophers lived in their 30's than in their 70's. In fact, philosophers who survived until their 70's made 22 per cent of their total contributions in that decade![30]

The need for help from employing organizations or professional associations is no one-sided argument, of course, especially because mid-life transition may mean radical mid-career change. It may seem perverse that an organization should apply its resources to create non-members, humanitarian motives aside. One can at least imagine, however, cases in which it is economically unsound to keep an individual in a job or profession that has lost its allure but which the individual cannot leave without help. Hence a few organizations have begun to subsidize mid-career changes for some of their employees, for multiple motives. Thus early, insistent attention to matching individual needs with career development can signal the mutual concern about personal development which is the bedrock of solid personnel management. Moreover, such subsidization acknowledges past employee contributions, while it can slip between the horns of this central dilemma: of tolerating relatively senior officials for whom the "go-go" has largely gone but who nonetheless provide unfortunate role-models for less-senior personnel; and of risking the spiritual and legal complications of purges via overt dismissals or "early retirement."

Paramountly, perhaps, subsidization of mid-career change—especially higher in the hierarchy—can contribute to the sense of a dynamic organization. That is, one mid-career change might permit a chain of promotions or reassignments. Dollars spent on mid-career change consequently can have a larger multiplier as far as creating positive motivational effects. This will be particularly the case when organizations are stabilizing or declining after a growth spurt, or during a recession.

Third, relatedly, great emphasis should be placed on continuous checks of career progress against individual needs. The goal is to do something about growing mismatches, and especially early in the game. That is, perhaps the crucial ingredient in making a successful mid-life transition is active reflection—isolating what is important and attainable for the individual, assessing whether those important things are being worked toward, and doing something when things go otherwise. Such active reflection does not just occur when it is needed. It must be encouraged and nourished over the long-run, until it becomes part of an individual's attitudes about self and about seeing self.

The prevailing bias in most organizations is more "go-go" than "look-see," of course, so this challenge is no easy piece. The emphasis on career planning in some organizations provides a major ray of hope here.

Fourth, the several rhythms of the life cycle must be acknowledged and responded to, both in individual behavior as well as in organization policies and procedures. "By recognizing the patterns," Gould notes, "we may gain some control over the forces by smoothing the transitions and muting the peaks and valleys of adult life phases." Without knowledge of the cycle, people are obliged to be its unknowing pawns. There is hope for making the inevitable somewhat more attractive. "While children mark the passing years by their changing bodies," Gould observes, "adults change their minds."[31]

The developmental profile in Exhibit 1 suggests that at different life-periods, individuals have different needs and expectations. Sensitivity to these life-period differences should underlie career planning. Illustratively, a career pattern that emphasizes the search for a "mentor" seems quite appropriate at stage 2 of Early Adulthood. By stage 4, however, a career pattern should emphasize humane and efficient ways for unbuckling from mentors, a delicate process that ideally should not meet developmental needs by a harsh rejection of the mentor's previous contributions and present needs.

Fifth, employing organizations and professional organizations should better tailor their various systems and policies to human cycles and needs. This tailoring could be both generic and specific, as it were. Organizations can generically permit easier responses to human cycles and needs at all life stages in such ways:

- by providing a cafeteria approach to benefits and fringes, from which assortment employees can pick-and-choose specific packages (up to some common dollar value) responsive to their individual life-situations
- by sponsoring activities—ranging from full-fledged sabbaticals to episodic "life planning experiences"—that encourage individuals to get in more intimate touch with their own needs/aspirations/abilities, and to do something with such clarifications to improve their worklife and homelife.

Organizations can also develop systems and policies for specific life-stages. For example, human cycles and needs during the child-rearing years can be responded to

- by hiring matched-pairs of employees, as in the case of two females with similar skills and young children who each work every second day and care for all of the children on alternative days
- by hiring husband-and-wife teams—often scientists or technicians with the same skills and training, no longer a rare occurrence—who share duties at work and at home, as when each works half-time
- by carefully monitoring transfers, relocations, and time-on-the-road when children are adolescents and seem especially vulnerable to trauma and may be especially needful of the availability of parents.

Finally, systems and policies also could be developed specifically for those in the mid-life transition, or just coming out of it. Illustratively, Exhibit 1 implies that the mid-life years enlarge the individual's focus from acquisition to integration, from a narrow emphasis on "making it," on acquiring or achieving one's key goals, to an emphasis on fulfillment of broader social and psychological needs. These subtle dynamics might be facilitated in several ways:

- by recognizing mid-life transitional phenomena and by providing resources to help employees cope and understand, as via training programs held in-house or sponsored by professional associations
- by subsidizing mid-career changes, the derivative benefits being most apparent in cases involving individuals at senior levels of responsibility whose departure requires a chain of promotions or reassignments
- by negotiating contracts with "permanent part-timers" at all levels of organization who are seeking some better balance between "making it" and satisfying broader needs or interests
- by helping employees cope with realities that can severely complicate mid-life transition, such as by subsidizing career-changes for individuals who have been passed-over for promotion

- by establishing procedures and traditions by which mid-life transitionists can devote greater attention to integrative and supportive activities that facilitate the development of others, as by serving as a mentor, in contrast to the emphasis on the competitiveness and development of self characteristic of earlier life-stages[32]
- by establishing policies and traditions whereby full-time employees can accept lesser job responsibilities at reduced compensation, as opposed to such approaches as "up or out" systems

These suggestions are easier made than accomplished, of course. Each would require appropriate policies and procedures, as well as the support of accepted values and traditions. The issues are often subtle. Consider the subsidization of mid-career change. Should support go only to those seeking additional education,[33] as for entry into a new career of public service? Or will entrepreneurial ventures also be subsidized? Relatedly, some argue that those passed over for promotion should get especial priority in such subsidies, the advantages to both individual and organization being most obvious in this case;[34] but would that encourage failure-on-purpose?

Similarly, prescribing that mid-career transitionists begin to serve as mentors is easier said than done. The prescription is sensitive to the "stage of generativity" of the mid-life years, when there is a growing emphasis on the development of others as well as on the important role of mediating between the requirements of younger personnel and the demands of their organization.[35] Most likely job requirements may have to be changed to aid transitionists in acting on their new urges. In addition, severe cross-pressures can be involved in developing one's own replacement, and especially so if organization norms and practices fixate on personal achievement and advancement only. Moreover, the required expressions of emotional support and affection may be inhibited by organizational norms and work pressures, as well as by the earlier experiences and reputation of the mid-life transitionist. Finally, the transitionist's own unbuckling from mentors may have been incomplete or traumatic, with any residual guilt or anger a probable contaminant of future service as mentor.

Conclusion

In sum, a new and subtle partnership will be required between the mid-life employee and his or her employing organizations and professional associations. The individual's organization patently will have to assume primary responsibility for helping directly with the mid-life transition, and especially for funding ameliorative efforts. Organizations also might adopt many systems and procedures to accommodate to this significant change in emphasis toward human fulfillment, as was illustrated above.

However, there seem real limits as to how far employing organizations can go or should go in such matters without raising specters of big brotherism or paternalism. This implies a very major role for outside contractors, and especially for professional associations serving in such learning/helping roles. They would be vital in raising awareness about the need to adapt systems and policies to human developmental sequences and phases, in documenting the effects of such efforts, and in sponsoring learning experiences which employing organizations might make available to their members. That would really make professional associations—I hesitate to even write the word, given the multiple usages of the past few years—relevant to the needs of their members.

That related duo—mid-life transition and mid-career crisis—seems like a high-priority target for a new cooperative humanism between employing organizations and professional associations.

Notes

1. Daniel J. Levinson, Charlotte M. Darrow, Edwin B. Klein, Maria H. Levinson, and Braxton McKee, "The Psychosocial Development of Men in Early Adulthood and Mid-Life Transition," p. 244, in David Ricks, Alexander Thomas, and Merrill Roff (eds.), *Life History Research in Psychopathology*, Vol. 3 (Minneapolis, Minn.: Univeristy of Minnesota Press, 1974).

2. Roger Gould, "Adult Life Stages: Growth Toward Self-Tolerance," *Psychology Today*, Vol. 9 (February, 1975), p. 78.

3. *Ibid.*, pp. 74, 76; and Elliot Jacques, "Death and the Mid-Life Crisis," *International Journal of Psychoanalysis*, Vol. 46 (October, 1965), p. 502.

4. Henry S. Maas and Joseph A. Kuypers, *From Thirty to Seventy* (San Francisco: Jossey-Bass Publishers, 1974), p. 2; and Jack Block, *Lives Through Time* (Berkeley, Cal.: [sic] pp. 137-88 and 189-246.

5. Jacques, *op. cit.*, p. 502.

6. *Ibid.*, p. 506.

7. Bernice L. Neugarten, *Personality in Middle and Late Life* (New York: Atherton Press, 1964), p. 192.

8. Richard Church, *The Voyage Home* (London: Heinemann, 1964), p. 127.

9. Jacques, *op. cit.*, p. 502.

10. Jacques, *op. cit.*, p. 511; and H. G. Kaufman, *Obsolescence and Professional Career Development* (New York: AMACOM, 1974), p. 47.

11. H. G. Kaufman, *op. cit.*, (New York, AMACOM, 1974), p. 47.

12. David Gutmann, "Aging Among the Highland Maya: A Comparative Study," *Journal of Personality and Social Psychology*, Vol. 7 (No. 1, 1967), pp. 28-35.

13. Levinson, Darrow, Klein, Levinson, and McKee, *op. cit.*, p. 244.

14. Gould, *op. cit.*

15. *Ibid.*, pp. 76-77.

16. *Ibid.*, p. 74.

17. Layne A. Longfellow, "Toward Understanding Societal Influences," n.p. Copyright 1975, Layne A. Longfellow, PhD., The Menninger Foundation.

18. T. George Harris, "Some Idiot Raised the Ante," *Psychology Today*, Vol. 5 (February, 1972), p. 40.

19. *Ibid.*, p. 40.

20. Longfellow, *op. cit.*, attributes the survey to Dean Dauw and Roy Horton, "Life-Style Transitions: Mid-Career Crises and Career Changes." Paper presented at the Annual Meeting, Association for Humanistic Psychology, Estes Park, Colo., August 1975.

21. "Don't Call it 'Early Retirement'," *Harvard Business Review*, Vol. 53 (September, 1975), pp. 103-118; and D. L. Hiestand, *Changing Careers After 35* (New York: Columbia University Press, 1971).

22. The malady was especially highlighted by the HEW report *Work in America*. For a more chilling description, see H. L. Sheppart and N. Q. Heverick, *Where Have All the Robots Gone? Worker Dissatisfaction in the 70's* (New York: Free Press, 1973).

23. Herbert A. Shepard, "Life Planning," pp. 240-51, in Kenneth D. Benne, Leland P. Bradford, Jack R. Gibb, and Ronald O. Lippitt (eds.), *The Laboratory Method of Changing and Learning: Theory and Application* (Palo Alto, Calif.: Science and Behavior Books, Inc., 1975).

24. The rigorous evidence is sparse and not consistent, but such blue-collar flame-out seems growing if perhaps not yet epidemic. For early hints, see Patricia Cain Smith, "The Prediction of Individual Differences in Susceptibility to Industrial Monotony," *Journal of Applied Psychology*, Vol. 39 (October, 1955), pp. 322-30. See also *Work in America*, pp. 122-26.

25. Allan J. Cox, "How to Love Your Job—And Yourself, Too," *Advertising Age*, Vol. 46 (June 23, 1975), p. 39. See also Kaufman, *op. cit.*, esp. pp. 46-48.

26. Britton and Britton, *op. cit.*, pp. 169-70.

27. Maas and Kuypers, *op. cit.*, pp. 200-201.

28. Harold Geist, *The Psychological Aspects of the Aging Process with Sociological Implications* (St. Louis, Mo.: Warren H. Green, 1968), pp. 36-37. Joseph H. Britton and Jean O. Britton, *Personality Changes in Aging* (New York: Springer Publishing Co., 1972), pp. 169-70.

29. The central study by Harvey C. Lehman is conveniently reprinted in Bernice Levin Neugarten (ed.), *Middle Age and Aging* (Chicago: University of Chicago Press, 1968). See esp. pp. 104-105.

30. See the study by Wayne David, esp. p. 113, in *ibid.*

31. Gould, *op. cit.*, p. 78.

32. Harry Levinson, *Psychological Man* (Cambridge, Mass.: The Levinson Institute, Inc., 1976), esp. pp. 45, 52, 97-98.

33. Career-switchers often go back to school to make their transition, and most studies deal with this sub-group. But some go directly into new businesses or ventures. For an interesting pilot study of the latter sub-group, see L. Eugene Thomas, Richard L. Meta, Paula I. Robbins, and David W. Harvey, "Corporate Dropouts: A Preliminary Typology," *Vocational Guidance Quarterly*, Vol. 24 (March, 1976), pp. 220-28.

34. Samuel R. Connor and John S. Fielden, "Rx for Managerial Shelf-Sitters," *Harvard Business Review*, Vol. 51, (November, 1973), pp. 113-20.

35. Levinson, *op. cit.*, esp. pp. 97-98.

The Androgynous Blend: Best of Both Worlds?

by Alice G. Sargent

To produce more effective managers, men and women need to develop behaviors traditionally assigned to the opposite sex. The concepts of "male" and "female" are certainly real enough, and their effects are felt on all levels of the business world. However, managers and their organizations could benefit from a blend of the two.

Managers have tended to value coolness, competitive power, charisma, toughness, resilience, external rather than intrinsic rewards, and logical problem-solving rather than an integrated approach relying on wants and needs as much as ideas. To categorize these qualities as "male" is probably less accurate than to say organizational norms are synonymous with male norms.

Indeed, our cultural norms seem to be divided into organization (male) norms and family (female) norms. Men have been taught to value task-oriented achieving and have been socialized to fill the needs of the organization. Women have been taught to be expressive, oriented toward the development of others as an extension of themselves and have been socialized to fill the needs of their families.

Yet, the concept of the manager as a rational and analytical problem-solver with predominantly "organization man" characteristics is shifting toward a managerial style that encompasses human relations skills in addition to problem-solving. Increasingly, organizations train for and reward both vicarious and direct achievement styles of leadership, and both instrumental and expressive behaviors. The effective manager is seen as someone with both leadership skills and supporting and helping behaviors.

Alice G. Sargent is a consultant, educator, trainee, and administrator. She resides in Washington, D.C.

Reprinted by permission of the publisher from *Management Review*, October, 1978, 60-65. ©1978 by AMACOM, a division of American Management Associations. All rights reserved.

Some evidence of changing managerial styles can be found in performance appraisal forms. For example, one major corporation includes several social skills among ten factors in evaluating managers. These are: (1) communicating expectations and standards; confronting problem situations and issues; (2) being open, honest, and fair with people, and developing trust regardless of racial, sexual, or cultural factors, (3) developing skills in groups and individual effectiveness—being a good coach and mentor; recognizing and molding skills of others, and (4) communicating well at all levels of the organization.

Developmental training efforts in this corporation and others include increasing managers' abilities to express feelings and teaching helping skills, such as attending behavior, active listening, paraphrasing, reflecting feelings, and influencing. Also, some participants in management training seminars have reported they attended to learn how to be more sensitive and to show their feelings more.

Furthermore, radical shifts in the composition of the workforce to include women in management have raised one more challenge to norms and values. If women managers are not simply to be forced into male management styles, the entire organizational culture needs to be studied. Also, women bring to the marketplace values, attitudes, and behaviors that run counter to the mainstream. Therefore, the significant questions for corporations are: Can female characteristics and behaviors become part of managerial style without jettisoning the best of male traits? And, can new attitudes toward the place of work in one's life, the role of intimacy, and a wider spectrum of attitudes toward time and success be included in organizational values?

The New Style

Changing values for managerial style are coalescing with the new composition of the workforce to create dual pressures for shifting mores. This could develop androgynous managers—people who have learned and value both "masculine" and "feminine" behaviors, fatherly styles *and* maternal behaviors, competition *and* cooperation. The concept of androgynous managers may enhance the ways we see managers, conduct training programs, and evaluate performance.

This androgyny is an archetype that represents the coming together of, for want of better terms, maleness and femaleness. The androgynous manager is both dominant and yielding, combining independence with playfulness and nurture. An androgynous manager is well-developed in both the right brain (creative skills, such as intuition, interrelationships, fantasy, and imagination) and the left brain (intellectual skills, such as linear, abstract, logical, and deductive thinking).

Changing Nature of Management

More and more, management is viewed as accomplishing tasks through building a set of relationships between boss and manager, manager and subordinates, and manager and peers. For example, managers spend between 50 and 90 percent of their time in interpersonal communication. Of that time, ten percent is spent communicating with bosses, 40 percent with subordinates, and 50 percent laterally throughout the organization. This kind of communication requires interpersonal skills and concern for relationships.

As a result of this emphasis, affiliation may become more important. Motivational psychologist David McClelland has noted that achievement was the motive of the '60's and power the major motive of the'70's, but the third interpersonal motive, affiliation, has yet to have its day in organizations.

Also, R. E. Boyatzis developed a two-factor motivation theory of affiliative assurance and affiliative interest. Managers with high affiliative assurance motives are concerned basically with the security and strength of their close relationships. Anxious about rejection, they tend to be jealous and possessive about subordinates and superiors and probably engage in sibling rivalry with peers. This form of motivation interferes with the work of managers, because it interferes with their perspective in making decisions about the quality of time spent with other workers.

The human relations components of managers' jobs require that they develop the potential of subordinates, give direct, sometimes critical, feedback about their work, build an effective work team, and help new employees join that team. Yet, the manager with high affiliation assurance needs may not be comfortable in giving negative feedback, may not be able to place goals in perspective when interpersonal issues are present, may not model a collaborative style in the face of competition, and may not be able to help subordinates change their behavior if they do not want to.

In contrast, the manager with high affiliative interest—a good concern for relationships as well as for tasks—could generate a climate of openness and compassion, and could communicate directly and openly with his or her boss without being overly concerned about approval and reassurance. Importantly, security with an authority figure generates more problems for most than does seeking reassurance from peers or subordinates.

If affiliation becomes a more valued part of the manager's style, "feminine" behaviors, such as being able to express feelings, show vulnerability, and ask for support, may become more valued in the marketplace. It would then be as relevant for men to increase their interper-

Pointers for an Androgynous Combination

Women should . . .

- Learn how to be powerful and forthright.
- Become entrepreneurial.
- Have a direct, visible impact on others, rather than just functioning behind the scenes.
- State their own needs and refuse to back down, even if the immediate response is not acceptance.
- Focus on a task and regard it as at least as important as the relationships with the people doing the task.
- Build support systems with other women and share competence with them, rather than competing with them.
- Build a sense of community among women instead of saying: "I pulled myself up by my bootstraps, so why can't you?"
- Intellectualize and generalize from experience.
- Behave "impersonally," rather than personalizing experience and denying another's reality because it is different.
- Stop turning anger, blame, and pain inward.
- Stop accepting feelings of suffering and victimization.
- Take the option of being invulnerable to destructive feedback.
- Stop being bitchy and passive-resistant about resentments and anger.
- Respond directly with "I" statements, rather than with blaming "you" ones.
- Become effective problem-solvers by being analytical, systematic, and directive.
- Stop self-limiting behaviors, such as allowing interruptions or laughing after making a serious statement.
- Become risk-takers (no matter that at this time each woman believes she is regarded as representative of all womankind).

Pointers for an Androgynous Combination (continued)

Men should . . .

- Become aware of, accept, and express feelings.
- Regard feelings as a basic and essential part of life, as guides to authenticity and effectiveness for a fully functioning person, rather than as impediments to achievement.
- Accept the vulnerability and imperfections that are part of all persons.
- Assert the right to work for self-fulfillment, rather than only playing the role of provider.
- Value an identity that is not defined totally by work.
- Learn how to fail at a task without feeling one has failed as a man.
- Accept and express the need to be nurtured when feeling hurt, afraid, vulnerable, or helpless, rather than hiding these feelings behind a mask of strength, rationality, and invulnerability.
- Touch and be close to both men and women, minimizing any inhibition over the presence or absence of sexuality in such contact.
- Listen empathetically and actively but without feeling responsible for solving others' problems.
- Share feelings as the most meaningful part of one's contact with others, accepting the risk and vulnerability that such sharing implies.
- Build support systems with other men, sharing competencies without competition, and feelings and needs without dissembling.
- Personalize experience, rather than assuming that the only valid approach to life and interpersonal contact is objective.
- Give up performance-oriented sexuality for a more sensual, less goal-oriented, personalized sexuality.
- Accept the emotional, spontaneous, and rational as valid parts of oneself to be explored and expressed as needed.
- Nurture and actively support other men and women in their efforts to change.

sonal competencies in affiliation and intimacy as for women to become more assertive and more effective in dealing with the realities of power.

Two Different Worlds

In many ways, it is as if women and men grew up in two different cultures in which both sexes developed and were rewarded for different skills, attitudes, and behaviors. For a healthy androgyny, both sexes need to temper their managerial styles with those of their counterparts. Women now need to develop behaviors that will enable them to be autonomous, powerful, and forthright as well as supportive; men need to learn to be more aware of their feelings instead of suppressing or avoiding them, to make greater emotional contact, to be more overtly dependent, and to build effective support systems. The boxes on the preceding pages detail some of the specifics of this "exchange" process.

The benefits of androgyny thus become clear. Women would benefit from the analytical skills and healthy assertiveness of males. And men could improve their managerial abilities by developing more effective intuition, improved ability to express emotion, and more effective support systems. Men could learn to decrease exhibitionism and jockeying for power with each other. Women could learn to share their competence with other women. If both sexes would participate in compensatory education programs designed to develop their human and managerial capacities more fully, we could have managers with a high concern for task and relationships and who, incidentally, would be androgynous.

Androgynous behavior impacts a range of managerial functions: giving performance appraisals, encouraging team effectiveness, assisting in the career development of other employees, developing a variety of decision-making styles, dealing with conflict, the capacity to generate a positive climate in the organization, and responses to new ideas and to stress.

In their quest to be taken seriously, many professional women go through a stage of becoming like the archetypical man before allowing themselves the tenderness and playfulness they abandoned. Women are often awkward as they search for role models, and they try to become like their male colleagues or mentors. They may try to take charge or express anger as some charismatic guru does, only to feel even more inept because they violate their own integrity.

In *The Managerial Woman*, M. Henning and A. Jardim note that the successful woman of 35 frequently tries to recapture her feminine side. As the pool of assertive women increases and the initial awkwardness of the new behavior is overcome, more women move to the next stage—

being assertive without being oppressive or non-caring.

If, as *MS* concludes (January 1977), it is possible to have "love after liberation," it may be all right to be both assertive *and* compassionate. Because women have for so long derived their style from the hostess role, it is almost a joy to see the disjointedness of the recent participant in assertiveness training.

Women have learned to be excessively pleasant, to smooth over conflict, to be preoccupied with bringing people together (often at the expense of substance), to be overly concerned with getting the job done, to smile too much, to allow themselves to be interrupted, to let their voices trail off when making an important point, to laugh at the end of an important sentence, and to require more expertise from themselves than a man would before venturing an opinion. In short, women have learned passivity, self-denigration, and vicarious satisfaction.

Because of socialization and continuing reinforcement, women are prone to abandon a position of strength in order to be charming and conciliatory. Rather than being concerned about whether they are being ignored or affirmed, women need to make their points and have their messages received openly. Also, they need to claim ownership for jobs well-done, to acknowledge errors in judgment, and to deal with instances where sexual attraction biased their responses to others.

Similarly, men tend to be awkward as they become aware of the need for more collaborative, less competitive behavior, and to commit themselves to greater openness rather than coolness. Men benefit when they are made aware that they are operating more out of need for power and control than a need to get the job done. On the basis that one should be rational, men typically act to the exclusion of needs for approval, closeness, and spontaneity, even to the extent of not recognizing the emotional content of a message or its relevance to a situation.

Power Relationships

Newer management styles tend to emphasize more collaboration and less competition, or at least different decision-making styles for different situations. Contingency decision making and situational leadership styles are becoming more wide-spread so that benevolent autocratic styles tend to be used in fire-fighting, and more consultative styles used for planning. Participative styles are not yet in widespread use.

A paramount issue for women is the exercise of power and the acceptance of any conflict that results. Many women avoid confrontation and competition in policymaking and goal setting, even to the point of not seeing issues in terms of power struggles and even though power

dynamics are rampant and frequently useful components in every organization. They may even spend their time in noninfluential roles in an
organization rather than seeing the system's real governance and
decision-making process as the issue.

Many women tend to be reluctant to take charge, even when appropriate, and to overuse the collaborative approach when it is inappropriate. As women become more comfortable leading, they undoubtedly will
be able to make judgments based on a correct reading of a situation. But
women managers now tend to be trained by subordinates rather than
singled out by top leaders and brought along. They are not seen to have,
nor do they have, as much access to information as male managers do.

Women managers also tend to give away their power. Women are
much more familiar with seeking help from others than with being
self-reliant. In one power-simulation game, which begins with the hand-
ing out of four pages of directions, it is not uncommon for a women
participant to glance at the directions, set them down, turn to the person
next to her, and ask, "What do they say?" Similarly, women have been
socialized to make do with what they have rather than to hustle for
themselves, and they fail to demand adequate resources for their programs or training for themselves and their subordinates.

In contrast, men have been taught to overemphasize power—and are
rewarded for doing so. Many men say they naturally slip into one-up/
one-down interactions, even when unnecessary, and that they distance
themselves in many of their relationships, business and social. Men
frequently use jokes and stories to regain control or enhance a point. Few
women use this approach, even when it might be helpful; they tend to
speak from a base of expertise or to talk more personally. In order to be
androgynous, and less isolated and lonely, men need to experience
situations that trigger the power responses and then allow and force
themselves to feel the discomfort of being less in control.

Another facet of the male manager style is the lack of reflection or
matching behavior. This is no surprise since organizations tend not to
reward this behavior among managers. Typically, male managers learn
from concrete experimentation and direct experience (doing), somewhat
less from abstract (feeling) conceptualization (thinking), and least of all
from reflective observation (watching).

Dynamics of Communication

Research on the impact of group composition on interaction patterns
demonstrates that men and women have indeed learned different sets of
behavior. Competition, aggression, violence, victimization, joking, identity
questions, and fear of self-disclosure have been shown to predominate in

all-male groups. For example, about one-third of the statements made in all-male groups tend to be addressed to the group as a whole, thus avoiding intimacy. Men also report that they do not usually get their intimacy needs met by men. All-female groups tend to stress themes of affiliation, family, conflicts about competition and leadership, and information about various relationships.

Women tend to deny the presence of power issues in a group. They want, instead, to feel part of a team where all are equal, whether this accords with reality or not.

In mixed groups, men tend to be more tense, serious, and self-conscious. They speak less of aggression and engage less in practical joking. Both sexes refer to the self and talk about feelings more, but women generally speak less than men by a significant amount: men get two-thirds of the air time. Sexual tensions are present in mixed groups, and people tend to express values and concerns about being attractive to the opposite sex.

Other research has demonstrated that a man in a female-dominated group is likely to be a central figure and to be deferred to and respected. On the other hand, a woman in a male-dominated group probably will be isolated and treated as trivial or as a mascot. Women express themselves more fully in a team situation if several women are part of the team. A woman alone on a team is less likely to make a full contribution because she tends to be invisible, isolated, and unsupported. This suggests the benefits of placing several rather than one woman on teams, even if other teams have no women members at all.

Toward Androgyny

The language of transactional analysis provides a useful communications model. TA views each person as a parent (critical and nurturing), an adult (problem-solving, rational thinker), and a child (free, natural, adaptive, rebellious, manipulative, creative).

If adult-adult or man-woman and woman-woman communication is the goal in most work interactions, then the following behaviors should be eliminated:

1. Men using women managers as mothers—telling them personal information but not treating them as real colleagues with whom they also solve problems and perform tasks. (Mother-boy pattern.)

2. Women managers not sharing their competence with each other but behaving instead in negative girl-girl or mother-girl patterns.

3. Men and women managers using sex to play out power and control issues, as in father-girl and mother-boy patterns.

4. Male managers being angry at women employees but protecting them. (Father-girl pattern.)

5. In emotional situations, the male manager deferring to the female manager if pain is expressed (woman manager comforts tearful woman secretary while the male manager steps aside). (Mother-boy pattern.)

6. Woman manager deferring to male manager on policy-making. (Father-girl pattern.)

The androgynous manager combines the adult problem-solving mode with the nurturance of the parent and the spontaneity, creativity, and playfulness of the child. The androgynous manager acting as adult is able to love, assert, express anger and fear, be caring, and solve problems.

New Life Patterns

To be more androgynous, women need to expand their repertoire of behavior for dealing with power and conflict. Men need to increase their capability for self-disclosure and for the spontaneous expressing of feelings. Our daily lives do not offer much support for seeing men and women through the transition to androgynous behavior in male-female relationships. Therefore, we all need to build better support systems to help deal with anxieties, to encourage risk taking, to help renew our energy and determination, and to encourage us to increase our opportunities for behavior that is free of sex-role stereotyping. These issues need to be talked about and explored in every aspect of organizational and family life.

We are building toward dramatically new patterns of interaction between men and men, between women and women, and between men and women. It is critical that both sexes have opportunities to develop androgynous behavior, free of sex-role constraints, if they are to work effectively within the new workforce and with human relations styles of management.

Part 3. The Person as a Manager

The focus of the book now shifts from the personal qualities and problems of individuals who function as managers to the managerial role itself. Part 3 is concerned with what managers do, what makes them effective, and how their performance can be improved. The role of the manager has been the subject of a great deal of investigation over the past four decades, and the readings included here represent some of the most useful insights.

The first article, "Managers and Leaders: Are They Different?," provides an in-depth look at two roles that are sometimes assumed to be synonymous. Management and leadership are two distinct executive functions, and Abraham Zaleznik explores the organizational need for both of them. The managerial role has evolved in response to organizational needs for rationality, systemization, distribution of power, and stability. Leadership, on the other hand, denotes a different set of characteristic behaviors—risk taking, personal power, and inspiration. Comparisons of leaders and managers reveal differences in style in interpersonal relationships, attitudes toward goals and work, and self-perceptions.

Zaleznik concludes the paper with a discussion of leadership development. Presumably, his psychoanalytic orientation influences him to emphasize early life experiences and the individual's identification with a mentor in a one-to-one relationship. An important consideration for organizations is whether their training programs are fostering management to the exclusion of leadership.

The second article, "To Achieve or Not: The Manager's Choice," is Jay Hall's report of his ambitious study of eleven thousand managers. Hall used a variety of questionnaires, most of which were developed by him, to measure such factors as work motivation, managerial style, and interpersonal competence; then he assessed them against the managers' levels of achievement. Hall's findings are generally supportive of a managerial stance that advocates integration of people and task emphases, openness and sensitivity to employees, and participatory practices.

Hall's study also indicates some interesting things about the motives of low-achieving managers. Low achievers are self-centered and primarily seek safety and comfort, while high achievers have markedly different motives. Furthermore, these attitudes are passed along to subordinates. It is Hall's conclusion that managerial achievement is a matter of behavior—of implementing practices that are known to lead to success—rather than catchy language or flashy programs.

In "Motivation: A Diagnostic Approach," Nadler and Lawler describe a line of research on another important aspect of the manager's role—understanding and influencing employees' *motivation*. Social science has provided the manager with some useful theories about human motivation (for example, see McGregor's "The Human Side of Enterprise" in part 4). However, these theories tend to be general and often are not very helpful to the manager in dealing with individual people and specific situations.

A new approach called *expectancy theory* has been developed and holds promise as a useful tool. Expectancy theory operates on the premise that employees make decisions about the degree and kind of performance they will undertake. These decisions are the results of weighing several expectations having to do with effort, likelihood of success, and payoff. Sets of guidelines and organizational strategies are provided by the authors to help managers select an optimal approach to employee motivation.

W. Warner Burke's article, "Developing and Selecting Leaders: What We Know," summarizes the state of the art of leadership research. He begins by tracing some historical views of leader effectiveness and ends with an integration of the important contemporary literature—including several of the studies in this volume. Although the findings are voluminous and complex, there are some consistent principles that emerge again and again, such as the need to balance concern for task accomplishment with concern for human relations.

Burke also explores the topic of nontraditional sources of leadership and the leadership styles of women. As Sargent reported in part 2, most women are socialized to rely on aspects of their personalities that are referred to as "feminine." However, behaviors traditionally considered to be "masculine," such as competitiveness, power-orientation, and rationality, are more often identified with leadership. Research on successful leaders cast doubt on the value of using either a masculine or a feminine style exclusively.

The article concludes with a summary of the ten functional characteristics prescribed by behavioral scientists as the best available model for effective leadership. The list is admittedly awesome, but it is an improvement over trial and error or conventional wisdom.

The readings in part 3 present a psychological and behavioral profile of the manager. Taken together they provide a useful model of the effective manager—her or his attitudes, styles, values, and skills. The articles also make it clear that successful managerial behavior does not occur in a vacuum. Each manager's *role* carries with it a unique set of demands, expectations, and problems that must be responded to. Flexibility and adaptability are essential.

The next section, part 4, will pick up the theme of the requirements of the work situation and extend it to some important view of the organization as an environment for humans.

10

Managers and Leaders:
Are They Different?

by Abraham Zaleznik

What is the ideal way to develop leadership? Every society provides its own answer to this question, and each, in groping for answers, defines its deepest concerns about the purposes, distributions, and uses of power. Business has contributed its answer to the leadership question by evolving a new breed called the manager. Simultaneously, business has established a new power ethic that favors collective over individual leadership, the cult of the group over that of personality. While ensuring the competence, control, and the balance of power relations among groups with the potential for rivalry, managerial leadership unfortunately does not necessarily ensure imagination, creativity, or ethical behavior in guiding the destinies of corporate enterprises.

Leadership inevitably requires using power to influence the thoughts and actions of other people. Power in the hands of an individual entails human risks: first, the risk of equating power with the ability to get immediate results; second, the risk of ignoring the many different ways people can legitimately accumulate power; and third, the risk of losing self-control in the desire for power. The need to hedge these risks accounts in part for the development of collective leadership and the managerial ethic. Consequently, an inherent conservatism dominates the culture of large organizations. In *The Second American Revolution*, John D. Rockefeller, 3rd. describes the conservatism of organizations:

"An organization is a system, with a logic of its own, and all the weight of tradition and inertia. The deck is stacked in favor of the tried and

Abraham Zaleznik is the Cahners-Rabb Professor of Social Psychology of Management at the Harvard Business School. He is also a psychoanalyst.

proven way of doing things and against the taking of risks and striking out in new directions."[1]

Out of this conservatism and inertia organizations provide succession to power through the development of managers rather than individual leaders. And the irony of the managerial ethic is that it fosters a bureaucratic culture in business, supposedly the last bastion protecting us from the encroachments and controls of bureaucracy in government and education. Perhaps the risks associated with power in the hands of an individual may be necessary ones for business to take if organizations are to break free of their inertia and bureaucratic conservatism.

MANAGER VS. LEADER PERSONALITY

Theodore Levitt has described the essential features of a managerial culture with its emphasis on rationality and control:

"Management consists of the rational assessment of a situation and the systematic selection of goals and purposes (what is to be done?); the systematic development of strategies to achieve these goals; the marshalling of the required resources; the rational design, organization, direction, and control of the activities required to attain the selected purposes; and finally, the motivating and rewarding of people to do the work."[2]

In other words, whether his or her energies are directed toward goals, resources, organization structures, or people, a manager is a problem solver. The manager asks himself, "What problems have to be solved, and what are the best ways to achieve results so that people will continue to contribute to this organization?" In this conception, leadership is a practical effort to direct affairs; and to fulfill his task, a manager requires that many people operate at different levels of status and responsibility. Our democratic society is, in fact, unique in having solved the problem of providing well-trained managers for business. The same solution stands ready to be applied to government, education, health care, and other institutions. It takes neither genius nor heroism to be a manager, but rather persistence, tough-mindedness, hard work, intelligence, analytical ability and, perhaps most important, tolerance and good will.

Another conception, however, attaches almost mystical beliefs to what leadership is and assumes that only great people are worthy of the drama of power and politics. Here, leadership is a psychodrama in

---

[1] John D. Rockefeller, 3rd., *The Second American Revolution* (New York: Harper-Row, 1973), p. 72.

[2] Theodore Levitt, "Management and the Post Industrial Society," *The Public Interest,* Summer 1976, p. 73.

which, as a precondition for control of a political structure, a lonely person must gain control of him- or herself. Such an expectation of leadership contrasts sharply with the mundane, practical, and yet important concept that leadership is really managing work that other people do.

Two questions come to mind. Is this mystique of leadership merely a holdover from our collective childhood of dependency and our longing for good and heroic parents? Or, is there a basic truth lurking behind the need for leaders that no matter how competent managers are, their leadership stagnates because of their limitations in visualizing purposes and generating value in work? Without this imaginative capacity and the ability to communicate, managers, driven by their narrow purposes, perpetuate group conflicts instead of reforming them into broader desires and goals.

If indeed problems demand greatness, then judging by past performance, the selection and development of leaders leave a great deal to chance. There are no known ways to train "great" leaders. Furthermore, beyond what we leave to chance, there is a deeper issue in the relationship between the need for competent managers and the longing for great leaders.

What it takes to ensure the supply of people who will assume practical responsibility may inhibit the development of great leaders. Conversely, the presence of great leaders may undermine the development of managers who become very anxious in the relative disorder that leaders seem to generate. The antagonism in aim (to have many competent managers as well as great leaders) often remains obscure in stable and well-developed societies. But the antagonism surfaces during periods of stress and change, as it did in the Western countries during both the Great Depression and World War II. The tension also appears in the struggle for power between theorists and professional managers in revolutionary societies.

It is easy enough to dismiss the dilemma I pose (of training managers while we may need new leaders, or leaders at the expense of managers) by saying that the need is for people who can be *both* managers and leaders. The truth of the matter as I see it, however, is that just as a managerial culture is different from the entrepreneurial culture that develops when leaders appear in organizations, managers and leaders are very different kinds of people. They differ in motivation, personal history, and in how they think and act.

A technologically oriented and economically successful society tends to depreciate the need for great leaders. Such societies hold a deep and abiding faith in rational methods of solving problems, including problems of value, economics, and justice. Once rational methods of solving problems are broken down into elements, organized, and taught as skills, then society's faith in technique over personal qualities in leadership remains the guiding conception for a democratic society contemplating its leadership requirements. But there are times when tinkering and trial and error prove inadequate to the emerging problems of selecting goals, allocating resources, and distributing wealth and opportunity. During such times, the democratic society needs to find leaders who use themselves as the instruments of learning and acting, instead of managers who use their accumulation of collective experience to get where they are going.

The most impressive spokesman, as well as exemplar of the managerial viewpoint, was Alfred P. Sloan, Jr. who, along with Pierre du Pont, designed the modern corporate structure. Reflecting on what makes one management successful while another fails, Sloan suggested that "good management rests on a reconciliation of centralization and decentralization, or 'decentralization with coordinated control' ".[3]

Sloan's conception of management, as well as his practice, developed by trial and error, and by the accumulation of experience. Sloan wrote:

"There is no hard and fast rule for sorting out the various responsibilities and the best way to assign them. The balance which is struck . . . varies according to what is being decided, the circumstances of the time, past experience, and the temperaments and skills of the executive involved."[4]

In other words, in much the same way that the inventors of the late nineteenth century tried, failed, and fitted until they hit on a product or method, managers who innovate in developing organizations are "tinkerers." They do not have a grand design or experience the intuitive flash of insight that, borrowing from modern science, we have come to call the "breakthrough."

Managers and leaders differ fundamentally in their world views. The dimensions for assessing these differences include managers' and leaders' orientations toward their goals, their work, their human relations, and their selves.

Attitudes Toward Goals

Managers tend to adopt impersonal, if not passive, attitudes toward goals. Managerial goals arise out of necessities rather than desires, and, therefore, are deeply embedded in the history and culture of the organization.

---

[3] Alfred P. Sloan, Jr., *My Years with General Motors* (New York: Doubleday & Co., 1964), p. 429.

[4] Ibid., p. 429.

Frederic G. Donner, chairman and chief executive officer of General Motors from 1958 to 1967, expressed this impersonal and passive attitude toward goals in defining GM's position on product development:

". . . To meet the challenge of the marketplace, we must recognize changes in customer needs and desires far enough ahead to have the right products in the right places at the right time and in the right quantity.

"We must balance trends in preference against the many compromises that are necessary to make a final product that is both reliable and good looking, that performs well and that sells at a competitive price in the necessary volume. We must design, not just the cars we would like to build, but more importantly, the cars that our customers want to buy."[5]

Nowhere in this formulation of how a product comes into being is there a notion that consumer tastes and preferences arise in part as a result of what manufacturers do. In reality, through product design, advertising, and promotion, consumers learn to like what they then say they need. Few would argue that people who enjoy taking snapshots *need* a camera that also develops pictures. But in response to novelty, convenience, a shorter interval between acting (taking the snap) and gaining pleasure (seeing the shot), the Polaroid camera succeeded in the marketplace. But it is inconceivable that Edwin Land responded to impressions of consumer need. Instead, he translated a technology (polarization of light) into a product, which proliferated and stimulated consumers' desires.

The example of Polaroid and Land suggests how leaders think about goals. They are active instead of reactive, shaping ideas instead of responding to them. Leaders adopt a personal and active attitude toward goals. The influence a leader exerts in altering moods, evoking images and expectations, and in establishing specific desires and objectives determines the direction a business takes. The net result of this influence is to change the way people think about what is desirable, possible, and necessary.

Conceptions of Work

What do managers and leaders do? What is the nature of their respective work?

Leaders and managers differ in their conceptions. Managers tend to view work as an enabling process involving some combination of people and ideas interacting to establish strategies and make decisions. Manag-

---

[5] Ibid. p. 440.

ers help the process along by a range of skills, including calculating the interests in opposition, staging and timing the surface of controversial issues, and reducing tensions. In this enabling process, managers appear flexible in the use of tactics: they negotiate and bargain, on the one hand, and use rewards and punishments, and other forms of coercion, on the other. Machiavelli wrote for managers and not necessarily for leaders.

Alfred Sloan illustrated how this enabling process works in situations of conflict. The time was the early 1920s when the Ford Motor Co. still dominated the automobile industry using, as did General Motors, the conventional water-cooled engine. With the full backing of Pierre du Pont, Charles Kettering dedicated himself to the design of an air-cooled engine, which, if successful, would have been a great technical and market coup for GM. Kettering believed in his product, but the manufacturing division heads at GM remained skeptical and later opposed the new design on two grounds: first, that it was technically unreliable, and second, that the corporation was putting all its eggs in one basket by investing in a new product instead of attending to the current marketing situation.

In the summer of 1923 after a series of false starts and after its decision to recall the copper-cooled Chevrolets from dealers and customers, GM management reorganized and finally scrapped the project. When it dawned on Kettering that the company had rejected the engine, he was deeply discouraged and wrote to Sloan that without the "organized resistance" against the project it would succeed and that unless the project were saved, he would leave the company.

Alfred Sloan was all too aware of the fact that Kettering was unhappy and indeed intended to leave General Motors. Sloan was also aware of the fact that, while the manufacturing divisions strongly opposed the new engine, Pierre du Pont supported Kettering. Furthermore, Sloan had himself gone on record in a letter to Kettering less than two years earlier expressing full confidence in him. The problem Sloan now had was to make his decision stick, keep Kettering in the organization (he was much too valuable to lose), avoid alienating du Pont, and encourage the division heads to move speedily in developing product lines using conventional water-cooled engines.

The actions that Sloan took in the face of this conflict reveal much about how managers work. First, he tried to reassure Kettering by presenting the problem in a very ambiguous fashion, suggesting that he and the Executive Committee sided with Kettering, but that it would not be practical to force the divisions to do what they were opposed to. He presented the problem as being a question of the people, not the product. Second, he proposed to reorganize around the problem by consolidating all functions in a new division that would be responsible for the design, production, and marketing of the new car. This solution, however, appeared as ambiguous as his efforts to placate and keep Kettering in General Motors. Sloan wrote: "My plan was to create an independent pilot operation under the sole jurisdiction of Mr. Kettering, a kind of copper-cooled-car division. Mr. Kettering would designate his own chief engineer and his production staff to solve the technical problems of manufacture."[6]

While Sloan did not discuss the practical value of this solution, which included saddling an inventor with management responsibility, he in effect used this plan to limit his conflict with Pierre du Pont.

In effect, the managerial solution that Sloan arranged and pressed for adoption limited the options available to others. The structural solution narrowed choices, even limiting emotional reactions to the point where the key people could do nothing but go along, and even allowed Sloan to say in his memorandum to du Pont, "We have discussed the matter with Mr. Kettering at some length this morning and he agrees with us absolutely on every point we made. He appears to receive the suggestion enthusiastically and has every confidence that it can be put across along these lines."[7]

Having placated people who opposed his views by developing a structural solution that appeared to give something but in reality only limited options, Sloan could then authorize the car division's general manager, with whom he basically agreed, to move quickly in designing water-cooled cars for the immediate market demand.

Years later Sloan wrote, evidently with tongue in cheek, "The cooper-cooled car never came up again in a big way. It just died out, I don't know why."[8]

In order to get people to accept solutions to problems, managers need to coordinate and balance continually. Interestingly enough, this managerial work has much in common with what diplomats and mediators do, with Henry Kissinger apparently an outstanding practitioner. The manager aims at shifting balances of power toward solutions acceptable as a compromise among conflicting values.

What about leaders, what do they do? Where managers act to limit choices, leaders work in the opposite direction, to develop fresh approaches to long-standing problems and to open issues for new options. Stanley and Inge Hoffmann, the political scientists, liken the leader's work to that of the artist. But unlike most artists, the leader himself is an

---

[6] Ibid. p. 91.

[7] Ibid. p. 91.

[8] Ibid, p. 93.

integral part of the aesthetic product. One cannot look at a leader's art without looking at the artist. On Charles de Gaulle as a political artist, they wrote: "And each of his major political acts, however tortuous the means or the details, has been whole, indivisible and unmistakably his own, like an artistic act."[9]

The closest one can get to a product apart from the artist is the ideas that occupy, indeed at times obsess, the leader's mental life. To be effective, however, the leader needs to project his ideas into images that excite people, and only then develop choices that give the projected images substance. Consequently, leaders create excitement in work.

John F. Kennedy's brief presidency shows both the strengths and weaknesses connected with the excitement leaders generate in their work. In his inaugural address he said, "Let every nation know, whether it wishes us well or ill, that we shall pay any price, bear any burden, meet any hardship, support any friend, oppose any foe, in order to assure the survival and the success of liberty."

This much-quoted statement forced people to react beyond immediate concerns and to identify with Kennedy and with important shared ideals. But upon closer scrutiny the statement must be seen as absurd because it promises a position which if in fact adopted, as in the Viet Nam War, could produce disastrous results. Yet unless expectations are aroused and mobilized, with all the dangers of frustration inherent in heightened desire, new thinking and new choice can never come to light.

Leaders work from high-risk positions, indeed often are temperamentally disposed to seek out risk and danger, especially where opportunity and reward appear high. From my observations, why one individual seeks risks while another approaches problems conservatively depends more on his or her personality and less on conscious choice. For some, especially those who become managers, the instinct for survival dominates their need for risk, and their ability to tolerate mundane, practical work assists their survival. The same cannot be said for leaders who sometimes react to mundane work as to an affliction.

Relations with Others

Managers prefer to work with people; they avoid solitary activity because it makes them anxious. Several years ago, I directed studies on the psychological aspects of career. The need to seek out others with whom to work and collaborate seemed to stand out as important characteristics of managers. When asked, for example, to write imaginative stories in

---

[9] Stanley and Inge Hoffmann, "The Will for Grandeur: de Gaulle as Political Artist," *Daedalus*, Summer 1968, p. 849.

response to a picture showing a single figure (a boy contemplating a violin, or a man silhouetted in a state of reflection), managers populated their stories with people. The following is an example of a manager's imaginative story about the young boy contemplating a violin:

"Mom and Dad insisted that Junior take music lessons so that someday he can become a concert musician. His instrument was ordered and had just arrived. Junior is weighing the alternatives of playing football with the other kids or playing with the squeak box. He can't understand how his parents could think a violin is better than a touchdown.

"After four months of practicing the violin, Junior has had more than enough, Daddy is going out of his mind, and Mommy is willing to give in reluctantly to the men's wishes. Football season is now over, but a good third baseman will take the field next spring."[10]

This story illustrates two themes that clarify managerial attitudes toward human relations. The first, as I have suggested, is to seek out activity with other people (i.e. the football team), and the second is to maintain a low level of emotional involvement in these relationships. The low emotional involvement appears in the writer's use of conventional metaphors, even clichés, and in the depiction of the ready transformation of potential conflict into harmonious decisions. In this case, Junior, Mommy, and Daddy agree to give up the violin for manly sports.

These two themes may seem paradoxical, but their coexistence supports what a manager does, including reconciling differences, seeking compromises, and establishing a balance of power. A further idea demonstrated by how the manager wrote the story is that managers may lack empathy, or the capacity to sense intuitively the thoughts and feelings of others. To illustrate attempts to be empathic, here is another story written to the same stimulus picture by someone considered by his peers to be a leader:

"This little boy has the appearance of being a sincere artist, one who is deeply affected by the violin, and has an intense desire to master the instrument.

"He seems to have just completed his normal practice session and appears to be somewhat crestfallen at his inability to produce the sounds which he is sure lie within the violin.

"He appears to be in the process of making a vow to himself to expend the necessary time and effort to play this instrument until he satisfies himself that he is able to bring forth the qualities of music which he feels within himself.

---

[10] Abraham Zaleznik, Gene W. Dalton, and Louis B. Barnes, *Orientation and Conflict in Career*, (Boston: Division of Research, Harvard Business School, 1970) p. 316.

"With this type of determination and carry through, this boy became one of the great violinists of his day."[11]

Empathy is not simply a matter of paying attention to other people. It is also the capacity to take in emotional signals and to make them mean something in a relationship with an individual. People who describe another person as "deeply affected" with "intense desire," as capable of feeling "crestfallen" and as one who can "vow to himself," would seem to have an inner perceptiveness that they can use in their relationships with others.

Managers relate to people according to the role they play in a sequence of events or in a decision-making *process*, while leaders, who are concerned with ideas, relate in more intuitive and empathetic ways. The manager's orientation to people, as actors in a sequence of events, deflects his or her attention away from the substance of people's concerns and toward their roles in a process. The distinction is simply between a manager's attention to *how* things get done and a leader's to *what* the events and decisions mean to participants.

In recent years, managers have taken over from game theory the notion that decision-making events can be one of two types: the win-lose situation (or zero-sum game) or the win-win situation in which everybody in the action comes out ahead. As part of the process of reconciling differences among people and maintaining balances of power, managers strive to convert win-lose into win-win situations.

As an illustration, take the decision of how to allocate capital resources among operating divisions in a large, decentralized organization. On the face of it, the dollars available for distribution are limited at any given time. Presumably, therefore, the more one division gets, the less is available for other divisions.

Managers tend to view this situation (as it affects human relations) as a conversion issue: how to make what seems like a win-lose problem into a win-win problem. Several solutions to this situation come to mind. First, the manager focuses others attention on procedure and not on substance. Here the actors become engrossed in the bigger problem of *how* to make decisions, not *what* decisions to make. Once committed to the bigger problem, the actors have to support the outcome since they were involved in formulating decision rules. Because the actors believe in the rules they formulated, they will accept present losses in the expectation that next time they will win.

Second, the manager communicates to his subordinates indirectly, using "signals" instead of "messages." A signal has a number of possible

---

[11] Ibid. p. 294.

implicit positions in it while a message clearly states a position. Signals are inconclusive and subject to reinterpretation should people become upset and angry, while messages involve the direct consequence that some people will indeed not like what they hear. The nature of messages heightens emotional response, and, as I have indicated, emotionally makes managers anxious. With signals, the question of who wins and who loses often becomes obscured.

Third, the manager plays for time. Managers seem to recognize that with the passage of time and the delay of major decisions, compromises emerge that take the sting out of win-lose situations; and the original "game" will be superseded by additional ones. Therefore, compromises may mean that one wins and loses simultaneously, depending on which one of the games one evaluates.

There are undoubtedly many other tactical moves managers use to change human situations from win-lose to win-win. But the point to be made is that such tactics focus on the decision-making process itself and interest managers rather than leaders. The interest in tactics involves costs as well as benefits, including making organizations fatter in bu-reaucratic and political intrigue and leaner in direct, hard activity and warm human relationships. Consequently, one often hears subordinates characterize managers as inscrutable, detached, and manipulative. These adjectives arise from the subordinates' perception that they are linked together in a process whose purpose, beyond simply making decisions, is to maintain a controlled as well as rational and equitable structure. These adjectives suggest that managers need order in the face of the potential chaos that many fear in human relationships.

In contrast, one often hears leaders referred to in adjectives rich in emotional content. Leaders attract strong feelings of identity and differ-ence, or of love and hate. Human relations in leader-dominated struc-tures often appear turbulent, intense, and at times even disorganized. Such an atmosphere intensifies individual motivation and often pro-duces unanticipated outcomes. Does this intense motivation lead to innovation and high performance, or does it represent wasted energy?

Senses of Self

In *The Varieties of Religious Experience*, William James describes two basic personality types, "once-born" and "twice-born."[12] People of the former personality type are those for whom adjustments to life have been straightforward and whose lives have been more or less a peaceful flow from the moment of their births. The twice-borns, on the other hand,

---

[12] William James, *Varieties of Religious Experience* (New York: Mentor Books, 1958).

have not had an easy time of it. Their lives are marked by a continual struggle to attain some sense of order. Unlike the once-borns they cannot take things for granted. According to James, these personalities have equally different world views. For a once-born personality, the sense of self, as a guide to conduct and atittude, derives from a feeling of being at home and in harmony with one's environment. For a twice-born, the sense of self derives from a feeling of profound separateness.

A sense of belonging or of being separate has a practical significance for the kinds of investments managers and leaders make in their careers. Managers see themselves as conservators and regulators of an existing order of affairs with which they personally identify and from which they gain rewards. Perpetuating and strengthening existing institutions enhances a manager's sense of self-worth: he or she is performing in a role that harmonizes with the ideals of duty and responsibility. William James had this harmony in mind—this sense of self as flowing easily to and from the outer world—in defining a once-born personality. If one feels oneself as a member of institutions, contributing to their well-being, then one fulfills a mission in life and feels rewarded for having measured up to ideals. This reward transcends material gains and answers the more fundamental desire for personal integrity which is achieved by identifying with existing institutions.

Leaders tend to be twice-born personalities, people who feel separate from their environment, including other people. They may work in organizations, but they never belong to them. Their sense of who they are does not depend upon memberships, work roles, or other social indicators of identity. What seems to follow from this idea about separateness is some theoretical basis for explaining why certain individuals search out opportunities for change. The methods to bring about change may be technological, political, or ideological, but the object is the same: to profoundly alter human, economic, and political relationships.

Sociologists refer to the preparation individuals undergo to perform in roles as the socialization process. Where individuals experience themselves as an integral part of the social structure (their self-esteem gains strength through participation and conformity), social standards exert powerful effects in maintaining the individual's personal sense of continuity, even beyond the early years in the family. The line of development from the family to schools, then to career is cumulative and reinforcing. When the line of development is not reinforcing because of significant disruptions in relationships or other problems experienced in the family or other social institutions, the individual turns inward and struggles to establish self-esteem, identity, and order. Here the psychological dynamics center on the experience with loss and the efforts at recovery.

In considering the development of leadership, we have to examine two different courses of life history: (1) development through socialization, which prepares the individual to guide institutions and to maintain the existing balance of social relations; and (2) development through personal mastery, which impels an individual to struggle for psychological and social change. Society produces its managerial talent through the first line of development, while through the second leaders emerge.

DEVELOPMENT OF LEADERSHIP

The development of every person begins in the family. Each person experiences the traumas associated with separating from his or her parents, as well as the pain that follows such frustration. In the same vein, all individuals face the difficulties of achieving self-regulation and self-control. But for some, perhaps a majority, the fortunes of childhood provide adequate gratifications and sufficient opportunities to find substitutes for rewards no longer available. Such individuals, the "once-borns," make moderate identifications with parents and find a harmony between what they expect and what they are able to realize from life.

But suppose the pains of separation are amplified by a combination of parental demands and the individual's needs to the degree that a sense of isolation, of being special, and of wariness disrupts the bonds that attach children to parents and other authority figures? Under such conditions, and given a special aptitude, the origins of which remain mysterious, the person becomes deeply involved in his or her inner world at the expense of interest in the outer world. For such a person, self-esteem no longer depends solely upon positive attachments and real rewards. A form of self-reliance takes hold along with expectations of performance and achievement, and perhaps even the desire to do great works.

Such self-perceptions can come to nothing if the individual's talents are negligible. Even with strong talents, there are no guarantees that achievement will follow, let alone that the end result will be for good rather than evil. Other factors enter into development. For one thing, leaders are like artists and other gifted people who often struggle with neuroses; their ability to function varies considerably even over the short run, and some potential leaders may lose the struggle altogether. Also, beyond early childhood, the patterns of development that affect managers and leaders involve the selective influence of particular people. Just as they appear flexible and evenly distributed in the types of talents available for development, managers form moderate and widely distributed attachments. Leaders, on the other hand, establish, and also break off, intensive one-to-one relationships.

It is a common observation that people with great talents are often only indifferent students. No one, for example, could have predicted Einstein's great achievements on the basis of his mediocre record in school. The reason for mediocrity is obviously not the absence of ability. It may result, instead, from self-absorption and the inability to pay attention to the ordinary tasks at hand. The only sure way an individual can interrupt reverie-like preoccupation and self-absorption is to form a deep attachment to a great teacher or other benevolent person who understands and has the ability to communicate with the gifted individual.

Whether gifted individuals find what they need in one-to-one relationships depends on the availability of sensitive and intuitive mentors who have a vocation in cultivating talent. Fortunately, when the generations do meet and the self-selections occur, we learn more about how to develop leaders and how talented people of different generations influence each other.

While apparently destined for a mediocre career, people who form important one-to-one relationships are able to accelerate and intensify their development through an apprenticeship. The background for such apprenticeships, or the psychological readiness of an individual to benefit from an intensive relationship, depends upon some experience in life that forces the individual to turn inward. A case example will make this point clearer. This example comes from the life of Dwight David Eisenhower, and illustrates the transformation of a career from competent to outstanding.[13]

Dwight Eisenhower's early career in the Army foreshadowed very little about his future development. During World War I, while some of his West Point classmates were already experiencing the war firsthand in France, Eisenhower felt "embedded in the monotony and unsought safety of the Zone of the Interior . . . that was intolerable punishment."[14]

Shortly after World War I, Eisenhower, then a young officer somewhat pessimistic about his career chances, asked for a transfer to Panama to work under General Fox Connor, a senior officer whom Eisenhower admired. The army turned down Eisenhower's request. This setback was very much on Eisenhower's mind when Ikey, his first-born son, succumbed to influenza. By some sense of responsibility for its own, the army transferred Eisenhower to Panama, where he took up his duties

---

[13] This example is included in Abraham Zaleznik and Manfred F. R. Kets de Vries, *Power and the Corporate Mind* (Boston: Houghton Mifflin, 1975).

[14] Dwight D. Eisenhower, *At Ease: Stories I Tell to Friends* (New York: Doubleday, 1967), p. 136.

[15] Ibid. p. 187.

under General Connor with the shadow of his lost son very much upon him.

In a relationship with the kind of father he would have wanted to be, Eisenhower reverted to being the son he lost. In this highly charged situation, Eisenhower began to learn from his mentor. General Connor offered, and Eisenhower gladly took, a magnificent tutorial on the military. The effects of this relationship on Eisenhower cannot be measured quantitatively, but, in Eisenhower's own reflections and the unfolding of his career, one cannot overestimate its significance in the reintegration of a person shattered by grief.

As Eisenhower wrote later about Connor, "Life with General Connor was a sort of graduate school in military affairs and the humanities, leavened by a man who was experienced in his knowledge of men and their conduct. I can never adequately express my gratitude to this one gentleman. . . . In a lifetime of association with great and good men, he is the one more or less invisible figure to whom I owe an incalculable debt."[15]

Some time after his tour of duty with General Connor, Eisenhower's breakthrough occurred. He received orders to attend the Command and General Staff School at Fort Leavenworth, one of the most competitive schools in the army. It was a coveted appointment, and Eisenhower took advantage of the opportunity. Unlike his performance in high school and West Point, his work at the Command School was excellent; he was graduated first in his class.

Psychological biographies of gifted people repeatedly demonstrate the important part a mentor plays in developing an individual. Andrew Carnegie owed much to his senior, Thomas A. Scott. As head of the Western Division of the Pennsylvania Railroad, Scott recognized talent and the desire to learn in the young telegrapher assigned to him. By giving Carnegie increasing responsibility and by providing him with the opportunity to learn through close personal observation, Scott added to Carnegie's self-confidence and sense of achievement. Because of his own personal strength and achievement, Scott did not fear Carnegie's aggressiveness. Rather, he gave it full play in encouraging Carnegie's initiative.

Mentors take risks with people. They bet initially on talent they perceive in younger people. Mentors also risk emotional involvement in working closely with their juniors. The risks do not always pay off, but the willingness to take them appears crucial in developing leaders.

CAN ORGANIZATIONS DEVELOP LEADERS?

The examples I have given of how leaders develop suggest the importance of personal influence and the one-to-one relationship. For organizations to encourage consciously the development of leaders as compared with managers would mean developing one-to-one relationships between junior and senior executives and, more important, fostering a culture of individualism and possibly elitism. The elitism arises out of the desire to identify talent and other qualities suggestive of the ability to lead and not simply to manage.

The Jewel Companies Inc. enjoy a reputation for developing talented people. The chairman and chief executive officer, Donald S. Perkins, is perhaps a good example of a person brought along through the mentor approach. Franklin J. Lunding, who was Perkins's mentor, expressed the philosophy of taking risks with young people this way:

"Young people today want in on the action. They don't want to sit around for six months trimming lettuce."[16]

This statement runs counter to the culture that attaches primary importance to slow progression based on experience and proved competence. It is a high-risk philosophy, one that requires time for the attachment between senior and junior people to grow and be meaningful, and one that is bound to produce more failures than successes.

The elitism is an especially sensitive issue. At Jewel the MBA degree symbolized the elite. Lunding attracted Perkins to Jewel at a time when business school graduates had little interest in retailing in general, and food distribution in particular. Yet the elitism seemed to pay off: not only did Perkins become the president at age 37, but also under the leadership of young executives recruited into Jewel with the promise of opportunity for growth and advancement, Jewel managed to diversify into discount and drug chains and still remain strong in food retailing. By assigning each recruit to a vice president who acted as sponsor, Jewel evidently tried to build a structure around the mentor approach to developing leaders. To counteract the elitism implied in such an approach, the company also introduced an "equalizer" in what Perkins described as "the first assistant philosophy." Perkins stated:

"Being a good first assistant means that each management person thinks of himself not as the order-giving, domineering boss, but as the first assistant to those who 'report' to him in a more typical organizational sense. Thus we mentally turn our organizational charts upside-down and challenge ourselves to seek ways in which we can lead ... by helping ... by teaching ... by listening ... and by managing in the true democratic sense ... that is, with the consent of the managed. Thus the satisfactions of leadership come from helping others to get things done and changed — and not from getting credit for doing and changing things ourselves."[17]

---

[16] "Jewel Lets Young Men Make Mistakes," *Business Week,* January 17, 1970, p. 90.

[17] "What Makes Jewel Shine so Bright," *Progressive Grocer,* September, 1973, p. 76.

While this statement would seem to be more egalitarian than elitist, it does reinforce a youth-oriented culture since it defines the senior officer's job as primarily helping the junior person.

A myth about how people learn and develop that seems to have taken hold in the American culture also dominates thinking in business. The myth is that people learn best from their peers. Supposedly, the threat of evaluation and even humiliation recedes in peer relations because of the tendency for mutual identification and the social restraints on authoritarian behavior among equals. Peer training in organizations occurs in various forms. The use, for example, of task forces made up of peers from several interested occupational groups (sales, production, research, and finance) supposedly removes the restraints of authority on the individual's willingness to assert and exchange ideas. As a result, so the theory goes, people interact more freely, listen more objectively to criticism and other points of view and, finally, learn from this healthy interchange.

Another application of peer training exists in some large corporations, such as Phillips, N.V. in Holland, where organization structure is built on the principle of joint responsibility of two peers, one representing the commercial end of the business and the other the technical. Formally, both hold equal responsibility for geographic operations or product groups, as the case may be. As a practical matter, it may turn out that one or the other of the peers dominates the management. Nevertheless, the main interaction is between two or more equals.

The principal question I would raise about such arrangements is whether they perpetuate the managerial orientation, and preclude the formation of one-to-one relationships between senior people and potential leaders.

Aware of the possible stifling effects of peer relationships on aggressiveness and individual initiative, another company, much smaller than Philips, utilizes joint responsibility of peers for operating units, with one important difference. The chief executive of this company encourages competition and rivalry among peers, ultimately appointing the one who comes out on top for increased responsibility. These hybrid arrangements produce some unintended consequences that can be disastrous. There is no easy way to limit rivalry. Instead, it permeates all levels of the operation and opens the way for the formation of cliques in an atmosphere of intrigue.

A large, integrated oil company has accepted the importance of developing leaders through the direct influence of senior on junior executives. One chairman and chief executive officer regularly selected one talented university graduate whom he appointed his special assistant, and with whom he would work closely for a year. At the end of the year, the junior executive would become available for assignment to one of the operating divisions, where he would be assigned to a responsible post rather than a training position. The mentor relationship had acquainted the junior executive firsthand with the use of power, and with the important antidotes to the power disease called *hubris* — performance and integrity.

Working in one-to-one relationships, where there is a formal and recognized difference in the power of the actors, takes a great deal of tolerance for emotional interchange. This interchange, inevitable in close working arrangements, probably accounts for the reluctance of many executives to become involved in such relationships. *Fortune* carried an interesting story on the departure of a key executive, John W. Hanley, from the top management of Procter & Gamble, for the chief executive officer position at Monsanto.[18] According to this account, the chief executive and chairman of P&G passed over Hanley for appointment to the presidency and named another executive vice president to this post instead.

The chairman evidently felt he could not work well with Hanley who, by his own acknowledgement, was aggressive, eager to experiment and change practices, and constantly challenged his superior. A chief executive officer naturally has the right to select people with whom he feels congenial. But I wonder whether a greater capacity on the part of senior officers to tolerate the competitive impulses and behavior of their subordinates might not be healthy for corporations. At least a greater tolerance for interchange would not favor the managerial team player at the expense of the individual who might become a leader.

I am constantly surprised at the frequency with which chief executives feel threatened by open challenges to their ideas, as though the source of their authority, rather than their specific ideas, were at issue. In one case a chief executive officer, who was troubled by the aggressiveness and sometimes outright rudeness of one of his talented vice presidents, used various indirect methods such as group meetings and hints from outside directors to avoid dealing with his subordinate. I advised the executive to deal head-on with what irritated him. I suggested that by direct, face-to-face confrontation, both he and his subordinate would learn to validate the distinction between the authority to be preserved and the issues to be debated.

To confront is also to tolerate aggressive interchange, and has the net effect of stripping away the veils of ambiguity and signaling so characteristic of managerial cultures, as well as encouraging the emotional relationship leaders need if they are to survive.

---

[18] "Jack Hanley Got There by Selling Harder," *Fortune*, November, 1976.

11

To Achieve or Not:
The Manager's Choice

by Jay Hall

Historically, ours has been an achievement-oriented culture. Our national archives fairly burst with tales of rugged men of purpose who tamed the frontier and moved mountains so that trains might run, and with stories of captains of industry who rose from the stockroom to the Boardroom in less time than it takes to mature medium-term bonds. Our ideals have been the leaders of men and we have recited until we believe the litany of leadership: plan, direct, control, organize, decide, win!

The need to achieve permeates our daily lives—all about us, we see books on how to succeed without really trying and advertisements aimed precisely at our very human desire to grow, to become better than we are. We have all, to some extent, been targeted for miracle cures for our frustrations; nowhere are preferred "solutions" more prevalent than in the field of management. Indeed, today's management literature is not unlike a smorgasbord from which each manager can choose according to his own appetite. He may read about winning through intimidation; on being an *OK* boss; how to avoid group think; and even how to say no convincingly.

Unfortunately, the effect on actual achievement is something less than that of a placebo. By relying on counterproductive rules of success, the modern manager in a hurry to succeed risks being stopped cold in his tracks. The problem is that most of the game plans turn out to have been conceived in a vacuum; they are, by and large, highly intuitive and subjective pronouncements of what should and should not be done.

Jay Hall, a social psychologist, is president and chief executive officer of Teleometrics International of The Woodlands, Texas.

They are long on inspiration but stingy where proof is concerned. But achievement, and one's need to feel that he can achieve, remains a serious matter; it deserves better treatment.

Those who have been stifled by the air of unfounded certainty surrounding many management offices or bruised by running into the invisible walls of orthodoxy founded on unsupported organizational myths may agree that the time has come to collect data rather than spin personally gratifying or corporately profitable yarns. Many of us have become increasingly curious—if not frankly contentious—about managerial achievement. Who are our achieving managers? What do they do to distinguish themselves from their less achieving cohorts? We need less speculation and more hard facts about the achieving condition.

That's what this article is about. It reports a systematic investigation of the achieving condition conducted according to the rules of scientific inquiry, tempered by the demands of rigorous statistical procedures. We have recently completed a five year research project on managerial achievement. We studied over 16,000 managers in the process and we discovered a number of factors which significantly distinguish those who achieve managerially from those who fail to do so. Our research was a partisan effort. Because we believe in focusing on things people can do something about, our studies were confined to the *behaviors* managers employ in administering the management process. Our findings are clear cut and straightforward: those who excel managerially behave differently than do those of only average or low achievement. In these differences lie the choice points for managers confronted with career planning. I would like to share our findings and, perhaps in the process, lay open some alternatives for those contemplating greater achievement.

The Achieving Manager Research Project

Our project began initially on a serendipitous note. We did not set out to prove anything or, for that matter, to study achievement. The nature of our business—we apply behavioral science technologies to organizational dynamics—is such that we routinely collect data on management groups from many different types of organizations and from all levels of management. These data concern the values, practices and day-to-day behavioral modes of those who make organizations function the way they do. It occurred to us that we were in a prime position to explore any number of heretofore unresearched relationships between managerial practices and other phenomena and, because of its obvious importance, we addressed ourselves to a systematic study of factors responsible for managerial achievement.

We adopted as our major objective in The Achieving Manager Project the isolation of the behavioral traits which not only appear to characterize achievers, but to distinguish them from other managers. We opted for one of the most basic and frequently encountered research procedures known to the social sciences, comparisons of groups identified as different on the basis of objective criteria and thought to be different in terms of several other dimensions. We were already busy collecting data on those dimensions we anticipated to underlie group differences; we needed a selection criterion which would allow us to categorize managers according to achievement level.

Identifying the Achieving Manager:
The Managerial Achievement Quotient

Achievement does not easily lend itself to measurement. Yet for our project we needed an achievement index that was objective and reflected the bench marks subjectively used as reference points by managers themselves. An obvious approach would be to confine ourselves to a study of those who have made it up the corporate ladder. Such an exemplary-case criterion, rooted solely in organizational rank, was rejected as an oversimplification on two grounds. First, rank attainment cannot be evaluated without some consideration of the manager's age; the issue of potential for achievement is at stake and it is obscured by a pure rank criterion. Second, we wanted information about managers who are not achievers; insight into counterproductive factors or ones which simply fail to work is just as important as data about factors responsible for achievement. Our search began, therefore, with a review of pertinent techniques for assessing managerial achievement which account for the effects of rank, age and varying levels of achievement status.

A formula for measuring achievement. We found that Blake and Mouton[1] conducted a study of managerial style and career accomplishment in which they used an achievement index developed by Dr. Benjamin Rhodes: the *Managerial Achievement Quotient* or MAQ, possesses all the properties of concern to us. It affords an evaluation of an individual's career progress in light of his chronological age much as the IQ ratio provides for assessments of one's mental age relative to his actual age. The MAQ takes into account such practical considerations as the number of career moves necessary to reach the top of an organization, the age span most germane to career planning and the time in grade.

The Blake and Mouton study was conducted within a single firm, allowing for considerable control over the number of levels comprising the organization's hierarchy and other features which differ from organization to organization. We desired an index with more generic application so that, through broader sampling, we might guard against any

Table 1. Summary of Managerial Style Assessments by
Subordinates of Low, Moderate, and High MAQ's

Style	Low	Moderate	High	Odds
9,9	44	52	56	3 in 100
5,5	44	46	51	ns
9,1	45	44	39	ns
1,9	45	44	50	ns
1,1	52	48	52	ns

uncontrolled effects traceable to unique organizational cultures through broader sampling. Our research plan called for the study of more than fifty different organizations and we adopted a variation of the basic MAQ which reflects our research aims more realistically. As an index of managerial achievement, therefore, we chose:

$$MAQ = \frac{5(6 - Rank)}{Age} \times 100$$

In the numerator of our revised formula, 5 is a constant progression factor—the time in grade per number of career moves available if one were to spend his work life in an eight-level organization—which reflects potential mobility upward in the absence of any other forces such as politics and chance. Also in the numerator, the quantity (6 - Rank) amounts to a rank index obtained by assigning numerical values of 1 to 5 to organizational levels ranging from top (L1) to nonmanagement (L5) and subtracting from the correction factor of 6.

In the denominator, age (20 to 50 years) represents a seniority index indicating the time, given a more or less standard entry age of twenty, in which an individual might advance from lowest to highest organizational levels if advancement were purely mechanical. Finally, we use the constant multiplier of *100* to eliminate decimals.

Normative data base for the MAQ. So that we might have confidence both in the selection mechanism and in the cutoff points we chose to identify individuals of high, average and low managerial achievement, we collected the necessary biographical data for computing the MAQ on a base sample of 5,451 managers. All organizational levels, from nonmanagement supervisory personnel to Chief Executive Officer, ages from 19 to 64 and 26 different types of organizations were represented. MAQ raw scores for this group ranged from 9 to 109.5. The average manager in this base sample had an MAQ of 39.4; he was approximately 38 years old and occupied a middle (L3) management position. This was a profile corresponding to that found in most organizations.

Raw scores were transformed to standard scores, affording a control for bias and allowing us to categorize managers with *standardized* MAQs of 60 or above as High Achievers, 41 to 59 as Average Achievers and those with 40 or below as Low Achievers. Finally, we conducted a number of pilot studies to determine the sensitivity and discriminant power of the index. Our results confirmed the standardized MAQ as a robust and reliable indicator of managerial achievement.

We were ready for the most important part of our search, that of finding out how managers high in achievement differ from lower achievers in administering the management process. As Blake and Mouton phrased it, we were ready to discover the factors *responsible* for managerial achievement.

Factors in Managerial Achievement

The work of several prominent behavioral theorists guided us in our study of managerial achievement as a function of behavioral factors. The issues pursuant to managerial effectiveness which have stemmed from behavioral theory and research essentially concern motivation, the participative ethic, interpersonal competence and managerial style. These areas have been the purview primarily of individuals like Maslow,[2] Herzberg,[3] McGregor,[4] Marrow, et al.,[5] Argyris,[6] Likert,[7] and Blake and Mouton.[8] Not only have they supplied most of the recorded examples of behavioral science applications to managerial and organizational dynamics, they have been most prescriptive as well. To follow their lead in investigating the factors responsible for managerial achievement, therefore, seems both natural and desirable from the standpoint of testing the validity of prescriptive rules.

As a point of logical departure, we focused first on managerial *and* subordinate motivational phenomena, and followed with an investigation of managers' employment of the participative ethic and its related involvement effects, as reported by their subordinates. Next, the issue of interpersonal competence, as reported by managers themselves and judged by their subordinates, was explored. And finally managerial style, that cluster of behaviors resulting from all the former, was studied as a predictor of managerial achievement.

In all, over 11,000 managers (all males) were studied in the Achieving Manager Project. All organizational levels, the full range of pertinent ages and over fifty actual organizations were represented. In each research instance, managers were assigned to High, Average or Low Managerial

Achievement groups on the basis of their standardized MAQ scores. We found, I think, not only what distinguishes the achiever from the non-achiever but a basis for exemplary management as well.

The Achieving Manager: What Makes Him Run?

Do most managers aspire to the same goals in an organization, but perceive different pathways to their attainment? Or do managers differ regarding the reasons they work and then employ practices best suited to attain their different objectives? Differences in achievement imply motivational differences, not so much in amount as in kind.

While a good deal of thought has been given to motivation in the work place, the dominant thrust has been one of better understanding—and therefore managing—the subordinate personnel who make up the great majority of any workforce. Implicit in such a focus is an assumption that managers—by virtue of occupying key slots in the organization—are somehow immune to the mundane world of work motivation. Yet, given differences in managerial performance, one must realize that managers are not above a "motivational analysis" and probably also differ in fundamental ways where needs, goals and personal drives are concerned. We can trace a manager's achievement to motivation just as we can the cooperativeness, dependability and overall productivity of his employees.

Managerial achievement and work motivation: One man's ceiling is another man's floor. To test this notion that our three groups differ with respect to the need profiles which make up "motivation," we administered the Hall and Williams *Work Motivation Inventory*[9] (WMI) to 1,265 managers. Based on a synthesis of the *need hierarchy* concept developed by Abraham Maslow[10] and the *hygiene-motivator* theory of Frederick Herzberg,[11] the WMI assesses the factors most important to an individual

Table 2. Study of Managerial Style Assessments
by Low, Moderate, and High MAQ Managers

Style	Low	Moderate	High	Odds
9,9	43	43	49	ns
5,5	37	42	40	ns
9,1	40	38	37	ns
1,9	45	37	45	4 in 1000
1,1	58	43	46	2 in 1000

in making decisions about and/or seeking satisfactions from his work. Five scores are generated from the instrument, each reflecting one of the five need systems Maslow postulated to characterize human motivation, i.e., basic creature comfort, safety, belongingness, ego-status and self-actualization. The creature comfort and safety needs, particularly, underlie a preoccupation with the incentives Herzberg has labeled hygiene or maintenance factors. Ego-status and actualization needs are linked to motivator incentives. So, the WMI yields both a need and a hygiene-motivator profile.

The higher a given score, the stronger the represented need and, as a result, the more the individual is motivated to pursue satisfaction of that particular need. Many of his behaviors and feelings, therefore, can best be understood in terms of his hygiene-seeking vis-à-vis motivator-seeking tendencies. The rationale, simply put, is that the individual primarily concerned with and motivated by safety and security needs will neither value the same incentives nor employ the same behaviors to attain his objectives as will the individual essentially motivated by an ego-status need. While the former is striving to avoid dissatisfaction, the latter is seeking to attain satisfaction. To the extent that both the form and quality of managerial behaviors can be traced to motivational dynamics, any differences found in a motivational analysis will prove significant for managerial performance in general and for achievement in particular. And differences there are!

Having sorted the 1,265 managers into their respective achievement groups, we ran a comparison of their WMI profiles. Substantial differences, in a statistical sense, were found between the motivational profiles of the three groups, revealing that the manager's own needs do indeed affect the level of achievement he will realize in his organization.

Table 3. Summary of Low, Moderate, and High Managerial Achievers'
Interpersonal Exposure/Feedback Use

Category	Low	Moderate	High	Odds
Exp: Sub.	40	52	54	8 in 1000
FB: Sub.	46	52	56	4 in 100
Exp: Col.	44	52	59	2 in 100
FB: Col.	52	55	61	1 in 100
Exp: Sup.	46	52	54	ns
FB: Sup.	48	56	55	6 in 100

Briefly, the need for self-actualization is the dominant motivational influence for High Achievers, while Average Achievers are most driven by ego-status needs. According to the WMI norms available, these two groups are substantially above the average in their respective need strengths and emerge as motivator seekers.

Low achievers, on the other hand, are caught up in a peculiar kind of double bind: at one and the same time they are most preoccupied with gaining satisfaction for basic creature comfort and ego-status needs. As Maslow has told us, it is highly unlikely that higher order needs, such as ego-status, will emerge until lower order needs like creature comfort have been adequately satisfied. When higher order needs arise in conjunction with lower order needs, as with Low Achievers, it therefore appears that we have a crisis of motivation in which neither motivator nor hygiene needs are being very well met.

We will return to this issue; for the moment, let it be said that managers differing in achievement have markedly different motivational profiles and pursue quite different incentives. Very likely, their practices differ too. Particularly, we would expect High, Average and Low Achieving managers to be characterized by different approaches to employee motivation. If this is the case, we reasoned, more serious implications than those initially apparent come into play. How do these groups of managers deal with the motivational processes within their organizations? What, then, are the motivational consequences among the organization's personnel? We conducted two more studies of motivational phenomena to answer these questions.

Achievement and the management of motives: High Achievers challenge while Low Achievers comfort. It is generally accepted that motivation is something the person brings with him to the organization, that managers cannot motivate their employees in any injective sense of the word. The best a manager can hope for is to accurately identify the incentives under his control which coincide with subordinate needs. He may then be able to harness the more constructive and contributive motives of his subordinates, thereby channeling those subordinates' activities toward the doing of the organization's work.

On the other hand, we know that the manager can greatly influence subordinate expectations and views of organizational reality by his actions and by the values he promulgates on behalf of the organization. Employee motives are probably some joint function of what they bring with them to the organization and the conditioning effects achieved by their managers as they mediate rewards and emphasize the practical utility of the organization's various incentives.

The manager's view of motivation—of what is important to his subordinates and of what is possible in the way of satisfactions within the organization—is a critical component of the motivational process. Depending upon his view, the manager can create conditions for need satisfaction coincidental to desired performance or he may frustrate and block needs along with the expression of the very skills of which his subordinates are most proud.

In effect, the manager's *personal theory* of motivation becomes a powerful force in the work place, shaping and facilitating subordinates' expression of some need related behaviors while blocking or denying that of others. Given the various need profiles which characterize High, Average and Low Achievers, we felt that managers differing in achievement are likely to have different "theories" about the motivational process. And indeed they do; the manager's view of the motivational process and the incentives he emphasizes in his management of that process differ greatly for the three groups.

The *Management of Motives Index* [12] (MMI), a companion piece to the WMI designed for use with managers, was administered to 664 individuals. As with the WMI, the MMI yields a score for each of the five need systems having hygiene-motivator significance; each score is an index of how much the manager emphasizes that particular need in his management of others. In mediating reality for their subordinates, High, Average and Low Achievers place significantly different emphases on four of the need systems. Moreover, these managers manage the motivational process for others *primarily as a function of their own needs!*

High Achievers place major emphasis on the actualization, belonging and ego-status needs comprising the motivator package, paying only average attention to hygiene factors. Low Achievers, on the other hand, virtually ignore motivators while stressing the importance of creature comfort and particularly safety and security issues having hygiene significance. Average Achievers stress ego-status, giving adequate attention to the actualization needs of their subordinates, essentially promoting motivator seeking among those they manage. As we expected, managerial achievement is linked to the motivational climate one creates for his subordinates as well as to personal striving.

Now the critical question. How does all this affect subordinates? If a manager's employees hear and heed his motivational message, the issue is broadened and goes beyond the mere consideration of his personal achievement to encompass the well-being of others, not to mention the probable success of their pursuit of organizational objectives. Argyris has cautioned us not to underestimate the power of the managerial self-fulfilling prophecy.

Managerial achievement and the fulfilling of motivational prophecies. To determine whether the effects of a manager's unique management of motives were strong enough to significantly influence the need profiles of his subordinates, we administered the WMI to over 3,500 subordinates of 1,291 managers. These subordinate data were separated according to the achievement rating of their managers and comparisons were run across the five need strengths. There are highly significant differences between the need profiles of High Achieving managers' subordinates and those of both Average and Low Achievers. Subordinates definitely hear and adopt as their own their manager's motivational message; managers create subordinates in their own image and the image definitely differs as a function of the manager's level of achievement.

Table 4. Summary of Analysis of Low, Moderate, and
High Managerial Achievers' Work Motivation Profiles

Motivation	Low	Moderate	High	Odds
Creature comfort	50	38	27	1 in 10,000
Safety-security	53	41	34	1 in 10,000
Belongingness	47	55	65	3 in 10,000
Ego status	52	52	46	ns
Self-actualization	43	56	71	1 in 10,000

Table 5. Summary of Analysis of Low, Moderate, and High Managerial
Achievers' Management of Motives

Motivation	Low	Moderate	High	Odds
Creature comfort	59	46	50	4 in 10,000
Safety-security	64	48	45	6 in 10,000
Belongingness	41	46	40	ns
Ego status	47	55	38	2 in 100
Self-actualization	42	53	59	1 in 10,000

To appreciate just how potent managerial prophecies about motivation are in our organizations, one has only to compare the need profiles of High, Average and Low Achievers with those of their subordinates. The statistical technique employed to analyze our data allows for simplifying the inputs from several sources so that we may obtain a distilled, concise and penetrating summary statement of differences. Dimensions along which achievement groups most differ are identified and give us a graphic depiction of the nature and degree of differences among groups. In this case, the dimensions are identical for managers and their subordinates and, as Figure 1 indicates, they allow for the creation of four motivational realms, each a unique portrayal of the need profile of those who fall into it.

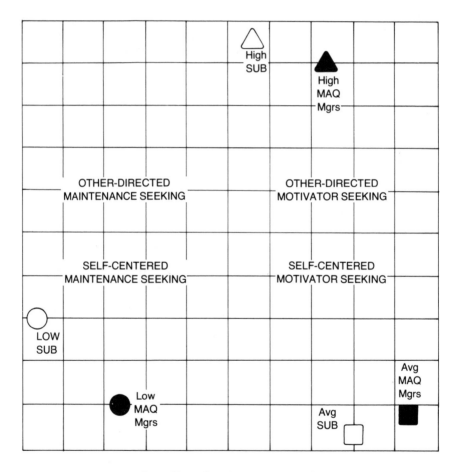

Figure 1. Motivational profiles of High, Average, and Low Achieving
            Managers and their subordinates

The dimensions which emerge from our analysis indicate the degree to which managers and their subordinates are: (1) *maintenance-seeking* or *motivator-seeking* and (2) either *self-centered* or *other-directed* in their orientations to attaining need satisfaction. It is readily apparent that subordinates occupy matrix positions similar to those occupied by their managers and, moreover, managers of different achievement levels and their subordinates occupy vastly different positions as well.

Low Achievers are *self-centered maintenance-seekers;* their subordinates display the same, assumedly conditioned, need properties. High Achievers are best characterized as *other-directed motivator-seekers* and so are their subordinates. Average Achievers are also *motivator-seeking,* but the nature of their quest is different from that of High Achievers in that it is *self-centered;* their subordinates are also *self-centered motivator seekers.*

Thus are motivational prophecies fulfilled. Not only does personal motivation affect a manager's achievement level, so does his perception of the motivational process and his consequent practices in the management of motives. Indeed, in what appears to be a causal fashion, a manager's achievement is directly linked to the motivational profile of his subordinates. A sobering thought is inferred: *the needs and quality of motivation characterizing a manager's subordinates may say more about the manager than about his subordinates.*

There are other implications. The motivational assumptions of Low Achieving managers correspond in significant ways to the pessimistic, reductive view of working man which Douglas McGregor[13] dubbed Theory X. High Achiever perspectives, on the other hand, are consistent with the more positive developmental beliefs embodied by McGregor's Theory Y. Average Achievers fall somewhere in between Theory X and Theory Y, portraying what Meyers[14] has called a Traditional view— essentially Theory X tempered by human relations training or related experiences. The point is, as McGregor contends, the view the manager holds of his subordinates affects in rather obvious ways the manner in which he manages.

Trust issues, for example, are rampant in the Theory X-Theory Y postures. The degree to which a manager trusts his subordinates influences which managerial options he considers viable, particularly where participative management is concerned. Indeed, many theorists have coordinated the use of participative practices with adherence to Theory Y, while avoidance or outright rejection of such practices has been linked with a Theory X value system. We reasoned that our managerial groups may very well differ along this dimension and moreover, if behavioral theory is valid, we may find employment of participative practices underlying achievement.

Participative Management and Managerial Achievement

Drawing on Kurt Lewin's action research strategy, Al Marrow, John R. P. French and their colleagues first demonstrated the efficacy of a participative approach to management in their studies of the Harwood Manufacturing Corporation.[15,16] Their subsequent application of participative techniques to Harwood's acquisition of the Weldon Corporation is a modern day classic of applied behavioral science. Marrow and his colleagues have probably done more than any others to advance participative management as a viable and feasible technique for organizational effectiveness, but no one before has directly linked the technique to individual career accomplishment and managerial achievement.

We have seen that there is reason to expect such a relationship. Participative management is founded on the belief that people directly affected by a decision should participate in that decision; the emphasis is on *joint* decision making about events which have future implications for the parties involved, and over which they can realistically exert influence. One has to be a manager to fully appreciate what a bone of contention such a work ethic can become; there are few who are neutral about the issue of participation. Originally embraced as a mechanism for countering the unilateral decision structure and authoritarian values often found in traditional organization theory, the participative ethic also positively affects loyalty and creativity. Now we find that it distinguishes between those who achieve managerially and those who do not.

To research the relationship between participative management practices and managerial achievement, we focused on subordinates; it is they, we felt, who are best equipped to report on their managers' use of participative practices and those all important feelings which they, the subordinates, experience as a result. We administered the *Personal Reaction Index*[17] to over 2,000 subordinates of 731 managers. The PRI, used extensively for training and research purposes, assesses the degree to which the manager allows a subordinate to participate and encourages him to influence work-related decisions. In addition, it gauges the amount of job satisfaction, sense of personal responsibility, commitment, pride in work and frustration experienced as a consequence of participation. Combined, the scales reflect an *involvement index* implying the kind of work *climate* a given manager creates.

Our results are presented graphically in Figure 2.

EGO-INVOLVEMENT VIA PARTICIPATION

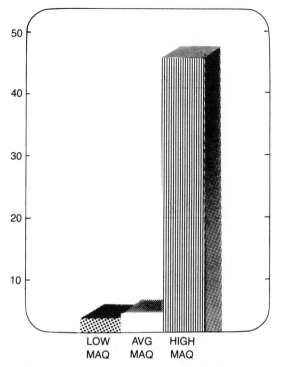

Figure 2. Subordinate ego involvement as a function of the participative management practices of High, Average, and Low Achieving Managers

Low Achievers, as reported by their subordinates, make minimal use of participative practices; Average Achievers make only slightly greater use. High Achievers, according to their subordinates, not only employ far and away greater amounts of the technique, but so much so that participative methods may be said to be a major characteristic of the High Achieving approach to management.

Of equal importance are the climate implications suggested in Figure 2. Our significant dimension is comprised of both participative opportunity data and feeling data. Only subordinates of High Achievers report the kind of satisfaction, commitment and pride in work that characterizes the work force of healthy organizations. Low Achievers, and to some extent Average Achievers, employ practices which result in repressive and frustrating circumstances typically found in neurotic organizations.

So the manager's use of participative practices also emerges as a factor responsible for managerial achievement, but it does not stand alone any more than did management of the motivational process. According to Marrow, we may expect its effectiveness to vary with the amount of mutual confidence found in the manager-subordinate relationship. In other words, to quote Marrow, participative management will only be successful when "... employees and managers are trusting and open, and problems can be approached in a spirit of joint inquiry and a consensus worked out." [16]

The stage must be set and a conducive climate prepared for participative management to succeed. Level of interpersonal competence, the management dynamic most stressed by Chris Argyris,[17] determines the nature of the climate within which participation is proffered. There is, therefore, ample reason to expect managerial achievement to be affected by the managerial level of interpersonal competence.

Achievement Via Interpersonal Competence: Managing the Interplay Among Ideas, Feelings and Norms

Interpersonal competence plays a vital role in the successful use of participative methods. Argyris has enumerated the outcomes of interpersonal competence: (1) greater awareness of relevant problems among parties to the problem-solving relationship, (2) increased problem-solving accuracy in that problems remain solved and (3) decreased likelihood for the problem-solving process to be negatively affected in any way.[19]

A manager involved in building and maintaining relationships with his subordinates achieves interpersonal competence through such behaviors as *owning up* to or accepting responsibility for his ideas and feelings, *being open* to his own thoughts and sentiments and those of others, *experimenting* with new ideas and feelings and *helping others* to own up, be open to and experiment with their concepts and attitudes. When he can accomplish these practices in such a way that norms of individuality, interpersonal concern and mutual trust are engendered, we may call that manager interpersonally competent.

Argyris has found that the required behaviors differ in their contribution to competence *and* in the frequency of their occurrence. For example, owning up to ideas is fairly common among managers, but it is not a strong predictor of competence. Actually it is a double-edged sword; an excessive preoccupation with his own ideas and feelings causes many a manager to forego participative methods in favor of more authoritarian practices. On the other hand, being open with others, willing to experiment with ideas and feelings as one helps others do the same, is an extremely potent predictor for competence but it is rare among managers. Implied, of course, is the fact that managers differ in the degree to which they perform all functions and hence, in interpersonal competence.

The *Personnel Relations Survey*,[20] based on the Luft-Ingram Johari Window[21] model of interpersonal processes, has proven to be an excellent device for assessing levels of interpersonal competence. In our investigation of achievement via competence, therefore, we first administered the PRS to 1,691 managers to discover how they handle interpersonal processes in relationships with their subordinates, colleagues, and superiors. Not content with self reports alone, we administered a PRS companion piece—the two part *Management Relations Survey*[22]—to 1,884 subordinates who were asked to appraise their managers' practices in Part I and, in Part II, to reveal their own practices in relating to those managers.

As Figure 3 shows, the differences in level of interpersonal competence are substantial between the managerial groups. Moreover, subordinate appraisals of competence level for the three groups are almost identical to those provided by managers themselves.

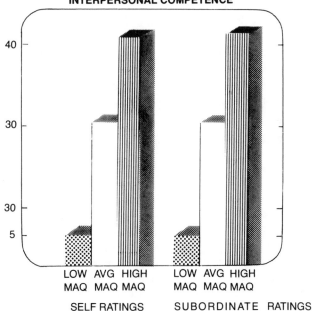

INTERPERSONAL COMPETENCE

Figure 3. Ratings of interpersonal competence for High, Average, and Low Achieving Managers as given by managers themselves and their subordinates

Not only do we find that level of interpersonal competence is directly bound to level of managerial achievement, but the link is so public and obvious that subordinates confirm it and report that their own interpersonal competence varies as a function of that evinced by their managers; they are well aware of the interplay. Competence and its norm-setting properties, as predicted by Argyris, is a powerful factor in determining the manager's career accomplishment and in shaping the nature and quality of subordinate practices as well.

The agreement between managers' and subordinates' reports is particularly noteworthy for it means that the behavioral messages sent by many managers come through loud and clear to subordinates who internalize them as their own. As with motivational dynamics, the competence of one's subordinates is a direct reflection of his managerial status.

But what about the organization's achievement of its production goals? What do the data have to say about that reality? Argyris has tied interpersonal competence of the executive system to organizational effectiveness, but how is competence linked with the management of technical, as well as interpersonal, facets of the enterprise? We have found in other studies that the level and type of interpersonal competence exhibited by managers coincides in predictable ways with their preferred manner for managing people-production interface in their organizations. It now appears, by logical extension, that managerial style may also be linked to managerial achievement in much the same way that both are joined to interpersonal competence. If this is so, we might just lay to rest some of those arguments about the merits of "ideal" style vis-à-vis situational or contingency approaches.

Achievement and Style:
The Manager's Choice

Because under a style rubric we can bring together and subsume so many complex, peripheral facets of a given process, the construct of *style* — an individual's preferred, relatively consistent approach to certain situations — has found acceptance as an analytic tool in discussions of decision making, leadership, sales and management. Style incorporates a whole cluster of behaviors and values which assume true operational significance only when they are considered in conjunction.

One of the more popular treatments of management style has been the managerial grid articulated by Blake and Mouton,[23] an elaboration of the work of Rensis Likert,[24] Fleischmann,[25] and others. With their model, we can account for those influences underlying an individual's selection of managerial behaviors: his values concerning task and social demands. We locate in the grid a manager's style as a function of his characteristic concerns; then we describe it in terms of the actual behaviors he is likely to employ in the service of such concerns. Production vis-à-vis people emphases serve as the point of departure for identifying the managerial styles and their attendant practices. The beauty of the model is that it brings together and explains, under a single unifying rationale, what appear to be vastly different approaches to management. Equally important is the fact that the grid affords a very workable, evaluative framework in terms of assessment as well as prediction of managerial effectiveness.

Obviously, the managerial grid seemed to us a perfect vehicle for exploring the relationship of style to managerial achievement; two assessment instruments based on its format, the *Styles of Management Inventory*[26] and the *Management Appraisal Survey*,[27] were used to identify most preferred styles. In the first instance, managers gave self reports and in the second case their subordinates evaluated them. The SMI was administered to 1,878 managers and the MAS was given to the subordinates of over 2,000 managers. In both instances, we find managerial style significantly tied to managerial achievement.

Those managers identified as High Achievers, according to their own reports, emphasize an *integration* of production-people issues, avoiding those impersonal and bureaucratic practices most favored by Low Achievers. Average Achievers are not distinguished by such clear choices, but by their aversion to any management style devoted to maintaining the human system. In general, we found that managers' self reports are more suggestive than definitive, despite the statistical significance of the differences, and again we turned to those on the receiving end.

In Figure 4 we present graphically the two dimensional nature of our results. The subordinate appraisals of their managers' practices are much more revealing: they flesh out and define the nature of differences only implied in the managers' self reports. Consistent with the grid model and numerous pieces of social research, we find two dimensions reflecting task and social demands; their existence allows us to assess managerial achievement as a joint function of task and relationship emphases.

By orienting the task dimension at right angles to that of relationship, we are able to construct a grid-like model in which four general approaches or "styles" of management are defined: Low Task-Low Relationship, High Task-Low Relationship, Low Task-High Relationship and High Task-High Relationship. Such qualitative labels capture the general focus of a given style; whether or not the style corresponds to a Blake 9/9 or a Likert System 4 is far less important than the fact that the style of High Achievers is different from that of Average or Low Achievers.

As the MAQ data plots in Figure 4 reveal, subordinates say their High Achieving managers are High Task-High Relationship oriented; in essence, a collaborative and participative managerial style typifies High Achievers. Average Achieving managers are placed by their subordinates

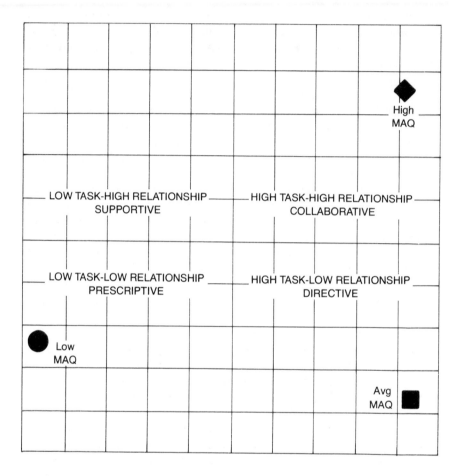

Figure 4: The relationship of managerial style to managerial achievement

in the style quadrant denoting a High Task-Low Relationship focus; they are so preoccupied with production goals that they give minimal attention to the dynamics of those who must ultimately do the work, that is, they are directive and self-authorizing. Finally, we find that Low Achieving managers employ practices pursuant to a Low Task-Low Relationship focus. Probably rooted in cultural imperatives, the personnel manual and standard operating procedures, such a style is mechanical and prescriptive in its implementation.

So it is that one's achievement is linked to his choice of management style. While there are undoubtedly cultural mandates and subtle incentives for managing in one way as opposed to another, our data reveal a generic basis for achievement. Our High Achievers and their less fortunate cohorts came from numerous organizations and cultural settings; it is perhaps a commentary on organizational mythology that those managers who achieve are most characterized by a High Task-High Relationship management style. The issue as I see it is not so much a matter of fitting one's style to the organization as a matter of choosing whether or not to achieve. Would that the solution were so simple.

Point and Counterpoint.
Now for the Achievement Paradox

The portrait of the Achieving Manager which emerges from our study is that of an individual employing an integrative style of management. He values people just as highly as the accomplishment of production goals. Candor, openness, sensitivity and receptivity comprise the rule in his interpersonal relationships rather than its exception. Participative practices are favored by him over unilaterally directive or lame duck prescriptive measures. Moreover, from a motivational standpoint the Achieving Manager needs to find meaning in his work and strives to afford such meaning to others. Higher order, constructive incentives are his motivational preoccupations, while his less achieving comrades remain mired in fantasies of defense and self-preservation.

But the results of our study go beyond an impressionistic, ill-defined treatment of the achieving condition. Their statistical level of confidence is such that we may say with assurance that if a manager is more concerned about factors that are peripheral to his work than he is about the nature of the work itself; if he is under wraps, secretive, unconfronting, and insensitive in his relationships with others; if his subordinates, while mirroring his motives and interpersonal practices, reap none of the rewards associated with that sense of proprietorship which participation affords; and if the manager remains more concerned about procedures and precedence than about productivity and the quality of life in his organization *there is a significant probability that he is a Low Achiever.* But, given a willingness to change, he need not remain so.

We are just as secure in our observation that to achieve, one must employ achieving practices and eschew self-serving, defensive self-authorized techniques. He must first embrace that collaborative stance which flows from the view that work—his own and that of his subordinates—is the source of challenge, meaning and opportunity for self-expansion. Through his practices he must acknowledge that his subordinates, as people at work, possess interests and expertise and he must create openings for their expression and incorporation into the work flow. He must be receptive to innovation, sensitive to the dynamics of relating and willing to take risks. And finally, ever conscious of his role of norm setter, the manager must look to his subordinates for his reflection: *truly achieving managers produce achievers.* The data could not be more clear.

Yes, but. . . . It is noteworthy that, in most major respects, the behaviors of Achieving Managers coincide with the very ones the behaviorist school might "prescribe." For the past several years, the literature has been filled by behavioral scientists and aimed at practicing managers. However, there have also been more than a few rebuttals aimed at the same group, authored by those of a different persuasion. These detractors more often than not dismiss the contributions of psychologists, sociologists and cultural anthropologists as being impractical for an organizational world filled with excruciating pressures for production, or as the theoretical ramblings of well-intentioned but appallingly naive spokesmen for the "soft sciences." Al Marrow,[28] a psychologist and Chief Executive Officer of Harwood, has commented at length on managers' resistance to behavioral science concepts; even when these theories are successfully applied, managers remain unpersuaded—the paradoxical failure of success!

Non-behavioral consultants, meanwhile, going for the soft underbelly, are quick to undermine the "foreign" field which intrudes. Charles Bowen,[29] CEO of a major management consulting firm, has suggested that there is an aura of fantasy surrounding most of the ideas and methods for upgrading managerial performance within a behaviorist framework. All that is needed for management development is an atmosphere in which managers can make hard decisions and make them right. That's putting realism into management development . . . or is it? What could be more realistic or practical than career accomplishment? And that's what we're talking about.

The Achieving Managers in our study are individuals who, compared to their management cohorts, are excelling in their managerial roles and making major contributions to their organizations. We have discovered that these same individuals embrace philosophies and practices fully consistent with the erstwhile impractical prescriptions of those maligned purveyors of soft science "who never had to make a payroll"!

The irony is that in this day when the medium is the message, many managers are more receptive to magic elixirs of success: "cute" treatments of mundane phenomena found in any human organization, grossly oversimplified versions of personal success formulae, popularly packaged and dispensed over the counter with no prescription necessary. Charm schools, rules for making it up the organization, encounter groups, computer games, key principles for avoiding incompetence . . .

they all sell. But where is the proof? How do these *really* relate to managerial achievement? Managers might profitably ask such questions. Of prime importance in our study of achievement is the fact that we are able to speak from data rather than from intuition; we are bound by our results rather than by our prejudices.

Who shall achieve, the Dilettante or the Doer? A related issue is raised by those pragmatists who ask, "Why should we invest time, energy and money to learn more about something that every business administration student picks up on his way to the real world?" Well ... if *everyone* already knows the jargon of the human side of enterprise, *someone* isn't putting his knowledge to work. Achieving Managers account for only 13 percent of all the managers we studied. It seems, as Marvin Weisbord[30] has observed, that there exists a vast gap between managers' glib mention of concepts and dropping of names and their creative use of science-based theories to improve the management of their organizations. And yet, from a purely selfish point of view, it must occur to some managers that a few of their colleagues are doing something about putting theory into practice. These individuals we have identified as Achieving Managers, but in their organizations they may simply be called the movers and shakers: those who, through some uncanny streak of luck, just happen to get ahead.

Dreaming of things that never were. ... The results of the Achieving Manager Research Project may, upon reflection, be seen to address the future, the prospect of not how things are but of what they may become. Chris Argyris[31] has pointedly referred to the capacity of people to go either way—toward growth or toward stagnation. And it is this theme which emerges most strongly from a study of managerial achievement. Managers have a choice. They may decide which way they will go— toward growth and achievement or toward stagnation and accommodation—just as surely as they decide where to live or what career to pursue.

The High Achiever's approach to management can result in not only sweet dreams of success, but true excellence—be it in a small firm, one of *Fortune*'s 500 or the Oval Office. Each of us has the option of becoming an Achieving Manager because the manager's achievement may be traced to the behaviors he employes. If we would make one impression, let it be this: managerial achievement does not depend upon the existence of personal traits and extraordinary skills unique to outstanding individuals. It depends on the manner in which the manager *behaves* in conducting organizational affairs and on the values he holds regarding personal and interpersonal potentials. All of which can be learned. *The key to becoming an Achieving Manager is to learn to behave like one.*

References

1. R. R. Blake and J. S. Mouton, *The Managerial Grid* (Houston, Texas: Gulf Publishing Co., 1964), 225-246.

2. A. Maslow, *Personality and Motivation* (New York: Harper, 1954).

3. F. Herzberg, *Work and the Nature of Man* (New York: Wiley, 1966).

4. D. McGregor, *The Human Side of Enterprise* (New York: McGraw-Hill, 1960).

5. A. J. Marrow, D. G. Bowers and S. E. Seashore, *Management by Participation* (New York: Harper & Row, 1967).

6. C. Argyris, *Personality and Organization* (New York: Harper & Row, 1957).

7. R. Likert, *The Human Organization* (New York: McGraw-Hill, 1967).

8. R. R. Blake and J. S. Mouton, op. cit.

9. J. Hall and M. S. Williams, *Work Motivation Inventory* (Conroe, Texas: Teleometrics International, Inc., 1967).

10. A. Maslow, op. cit.

11. F. Herzberg, op. cit.

12. J. Hall, *Management of Motives Index* (Conroe, Texas: Teleometrics International, Inc., 1968).

13. D. McGregor, op. cit.

14. M. S. Myers, "Conditions for Manager Motivation," *Harvard Business Review* (January-February 1966).

15. L. Coch and J. R. P. French, "Overcoming Resistance to Change," *Human Relations* (1948), 512-532.

16. Marrow, op. cit.

17. J. Hall, *Personal Reaction Index*. In "Models for Management" (seminar) (Conroe, Texas: Teleometrics International, Inc., 1971).

18. C. Argyris, *Interpersonal Competence and Organizational Effectiveness* (Homewood, Illinois: Dorsey, 1962).

19. Ibid.

20. J. Hall and M. S. Williams, *Personnel Relations Survey* (Conroe, Texas: Teleometrics International, Inc., 1967).

21. J. Luft, *Of Human Interaction* (Palo Alto, Calif.: National Press Books, 1969).

22. J. Hall and M. S. Williams. *Management Relations Survey* (Conroe, Texas: Teleometrics International, Inc., 1970).

23. R. R. Blake, et al., op. cit.

24. R. Likert, *New Patterns of Management* (New York: McGraw-Hill, 1961).

25. E. A. Fleischman, E. F. Harris, and H. E. Burt, *Leadership and Supervision in Industry* (Columbus: Bureau of Educational Research, Ohio State University, 1955).

26. J. Hall, J. B. Harvey and M. S. Williams, *Styles of Management Inventory* (Conroe, Texas: Teleometrics International, Inc., 1963).

27. J. Hall, J. B. Harvey, and M. S, Williams, *Management Appraisal Survey* (Conroe, Texas: Teleometrics International, Inc., 1970).

28. A. J. Marrow, *The Failure of Success* (New York: AMACOM, 1972).

29. C. P. Bowen, "Let's Put Realism into Management Development," *Harvard Business Review* (July-August 1973, 81-87).

30. M. R. Weisbord, "What, Not Again! Manage People Better?" *Think* (January-February 1970).

31. C. Argyris, "A Few Words in Advance," in A. J. Marrow, ed., *The Failure of Success* (New York: AMACOM, 1972).

Motivation: A Diagnostic Approach

by David A. Nadler and Edward E. Lawler III

- What makes some people work hard while others do as little as possible?
- How can I, as a manager, influence the performance of people who work for me?
- Why do people turn over, show up late to work, and miss work entirely?

These important questions about employees' behavior can only be answered by managers who have a grasp of what motivates people. Specifically, a good understanding of motivation can serve as a valuable tool for *understanding* the causes of behavior in organizations, for *predicting* the effects of any managerial action, and for *directing* behavior so that organizational and individual goals can be achieved.

EXISTING APPROACHES

During the past twenty years, managers have been bombarded with a number of different approaches to motivation. The terms associated with these approaches are well known—"human relations," "scientific management," "job enrichment," "need hierarchy," "self-actualization," etc. Each of these approaches has something to offer. On the other hand, each of these different approaches also has its problems in both theory and practice. Running through almost all of the approaches with which managers are familiar are a series of implicit but clearly erroneous assumptions.

David A. Nadler is associate professor, Graduate School of Business, Columbia University in the City of New York. Edward E. Lawler III is professor, Department of Organizational Behavior, Graduate School of Business Administration, University of Southern California.

Assumption 1: All Employees Are Alike Different theories present different ways of looking at people, but each of them assumes that all employees are basically similar in their makeup: Employees all want economic gains, or all want a pleasant climate, or all aspire to be self-actualizing, etc.

Assumption 2: All Situations Are Alike Most theories assume that all managerial situations are alike, and that the managerial course of action for motivation (for example, participation, job enlargement, etc.) is applicable in all situations.

Assumption 3: One Best Way Out of the other two assumptions there emerges a basic principle that there is "one best way" to motivate employees.

When these "one best way" approaches are tried in the "correct" situation they will work. However, all of them are bound to fail in some situations. They are therefore not adequate managerial tools.

A NEW APPROACH

During the past ten years, a great deal of research has been done on a new approach to looking at motivation. This approach, frequently called "expectancy theory," still needs further testing, refining, and extending. However, enough is known that many behavioral scientists have concluded that it represents the most comprehensive, valid, and useful approach to understanding motivation. Further, it is apparent that it is a very useful tool for understanding motivation in organizations.

The theory is based on a number of scientific assumptions about the causes of behavior in organizations.

Assumption 1: Behavior Is Determined by a Combination of Forces in the Individual and Forces in the Environment Neither the individual nor the environment alone determines behavior. Individuals come into organizations with certain "psychological baggage." They have past experiences and a developmental history which has given them unique sets of needs, ways of looking at the world, and expectations about how organizations will treat them. These all influence how individuals respond to their work environment. The work environment provides structures (such as a pay system or a supervisor) which influence the behavior of people. Different environments tend to produce different behavior in similar people just as dissimilar people tend to behave differently in similar environments.

Assumption 2: People Make Decisions about Their Own Behavior in Organizations While there are many constraints on the behavior of individuals in organizations, most of the behavior that is observed is the result of individuals' conscious decisions. These decisions usually fall into two categories. First, individuals make decisions about *membership behavior*—coming to work, staying at work, and in other ways being a member of the organization. Second, individuals make decisions about the amount of *effort* they will direct *towards performing their jobs*. This includes decisions about how hard to work, how much to produce, at what quality, etc.

Assumption 3: Different People Have Different Types of Needs, Desires and Goals Individuals differ on what kinds of outcomes (or rewards) they desire. These differences are not random; they can be examined systematically by an understanding of the differences in the strength of individuals' needs.

Assumption 4: People Make Decisions among Alternative Plans of Behavior Based on Their Perceptions (Expectancies) of the Degree to Which a Given Behavior Will Lead to Desired Outcomes In simple terms, people tend to do those things which they see as leading to outcomes (which can also be called "rewards") they desire and avoid doing those things they see as leading to outcomes that are not desired.

In general, the approach used here views people as having their own needs and mental maps of what the world is like. They use these maps to make decisions about how they will behave, behaving in those ways which their mental maps indicate will lead to outcomes that will satisfy their needs. Therefore, they are inherently neither motivated nor unmotivated; motivation depends on the situation they are in, and how it fits their needs.

THE THEORY

Based on these general assumptions, expectancy theory states a number of propositions about the process by which people make decisions about their own behavior in organizational settings. While the theory is complex at first view, it is in fact made of a series of fairly straightforward observations about behavior. . . . Three concepts serve as the key building blocks of the theory:

Performance-Outcome Expectancy Every behavior has associated with it, in an individual's mind, certain outcomes (rewards or punishments). In other words, the individual believes or expects that if he or she behaves in a certain way, he or she will get certain things.

Examples of expectancies can easily be described. An individual may have an expectancy that if he produces ten units he will receive his normal hourly rate while if he produces fifteen units he will receive his hourly pay rate plus a bonus. Similarly an individual may believe that certain levels of performance will lead to approval or disapproval from members of her work group or from her supervisor. Each performance can be seen as leading to a number of different kinds of outcomes and outcomes can differ in their types.

Valence Each outcome has a "valence" (value, worth, attractiveness) to a specific individual. Outcomes have different valences for different individuals. This comes about because valences result from individual needs and perceptions, which differ because they in turn reflect other factors in the individual's life.

For example, some individuals may value an opportunity for promotion or advancement because of their needs for achievement or power, while others may not want to be promoted and leave their current work group because of needs for affiliation with others. Similarly, a fringe benefit such as a pension plan may have great valence for an older worker but little valence for a young employee on his first job.

Effort-Performance Expectancy Each behavior also has associated with it in the individual's mind a certain expectancy or probability of success. This expectancy represents the individual's perception of how hard it will be to achieve such behavior and the probability of his or her successful achievement of that behavior.

For example, you may have a strong expectancy that if you put forth the effort, you can produce ten units an hour, but that you have only a fifty-fifty chance of producing fifteen units an hour if you try.

Putting these concepts together, it is possible to make a basic statement about motivation. In general, the motivation to attempt to behave in a certain way is greatest when:

a. The individual believes that the behavior will lead to outcomes (performance-outcome expectancy)

b. The individual believes that these outcomes have positive value for him or her (valence)

c. The individual believes that he or she is able to perform at the desired level (effort-performance expectancy)

Given a number of alternative levels of behavior (ten, fifteen, and twenty units of production per hour, for example) the individual will choose that level of performance which has the greatest motivational force associated with it, as indicated by the expectancies, outcomes, and valences.

In other words, when faced with choices about behavior, the individual goes through a process of considering questions such as, "Can I perform at that level if I try?" "If I perform at that level, what will happen?" "How do I feel about those things that will happen?" The individual then decides to behave in that way which seems to have the best chance of producing positive, desired outcomes.

A General Model

On the basis of these concepts, it is possible to construct a general model of behavior in organizational settings (see Figure 3-1). Working from left to right in the model, motivation is seen as the force on the individual to expend effort. Motivation leads to an observed level of effort by the individual. Effort, alone, however, is not enough. Performance results from a combination of the effort that an individual puts forth *and* the level of ability which he or she has (reflecting skills, training, information, etc.). Effort thus combines with ability to produce a given level of performance. As a result of performance, the individual attains certain outcomes. The model indicates this relationship in a dotted line, reflecting the fact that sometimes people perform but do not get desired outcomes. As this process of performance-reward occurs, time after time, the actual events serve to provide information which influences the individual's perceptions (particularly expectancies) and thus influences motivation in the future.

Outcomes, or rewards, fall into two major categories. First, the individual obtains outcomes from the environment. When an individual performs at a given level he or she can receive positive or negative outcomes from supervisors, coworkers, the organization's rewards systems, or other sources. These environmental rewards are thus one source of outcomes for the individual. A second source of outcomes is the individual. These include outcomes which occur purely from the performance of the task itself (feelings of accomplishment, personal worth, achievement, etc.). In a sense, the individual gives these rewards to himself or herself. The environment cannot give them or take them away directly; it can only make them possible.

Supporting Evidence

Over fifty studies have been done to test the validity of the expectancy-theory approach to predicting employee behavior.[1] Almost without exception, the studies have confirmed the predictions of the theory. As the theory predicts, the best performers in organizations tend to see a strong relationship between performing their jobs well and receiving rewards they value. In addition they have clear performance goals and feel they can perform well. Similarly, studies using the expectancy theory to pre-

---

[1]For reviews of the expectancy theory research see Mitchell, T. R. Expectancy models of job satisfaction, occupational preference and effort: A theoretical methodological, and empirical appraisal. *Psychological Bulletin*, 1974. *81*. 1053-1077. For a more general discussion of expectancy theory and other approaches to motivation see Lawler, E. E. *Motivation in work organizations*, Belmont Calif.: Brooks/Cole, 1973.

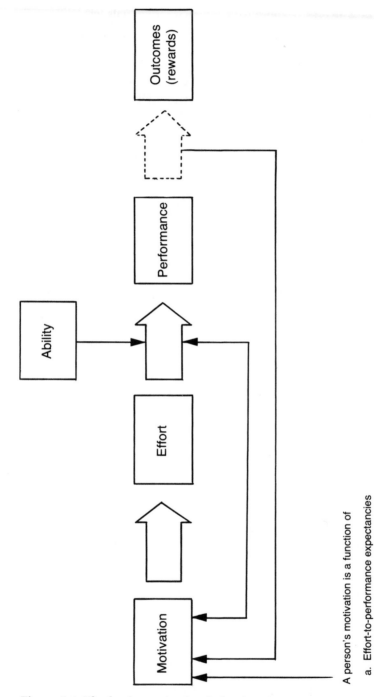

Figure 3-1. The basic motivation-behavior sequence

dict how people choose jobs also show that individuals tend to interview for and actually take those jobs which they feel will provide the rewards they value. One study, for example, was able to correctly predict for 80 percent of the people studied which of several jobs they would take.[2] Finally, the theory correctly predicts that beliefs about the outcomes associated with performance (expectancies) will be better predictors of performance than will feelings of job satisfaction since expectancies are the critical causes of performance and satisfaction is not.

Questions about the Model

Although the results so far have been encouraging, they also indicate some problems with the model. These problems do not critically affect the managerial implications of the model, but they should be noted. The model is based on the assumption that individuals make very rational decisions after a thorough exploration of all the available alternatives and on weighing the possible outcomes of all these alternatives. When we talk to or observe individuals, however, we find that their decision processes are frequently less thorough. People often stop considering alternative behavior plans when they find one that is at least moderately satisfying, even though more rewarding plans remain to be examined.

People are also limited in the amount of information they can handle at one time, and therefore the model may indicate a process that is much more complex than the one that actually takes place. On the other hand, the model does provide enough information and is consistent enough with reality to present some clear implications for managers who are concerned with the question of how to motivate the people who work for them.

Implications for Managers

The first set of implications is directed toward the individual manager who has a group of people working for him or her and is concerned with how to motivate good performance. Since behavior is a result of forces both in the person and in the environment, you as manager need to look at and diagnose both the person and the environment. Specifically, you need to do the following:

Figure out what outcomes each employee values As a first step, it is important to determine what kinds of outcomes or rewards have valence for your employees. For each employee you need to determine "what turns him or her on." There are various ways of finding this out, including (a) finding out employees' desires through some structured

---

[2]Lawler, E. E., Kuleck, W. J., Rhode, J. G., & Sorenson, J. E. Job choice and post-decision dissonance. *Organizational Behavior and Human Performance*, 1975, *13*, 133-145.

method of data collection, such as a questionnaire, (b) observing the employees' reactions to different situations or rewards, or (c) the fairly simple act of asking them what kinds of rewards they want, what kind of career goals they have, or "what's in it for them." It is important to stress here that it is very difficult to change what people want, but fairly easy to find out what they want. Thus, the skillful manager emphasizes diagnosis of needs, not changing the individuals themselves.

Determine what kinds of behavior you desire Managers frequently talk about "good performance" without really defining what good performance is. An important step in motivating is for you yourself to figure out what kinds of performances are required and what are adequate measures or indicators of performance (quantity, quality, etc.). There is also a need to be able to define those performances in fairly specific terms so that observable and measurable behavior can be defined and subordinates can understand what is desired of them (e.g., produce ten products of a certain quality standard—rather than only produce at a high rate).

Make sure desired levels of performance are reachable The model states that motivation is determined not only by the performance-to-outcome expectancy, but also by the effort-to-performance expectancy. The implication of this is that the levels of performance which are set as the points at which individuals receive desired outcomes must be reachable or attainable by these individuals. If the employees feel that the level of performance required to get a reward is higher than they can reasonably achieve, then their motivation to perform well will be relatively low.

Link desired outcomes to desired performances The next step is to directly, clearly, and explicitly link those outcomes desired by employees to the specific performances desired by you. If your employee values external rewards, then the emphasis should be on the rewards systems concerned with promotion, pay, and approval. While the linking of these rewards can be initiated through your making statements to your employees, it is extremely important that employees see a clear example of the reward process working in a fairly short period of time if the motivating "expectancies" are to be created in the employees' minds. The linking must be done by some concrete public acts, in addition to statements of intent.

If your employee values internal rewards (e.g., achievement), then you should concentrate on changing the nature of the person's job, for he or she is likely to respond well to such things as increased autonomy, feedback, and challenge, because these things will lead to a situation where good job performance is inherently rewarding. The best way to check on the adequacy of the internal and external reward system is to ask people what their perceptions of the situation are. Remember it is the perceptions of the people that determine their motivation, not reality. It doesn't matter for example whether you feel a subordinate's pay is related to his or her motivation. Motivation will be present only if the subordinate sees the relationship. Many managers are misled about the behavior of their subordinates because they rely on their own perceptions of the situation and forget to find out what their subordinates feel. There is only one way to do this: ask. Questionnaires can be used here, as can personal interviews. . . .

Analyze the total situation for conflicting expectancies Having set up positive expectancies for employees, you then need to look at the entire situation to see if other factors (informal work groups, other managers, the organization's reward systems) have set up conflicting expectancies in the minds of the employees. Motivation will only be high when people see a number of rewards associated with good performance and few negative outcomes. Again, you can often gather this kind of information by asking your subordinates. If there are major conflicts, you need to make adjustments, either in your own performance and reward structure, or in the other sources of rewards or punishments in the environment.

Make sure changes in outcomes are large enough In examining the motivational system, it is important to make sure that changes in outcomes or rewards are large enough to motivate significant behavior. Trivial rewards will result in trivial amounts of effort and thus trivial improvements in performance. Rewards must be large enough to motivate individuals to put forth the effort required to bring about significant changes in performance.

Check the system for its equity The model is based on the idea that individuals are different and therefore different rewards will need to be used to motivate different individuals. On the other hand, for a motivational system to work it must be a fair one—one that has equity (not equality). Good performers should see that they get more desired rewards than do poor performers, and others in the system should see that also. Equity should not be confused with a system of equality where all are rewarded equally, with no regard to their performance. A system of equality is guaranteed to produce low motivation.

Implications for Organizations

Expectancy theory has some clear messages for those who run large organizations. It suggests how organizational structures can be designed so that they increase rather than decrease levels of motivation of organization members. While there are many different implications, a few of the major ones are as follows:

Implication 1: The design of pay and reward systems Organizations usually get what they reward, not what they want. This can be seen in many situations, and pay systems are a good example.[3] Frequently, organizations reward people for membership (through pay tied to seniority, for example) rather than for performance. Little wonder that what the organization gets is behavior oriented towards "safe," secure employment rather than effort directed at performing well. In addition, even where organizations do pay for performance as a motivational device, they frequently negate the motivational value of the system by keeping pay secret, therefore preventing people from observing the pay-to-performance relationship that would serve to create positive, clear, and strong performance-to-reward expectancies. The implication is that organizations should put more effort into rewarding people (through pay, promotion, better job opportunities, etc.) for the performances which are desired, and that to keep these rewards secret is clearly self-defeating. In addition, it underscores the importance of the frequently ignored performance evaluation or appraisal process and the need to evaluate people based on how they perform clearly defined specific behaviors, rather than on how they score on ratings of general traits such as "honesty," cleanliness," and other, similar terms which frequently appear as part of the performance appraisal form.

Implication 2: The design of tasks, jobs, and roles One source of desired outcomes is the work itself. The expectancy-theory model supports much of the job enrichment literature, in saying that by designing jobs which enable people to get their needs fulfilled, organizations can bring about higher levels of motivation.[4] The major difference between the traditional approaches to job enlargement or enrichment and the expectancy-theory approach is the recognition by the expectancy theory that different people have different needs and, therefore, some people may not want enlarged or enriched jobs. Thus, while the design of tasks that have more autonomy, variety, feedback, meaningfulness, etc., will lead to higher motivation in some, the organization needs to build in the opportunity for individuals to make choices about the kind of work they will do so that not everyone is forced to experience job enrichment.

Implication 3: The importance of group structures Groups, both formal and informal, are powerful and potent sources of desired out-

---

[3]For a detailed discussion of the implications of expectancy theory for pay and reward systems, see Lawler, E. E. *Pay and organizational effectiveness: A psychological view.* New York: McGraw-Hill, 1971.

[4]A good discussion of job design with an expectancy theory perspective is in Hackman, J. R., Oldham, G. R., Janson, R., & Purdy, K. A new strategy for job enrichment. *California Management Review*, Summer, 1975, p. 57.

comes for individuals. Groups can provide or withhold acceptance, approval, affection, skill training, needed information, assistance, etc. They are a powerful force in the total motivational environment of individuals. Several implications emerge from the importance of groups. First, organizations should consider the structuring of at least a portion of rewards around group performance rather than individual performance. This is particularly important where group members have to cooperate with each other to produce a group product or service, and where the individual's contribution is often hard to determine. Second, the organization needs to train managers to be aware of how groups can influence individual behavior and to be sensitive to the kinds of expectancies which informal groups set up and their conflict or consistency with the expectancies that the organization attempts to create.

Implication 4: The supervisor's role The immediate supervisor has an important role in creating, monitoring, and maintaining the expectancies and reward structures which will lead to good performance. The supervisor's role in the motivation process becomes one of defining clear goals, setting clear reward expectancies, and providing the right rewards for different people (which could include both organizational rewards and personal rewards such as recognition, approval, or support from the supervisor). Thus, organizations need to provide supervisors with an awareness of the nature of motivation as well as the tools (control over organizational rewards, skill in administering those rewards) to create positive motivation.

Implication 5: Measuring motivation If things like expectancies, the nature of the job, supervisor-controlled outcomes, satisfaction, etc., are important in understanding how well people are being motivated, then organizations need to monitor employee perceptions along these lines. One relatively cheap and reliable method of doing this is through standardized employee questionnaires. A number of organizations already use such techniques, surveying employees' perceptions and attitudes at regular intervals (ranging from once a month to once every year-and-a-half) using either standardized surveys or surveys developed specifically for the organization. Such information is useful both to the individual manager and to top management in assessing the state of human resources and the effectiveness of the organization's motivational systems.[5] . . . Appendix B for excerpts from a standardized survey.)

Implication 6: Individualizing organizations Expectancy theory leads to a final general implication about a possible future direction for

---

[5]The use of questionnaires for understanding and changing organizational behavior is discussed in Nadler, D. A. *Feedback and organizational development: Using data-based methods*. Reading, Mass.: Addison-Wesley, 1977.

the design of organizations. Because different people have different needs and therefore have different valences, effective motivation must come through the recognition that not all employees are alike and that organizations need to be flexible in order to accommodate individual differences. This implies the "building in" of choice for employees in many areas, such as reward systems, fringe benefits, job assignments, etc., where employees previously have had little say. A successful example of the building in of such choice can be seen in the experiments at TRW and the Educational Testing Service with "cafeteria fringe-benefits plans" which allow employees to choose the fringe benefits they want, rather than taking the expensive and often unwanted benefits which the company frequently provides to everyone.[6]

SUMMARY

Expectancy theory provides a more complex model of man for managers to work with. At the same time, it is a model which holds promise for the more effective motivation of individuals and the more effective design of organizational systems. It implies, however, the need for more exacting and thorough diagnosis by the manager to determine (a) the relevant forces in the individual, and (b) the relevant forces in the environment, both of which combine to motivate different kinds of behavior. Following diagnosis, the model implies a need to act—to develop a system of pay, promotion, job assignments, group structures, supervision, etc.—to bring about effective motivation by providing different outcomes for different individuals.

   Performance of individuals is a critical issue in making organizations work effectively. If a manager is to influence work behavior and performance, he or she must have an understanding of motivation and the factors which influence an individual's motivation to come to work, to work hard, and to work well. While simple models offer easy answers, it is the more complex models which seem to offer more promise. Managers can use models (like expectancy theory) to understand the nature of behavior and build more effective organizations.

---

[6]The whole issue of individualizing organizations is examined in Lawler, E. E. The individualized organization: Problems and promise. *California Management Review*, 1974, 17(2), 3139.

Developing and Selecting Leaders: What We Know

by W. Warner Burke

When I give a talk on leadership, I typically ask members of the audience to individually make a list of the five personal characteristics they consider most important for successful leadership. After they have completed their lists, I ask whether anyone would like to make a small wager with me. My side of the wager is that there will be no two lists with the same five charateristics. If an individual takes me up on the bet, we then agree on some third party to serve as judge and to hold the money (sometimes as much as a dollar). Although I have made this bet dozens of times, I lost it only once. And even in that instance, I considered the judge to be on shaky ground! This is an engaging way to begin a session on leadership and to dramatically illustrate that in an audience of, say, thirty-five people there will be at least that many different opinions about the key ingredients of successful leadership.

The point is that all of us have experienced leadership firsthand in one form or the other and, therefore, we believe that we understand it. But when it comes to defining leadership, we can produce a myriad of answers. In his magnum opus, *Handbook of Leadership*, the late Ralph Stogdill (1974) examined ten different definitions of leadership, ranging from leadership as a focus of group processes to leadership as the exercise of influence. Stogdill's own definition is the one most appropriate to this research:

> Leadership is the process (act) of influencing the activities of an organized group in its efforts toward goal setting and goal achievement. (p. 10)[1]

I wish to acknowledge the valuable assistance and comment of Eileen Morley in the writing of this chapter.

W. Warner Burke is professor of psychology and education, Department of Educational Psychology, Teachers College, Columbia University.

We can see immediately that even Stogdill's definition is limiting. He does not account for the possibility of an emergent leader in an unorganized situation. However, since we are concerned here with leaders and organizations, Stogdill's definition will serve our purposes.

The purposes of this paper, therefore, are to (a) provide a synopsis of leadership research over the past sixty or so years, (b) update past research and theory with more recent findings, and (c) consider the applicability of what evidence we have for the selection and development of leaders for organizations.

A SYNOPSIS OF LEADERSHIP RESEARCH

Great-Man Theories of Leadership

According to Stogdill (1974), "A preoccupation with leadership occurs predominantly in countries with an Anglo-Saxon heritage." (p. 7) This observation is valid provided that our point of reference is the written word. A similar preoccupation may have occurred but been lost in other cultures because the communication process was oral rather than written. Historians and biographers of the Western world wrote about great leaders long before the invention of the printing press. If not outright, at least implicitly, these early writers made comparisons of important leaders. What did Caesar have in common with Alexander the Great? And what did these two luminaries have in common with, say, Napoleon? The so-called *great-man theory* of leadership was based on this comparative approach; the common denominator for distinction was that of inherited capabilities. That is, the great-man theory held that leaders were endowed with capabilities (such as being more intelligent) that set them apart from common men.

Trait Theory

The great-man theory influenced the early investigators of leadership to ask exactly what it was that distinguished great from lesser men. As a result, the next theory to guide initial research was the *trait theory*.

What traits were held in common by the three aforementioned notables—Caesar, Alexander the Great, and Napoleon? Besides being military leaders, they had the common characteristic of being short of stature, even for their time, and all three contracted venereal disease.

---

[1]From R. J. Stogdill, *Handbook of Leadership: A Survey of Theory and Research*, pp. 7, 63-64. Copyright © 1974 by The Free Press. Reprinted by permission.

Does this mean that short and sexually active people are more likely to ascend to positions of leadership? Much as some of us might like to believe that, no such evidence exists. But, nevertheless, the trait theory was based on the assumption that there were certain characteristics, mostly in the realm of personality, that would predict leadership success when combined within the same individual. In other words, successful leaders were presumed to be persons who are more intelligent, courageous, risk taking, verbal, and extroversive than other people.

In the 1920s, predominantly in the United States, trait theory provided the frame of reference and impetus for leadership research. It is interesting to note that the first systematic study of leadership began in the U.S. "Systematic" in this case means that the research was empirical. Most of the investigations of that era were characterized by correlational analyses. That is, they were not cause-and-effect studies but were investigations of which trait(s) related in a systematic way to leadership success. Successful leadership was typically defined in terms of group performance or in terms of the degree to which the leader influenced his or her followers.

Trait-theory research produced somewhat confusing results:

- Leaders are typically more intelligent than the average person, but above an IQ level of about 115 there is no positive correlation between leadership and intelligence whatsoever.
- Successful leaders are more extroversive than their followers in certain situations, but not in others.
- Taller people are not more likely to be successful leaders, although the research shows that they are more likely to have an opportunity for leadership.

During the late 1940s and early 1950s, psychologists and sociologists began to abandon the fruitless examination of traits and to take different approaches to the study of leadership. There seemed to be implicit agreement that effective leadership must be more than a function of the leader's personality; situational differences are involved.

The Situationist Approach

Beginning in the late 1950s and extending to the present, a *situationist approach* to leadership has been popular. It is epitomized in the writings of Hersey and Blanchard (1977). This approach asserts that the successful leader adapts behavior to fit the demands of a given situation; being able to adapt is the key. The situationists, however, overreacted to the unfruitfulness of the trait approach. They denied that leaders show a certain amount of behavioral consistency across situations—portraying them as chameleons.

Although the trait approach has lost favor, certain research results that reflect uniformity are noteworthy, even though they are fairly general. The early trait research was atomistic, looking at discrete characteristics. Later studies, which used more sophisticated research methodology, such as factor analysis, and benefited from computer technology, began to show which traits grouped together.

As Stogdill (1974) has summarized, the average leader tends to be superior to the average follower in the following traits:

- Intelligence (but not significantly more);
- Achievement and knowledge;
- Dependability in exercising responsibility;
- Activity and promoting participation;
- Socio-economic status; and
- Sense of humor.

Stogdill goes on to say:

> A person does not become a leader by virtue of the possession of some combination of traits, but the pattern of personal characteristics of the leader must bear some relevant relationship to the characteristics, activities, and goals of the followers. (pp. 63-64)

The interaction, therefore, of the leader's personal characteristics, the needs and goals of the followers, and the situational demands is the key to understanding leadership (Burke, 1965).

Leadership Behavior

In the late 1940s, trait theory began to be displaced by the study of leaders' *behavior* rather than their personalities. As a result of several factor-analytic studies, Hemphill (1950) identified two primary factors that clearly differentiated leader behavior from other behavior along two dimensions—*consideration* and *initiation of structure*.

During the 1950s, numerous investigations were conducted to clarify the meaning of these two factors. Most of this work emanated from the Ohio State Leadership Studies, led by Hemphill, Halpin, Fleishman, and Stogdill, among others. *Consideration* came to be defined as follower-oriented behavior, i.e., consideration of followers' needs and goals and recognition of their accomplishments. *Initiation of structure* came to be defined as communication of what is expected of the followers by their leaders and what the followers can expect from the leader. The former concerns the human element and the latter the task. Not surprisingly, multiple studies show that these two elements—consideration and initiation of structure—interact directly to influence work-group performance and satisfaction. Moreover, the performances of the most effective leaders are high in both elements.

In the early 1960s, Blake and Mouton, two psychologists on the faculty of the University of Texas (at that time), aware of the Ohio State Leadership Studies, postulated that managers simultaneously have two concerns—a concern for *production or results* and a concern for *people*—and that managers differ with respect to how much they are concerned with each of the two. That is, some managers are more concerned with getting results than they are with the people involved; for some other managers, the concern is reversed. Blake and Mouton (1978) graphically arranged these two concerns on two nine-point scales, resulting in what they called the Managerial Grid® (see chapter 15), a two-dimensional model that describes managerial style.

A Grid score for any given manager shows how the two concerns combine to determine his or her style of management. The greater the concern for production, the more autocratic the manager's style tends to be. The greater the manager's concern for people, the more the style can be characterized as permissive. Blake and Mouton argued that the higher the manager's simultaneous concern for both production and people (what they labeled as a 9,9 style), the more effective the manager is likely to be.

Contingency Theory of Leadership

Another development in the 1960s was Fiedler's (1967) *contingency theory of leadership.* Fiedler contends that leadership is contingent on the personal characteristics of the leader and on certain situational factors, the latter defined in terms of how much control the leader can exercise over the situation.

In terms of personality, Fiedler divides leaders into two categories—those who are primarily task motivated and those who are primarily relationship motivated. These two categories are, of course, similar to, if not the same as, the original concepts of initiation of structure and consideration.

Fiedler categorizes situations along three dimensions:

1. Leader-member relations, ranging from good to poor;
2. Task structure, from high (clear) structure to low (ambiguous); and
3. The leader's position-power from strong to weak.

The cumulative results of more than fifty separate research studies show an interactive effect. Task-motivated leaders perform best under two sets of conditions: (a) when the leader has high control over the situation due to good relations with subordinates, high task structure, or a high degree of power, and (b) when the leader has very low control. When the leader has intermediate control, neither very high nor very low, relationship-motivated leaders outperform the task-motivated leaders (Fiedler, 1974). Fiedler argues, with good evidence, that effective leaders are those whose style and characteristics fit their situation well, either by good luck or because they can find ways to change the situation to match their personalities.

Fiedler is pessimistic about the possibility of changing the personal characteristics of a leader to fit a situation (short of long-term therapy, which is an unrealisitic business proposition). Therefore, he is neither a situationist nor an advocate of training people to adopt a particular (e.g., 9,9) style of management. Successful leaders, according to Fiedler, are those who shape the situations in which they find themselves to match their personalities more effectively. He suggests that is is far easier to change situations than personalities.

In another independent domain of research into small-group behavior, Bales (1950) observed scores of problem-solving groups. He concluded that two types of leadership behavior are essential for effective group functioning: *task behavior* and *maintenance or socio-emotional behavior*.

Current Research and Theory

To summarize, a number of different schools of research, theorists, and practitioners (some independently) have found that two elements are critically important in leadership effectiveness. Whether these two elements are named initiation of structure and consideration, a concern for production and a concern for people, or task behavior and socio-emotional behavior, the consensual validation among the investigators is no small matter.

What else can be concluded? A debate still continues among psychologists and sociologists concerning whether a contingency theory or a normative ("one best way") approach is more valid. Currently, contingency theorists appear to have more support. However, Stogdill's (1974) conclusion, based on his massive survey of leadership research, is that *leaders who rate high in both initiation of structure and consideration are more successful*. Other more recent evidence also leans toward the normative conclusion that, under most conditions, a leader who integrates the two dimensions and does not utilize one at the expense of the other is more effective.

RECENT FINDINGS

In a study of some sixteen thousand managers from a variety of organizations, Hall (1976) (see chapter 11) found that those who rose most rapidly to top-management ranks were significantly more (a) integrative in their managerial styles, i.e., not permissive but combining concern for production and for people, (b) open and solicitous of feedback in their communication processes and interpersonal relationships, (c) self-actualizing, and (d) apt to utilize motivators as opposed to hygiene factors (Herzberg, 1966) in their motivational approach to subordinates. In other words, it can be stated with a great deal of statistical confidence that successful managers are:

- More concerned with the work and the job itself than with the peripheral factors, such as fringe benefits;
- More likely to communicate openly and straightforwardly than to be secretive and political;
- More willing to confront other people regarding work-related issues than to ignore or suppress potential conflict;
- More likely to involve their subordinates in problem solving, planning, and decision making than to be unilateral;
- More concerned with getting results and achieving goals than with procedure and policy.

These findings may seem self-evident when successful managers are compared with less successful ones, but they are much more than self-evident. These findings are based on sound empirical evidence, and they corroborate results from other independent studies.

RELEVANCE OF RESEARCH TO NONTRADITIONAL SOURCES OF LEADERSHIP

Virtually all research on leadership has been on the leadership roles played by men. This limits the usefulness of this literature in enabling us to understand how best to develop future leaders from nontraditional sources, which include women, or what particular strengths women can bring to leadership roles.

The reason for this bias in leadership research is due to the fact that, in North American society, concepts of leadership and masculine behavior overlap a good deal. While not all men engage in leadership behavior, to a large extent the qualities and behaviors that are associated in most people's minds with effective leadership are masculine. And, until recently, most people made the assumption that individuals have to be *either* masculine *or* feminine—that it is not possible or appropriate to be both aggressive *and* nurturant, analytical *and* expressive, independent *and* cooperative, power-oriented *and* caring.

As a result of this cultural bias, when put into situations in which they are expected to be nurturant and expressive, many men experience considerable anxiety; as much, in fact, as do women in situations in which they are expected to be assertive or sophisticated about the use of power. In both cases, the anxiety stems from two concerns. One is that the individuals are being expected to do something their sex is not supposed to do. The other is that, given a traditional upbringing, they also do not know how to do it.

Recently, important research into the nature of the kinds of behaviors that characterize each sex and the extent to which these are intrinsic or simply learned has come from two sources. Sandra Bem (1975) has conducted a series of studies in which she has explored the extent to which masculine and feminine behaviors are, in fact, distinct separate clusters that all of us possess to greater or lesser degree. This approach has enabled her to study the behavior of individuals, independent of their physiological sex.

A parallel line of research has been conducted by two psychologists at the University of Texas. In a highly significant and rigorous series of studies, Janet Spence and Robert Helmreich (1978) have disproved the popular belief that masculinity and femininity are opposite ends of the same continuum. They have demonstrated that both characteristics are present to some degree within all of us, regardless of sex. These characteristics are dualistic, not opposite.

Spence and Helmreich found that some men scored high on both masculine and feminine traits; so did some women. To describe these people, Spence and Helmreich used the word *androgynous*, meaning a person who can behave in ways that are traditionally characteristic of both sexes. For example, men with high scores in masculinity *and* femininity can, as circumstances require, be both independent *and* tender, assertive *and* compassionate, tough *and* sensitive. So can women with high feminine and masculine scores.

Spence and Helmreich found other men who scored high on masculine traits and low on feminine traits, and they found women who scored high on feminine traits and low on masculine ones. These people defined themselves as being much more closely tied to one set of sex-related behaviors than the people in the first group. They did not have so wide a range of behavior nor the same flexibility to adapt their behavior according to circumstance. Finally, a third group of people scored low on both masculine and feminine behaviors.

What has all this got to do with leadership? While Spence and Helmreich did not specifically study leaders, they did study successful people in three different fields:

- MBA students
- MBA alumni (by definition including some business managers and leaders)
- Scientists

Their results showed that the more successful the individual, the higher the need for achievement, the higher the score on both masculine and feminine measures (i.e., high on androgyny), and the lower the need for competitiveness.

This finding is consistent with all the leadership research that has been reported until now and that has indicated the importance of the two key leadership attributes: *structure* and *consideration*. The ability to define a task, to give concrete instructions about what must be done, and to direct its completion certainly fits our traditional notions of masculine instrumental and assertive behavior. However, the ability to know what is going on with the people one supervises and to be sensitive to their needs and considerate of them in carrying out the leadership role is more in harmony with our notion of the feminine characteristics of sensitivity, intuition, and caring.

Hall (1976) found that successful managers are more disclosing and communicative in general (more expressive) and encourage more feed-back than less successful managers. Hall's discovery reinforces the importance in the successful manager's behavior of elements that can be viewed as feminine; yet most men look for these elements in male leaders. Certainly, few successful male leaders reach positions of eminence without having experienced relationships with more senior men in which they benefited from much personal caring and concern.

From this research, and from the article by Sargent in chapter 11, we learn that the most successful manager and leader will be the person who has best command of a broad range of both "feminine" and "masculine" behaviors and can call on them as needed. We learn that people who are more rigidly tied to either masculine or feminine behavior will be less successful. The successful manager, and perhaps the successful person in general, is one whose behavior is versatile, at times assertive—even aggressive—and at other times caring and supportive.

The work of Hall, Spence and Helmreich, Bem, and Sargent adds considerably to our understanding of the complicated mosaic of leadership. It also has important implications for the personal growth and learning of men and women with leadership potential. Their different socialization has led most men and women to develop opposite, although complementary, strengths and limitations. Male managers are more likely to need help in developing interpersonal sensitivity and expressiveness. Female managers may need to cultivate assertiveness, the ability to instruct and direct, and an understanding of power. Although large areas of the managerial training of men and women may overlap, it is crucial to address these differential needs and to assess performance by results, rather than by the extent to which a leader follows a strictly "masculine" method.

CHARACTERISTICS OF EFFECTIVE ORGANIZATIONAL LEADERS

The model of leadership covered here applies to abilities that can be exercised at any level of the organization and at any stage of leadership development. Leadership does not, nor should it, exist at top levels only. Effective leadership should exist at all levels in organizations, and effective top-management leadership is most likely to result from an evolving leadership capability practiced over a long period of time in a sequence of graduated responsibilities. At any level, therefore, effective leadership requires the following personal and functional characteristics.

Personal Characteristics

Successful leaders are those who:

- Are above average intellectually;
- Are knowledgeable, capable of achieving, and like to achieve;
- Are dependable in exercising responsibility;
- Shape situations to fit their personality traits;
- Seek feedback and communicate openly;
- Confront issues;
- Tend to be more participative than autocratic in their approach to the management of people;
- Are not overly competitive;
- Rate high on both masculine and feminine characteristics (that is, they are androgynous—characterized by neither competitive nor very dependent characteristics—and able to be both assertive and caring);
- Have a high motivation for power but a low need for affiliation;
- Enjoy work and organizational life;
- Are judicious and mature; and
- Understand power and how to exercise it for the ultimate good of all concerned.

This list of the personal characteristics of leaders is based on sound theoretical and research evidence and can be used, at a minimum, as a checklist for selection and planning purposes.

Functional Characteristics

1. Initiation of Structure

Successful leaders are effective at initiating task structure and setting expectations. They are able to articulate clear, although not necessarily detailed, expectations and to understand their effects on the behavior of others. In communicating expectations, leaders need to understand both the importance of their own confidence and of having confidence in others—genuinely believing in their potential and providing support for that potential to be recognized.

2. Provision of Consideration

Effective leaders are aware of their subordinates' morale—have an intuitive or empathic sense of how their subordinates are feeling—and take these factors into account as they manage the task. Schrage (1965) found that in small entrepreneurships such consideration was one of the three characteristics that correlated directly with profitability.

The more these first two leadership functions are blended and integrated within the individual leader, the better.

3. Understanding and Effective Use of Power

An understanding of the nature and use of power is crucial to a manager, and top-management and board members, in particular, have two important functions here. One function is to identify as early as possible those managers who seem able to use power. The second is to monitor managers' healthy use of power as they progress in the organization. The monitoring process can be another key source of information concerning the healthy or self-serving use of power by younger managers.

4. Awareness of Self and Situation

Effective leaders are highly aware people. They are aware of themselves, what motivates them, their essential values, strengths, and limitations, and how best to use themselves in a variety of situations. Equally important is the leader's awareness of others, particularly what motivates, frustrates, or stimulates them. At this time in our society, it appears that people—potential followers—are placing a strong value on awareness by their leaders.

5. Diagnosis and Priority Setting

Leaders can use awareness of self, others, and situation to be effective diagnosticians and priority setters. They need to know not only what problems exist, but which require highest priority and which can safely be ignored, at least temporarily. Organizations can suffer significant losses by working efficiently on the wrong problem.

6. Conflict Management and Concern for Collaboration

To be effective, leaders need to be skilled not only in the management of conflict but in collaborating with others. One reason for this, according to

Bennis (1976), is that many groups join an "unconscious conspiracy" of self-interest, which prevents them from subordinating their desires to the good of the whole and pulling together. Each group goes its own way with quiet resistance to demands for collaboration. These demands, if imposed, would surface intergroup animosities. In fact, the surfacing and working through of such animosities leads to a much more effective group, but this is avoided by many leaders who are uncomfortable with personal confrontations.

Another reason for developing conflict-management skills is that fewer people are willing to acknowledge and respond obediently to authority today than formerly, and managers will face many more occasions in which confrontation is unavoidable.

In addition to a concern for collaboration in the areas they supervise, leaders should understand how their units, operations, or businesses fit into the larger organization. They need to have skill in integrating or collaborating with others who manage interactive units.

7. Guided Autonomy

Leaders need to value guided autonomy and have a zest for operating independently and trying out the limits of skills, knowledge, and insight. But at the same time, leaders must be able to use the guidance of more experienced people to review problems or accomplishments and to learn better ways of handling them. In addition, as the individual matures, he or she must be equally willing and able to provide guidance to the next generation.

Here again, research has shown that the ability to value advice and to operate successfully under conditions of guided autonomy are characteristic, not only of leaders, but of entrepreneurs as well.

8. Time Perspective

Successful leaders possess a time perspective appropriate to the time span of responsibility implicit in their roles. They are able to resist over-involvement in the present or immediate future.

Elliott Jaques' (1976) research has impressively demonstrated that chief executive officers of organizations with over 100,000 people have a future time perspective of up to twenty years. At senior levels in any organization, a time span of ten years appears to be the acceptable minimum.

9. Cross-Cultural Perspective

For multinational organizations, be they corporations or federal agencies, cross-cultural experience is a critical prerequisite to top-management positions. Cross-cultural experience develops a perspective on world affairs, a sensitivity to the nature of different people, and an understanding of the varying roles of international affairs that no other experience can provide.

10. Entrepreneurial Capacity

Finally, and, of course, most importantly for a business organization, people who have an entrepreneurial flair should be identified as early as possible and given a piece of the business to lead. According to Glueck (1977), there are five requirements for successful entrepreneurship, which in part overlap the requirements for leadership. They are as follows:

Entrepreneurial Ability. This is primarily the ability to conceptualize and organize a business; to be able to perceive business opportunities and communicate these perceptions and ideas effectively to others; and to be flexible in the face of change.

Entrepreneurial Attitudes, Motivation, and Personality. Entrepreneurs should have high energy, capacity for hard work, high achievement motivation, and the willingness to defer reward and gratification to the future.

Encouraging Environment. Entrepreneurs need support, especially from family and friends, and, of course, from the work environment. This means the provision of autonomy, freedom, and independence. Equally important are advice, consultation, and counseling (these match the aforementioned ability to use *guided autonomy*). Entrepreneurs want to run their own show, but they desire advice just as strongly. The more this advice is consultative, as opposed to controlling, the more acceptable it is likely to be.

Adequate Capital. Resources are required—money, materials, people— for entrepreneurs, and the provision of a budget over which they have maximum control is important. Therefore, freedom and self-control should be provided within appropriate and reasonable time frames and deadlines.

Genuine Business Opportunity and Understanding of the Market Environment. There are two types of opportunity—the creation of a new type of business or the development of an existing business to compete with other less effective firms. In either case, a thorough knowledge of the market(s) is needed. Leaders need to understand their markets well and be in close touch with them so that they are attuned to evolving customer needs and can translate them into opportunities for new business. Knowledge of the market is the second quality that Schrage (1965) found to be directly correlated with entrepreneurial profitability. If entrepreneurs can do market research and planning themselves, so much the better.

SUMMARY

Considering the sizable lists of leadership characteristics, it might appear to the reader that effective leaders are those who can walk on water. No individual is likely to score highly positively on all personal and functional characteristics. But after more than a half-century of systematic research and theory development, it is possible to delineate attributes of people and conditions within an organization (e.g., good career-development programs) and use the data as key guidelines for the development of effective leadership. Although there is much more that is unknown, we do know some things. Not to capitalize on the evidence that does exist is to continue to rely on conventional wisdom and on trial-and-error learning, neither of which is as reliable as the behavioral science knowledge we have now accumulated.

References

Bales, R. F. *Interaction process analysis*. Reading, MA: Addison-Wesley, 1950.

Bem, S. L. Androgyny vs. the tight little lives of fluffy women and chesty men. *Psychology Today*, 1975, *9*, 58-62.

Bennis, W. G. *The unconscious conspiracy: Why leaders can't lead*. New York: AMACOM, 1976.

Blake, R. R., & Mouton, J. S. *The new managerial grid*. Houston, TX: Gulf Publishing Co., 1978.

Burke, W. W. Leadership behavior as a function of the leader, the follower, and the situation. *Journal of Personality*, 1965, *33*, 60-81.

Fiedler, F. E. *A theory of leadership effectiveness*. New York: McGraw-Hill, 1967.

Fiedler, F. E. The contingency model—New directions for leadership utilization. *Journal of Contemporary Business*, Autumn, 1974, *3* (4), 65-80.

Glueck, W. F. *Management*. Hinsdale, IL: Dryden Press, 1977.

Hall, J. To achieve or not: The manager's choice. *California Management* Review, 1976, *18* (4), 5-18.

Hemphill, J. K. *Leader behavior description*. Columbus, OH: Ohio State University, Personnel Research Board, 1950 (mimeo).

Hersey, P., & Blanchard, K. H. *Management of organizational behavior* (3rd ed.). Englewood Cliffs, NJ: Prentice-Hall, 1977.

Herzberg, F. *Work and the nature of man*. Cleveland, OH: World, 1966.

Jaques, E. *A general theory of bureaucracy*. New York: Halstead Press, 1976.

Schrage, H. The R & D entrepreneur: Profile of success. *Harvard Business Review*, 1965, *43* (6), 56-69.

Spence, J. T., & Helmreich, R. L. *Masculinity and femininity: Their psychological dimensions, correlates and antecedents*. Austin, TX: University of Texas Press, 1978.

Stogdill, R. J. *Handbook of leadership: A survey of theory and research*. New York: The Free Press, 1974.

Part 4. The Manager in the Organization

From a variety of perspectives this section examines managers' influence on the organization and, in turn, the effect the organization has on their behavior, attitudes, and styles of managing. It presents a theory about managers' assumptions about others in the organization, especially those who are lower in the managerial hierarchy. Styles of management are explained in terms of how much managers concern themselves with production and with people. Managerial careers are charted from the standpoint of how persons "move" within the organization, that is, how they enter in the first place and how they may progress managerially. Finally, managers' behavior and style are seen as a consequence of type of organizational structure and design.

Part 4 begins with Douglas McGregor's classic—"The Human Side of Enterprise." It has been retained in the second edition of this book because of the enduring nature of its message and the continuing impact of McGregor's thinking. For example, in a study conducted by the Conference Board (Rush, 1969), of 202 behavioral scientists listed by the 302 respondents as having influenced them personally, Douglas McGregor was listed most frequently (134 times).

Practically everyone who has had any training in management has heard of Douglas McGregor's Theory X and Theory Y, but many of those who have heard have misunderstood. Some common misunderstandings of McGregor's theory include the following:

1.   X and Y represent *styles* of management.
2.   X is *hard* while Y is *soft*.
3.   X and Y represent polar opposites of a *single* continuum.

The reader can note that, in McGregor's chapter, X and Y are arbitrary labels for two different views of human behavior in an organization. These views are based on assumptions and beliefs that people hold about others, especially within the framework of organizational life. Doubtlessly, the way a person manages others reflects a set of assumptions and beliefs, but the managers' behavior may take more than one form stylistically. A manager may assume Theory X (e.g., people are inherently lazy), but in handling subordinates that manager may either be autocratic ("You have to push people to get work out of them") or highly benevolent ("You have to nurture and coddle people to get work out of them"). The underlying assumption is the same for the different styles of management (see chapter 11 by Hall). Moreover, one can believe Theory X and still be "soft" with respect to managerial approach. A manager who is highly permissive and supportive may act that way because he or she believes that people in organizations are not quite capable of taking care of themselves (a Theory-X assumption) and, therefore, must be watched over by management.

Since McGregor postulated that Theory-X and Theory-Y assumptions represent separate and mutually exclusive sets of beliefs (he called them "cosmologies"), and assuming that he was correct, then a single, bipolar continuum is not logical. In fact, research has shown that people may hold both sets of assumptions simultaneously, even though the different beliefs contradict one another (again, see chapter 11 by Hall).

McGregor's thinking was seminal, his impact pervasive. And as more evidence and experience are accumulated, it is our prediction that McGregor's bias for Theory Y as a more effective way to believe and to act will be supported accordingly.

The actions of managers in relation to their subordinates have become the domain of Blake and Mouton, authors of "An Overview of the Grid." Two dimensions of leadership—task and relationships—have emerged over time and through research again and again (see chapter 6 by Burke). By arranging these dimensions into graph form with one axis representing concern for production-task and the other axis representing concern for people, Blake and Mouton created a model of managerial style, the Managerial Grid.® This model has had a major influence on managers' language; at times, they speak to each other in numbers, e.g., 9,1; 5,5; 9,9. The numbers mark five different positions on the Grid and represent distinct styles of managerial behavior. A significant contribution of Blake and Mouton's model is its shorthand language and quick and simple way of understanding different styles of management.

Since the model was originally introduced in the early 1960s, Blake and Mouton have developed a six-phase Grid approach to organization development, which is summarized in their chapter. More recently, they have updated their original assumptions regarding the model and revised their 1964 book (Blake & Mouton, 1978). Although the Grid model itself has not been changed in their revised work, additions have been made. With each of the five primary styles of management, Blake and Mouton have now included motivations. They hypothesize that each of the five styles represents different motivations on the part of the manager. There are differences among the types of managers, in what each is striving to reach and, at the same time, seeking to avoid. For example, the 9,1 manager, or authority-obedience style, is striving to control and dominate while seeking to avoid failure and feelings of weakness. Whereas the 9,9 manager, or participative style, strives to achieve self-actualization and organizational goals while trying to avoid demonstrating undue selfishness.

Blake and Mouton contend that evidence is now heavily weighted toward a "one best way" of management, the 9,9 style, as opposed to a contingency ("it all depends") or situational viewpoint (see Blake & Mouton, 1978, and Hall's chapter in part 3).

Regardless of how long they may stay with an organization, all managers have careers, at least as Edgar Schein defines the concept of a career in "The Individual, the Organization, and the Career: A Conceptual Scheme." The "movement" of individuals through their respective organizations constitutes their careers. Schein presents a conceptual scheme for understanding how people relate to an organization regarding their entry, movement through, and eventual departure, and how organizations establish expectations concerning this series of events or career progress.

Schein has been a student of organizational careers for more than twenty years, and he recently completed a book that culminates much of his work in this field (Schein, 1978). His model for understanding careers is three-dimensional and shaped like a cone with the apex representing the top of the organizational structure or pyramid. Career movement by a manager occurs (1) vertically via rank or level; (2) radially by becoming closer to or farther from the center of the organization, i.e. "being on the inside"; and (3) circumferentially via functional changes and/or by moving to another department or division. A manager's career, threfore, is comprised of some combination of movement in all three of these dimensions. Schein states the implications of this model for career development. The usefulness of the model is his clarification of how an organization shapes a person's career and where an individual has control over his or her destiny.

Chris Argyris also relates organizational structure with individual behavior in "Today's Problems with Tomorrow's Organizations." Moreover, he contends that with the increasing rate of change and the consequent need for organizational flexibility, the traditional, pyramidal structure of organizational design is out-of-date. With its continual interdepartmental conflict, top-down decision making and communication flow, and the inherent climate of win-lose competition, the pyramidal structure does not foster the kinds of internal conditions that foster adaptability to a rapidly changing environment. The matrix organizational structure is more adapatable but is difficult to implement, especially when the former structure has been traditional and pyramidal.

The primary message of Argyris is that organizational structure has more influence on individual behavior than the other way around. To change the organization one must change the structure, he argues. And the *way* this change is implemented sets the stage for whether the new structure will work effectively. Attempting in an autocratic , top-down fashion to move an organization from a pyramidal structure to a more decentralized and collaborative one will cause the change effort to fail.

Part 4 ends with the Argyris chapter which, in turn, establishes a bridge to the next section on organization design and change.

References

Blake, R. R., & Mouton, J. S. *The new managerial grid.* Houston, TX: Gulf Publishing, 1978.

Schein, E. H. *Career dynamics: Matching individual and organizational needs.* Reading, MA: Addison-Wesley, 1978.

The Human Side
of Enterprise

by Douglas M. McGregor

It has become trite to say that industry has the fundamental know-how to utilize physical science and technology for the material benefit of mankind, and that we must now learn how to utilize the social sciences to make our human organizations truly effective.

To a degree, the social sciences today are in a position like that of the physical sciences with respect to atomic energy in the thirties. We know that past conceptions of the nature of man are inadequate and, in many ways, incorrect. We are becoming quite certain that, under proper conditions, unimagined resources of creative human energy could become available within the organizational setting.

We cannot tell industrial management how to apply this new knowledge in simple, economic ways. We know it will require years of exploration, much costly development research, and a substantial amount of creative imagination on the part of management to discover how to apply this growing knowledge to the organization of human effort in industry.

MANAGEMENT'S TASK:
THE CONVENTIONAL VIEW

The conventional conception of management's task in harnessing human energy to organizational requirements can be stated broadly in terms of three propositions. In order to avoid the complications introduced by a label, let us call this set of propositions "Theory X":

Douglas M. McGregor is deceased. He was Sloan Professor of Management, Massachusetts Institute of Technology.

Reprinted by permission of the publisher from *Management Review*, November 1957, ©1957 by the American Management Association, Inc. All rights reserved.

1. Management is responsible for organizing the elements of productive enterprise—money, materials, equipment, people—in the interest of economic ends.

2. With respect to people, this is a process of directing their efforts, motivating them, controlling their actions, modifying their behavior to fit the needs of the organization.

3. Without this active intervention by management, people would be passive—even resistant—to organizational needs. They must therefore be persuaded, rewarded, punished, controlled—their activities must be directed. This is management's task. We often sum it up by saying that management consists of getting things done through other people.

Behind this conventional theory there are several additional beliefs—less explicit, but widespread:

4. The average man is by nature indolent—he works as little as possible.

5. He lacks ambition, dislikes responsibility, prefers to be led.

6. He is inherently self-centered, indifferent to organizational needs.

7. He is by nature resistant to change.

8. He is gullible, not very bright, the ready dupe of the charlatan and the demagogue.

The human side of economic enterprise today is fashioned from propositions and beliefs such as these. Conventional organization structures and managerial policies, practices, and programs reflect these assumptions.

In accomplishing its task—with these assumptions as guides—management has conceived of a range of possibilities.

At one extreme, management can be "hard" or "strong." The methods for directing behavior involve coercion and threat (usually disguised), close supervision, tight controls over behavior. At the other extreme, management can be "soft" or "weak." The methods for directing behavior involve being permissive, satisfying people's demands, achieving harmony. Then they will be tractable, accept direction.

This range has been fairly completely explored during the past half century, and management has learned some things from the exploration. There are difficulties in the "hard" approach. Force breeds counterforces: restriction of output, antagonism, militant unionism, subtle but effective sabotage of management objectives. This "hard" approach is especially difficult during times of full employment.

There are also difficulties in the "soft" approach. It leads frequently to the abdication of management—to harmony, perhaps, but to indifferent performance. People take advantage of the soft approach. They continually expect more, but they give less and less.

Currently, the popular theme is "firm but fair." This is an attempt to gain the advantages of both the hard and soft approaches. It is reminiscent of Teddy Roosevelt's "speak softly and carry a big stick."

IS THE CONVENTIONAL VIEW CORRECT?

The findings which are beginning to emerge from the social sciences challenge this whole set of beliefs about man and human nature and about the task of management. The evidence is far from conclusive, certainly, but it is suggestive. It comes from the laboratory, the clinic, the schoolroom, the home, and even to a limited extent from industry itself.

The social scientist does not deny that human behavior in industrial organization today is approximately what management perceives it to be. He has, in fact, observed it and studied it fairly extensively. But he is pretty sure that this behavior is *not* a consequence of man's inherent nature. It is a consequence rather of the nature of industrial organizations, of management philosophy, policy, and practice. The conventional approach of Theory X is based on mistaken notions of what is cause and what is effect.

Perhaps the best way to indicate why the conventional approach of management is inadequate is to consider the subject of motivation.

PHYSIOLOGICAL NEEDS

Man is a wanting animal—as soon as one of his needs is satisfied, another appears in its place. This process is unending. It continues from birth to death.

Man's needs are organized in a series of levels—a hierarchy of importance. At the lowest level, but pre-eminent in importance when they are thwarted, are his *physiological needs*. Man lives for bread alone, when there is no bread. Unless the circumstances are unusual, his needs for love, for status, for recognition are inoperative when his stomach has been empty for a while. But when he eats regularly and adequately, hunger ceases to be an important motivation. The same is true of the other physiological needs of man—for rest, exercise, shelter, protection from the elements.

A satisfied need is not a motivator of behavior! This is a fact of profound significance that is regularly ignored in the conventional approach to the management of people. Consider your own need for air:

Except as you are deprived of it, it has no appreciable motivating effect upon your behavior.

SAFETY NEEDS

When the physiological needs are reasonably satisfied, needs at the next higher level begin to dominate man's behavior—to motivate him. These are called *safety needs.* They are needs for protection against danger, threat, deprivation. Some people mistakenly refer to these as needs for security. However, unless man is in a dependent relationship where he fears arbitrary deprivation, he does not demand security. The need is for the "fairest possible break." When he is confident of this, he is more than willing to take risks. But when he feels threatened or dependent, his greatest need is for guarantee, for protection, for security.

The fact needs little emphasis that, since every industrial employee is in a dependent relationship, safety needs may assume considerable importance. Arbitrary management actions, behavior which arouses uncertainty with respect to continued employment or which reflects favoritism or discrimination, unpredictable administration of policy— these can be powerful motivators of the safety needs in the employment relationship *at every level*, from worker to vice president.

SOCIAL NEEDS

When man's physiological needs are satisfied and he is no longer fearful about his physical welfare, his *social needs* become important motivators of his behavior—needs for belonging, for association, for acceptance by his fellows, for giving and receiving friendship and love.

Management knows today of the existence of these needs, but it often assumes quite wrongly that they represent a threat to the organization. Many studies have demonstrated that the tightly knit, cohesive work group may, under proper conditions, be far more effective than an equal number of separate individuals in achieving organizational goals.

Yet management, fearing group hostility to its own objectives, often goes to considerable lengths to control and direct human efforts in ways that are inimical to the natural "groupiness" of human beings. When man's social needs—and perhaps his safety needs, too—are thus thwarted, he behaves in ways which tend to defeat organizational objectives. He becomes resistant, antagonistic, uncooperative. But this behavior is a consequence, not a cause.

EGO NEEDS

Above the social needs—in the sense that they do not become motivators until lower needs are reasonably satisfied—are the needs of greatest significance to management and to man himself. They are the *egoistic needs*, and they are of two kinds:

1. Those needs that relate to one's self-esteem—needs for self-confidence, for independence, for achievement, for competence, for knowledge.

2. Those needs that relate to one's reputation—needs for status, for recognition, for appreciation, for the deserved respect of one's fellows.

Unlike the lower needs, these are rarely satisfied; man seeks indefinitely for more satisfaction of these needs once they have become important to him. But they do not appear in any significant way until physiological, safety, and social needs are all reasonably satisfied.

The typical industrial organization offers few opportunities for the satisfaction of these egoistic needs to people at lower levels in the hierarchy. The conventional methods of organizing work, particularly in mass-production industries, give little heed to these aspects of human motivation. If the practices of scientific management were deliberately calculated to thwart these needs, they could hardly accomplish this purpose better than they do.

SELF-FULFILLMENT NEEDS

Finally—a capstone, as it were, on the hierarchy of man's needs—there are what we may call the *needs for self-fulfillment*. These are the needs for realizing one's own potentialities, for continued self-development, for being creative in the broadest sense of that term.

It is clear that the conditions of modern life give only limited opportunity for these relatively weak needs to obtain expression. The deprivation most people experience with respect to other lower-level needs diverts their energies into the struggle to satisfy *those* needs, and the needs for self-fulfillment remain dormant.

MANAGEMENT AND MOTIVATION

We recognize readily enough that a man suffering from a severe dietary deficiency is sick. The deprivation of physiological needs has behavioral consequences. The same is true—although less well recognized—of deprivation of higher-level needs. The man whose needs for safety, association, independence, or status are thwarted is sick just as surely as the man who has rickets. And his sickness will have behavioral consequences. We will be mistaken if we attribute his resultant passivity, his hostility, his refusal to accept responsibility to his inherent "human nature." These forms of behavior are *symptoms* of illness—of deprivation of his social and egoistic needs.

The man whose lower-level needs are satisfied is not motivated to satisfy those needs any longer. For practical purposes they exist no longer. Management often asks, "Why aren't people more productive? We pay good wages, provide good working conditions, have excellent fringe benefits and steady employment. Yet people do not seem to be willing to put forth more than minimum effort."

The fact that management has provided for these physiological and safety needs has shifted the motivational emphasis to the social and perhaps to the egoistic needs. Unless there are opportunities *at work* to satisfy these higher-level needs, people will be deprived, and their behavior will reflect this deprivation. Under such conditions, if management continues to focus its attention on physiological needs, its efforts are bound to be ineffective.

People *will* make insistent demands for more money under these conditions. It becomes more important than ever to buy the material goods and services which can provide limited satisfaction of the thwarted needs. Although money has only limited value in satisfying many higher-level needs, it can become the focus of interest if it is the *only* means available.

THE CARROT-AND-STICK APPROACH

The carrot-and-stick theory of motivation (like Newtonian physical theory) works reasonably well under certain circumstances. The *means* for satisfying man's physiological and (within limits) his safety needs can be provided or withheld by management. Employment itself is such a means, and so are wages, working conditions, and benefits. By these means the individual can be controlled so long as he is struggling for subsistence.

But the carrot-and-stick theory does not work at all once man has reached an adequate subsistence level and is motivated primarily by higher needs. Management cannot provide a man with self-respect, or with the respect of his fellows, or with the satisfaction of needs for self-fulfillment. It can create such conditions that he is encouraged and enabled to seek such satisfaction for *himself,* or it can thwart him by failing to create those conditions.

But this creation of conditions is not "control." It is not a good device for directing behavior. And so management finds itself in an odd position. The high standard of living created by our modern technological know-how provides quite adequately for the satisfaction of physiological and safety needs. The only significant exception is where management practices have not created confidence in a "fair break"—and thus where safety needs are thwarted. But by making possible the satisfaction of low-level needs, management has deprived itself of the ability to use as motivators the devices on which conventional theory has taught it to rely—rewards, promises, incentives, or threats and other coercive devices.

The philosophy of management by direction and control—*regardless of whether it is hard or soft*—is inadequate to motivate because the human needs on which this approach relies are today unimportant motivators of behavior. Direction and control are essentially useless in motivating people whose important needs are social and egoistic. Both the hard and the soft approach fail today because they are simply irrelevant to the situation.

People, deprived of opportunities to satisfy at work the needs which are now important to them, behave exactly as we might predict—with indolence, passivity, resistance to change, lack of responsibility, willingness to follow the demagogue, unreasonable demands for economic benefits. It would seem that we are caught in a web of our own weaving.

A NEW THEORY OF MANAGEMENT

For these and many other reasons, we require a different theory of the task of managing people based on more adequate assumptions about human nature and human motivation. I am going to be so bold as to suggest the broad dimensions of such a theory. Call it "Theory Y," if you will.

1. Management is responsible for organizing the elements of productive enterprise—money, materials, equipment, people—in the interest of economic ends.

2. People are *not* by nature passive or resistant to organizational needs. They have become so as a result of experience in organizations.

3. The motivation, the potential for development, the capacity for assuming responsibility, the readiness to direct behavior toward organizational goals are all present in people. Management does not put them there. It is a responsibility of management to make it possible for people to recognize and develop these human characteristics for themselves.

4. The essential task of management is to arrange organizational conditions and methods of operation so that people can achieve their

own goals *best* by directing *their own* efforts toward organizational objectives.

This is a process primarily of creating opportunities, releasing potential, removing obstacles, encouraging growth, providing guidance. It is what Peter Drucker has called "management by objectives" in contrast to "management by control." It does *not* involve the abdication of management, the absence of leadership, the lowering of standards or the other characteristics usually associated with the "soft" approach under Theory X.

SOME DIFFICULTIES

It is no more possible to create an organization today which will be a full, effective application of this theory than it was to build an atomic power plant in 1945. There are many formidable obstacles to overcome.

The conditions imposed by conventional organization theory and by the approach of scientific management for the past half century have tied men to limited jobs which do not utilize their capabilities, have discouraged the acceptance of responsibility, have encouraged passivity, have eliminated meaning from work. Man's habits, attitudes, expectations—his whole conception of membership in an industrial organization—have been conditioned by his experience under these circumstances.

People today are accustomed to being directed, manipulated, controlled in industrial organizations and to finding satisfaction for their social, egoistic, and self-fulfillment needs away from the job. This is true of much of management as well as of workers. Genuine "industrial citizenship"—to borrow again a term from Drucker—is a remote and unrealistic idea, the meaning of which has not even been considered by most members of industrial organizations.

Another way of saying this is that Theory X places exclusive reliance upon external control of human behavior, while Theory Y relies heavily on self-control and self-direction. It is worth noting that this difference is the difference between treating people as children and treating them as mature adults. After generations of the former, we cannot expect to shift to the latter overnight.

STEPS IN THE RIGHT DIRECTION

Before we are overwhelmed by the obstacles, let us remember that the application of theory is always slow. Progress is usually achieved in small steps. Some innovative ideas which are entirely consistent with Theory Y are today being applied with some success.

Decentralization and Delegation

These are ways of freeing people from the too-close control of conventional organization, giving them a degree of freedom to direct their own activities, to assume responsibility, and, importantly, to satisfy their egoistic needs. In this connection, the flat organization of Sears, Roebuck and Company provides an interesting example. It forces "management by objectives," since it enlarges the number of people reporting to a manager until he cannot direct and control them in the conventional manner.

Job Enlargement

This concept, pioneered by I.B.M. and Detroit Edison, is quite consistent with Theory Y. It encourages the acceptance of responsibility at the bottom of the organization; it provides opportunities for satisfying social and egoistic needs. In fact, the reorganization of work at the factory level offers one of the more challenging opportunities for innovation consistent with Theory Y.

Participation and Consultative Management

Under proper conditions, participation and consultative management provide encouragement to people to direct their creative energies toward organizational objectives, give them some voice in decisions that affect them, provide significant opportunities for the satisfaction of social and egoistic needs. The Scanlon Plan is the outstanding embodiment of these ideas in practice.

Performance Appraisal

Even a cursory examination of conventional programs of performance appraisal within the ranks of management will reveal how completely consistent they are with Theory X. In fact, most such programs tend to treat the individual as though he were a product under inspection on the assembly line.

A few companies — among them General Mills, Ansul Chemical, and General Electric — have been experimenting with approaches which involve the individual in setting "targets" or objectives *for himself* and in a *self*-evaluation of performance semiannually or annually. Of course, the superior plays an important leadership role in this process — one, in fact, which demands substantially more competence than the conventional approach. The role is, however, considerably more congenial to many managers than the role of "judge" or "inspector" which is usually forced upon them. Above all, the individual is encouraged to take a greater responsibility for planning and appraising his own contribution to organizational objectives; and the accompanying effects on eogistic and self-fulfillment needs are substantial.

APPLYING THE IDEAS

The not infrequent failure of such ideas as these to work as well as expected is often attributable to the fact that a management has "bought the idea" but applied it within the framework of Theory X and its assumption.

Delegation is not an effective way of exercising management by control. Participation becomes a farce when it is applied as a sales gimmick or a device for kidding people into thinking they are important. Only the management that has confidence in human capacities and is itself directed toward organizational objectives rather than toward the preservation of personal power can grasp the implications of this emerging theory. Such management will find and apply successfully other innovative ideas as we move slowly toward the full implementation of a theory like Y.

THE HUMAN SIDE OF ENTERPRISE

It is quite possible for us to realize substantial improvements in the effectiveness of industrial organizations during the next decade or two. The social sciences can contribute much to such developments; we are only beginning to grasp the implications of the growing body of knowledge in these fields. But if this conviction is to become a reality instead of a pious hope, we will need to view the process much as we view the process of releasing the energy of the atom for constructive human ends—as a slow, costly, sometimes discouraging approach toward a goal which would seem to many to be quite unrealistic.

The ingenuity and the perseverance of industrial management in the pursuit of economic ends have changed many scientific and technological dreams into commonplace realities. It is now becoming clear that the application of these same talents to the human side of enterprise will not only enhance substantially these materialistic achievements, but will bring us one step closer to "the good society."

An Overview of the Grid®

by Robert R. Blake and Jane Srygley Mouton

Dramatic changes are occurring in the way Americans handle their affairs. This is true across the spectrum, from commercial firms to government agencies, to schools and universities. What these are, and how they can be met and brought under management is discussed below.

Breakdown of Authority and Obedience

In the past, bosses could exercise work-or-starve authority over their subordinates. They expected and got obedience from them. Authority-obedience was the basis for supervision that built pyramids, big ships, great armies and that made Prussia famous.

But authority-obedience as a way of life has been under greater and greater attack for the past hundred years. Though wars tended to bring it back, during peacetime it became more and more objectionable as a basis for getting people to cooperate. But today, in an environment of vastly improved education and of relative affluence, many are rejecting traditional authority and trying to set up and act upon their own.

The year 1968 might be taken as the beginning of the end for authority-obedience as the control mechanism of American society. That was the year when Detroit and Watts burned. It was when young people were burning their draft cards and dodging the draft by heading for Canada, Sweden and elsewhere. And it was when several universities' presidents were held as hostages in their offices. Furthermore, truancy, runaways and drug problems tell us that the old family pattern where father was boss and the children complied with his authority has crumbled too.

Robert R. Blake and Jane S. Mouton are president and vice president, respectively, of Scientific Methods, Inc., Austin, Tex.

Reproduced by special permission from the May, 1975 *Training and Development Journal.* Copyright 1975 by the American Society for Training and Development, Inc.

The 1964 Civil Rights Act put society on notice that equality, not authority and obedience, was to be the basis for race relations in the future. Other federal legislation established standards for organizations to be more responsible for the safety of their employees, for their customers and for the everyday citizen as well. Understanding all this new-found and partly enforced equality and social justice and the motivations that underlie it is important for comprehending the new day that is emerging.

These many influences tell us as far as bosses and subordinates are concerned that authority and obedience is no longer the name of the game.

The new relationship between a "boss" and a "subordinate" is such that they seek to reach mutual understanding and agreement as to the course of action to be taken, as well as how to go about it. Before coming to any conclusion on the "how," though, the *main* alternative ways of managing will be presented. First examined is how management occurs under an authority-obedience system and its strengths and weaknesses. Then the "love conquers all" proposition will be considered. This is where the boss says, "If my subordinates love me, they'll do what I want without me having to tell them."

Then those hard-to-notice managers who are doing the least amount to get by on a "see no evil, speak no evil, hear no evil" basis will be viewed. Next to be described is the "halfway is far enough" manager who deals with problems by compromise, adjustment, and accommodation of differences, by being willing to do what's "practical." Finally the possibility already introduced, seeking for excellence through getting the highest possible involvement-participation-commitment to organization purpose up and down the line, is evaluated.

The Grid®

The Grid is a way of sorting out all these possibilities and seeing how each compares with the others. What is involved is this:

The Grid, shown in Figure 1, clarifies and crystallizes many of the different possible ways of supervision. Here is the basis of it. Any person who is working has some assigned responsibilities. This is true whether he or she works very low on the job ladder or high up in the organization. There are two matters on his or her mind whenever acting as a manager. One is *production* — getting results, or accomplishing the mission. How intensely he or she thinks about results can be described as a degree of concern for production. On the Grid, the horizontal axis stands for concern for production. It is a nine-point scale where 9 shows high concern for production and 1, low concern.

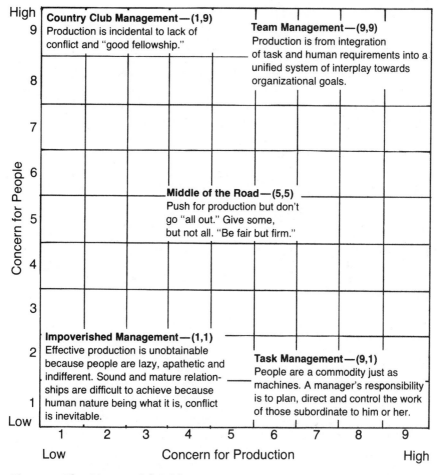

Figure 1. The Managerial Grid

A manager is also thinking about those whose work he or she directs, because he or she has to get results through people. The Grid's vertical axis represents this concern for people. This, too, is on a nine-point scale with 9 a high degree and 1 a low degree.

The Grid identifies these two concerns. It does so in a way that enables a person to see how the two concerns interact. Various "theories" are found at points of intersection of the two scales. Whether he or she realizes it or not, these are theories that different managers use when they think about how to get results through people. Five of the many possible theories or styles of management mentioned earlier stand out clearly. They appear in the four corners and in the center of the Grid.

Going Around the Grid

As can be seen from the Grid figure, in the lower right corner, 9,1 represents a great deal of concern for output but little for the people who are expected to produce. 9,1 is the authority-obedience theory. At the opposite corner of the Grid, the top left, is the 1,9 theory. It's the "love conquers all" approach. In the lower left Grid corner is 1,1. It might seem odd that a manager could have almost no concern for either production or people. He or she goes through the motions of being part of the organization but is not really contributing to it. But such managers do exist, even though they may not be easy to notice until you know their theory. They are not doers but freeloaders, getting by on a "speak no, hear no, see no evil" basis. They have not physically quit the firm, but they walked out mentally, perhaps many years ago.

In the center is the 5,5 style. The manager with this approach is going up the middle of the road. His or her attitude is, "Get results but don't kill yourself! Don't push too much or you will be seen as a 'hard nose.' Don't let people off too easily or they will think you are soft. Be fair but firm. Do the job but find a comfortable tempo." The 5,5 manager is an "organization man."

The upper right corner, the 9,9 position, is high concern for production united with high concern for people. A person who manages according to this theory stresses understanding and agreement through involvement-participation-commitment as the key to solving boss-subordinate problems. Whenever disagreements arise, he or she sees to it that facts are examined. The problem is thrashed through to solution in an open and aboveboard way that can result in mutual understanding with full commitment to conclusions reached. People working together in 9,9 manner know that they have a common stake in the outcome of their endeavors. They mesh effort in an interdependent way. The 9,9 theory doesn't abide by the laws of simple arithmetic. On the joining of contributions, "one" plus "one" can add up to "three."

You may have figured out that there are 81 combinations of concerns represented on the Grid. Adjacent to 9,1 are 8,2 and 7,3. And 1,9 has 2,8 and 3,7 near it. There are 3,3, 4,4, 6,6, 7,7 along the diagonal between 1,1 and 9,9 and so on. But our main emphasis is on the theories in the corners and at the middle of the Grid. These are the most distinct styles. They're the ones you see most often. But you might think of a Grid style as you do shades of hair—black, brown, red, blond and white.

Within each hair shade there's a variety—for example, twenty-seven different ways to be blond—yet on your driver's license the outstanding feature is enough for identification. The five main Grid styles, too, are broadly descriptive. We'll use them in much the same way. While talking about 9,1, remember it's just a tinge away to 8,2 or 7,3, or a halftone or so to 6,4, but all these neighboring combinations describe behavior in broadly similar ways.

Basic Assumptions

Grid theories describe sets of basic assumptions under which people deal with one another. An *assumption* is what you take for granted as being true or reliable. Maybe you learned most of your present-day assumptions as you grew up. "I have to be ... (a tough character or nice person) ... to get what I want," illustrates some assumptions from childhood that persist. In supervision they lay down the pathway of the boss' everyday approach. Managers act on the assumptions they hold even though it may be rare for you to put them into words. The same set of assumptions usually underlies a whole range of attitudes and activities.

For example, a 1,9-oriented boss who wants to please subordinates may be quite inventive in finding all sorts of ways to show personal warmth. His or her behavior may not be so simple as to say "I appreciate you and everything you do" 25 times a day, but, nonetheless, the subordinate dominates his or her thoughts and concerns. His or her subordinate might say, "I never know what nice surprise the boss will think up next," and yet the manager's core assumptions are remarkably consistent—to please his or her subordinate and win their appreciation.

Were persons to act without assumptions, their behavior would be random, purposeless; it would make no sense in any predictable way. Even so, it is not enough just to have a set of assumptions—any old set. Faulty assumptions can ruin a manager. More reliable ones can enhance his or her work and enrich his or her life on the job, not to mention elsewhere. When a person acting under any set of assumptions understands them, this Grid knowledge can aid him or her to predict what the impact of his or her behavior will be on colleagues and subordinates. Thus, learning the Grid framework will help you understand what kinds of actions are likely to lead to what kind of results.

"Dominants" and "Backups"

Does a manager have just one Grid style strategy or does he or she skip over the surface of the Grid, shifting and adapting according to how he or she sees the situation?

All but a very few do have characteristic styles which, presently, they are using most of the time. Let's call this the manager's *dominant* style. Each boss' basic approach resembles one that is founded on either 9,1; 1,9; 5,5; 1,1; or 9,9 assumptions. How can the idea that a person has a dominant Grid style be squared with the fact that people observably do shift and change? It can be understood in the following way. Not only does a supervisor have a dominant style, he or she also has a back-up strategy, and sometimes a third strategy to fall back on even beyond the second way of operating.

The back-up strategy is likely to show when a manager runs up against difficulty in using the dominant strategy. A back-up Grid strategy is the one he or she falls back on, particularly when feeling the strain of tension, frustration or conflict. This can happen when initial efforts meet nothing but resistance or when, at the point of getting down to working on a project the subordinate's enthusiasm turns to stubborn reluctance.

Apparent complexity, when you first encounter it, can be confusing. Maybe you have played with a kaleidoscope. It contains bits of glass, not many, of different shapes and colors, and these can arrange themselves in an endless variety of patterns that you see reflected from its mirrors. Children are fascinated yet bewildered by this. When the key to understanding has been found, however, what previously appeared bewildering now makes sense.

Any Grid style can be a back-up to any other. For example, even a 1,9-oriented manager, when sharply challenged, might turn stubborn and go 9,1. Again, a person who normally deals in a 9,9 way may meet continued resistance from a subordinate. Unable to find a way of getting on to an action basis with him or her, he or she may shift to a 5,5 approach, negotiating for some kind of compromise where both boss and subordinate will be partially satisfied.

There are no natural links between one particular Grid style and another in terms of dominant-to-back-up. It all depends on the individual and his or her situation. You may sometimes see a person who habitually comes on in a 9,1 way, pressing hard for a time, then breaking off, crestfallen. He or she has switched to a different set of assumptions and moved back to a 1,1 stage of resignation, feeling a sense of powerlessness, feeling that he or she is a victim of hostile fate. Who knows, had he or she used a different style from the beginning, or another set of back-up assumptions, and continued talking with the subordinate, he or she might have gotten the reaction desired.

The 9,9 approach is acknowledged by managers as the soundest way to achieve excellence. This conclusion has been verified from studies throughout the U.S. and around the world. The 9,9 theory defines a model that people say with conviction they want, not only for a guide to their own conduct but also as a model of what they want their organization and agencies to become.

That's what the Grid is. The Grid can be used to investigate how a boss supervises in everyday work. There are many boss-subordinate issues that can be looked at in this way. How boss and subordinate communicate is one. Another is the manner in which the boss gives work directions. Others involve managing mistakes, dealing with complaints, and how the boss reacts to hostile feelings.

Change

There are many approaches to change and development, but two are of particular importance in business, industry and government. One critical development step involves the matter of performance evaluation, i.e., how the boss talks with a subordinate to help him or her increase effectiveness. This is individual development. The other, to be treated later, involves *organization development.*

Individual Development

A special word needs to be said about person-to-person individual development. One of the major approaches used today to help people develop involves having bosses interview their subordinates, usually once a year but with the option of doing so more frequently, to help each subordinate see how he or she is performing and how he or she might do better.

This performance review and evaluation involves a more or less prescribed procedure. It starts with the boss and (in principle) the subordinate mutually setting up performance standards and measures of results. The second step, perhaps a year later, or at the end of a briefer period, is for the boss and subordinate to hold another session to review how well the subordinate did in meeting specific and agreed performance standards.

Then, whether simultaneously at annual performance rating time or not, the boss, working alone, also calibrates subordinate performance in terms of standard categories on a rating for such as "responsibility" and "initiative," which apply to all jobs. These evaluations are intended to be used for several purposes. One is for aiding a subordinate to see how he or she can improve performance. Another is to identify special training and development opportunities. Most generally they are used as the basis for pay raises, promotion and termination.

A boss can do any one of these things in a 9,1, 1,9, 1,1, 5,5, or 9,9 way, and, as you can well appreciate, the quality of individual development, if any, hangs in the balance.

Organization Development

Sound management can only meet the challenge of change by seeing the deeper issue: organization development. But a blueprint of an excellent organization is needed to describe an organization so well managed that it can grasp opportunity from the challenge of change. What would such an organization be like?

1. *Its objectives would be sound, strong and clear.* Its leaders would know where it was headed and how to get there. Its objectives would also be understood and embraced by all members of the management body. These persons would strive to contribute because the organization's objectives and their own goals would be consistent. There would be a high level of commitment to organization goals as well as to personal goals. Commitment would be based on understanding. To be understood, goals would be quite specific.

Every business has an objective "profit." But this is too vague to motivate persons to greater effectiveness. Profit needs to be converted into concrete objectives. One might be, "To develop a position in the plastic industry which will service 20 percent of this market within the next five years." In a government organization, a specific objective might be "To establish six urban renewal demonstration projects distributed by regions and by city size within 10 months." Government objectives would be implemented through program planning and budgeting rather than the profit motive.

2. *Standards of excellence would be high.* Managers would be thoroughly acquainted with their areas of operation. A premium would be placed on knowledge and thorough analysis rather than on opinion and casual thought.

3. *The work culture would support the work.* It would be an organization culture in which the members would be highly committed to achieving the goals of the organization, with accomplishment the source of individual gratification.

4. *Teamwork would increase individual initiative.* There would be close cooperation within a work team, each supporting the others to get a job done. Teamwork would cut across department lines.

5. *Technical business knowledge is needed.* This is critical for valid decision-making and problem-solving and would come through coaching, developmental assignments, on-the-job training and special courses.

6. *Leadership would be evident.* With sound objectives, high standards of excellence, a culture characterized by high commitment, sound teamwork and technical know-how, productivity would increase.

The way of life or culture of an organization can be a barrier to effectiveness. Barriers may stem from such elements of culture as the attitudes or traditions present in any unit of the organization. Culture both limits and guides the actions of the persons in the organization. Because of traditional ways and fear of change, an organization's leaders may be reluctant to apply modern management science. Yet, the need for change may be quite evident.

Criteria for Change

A sound approach to introducing change and improvement is a *Grid Organization Development* effort. It should:

1. *Involve the widest possible participation of executives, managers and supervisors* to obtain a common set of concepts about how management can be improved.

2. *Be carried out by the organization itself.* The development of subordinates is recognized as part of the manager's job. When organization members from the line become the instructors, higher management's commitment, understanding and support for on-the-job application and change are ensured.

3. *Aim to improve the skills of executives and supervisors who must work together to improve management.* This means the skills of drawing on each other's knowledge and capacities, of making constructive use of disagreement and of making sound decisions to which members become committed.

4. *Aim to improve the ability of all managers to communicate better* so that genuine understanding can prevail.

5. *Clarify styles of management* so that managers learn how the elements of a formal management program (e.g., planned objectives, defined responsibilities, established policies) can be used without the organization's becoming overly formal and complex or unduly restricting personal freedom and needed individual initiative.

6. *Aid each manager to investigate managerial style* to understand its impact and learn to make changes to improve it.

7. *Provide for examination of the organization's culture* to develop managers' understanding of the cultural barriers to effectiveness and how to eliminate them.

8. *Constantly encourage managers to plan and introduce improvements* based on their learnings and analysis of the organization.

How To Get There

Grid Organization Development is one way of increasing the effectiveness of an organization, whether it is a company, a public institution or a government agency. The behavioral science concepts on which organization development is based reach back more than 50 years. Because organization development itself is only a decade or so old, those unfamiliar with its rationale may look upon it with doubt or skepticism, see it as a mystery or a package, a gimmick or a fad. Experience pinpoints which behavioral science concepts are tied to the struggle for a more effective organization. This has done much to help managers apply the pertinent concepts to everyday work.

There are several questions preceding the definition of organization development as it is applied to raise an organization's capacity to operate by using behavioral science concepts. One question is, "What is an organization?" Another is, "What is meant by development?" Finally, "What is it that organization development adds to the organization, that it lacks without it?" The goal of organization development is to increase operational effectiveness by increasing the degree of integration of the organization around its profit/production/or service purpose.

It seems almost self-evident that everyone in an organization would have a clear idea of the *purpose* toward which its efforts were being directed. Yet this is seldom true. For many persons, an organization's purpose is fuzzy, unrealistic and with little force as a motivator. A major organization development contribution is to clarify organization purposes and identify individual goals with them to increase efforts toward their attainment.

As for the *human interaction* process, some styles of managing may decrease a person's desire to contribute to the organization's purpose. The kind of supervision exercised not only fails to make a subordinate feel "in" but even serves to make him or her feel "out." His or her efforts are alienated rather than integrated. This may hold true in the coordination of efforts between organized units. Relationships between divisions, for example, may deteriorate into the kind of disputes that can be reconciled only through arbitration by higher levels of management. At best, they are likely to encourage attitudes of appeasement and compromise.

The organization's *culture*, its history, its traditions, its customs and habits which have evolved from earlier interaction and have become norms regulating human actions and conduct may be responsible for many of the organization's difficulties and a low degree of integration within it.

Organization development deliberately shifts the emphasis away from the organization's structure, from human technical skill, from wherewithal and results *per se* as it diagnoses the organization's ills. Focusing on organization purpose, the human interaction process and organization culture, it accepts these as the areas in which problems are preventing the fullest possible integration within the organization. Once an organization has moved to the point of which the three key properties are fully developed the problems that originally seemed to be related to the others are more easily corrected.

Six-Phase Approach

How, specifically, does one go about organization development? The Managerial Grid is one way of achieving it. The six-phase approach provides the various methods and activities for doing so.

Phase 1 of the six-phase approach involves study of *The Managerial Grid.* Managers learn the Grid concepts in seminars of a week's length.

These seminars are conducted both on a "public" and on an internal basis. They involve hard work. The program requires 30 or more hours of guided study before the beginning of the seminar week. A seminar usually begins Sunday evening, and participants work morning, afternoon and evening through the following Friday.

The sessions include investigation by each person of his or her own managerial approach and alternative ways of managing which he or she is able to learn, experiment with and apply. He or she measures and evaluates team effectiveness in solving problems with others. He or she also studies methods of team action. A high point of Grid Seminar learning is when he or she receives a critique of style of managerial thoughts and performance from other members of his or her team. The emphasis is on personal style of managing, not on character or personality traits. Another high point of the Grid Seminar is when the manager critiques the style of his or her organization's culture, its traditions, precedents and past practices, and begins to consider steps for increasing the effectiveness of the whole organization.

Participants in a Grid Seminar can expect to gain insight into their own and other managerial approaches and develop new ways to solve managerial problems. They can expect to improve team effectiveness skills. They will on completion of Phase 1 have new standards of candor to bring to work activities and a greater awareness of the effects of his company's culture upon the regulation of work.

Comments are often heard to the effect, "The Grid has helped me to better understanding and is useful in many aspects of my life." But the vital question is in the use made of Phase 1 learning. The test for the manager is usefulness on the job. To direct this usefulness to the work situation, and incidentally enhance it from a personal point of view, one proceeds to Phase 2.

Work Team Development

Phase 2 is Work Team Development. As the title suggests, work team development is concerned with development of the individual and the work team. Phases 1 and 2 are often viewed as *management* development, while Phases 3 through 6 move into true *organization development.* The purpose of Phase 2 is to aid work team members to apply their Phase 1 learning directly to the operation of their team.

Individual effort is the raw material out of which sound teamwork is built! It cannot be had just for the asking. Barriers that prevent people from talking out their problems need to be overcome before their full potential can be realized.

Work team development starts with the key executive and those who report to him or her. It then moves down through the organization. Each supervisor sits down with subordinates as a team. They study their barriers to work effectiveness and plan ways to overcome them.

An important result to be expected from the Phase 2 effort is team-wide agreement on ground rules for team operation. The team may also be expected to learn to use critique to improve teamwork on the job. Teamwork is increased through improving communication, control and problem-solving. Getting greater objectivity into work behavior is vital to improved teamwork.

A team analysis of the team culture and operating practices precedes the setting of goals for improvement of the team operation along with a time schedule for achieving these goals. Tied into the goal-setting for the team is personal goal-setting by team members. This might be a goal for trying to change aspects of behavior so as to increase a member's contribution to teamwork. Setting standards for achieving excellence are involved throughout the process.

Intergroup Development

Phase 3 is Intergroup Development. It represents the first step in Grid OD that is applied to organization components rather than to individuals. Its purpose is to achieve *better problem-solving between groups through a closer integration of units that have working interrelationships!*

Managers examine and analyze these working relationships to strengthen and unify the organization across the board. Some dramatic examples of successful Phase 3 applications between labor and management groups are on record. Other units that might appropriately be involved in Phase 3 would be a field unit and the headquarters group to whom it reports, or two sections within a division, or a region and its reporting parent group. It is the matter of coordination between such units that is the target of Phase 3. Problems of integration may be problems of function or merely problems in terms of level.

Management is inclined to solve the problem of functional coordination by setting up systems of reporting and centralized planning. Misunderstandings or disagreements between levels are often viewed as "a communications problem." Phase 3, in recognition that many problems are relationship problems, seeks closer integration of units through the exchange and comparison of group images as set forth by the members of two groups.

Areas of misunderstandings are identified while conditions are created to reduce such intergroup problems and plan steps of operational coordination between the groups. Only groups that stand in a direct, problem-solving relationship with one another and share a need for improved coordination participate in Phase 3 intergroup development. And only those members with key responsibilities for solving the coordination problem are participants.

The activities of Phase 3 naturally follow Phase 2 because when there is conflict between working teams, if the teams themselves have already had the opportunity to solve their internal problems, they are prepared to engage in activities designed to solve their problem of working together. Phase 3 also can be expected to clear the decks for Phases 4 and 5. Any past intergroup problems that were barriers to coordinated effort are solved before the total organization development effort is launched in the latter phases.

A successful Phase 3 will link groups vertically and horizontally and reduce intergroup blockages. This increases the problem-solving between departments, divisions and other segments wherever coordination of effort is a vital necessity. Persons who have participated in Phase 3 report improved intergroup relationships and express appreciation of the team management concept, pointing out that it reverses the traditional procedure in which criticism flows from one level of management down to the next.

Organization Blueprint

Phase 4 calls for the Production of an Organization Blueprint. If Phases 1, 2 and 3 represent pruning the branches, Phase 4 gets at the *root structure.* A long-range blueprint is developed to ensure that the basic strategies of the organization are "right." The immediate goal is to set up a model that is both realistic and obtainable for an organization's system for the future. How is this done? The existing corporate entity is momentarily set aside while an ideal concept is drawn up representing how it would be organized and operated if it were truly effective. The optimal organization blueprint is produced as a result of a policy diagnosis based on study of a model organization culture. The blueprint is drawn up by the top team and moves down through lower levels. The outcome is organization-wide understanding of the blueprint for the future.

It can be expected that as a result of Phase 4, the top team will have set a direction of performance goals to be achieved. Individuals and work teams will have developed understanding and commitment to both general and specific goals to be achieved.

Blueprint Implementation

Phase 5 is Blueprint Implementation. That is, Phase 5 is designed for the carrying out of the organizational plan through activities that change the organization from what it "is" to what it "should be." A Phase 5 may spread over several years, but as a result there comes about the effective realization of the goals that have been set in Phase 4 and specific accomplishments, depending on concrete issues facing the organization. During Phase 5, the members who are responsible for the organization achieve agreement and commitment to courses of action that represent steps to implement the Phase 4 blueprint for the future.

Stabilization

Phase 6 is Stabilization. It is for reinforcing and making habitual the new patterns of management achieved in Phases 1 through 5. Organization members identify tendencies to slip back into the older and less effective patterns of work and take corrective action. Phase 6 involves an overall critique of the state of the OD effort for the purpose of replanning for even greater effectiveness. It is not only to support and strengthen the changes achieved through earlier activities, but also to identify weaknesses and plan ways of eliminating them.

By the time Phase 6 is under way, the stabilization of new communication, control and problem-solving approaches should be evident. Moreover, there should be complete managerial confidence and competence in resisting the pressures to revert to old managerial habits.

As we see our business, government and educational institutions facing crisis after crisis, we realize the need for change becomes more imperative with each passing day. Behavioral science ideas and technology now provide a way through which need can become actuality.

"Organizations *can* change!" This issue is *will* they? Problems are inherent in every organization. What is needed is the will, determination and effort to solve them.

Reference

1. Robert R. Blake and Jane Srygley Mouton, The Managerial Grid Laboratory-Seminar Materials, Austin, Texas. Scientific Methods, Inc., 1962.

16

The Individual, the Organization, and the Career: A Conceptual Scheme

by Edgar H. Schein

INTRODUCTION

The purpose of this paper is to present a conceptual scheme and a set of variables which make possible the description and analysis of an individual's movement through an organization. We usually think of this set of events in terms of the word "career," but we do not have readily available concepts for describing the multitude of separate experiences and adventures which the individual encounters during the life of his organizational career. We also need concepts which can articulate the relationship between 1) the career seen as a set of attributes and experiences of the *individual* who joins, moves through, and finally leaves an organization, and 2) the career as defined by the *organization*—a set of expectations held by individuals inside the organization which guide their decisions about whom to move, when, how, and at what "speed." It is in the different perspectives which are held toward careers by those who act them out and those who make decisons about them, that one may find some of the richest data for understanding the relationship between individuals and organizations.

The ideas in this paper derive from research conducted from 1958-1964 with funds from the Office of Naval Research, Contract NONR 1841 (83) and subsequently with funds from the Sloan Research Fund, M.I.T.

Edgar H. Schein is professor of organizational psychology and management, Sloan School of Management, Massachusetts Institute of Technology.

Reproduced by special permission from the *Journal of Applied Behavioral Science*, "The Individual, the Organization and the Career: A Conceptual Scheme," by Edgar H. Schein, volume 7, number 4, pp. 401-426, 1971, NTL Institute for Applied Behavioral Science.

The ensuing discussion will focus first on structural variables, those features of the organization, the individual, and the career which are the more or less stable elements. Then we will consider a number of "process" variables which will attempt to describe the dynamic interplay between parts of the organization and parts of the individual in the context of his ongoing career. Basically there are two kinds of processes to consider: 1) the influence of the organization on the individual, which can be thought of as a type of *acculturation* or *adult socialization*; and 2) the influence of the individual on the organization, which can be thought of as a process of *innovation* (Schein, 1968).

Both the socialization and innovation involve the relationship between the individual and the organization. They differ in that the former is initiated by the organization and reflects the relatively greater power of the social system to induce change in the individual, whereas the latter is initiated by the individual and reflects his power to change the social system. Ordinarily these two processes are discussed as if they were mutually exclusive of each other and as if they reflected *properties* of the organization or the individual. Thus certain organizations are alleged to produce conformity in virtually all of their members, while certain individuals are alleged to have personal strengths which make them innovators wherever they may find themselves. By using the concept of career as a process over time which embodies many different kinds of relationships between an organization and its members, I hope it can be shown that typically the same person is both influenced (socialized) and in turn influences (innovates), and that both processes coexist (though at different points in the life of a career) within any given organization.

I. THE STRUCTURE OF THE ORGANIZATION

Organizations such as industrial concerns, government agencies, schools, fraternities, hospitals, and military establishments which have a continuity beyond the individual careers of their members can be characterized structurally in many different ways. The particular conceptual model one chooses will depend on the purposes which the model is to fulfill. The structural model which I would like to propose for the analysis of careers is not intended to be a general organizational model; rather, it is designed to elucidate that side of the organization which involves the movement of people through it.

My basic proposition is that the organization should be conceived of as a three-dimensional space like a cone or cylinder in which the external vertical surface is essentially round and in which a core or inner center can be identified. What we traditionally draw as a pyramidal organization on organization charts should really be drawn as a cone in which the various boxes of the traditional chart would represent adjacent sectors of the cone but where movement would be possible within each sector toward or away from the center axis of the cone. Figure 1 shows a redrawing of a typical organization chart according to the present formulation.

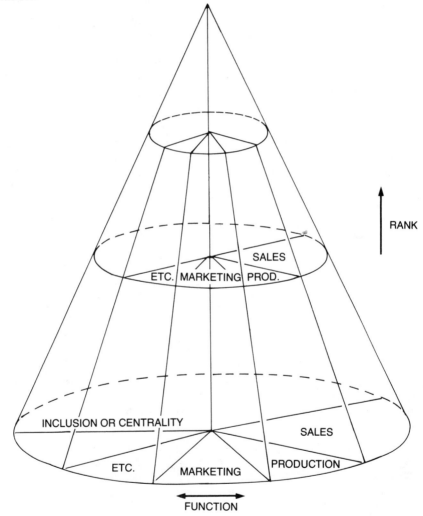

Figure 1. A three-dimensional model of an organization

Movement within the organization can then occur along three conceptually distinguishable dimensions:

  a. *Vertically*—corresponding roughly to the notion of increasing or decreasing one's *rank* or *level* in the organization;
  b. *Radially*—corresponding roughly to the notion of increasing or decreasing one's *centrality* in the organization, one's degree of being more or less "on the inside";
  c. *Circumferentially*—corresponding roughly to the notion of changing one's function or one's division of the organization.

Whether movement along one of these dimensions is ever independent of movement along another one is basically an empirical matter. For present purposes it is enough to establish that it would be, in principle, possible for an individual to move along any one of the dimensions without changing his position on either of the other ones.

Corresponding to the three types of movement one can identify three types of *boundaries* which characterize the internal structure of the organization:

  a. *Hierarchical boundaries*—which separate the hierarchical levels from each other;
  b. *Inclusion boundaries*—which separate individuals or groups who differ in the degree of their centrality;[1]
  c. *Functional or departmental boundaries*—which separate departments, divisions, or different functional groupings from each other.

Boundaries can vary in 1) *number*, 2) *degree of permeability*, and 3) type of *filtering properties* they possess. For example, in the military there are a great many functional boundaries separating the different line and staff activities, but the overall policy of rotation and keeping all officers highly flexible makes these boundaries highly permeable in the sense that people move a great deal from function to function. On the other hand, a university would also have many functional boundaries corresponding to the different academic departments, but these would be highly impermeable in the sense that no one would seriously consider the movement of an English professor to a Chemistry department, or vice versa. A small family-run business, to take a third example, is an organization with very few functional boundaries in that any manager performs all of the various functions.

---

[1]The organization as a multi-layered system corresponds to Lewin's concept of the personality as a multi-layered system like an onion (Lewin, 1948).

Similarly, with respect to hierarchial or inclusion boundaries one can find examples of organizations in which there are many or few levels, many or few degrees of "being in," with the boundaries separating the levels or inner regions being more or less permeable. The external inclusion boundary is, of course, of particular significance, in that its permeability defines the ease or difficulty of initial entry into the organization. Those companies or schools which take in virtually anyone but keep only a small percentage of high performers can be described as having a highly permeable external inclusion boundary, but a relatively impermeable inclusion boundary fairly close to the exterior. On the other hand, the company or school which uses elaborate selection procedures to take in only very few candidates, expects those taken in to succeed, and supports them accordingly, can be described as having a relatively impermeable inclusion boundary fairly close to the exterior. On the other hand, the company or school which uses elaborate selection procedures to take in only very few candidates, expects those taken in to succeed, and supports them accordingly, can be described as having a relatively impermeable external inclusion boundary but no other impermeable boundaries close to the exterior.

Further refinement can be achieved in this model if one considers the particular types of filters which characterize different boundaries, i.e., which specify the process or set of rules by which one passes through the boundary. Thus hierarchical boundaries filter individuals in terms of attributes such as seniority, merit, personal characteristics, types of attitudes held, who is sponsoring them, and so on. Functional boundaries filter much more in terms of the specific competencies of the individual, or his "needs" for broader experience in some scheme of training and development (the latter would certainly not be considered in reference to a hierarchical boundary). Inclusion boundaries are probably the most difficult to characterize in terms of their filtering system in that the system may change as one gets closer to the inner core of the organization. Competence may be critical in permeating the external boundary, but factors such as personality, seniority, and willingness to play a certain kind of political game may be critical in becoming a member of the "inner circle."[2] Filter properties may be formally stated requirements for admission or may be highly informal norms shared by the group to be entered.

With reference to individual careers, organizations can be analyzed and described on the basis of 1) number of boundaries of each type, 2) the

---

[2]One of the best descriptions of such filters in an organization can be found in Dalton's (1959) discussion of career advancement in the companies to be studied.

boundary permeability of the different boundaries, and 3) the filtering system which characterizes them. For example, most universities have two hierarchical boundares (between the ranks of assistant, associate, and full professor), two inclusion boundaries (for initial entry and tenure), and as many functional boundaries as there are departments and schools. Filters for promotion and tenure may or may not be the same depending on the university, but will generally involve some combination of scholarly or research publication, teaching ability, and "service" to the institution. Organizations like industrial ones which do not have a tenure system will be harder to diagnose as far as inclusion filters go, but the inclusion boundaries are just as much a part of their system. The variables identified thus far are basically intended as a set of categories in terms of which to describe and compare different types of organizations in respect to the career paths they generate.

A final variable which needs to be considered is the *shape* of the three-dimensional space which characterizes the organization. The traditional pyramidal organization would presumably become in this scheme a cone. An organization with very many levels could be thought of as a very steep cone, while one with few levels could be thought of as a flat cone. The drawing of the organization as a cone implies, however, that the highest level person is also the most central which is, of course, not necessarily the case. If the top of the organization is a management team, one might think of a truncated cone; if there is a powerful board of directors who represent a higher level but a wider range of centrality one might think of an inverted cone, the point of which touches the apex of the main cone and which sits on top of the main one. In universities where the number of full professors is as large as the number of assistant professors, one might think of the organization more as a cylinder with a small cone on top of it representing the administration.

I am not stating any requirements that the shape of the organization be symmetrical. If a certain department is very large but very peripheral, it might best be thought of as a large bulge on an otherwise round shape. If one considers internal inclusion boundaries one may have some departments which are in their entirety very central and thus reach the vertical axis (core), while other departments do not contain anyone who is very central in the organization and thus do not reach the core at all. The shape of the inner core is also highly variable. It may be an inverted cone which would imply that the number of central people *increases* with rank. Or it might be a cylinder which would imply that there are equal numbers of central people at all ranks. Or it might be some highly asymmetrical shape reflecting the reality that the number of central people varies with length of service, department, political connections with higher ranks, access to critical company informations, etc.[3]

Some Problems of Measuring Organizational Structure

The problem of measurement varies greatly as a function of the degree to which boundaries and their filtering characteristics are explicitly acknowledged by a given organization and by the wider society. Thus, hierarchical boundaries which separate levels are a widely accepted fact of organizational life and the rules for permeating them tend to be fairly explicit. To the extent that implicit informal factors do operate it becomes more difficult to measure the filtering properties of the hierarchical boundaries in any given organization.

Functional boundaries are generally the easiest to identify because our typical analysis of organizations emphasizes different functions and departments. Similarly, the rules of entry to a function or department tend to be fairly explicit.

The inclusion boundaries are the hardest to identify and measure because to a considerable extent their very existence usually remains implicit. While it may be clear to everyone in a company that there is an inner circle (which may cut across many rank levels), this fact may be denied when an outsider probes for the data. The filtering mechanism may be even more difficult to identify because even the willing informant, including members of the inner circle, may be unclear about the actual mechanisms by which people move toward the center. Even the *concept* of centrality is unclear in that it does not discriminate between a) an individual person's *feeling* of being central or peripheral, and b) some *objective criterion* of his actual position in the organization's social structure.

In the discussion thus far I have meant by the term "centrality" the person's objective position as measured by the degree to which company secrets are entrusted to him, by ratings of others of his position, and by his power. His subjective rating of himself might correlate highly with these other measures and thus might prove to be a simpler measuring device, but it does not basically define centrality because a person may misperceive his own position.

It may be argued that I have over-stated the assumption that an organization is an integrated unified entity. It may after all be only a

---

[3]Dalton (1959) has identified what he calls "vertical cliques" which cover different ranks as well as departments of an industrial organization.

group of individual people or sub-groups coordinating their activities to some degree but operating from quite different premises. Therefore there are no "organizational" boundaries, only individual approaches to the movement and promotion of their subordinates.

There is ample evidence for the assertion that people who associate with each other around a common task for any length of time *do* develop group boundaries of various sorts and a set of norms which define their probability and filtering properties (e.g. Homans, 1950). But it is quite possible that several such groups co-exist within a larger social system and develop different norms. In applying the concepts which I am outlining in this paper it is therefore necessary to identify as the "organization" a group which has interacted for a sufficient length of time to have developed some common norms. Later, in analyzing the progress of a career, it will of course be necessary to consider the difficulties which are created for the individual as he moves from a group with one set of norms about boundaries to another group with a different set of norms about boundaries, even though both groups are part of the same larger organization.

II. THE STRUCTURE OF THE INDIVIDUAL

Any given individual can be thought of as a more or less integrated set of social selves organized around a basic image or concept of self. His basic temperament, intellectual equipment, learned patterns of feeling expression, and psychological defenses underlie and partially determine this self-image and the kinds of social selves which the individual constructs for himself to deal with his environment. But our focus is on the constructed selves which make it possible for the individual to fulfill various role expectations in his environment, not on the more enduring underlying qualities.

I am using the concept of a constructed social self in the sense of Mead (1934) and more recently Becker (1961) and Goffman (1955, 1957, 1959), as a set of assumptions about, perceptions of, and claims on a given social situation in which role expectations may be more or less well defined. The basic rules of conduct and interaction in terms of which the person orients himself to any social situation are largely culturally determined, but these basic rules still leave each individual a wide latitude in how he will choose to present himself in any given situation (the "line" he will take), and how much social value or status he will claim for himself (his "face").

This conception of the individual places primary emphasis on those aspects of his total being which are the most immediate product of socialization, which most immediately engage other persons in daily life, and which are most dependent on the reinforcement or confirmation of others. For example, at a *basic* level, a person may be temperamentally easily frustrated, may have developed a character structure around the repression of strong aggressive impulses, and may rely heavily on denial and reaction-formation as defense mechanisms. These characteristics describe his basic underlying personality structure but they tell us practically nothing of how he presents himself to others, what his self-image is, how he takes characteristic occupational or social roles, how much value he places on himself, and what kind of interaction patterns he engages in with others.

Focusing on his constructed selves, on the other hand, might show us that this person presents himself to others as very even tempered and mild mannered, that in group situations he takes a role of harmonizing any incipient fights which develop between others, that he tries to appear as the logical voice of reason in discussions and is made uneasy by emotions, that he prefers to analyze problems and advise others rather than getting into action situations (i.e., he prefers some kind of "staff" position), and that he does not get too close to people or depend too heavily upon them. None of the latter characteristics are inconsistent with the basic structure, but they could not have been specifically predicted from the basic structure. Persons with the same kind of underlying character structure might enter similar interactive situations quite differently. In other words, I am asserting that it is not sufficient to describe a person in terms of basic personality structure, if we are to understand his relationship to organizations. Furthermore, it is possible to analyze the person's functioning at the social self level and this level of analysis is most likely to be productive for the understanding of career patterns and the reciprocal influence process between individual and organization.

Each of us learns to construct somewhat different selves for the different kinds of situations in which we are called on to perform, and for the different kinds of roles we are expected to take. Thus, I am a somewhat different person at work than at home; I present myself somewhat differently to my superior than to my subordinate, to my wife than to my children, to my doctor than to a salesman, when I am at a party than when I am at work, and so on. The long and complex process of socialization teaches us the various norms, rules of conduct, values and attitudes, and desirable role behaviors through which one's obligations in situations and roles can be fulfilled. All of these patterns become part of us so that to a large extent we are not conscious of the almost instantaneous choices we make among possible patterns as we "compose ourselves" for entry into a new social situation. Yet these patterns can be immediately brought to consciousness if the presented self chosen is one which does not fit the situation, that is, fails to get confirmation from others.

Failure to get confirmation of a self which involves a certain claimed value is felt by the actor as a threat to his face; he finds himself in a situation in which he is about to lose face if he and the others do not take action to reequilibrate the situation (Goffman, 1955). A simple example of this process can be seen if a person presents himself to others as a humorous fellow who can tell a good joke, tries telling a joke which turns out not to be seen as funny, and "recoups" or avoids the loss of face which is threatened by the silence of others by humorously derogating his own joke telling ability, thereby signalling to the others that he is now claiming a differing and somewhat less "valuable" (i.e., more humble) self. The others may signal their acceptance of the latter self by various reassurances, but all parties know very well the unmistakeable meaning of the silence following the first joke.

The various selves which we bring to situations and from which we choose as we present ourselves to others, overlap in varying degrees in that many of the attributes possessed by the person are relevant to several of his selves. Thus, emotional sensitivity may be just as relevant when a person is dealing with a customer in a sales relationship as it is with his wife and children in a family relationship. The person's attributes and underlying character structure thus provide some of the common threads which run through the various social selves he constructs, and provide one basis for seeking order and consistency among them.

Another basis for such order and consistency is to be found in the role demands the person faces. That is, with respect to each role which the person takes or to which he aspires, one can distinguish certain central expectations, certain essential attributes which the person must have or certain behaviors he must be willing to engage in, in order to fulfill the role minimally (pivotal attributes or norms). Other attributes and behaviors are desirable and relevant though not necessary (*relevant* attributes or norms), while still another set can be identified as irrelevant with respect to the role under analysis, though this other set may define various "latent" role capacities the person may have (*peripheral* attributes or norms).[4] The pivotal, relevant, and peripheral attributes of a role will define to some degree the filters which operate at the boundary guarding access to that role.

These changes which occur in a person during the course of his career, as a result of adult socialization or acculturation, are changes in the nature and integration of his social selves. It is highly unlikely that he will change substantially in his basic character structure and his pattern

---

[4]This analysis is based on the distinction made by Nadel (1957) and utilized in a study of out-patient nurses by Bennis *et al.* (1959).

of psychological defenses, but he may change drastically in his social selves in the sense of developing new attitudes and values, new competencies, new images of himself, and new ways of entering and conducting himself in social situations. As he faces new roles which bring new demands, it is from his repertory of attributes and skills that he constructs or reconstructs himself to meet these demands.

A final point concerns the problem of locating what we ordinarily term as the person's beliefs, attitudes, and values at an appropriate level of his total personality. It has been adequately demonstrated (e.g., Adorne et al., 1950; Smith, Bruner, and White, 1956; Katz, 1960) that beliefs, attitudes, and values are intimately related to basic character structure and psychological defenses. But this relationship differs in different people according to the functions which beliefs, attitudes, and values serve for them. Smith et al. distinguish three such functions: 1) reality testing —where beliefs and attitudes are used by the person to discover and test the basic reality around him; 2) social adjustment —where beliefs and attitudes are used by the person to enable him to relate comfortably to others, express his membership in groups, and his social selves; and 3) externalization —where beliefs and attitudes are used to express personal conflicts, conscious and unconscious motives, and feelings.

The kind of function which beliefs and attitudes serve for the individual and the kind of flexibility he has in adapting available social selves to varying role demands will define for each individual some of his strengths and weaknesses with respect to organizational demands and the particular pattern of socialization and innovation which one might expect in his career.

For example, a given individual might well have a number of highly labile social selves in which his beliefs and attitudes serve only a social adjustment function. At the same time, he might have one or more other highly stable selves in which he shows a great rigidity of belief and attitude. The process of socialization might then involve extensive adaptation and change on the part of the person in his "labile" social selves without touching other more stable parts of him. He might show evidence of having been strongly influenced by the organization, but only in certain areas.[5] Whether this same person would be capable of innovating during his career would depend on whether his job would at any time call on his more stable social selves. The activation of such stable selves might occur only with promotion, the acquisition of increasing responsibility, or acceptance into a more central region of the organization.

---

[5]For a relevant analysis of areas which the organization is perceived to be entitled to influence see Schein and Ott (1962) and Schein and Lippitt (1965).

When we think of organizations infringing on the private lives of their members we think of a more extensive socialization process which involves changes in more stable beliefs and attitudes which are integrated into more stable social selves. Clearly it is possible for such "deeper" influence to occur, but in assessing depth of influence in any given individual-organizational relationship we must be careful not to overlook adaptational patterns which look like deep influence but are only the activation of and changes in relatively more labile social selves.

Some Problems of Measuring Individual Structure

I do not know of any well worked out techniques for studying a person's repertory of social selves, their availability, lability, and associated beliefs and attitudes. Something like rating behavior during role-playing or socio-drama would be a possible method but it is difficult to produce in full force the situational and role demands which elicit from us the social selves with which we play for keeps. Assessment techniques which involve observing the person in actual ongoing situations are more promising but more expensive. It is possible that a well motivated person would find it possible to provide accurate data through self-description, i.e. tell accurately how he behaves in situations that he typically faces.

If observation and interview both are impractical, it may be possible to obtain written self-descriptions or adjective check-list data (where the adjectives are specifically descriptive of interactional or social behavior) in response to hypothetical problem situations which are posed for the individual. The major difficulty with this technique would be that it is highly likely that much of the taking of a social self is an unconscious process which even a well-motivated subject could not reconstruct accurately. Hence his data would be limited to his conscious self-perceptions. Such conscious self-perceptions could, of course, be supplemented by similar descriptions of the subject made by others.

III. THE STRUCTURE OF THE CAREER

The career can be looked at from a number of points of view. The individual moving through an organization builds certain perspectives having to do with advancement, personal success, nature of the work, and so on (Becker *et al.*, 1961). Those individuals in the organization who take the "organizational" point of view, build perspectives in terms of the development of human resources, allocation of the right people to right slots, optimum rates of movement through departments and levels, and so on. A third possible perspective which one can take toward the career is that of the outside observer of the whole process, in which case one is struck by certain basic similarities between organizational careers and other transitional processes which occur in society such as socialization, education, the acculturation of immigrants, initiation into groups, etc. If one takes this observer perspective one can describe the structure and process of the career in terms of a set of basic *stages* which create transitional and terminal *statuses* or *positions*, and involve certain psychological and organizational processes (see Table 1).

In the first column of the Table 1, I have placed the basic stages as well as the key transitional events which characterize movement from one stage to another. The terminology chosen deliberately reflects events in organizations such as schools, religious orders, or fraternities where the stages are well articulated. These same stages and events are assumed to exist and operate in industrial, governmental, and other kinds of organizations even though they are not as clearly defined or labelled. Where a stage does not exist for a given organization, we can ask what the functional equivalent of that stage is. For example, the granting of tenure and the stage of permanent membership is not clearly identified in American business or industrial concerns, yet there are powerful norms operating in most such organizations to retain employees who have reached a certain level and/or have had a certain number of years of service. These norms lead to personnel policies which on the average guarantee the employee a job and thus function as equivalents to a more formal tenure system.

It should be noted that the kind of stages and terminology chosen also reflects the assumption that career movement is basically a process of learning or socialization (during which organizational influence is at a maximum), followed by a process of performance (during which individual influence on the organization is at a maximum), followed by a process of either becoming obsolete or learning new skills which lead to further movement. These are relatively broad categories which are not fully refined in the table. For example, in the case of becoming obsolete a further set of alternative stages may be provided by the organizational structure — 1) retraining for new career; 2) lateral transfer and permanent leveling off with respect to rank, but not necessarily with respect to inclusion; 3) early forced exit (early "retirement"); 4) retention in the given stage in spite of marginal performance (retaining "dead wood" in the organization).

In the second column of the table are found the kinds of terms which we use to characterize the statuses or positions which reflect the different stages of the career. In the third column I have tried to list the kinds of interactional processes which occur between the individual and the organization. These processes can be thought of as reflecting preparation of the incumbent for boundary transition, preparation of the group for

Table 1
Basic Stages, Positions, and Processes Involved in a Career

Basic Stages and Transitions	Statuses or Positions	Psychological and Organizational Processes transactions between individual and organization
1. Pre-entry Entry (trans.)	Aspirant, applicant, rushee Entrant, postulant, recruit	Preparation, education, anticipatory socialization Recruitment, rushing, testing, screening, selection, acceptance ("hiring"); passage through external inclusion boundary; rites of entry; induction and orientation
2. Basic training, novitiate	Trainee, novice, pledge	Training, indoctrination, socialization, testing of the man by the organization, tentative acceptance into group
Initiation, first vows (trans.)	Initiate, graduate	Passage through first inner inclusion boundary, acceptance as member and conferring of organizational status, rite of passage and acceptance
3. First regular assignment	New member	First testing by the man of his own capacity to function; granting of real responsibility (playing for keeps); passage through functional boundary with assignment to specific job or department
Sub-stages 3a. Learning the job 3b. Maximum performance 3c. Becoming obsolete 3d. Learning new skills, etc. Promotion or leveling off (trans.)		Indoctrination and testing of man by immediate work group leading to acceptance or rejection; if accepted further education and socialization (learning the ropes); preparation for higher status through coaching, seeking visibility, finding sponsors, etc. Preparation, testing, passage through hierarchical boundary, rite of passage; may involve passage through functional boundary as well (rotation)
4. Second assignment	Legitimate member (fully accepted)	Processes under no. 3 repeat
Sub-stages 5. Granting of tenure Termination and exit (trans.)	Permanent member Old timer, senior citizen	Passage through another inner conclusion boundary Preparation for exit, cooling the mark out, rites of exit (testimonial dinners, etc.)
6. Post-exit	Alumnus emeritus, retired	Granting of peripheral status

his arrival, actual transition processes such as tests, rites of passage, status conferring ceremonies, and post transition processes prior to preparation for new transitions.[6]

Basically the dynamics of the career can be thought of as a *sequence of boundary passages*. The person can move up, around, and in, and every career is some sequence of moves along these three paths. Thus, it is possible to move primarily inward without moving upward or around as in the case of the janitor who has remained a janitor all of his career but, because of association with others who have risen in the hierarchy, enjoys their confidences and a certain amount of power through his opportunities to coach newcomers.

It is also possible to move primarily upward without moving inward or around, as in the case of the scarce highly trained technical specialist who must be elevated in order to be held by the organization but who is given little administrative power or confidential information outside of his immediate area. Such careers are frequently found in universities where certain scholars can become full professors without ever taking the slightest interest in the university as an organization and where they are not seen as being very central to its functioning.

The problem of the professional scientist or engineer in industry hinges precisely on this issue, in that the scientist often feels excluded in spite of "parallel ladders," high salaries, frequent promotions, and fancy titles. Moving in or toward the center of an organization implies increase in power and access to information which enables the person to influence his own destiny. The "parallel ladder" provides rank but often deprives the professional in industry of the kind of power and sense of influence which is associated with centrality.

Finally, movement around without movement in or up is perhaps most clearly exemplified in the perpetual student, or the person who tries some new skill or work area as soon as he has reasonably mastered what he had been doing. Such circumferential or lateral movement is also a way in which organizations handle those whom they are unwilling to promote or get rid of. Thus, they get transferred from one job to another, often with the polite fiction that the transfers constitute promotions of a sort.

In most cases, the career will be some combination of movement in all three dimensions—the person will have been moved up, will have had experience in several departments, and will have moved into a more central position in the organization. Whether any given final position results from smooth or even movement or represents a zig-zagging course is another aspect to consider. Because sub-cultures always tend

---

[6]See Strauss (1959) for an excellent description of some of these processes.

to exist within a large organization, one may assume that any promotion or transfer results in some *temporary* loss of centrality, in that the person will not immediately be accepted by the new group into which he has been moved. In fact, one of the critical skills of getting ahead may be the person's capacity to regain a central position in any new group into which he is placed.[7] In the military service, whether a person is ultimately accepted as a good leader or not may depend upon his capacity to take a known difficult assignment in which he temporarily loses acceptance and centrality and to succeed in spite of this in gaining high productivity and allegiance from the men.

The attempt to describe the career in terms of sequential steps or stages introduces some possible distortions. For example, various of the stages may be collapsed in certain situations into a single major event. A young man may report for work and be given as his first assignment a highly responsible job, may be expected to learn as he actually performs, and is indoctrinated by his experiences at the same time that he is using them as a test of his self. The whole assignment may serve the function of an elaborate initiation rite during which the organization tests the man as well. The stages outlined in the chart all occur in one way or another, but they may occur simultaneously and thus be difficult to differentiate.

Another distortion is the implication in the chart that boundaries are crossed in certain set sequences. In reality it may be the case that the person enters a given department on a provisional basis before he has achieved any basic acceptance by the organization so that the functional boundary passage precedes inclusion boundary passage. On the other hand, it may be more appropriate to think of the person as being located in a kind of organizational limbo during his basic training, an image which certainly fits well those training programs which rotate the trainee through all of the departments of the organization without allowing him to do any real work in any of them.

A further complexity arises from the fact that each department, echelon, and power clique is a sub-organization with a sub-culture which superimposes on the major career pattern a set of, in effect, sub-careers within each of the sub-organizations. The socialization which occurs in sub-units creates difficulties or opportunities for the person to the degree that the sub-culture is well integrated with the larger organizational culture. If conflicts exist, the person must make a complex analysis of the

---

[7]In a fascinating experiment with children, Merei, 1941, showed that a strong group could resist the impact of a strong leader child and force the leader child to conform to group norms, but that the skillful leader child first accepted the norms, gained acceptance and centrality, and then began to influence the group toward his own goals.

major organizational boundaries to attempt to discover whether subsequent passage through a hierarchical boundary (promotion) for example, is more closely tied to acceptance or rejection of subcultural norms (i.e., does the filter operate more in terms of the person's capacity to show loyalty even in the face of frustration or in terms of disloyalty for the sake of larger organizational goals even though this entails larger personal risks?).

IV. IMPLICATIONS AND HYPOTHESES

Thus far I have tried to develop a set of concepts and a kind of model of the organization, the individual, and the career. The kinds of concepts chosen were intended to be useful in identifying the interactions between the individual and the organization as he pursues his career within the organization. We need concepts of this sort to make it possible to compare organizations with respect to the kinds of career paths they generate, and to make it possible to describe the vicissitudes of the career itself. Perhaps the most important function of the concepts, however, is to provide an analytical frame of reference which will make it possible to generate some hypotheses about the crucial process of organizational influences on the individual (socialization) and individual influences on the organization (innovation). Using the concepts defined above, I would now like to try to state some hypotheses as a first step toward building a genuinely socio-psychological theory of career development.

Hypothesis 1. Organizational *socialization* will occur primarily in connection with the passage through hierarchical and inclusion boundaries; efforts at *education* and *training* will occur primarily in connection with the passage through functional boundaries. In both instances, the amount of effort at socialization and/or training will be at maximum just prior to boundary passage, but will continue for some time after boundary passage.

The underlying assumption behind this hypothesis is that 1) the organization is most concerned about correct values and attitudes at the point where it is granting a member more authority and/or centrality, and 2) the individual is most vulnerable to socialization pressures just before and after boundary passage. He is vulnerable before because of the likelihood that he is anxious to move up or in and is therefore motivated to learn organizational norms and values; he is vulnerable after boundary passage because of the new role demands and his needs to reciprocate with correct attitudes and values for having been passed. It is a commonly observed organizational fact that a griping employee often becomes a devoted, loyal follower once he has been promoted and has acquired responsibility for the socialization of other employees.[8]

Hypothesis 2. Innovation, or the individual's influence on the organization, will occur *in the middle* of a given stage of the career, at a maximum distance from boundary passage.

The person must be far enough from the earlier boundary passage to have learned the requirements of the new position and to have earned centrality in the new sub-culture, yet must be far enough from his next boundary passage to be fully involved in the present job without being concerned about preparing himself for the future. Also, his power to induce change is lower if he is perceived as about to leave (the lame duck phenomenon). Attempts to innovate closer to boundary passage either will meet resistance or will produce only temporary change.

Hypothesis 3. In general, the process of socialization will be more prevalent in the early stages of a career and the process of innovation late in the career, *but both processes occur at all stages.*

Figure 2 attempts to diagram the relationships discussed above. The boundaries that are most relevant to these influence processes are the hierarchical ones in that the power of the organization to socialize is most intimately tied to the status rewards it can offer. One cannot ignore, however, the crucial role which inclusion boundaries and centrality may play in affecting the amount of socialization or innovation. If it is a correct assumption that genuinely creative innovative behavior can occur only when the person is reasonably secure in his position, this is tantamount to saying that he has to have a certain amount of acceptance and centrality to innovate. On the other hand, if the acceptance and centrality involves a sub-culture which is itself hostile to certain organizational goals, it becomes more difficult for the person to innovate (except in reference to sub-cultural norms). This is the case of the men in the production shop with fancy rigs and working routines which permit them to get the job done faster and more comfortably (thus innovating in the service of sub-group norms), yet which are guarded from management eyes and used only to make life easier for the men themselves. One thing which keeps these processes from being shared is the sub-group pressure on the individual and his knowledge that his acceptance by the sub-group hinges on his adherence to its norms. Innovation by individuals will always occur to some degree, but it does not necessarily lead to any new ideas or processes which are functional for the total organization.

---

[8]See also Lieberman (1956) for an excellent research study demonstrating attitude change after promotion.

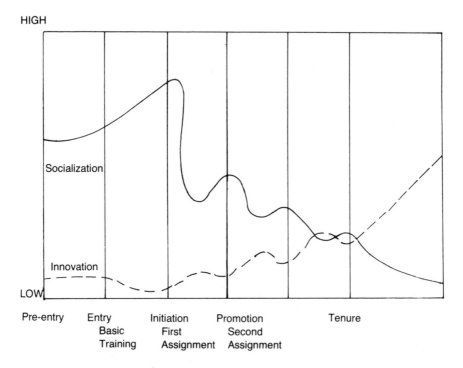

Figure 2. Socialization and innovation during the stages of the career

Whether or not organizational innovation occurs, then becomes more a function of the degree to which sub-group norms are integrated with the norms and goals of the total organization. In complex organizations there are many forces acting which tend to make groups defensive and competitive, thus increasing the likelihood of their developing conflicting norms (Schein, 1965). Where this happens the process of innovation can still be stimulated through something akin to the "heroic cycle" by which societies revitalize themselves. Campbell shows how the myth of the hero in many cultures is essentially similar (Campbell, 1956). Some respected member of the total organization or society is sent away (freed from the sub-group norms) to find a magic gift which he must bring back to revitalize the organization. By temporarily stepping outside the organization the person can bring back new ideas and methods without directly violating sub-group norms and thus protect his own position as well as the face of the other group members.

Hypothesis 4. Socialization or influence will involve primarily the more labile social selves of the individual, while innovation will involve primarily the more stable social selves of the individual, provided the individual is not held captive in the organization.

I am assuming that if socialization forces encounter a stable part of the person which he is unable or unwilling to change, he will leave the organization if he can. On the other hand, if a given way of operating which flows from a stable portion of the individual is incompatible with other organizational procedures or norms, i.e., if innovation is impossible, the individual will also leave. The only condition under which neither of these statements would hold is the condition in which the individual is physically or psychologically unable to leave.

Hypothesis 5. A change in the more stable social selves as a result of socialization will occur only under conditions of coercive persuasion, i.e., where the individual cannot or does not psychologically feel free to leave the organization.

Conditions under which coercive persuasion would operate can be produced by a variety of factors: a tight labor market in which movement to other organizations is constrained; an employment contract which involves a legal or moral obligation to remain with the organization; a reward system which subtly but firmly entraps the individual through stock options, pension plans, deferred compensation plans and the like.

If conditions such as those mentioned above do operate to entrap the individual and, if he in turn begins to conform to organizational norms even in terms of the more stable parts of his self, he will indeed become unable to innovate. It is this pattern which has been identified by Merton as operating in bureaucratic frameworks and which writers like W. H. Whyte have decried with the label of "organizational man." It should be noted, however, that this pattern occurs only under certain conditions; it should not be confused with normal processes of socialization, those involving the more labile parts of the person's self and the more pivotal role requirements or norms of the organization.

An important corrollary of this hypothesis is that if organizations wish to insure a high rate of innovation, they must also insure highly permeable external boundaries, i.e., must insure that employees feel free to leave the organization. The less permeable the exit boundary, the greater the pressures for total conformity.

SUMMARY

In this paper I have tried to present a set of concepts about the nature of the organization, the nature of the individual, and the nature of the career—the set of events which tie the individual and the organization together. My purpose has been to provide a frame of reference and a set of concepts which would make it possible to think in more empirical terms about a variable like "career," yet which would relate this variable both to organizational and psychological variables. Using concepts such as "organizational boundaries," labile and stabile "social selves," career stages and transitional processes, I have tried to identify some hypotheses about organizational influences on the individual (socialization) and individual influences on the organization (innovation).

References

Adorno, T. W. *The authoritarian personality.* New York: Harper, 1950.

Becker, H. S. *et al., Boys in white.* Chicago: University of Chicago Press, 1961.

Bennis, W. G. *et al.,* The role of the nurse in the OPD. Boston University Research Rept. No. 39, 1959.

Campbell, J. *The hero with a thousand faces.* New York: Meridian, 1956.

Dalton, M. *Men who manage.* New York: Wiley, 1959.

Goffman, E. On face work. *Psychiatry,* 1955, 18, 213-231.

Goffman, E. Alienation from interaction. *Human Relations,* 1957, 10, 47-60.

Goffman, E. *The presentation of self in everyday life.* Garden City, New York: Doubleday Anchor, 1959.

Homans, G. C. *The human group.* New York: Harcourt Brace, 1950.

Katz, D. (ed.) Attitude change. *Public Opinion Quarterly,* 1960, 24, 163-365.

Lewin, K. *Resolving social conflicts.* New York: Harper, 1948.

Lieberman, S. The effects of changes in roles on the attitudes of role occupants. *Human Relations,* 1956, 9, 385-402.

Mead, G. H. *Mind, self, and society.* Chicago, Ill.: University of Chicago Press, 1934.

Merei, F. Group leadership and institutionalization. *Human Relations,* 1941, 2, 23-39.

Nadel, F. *The theory of social structure.* Glencoe, Illinois: Free Press, 1957.

Schein, E. H. & Ott, J. S. The legitimacy of organizational influence. *Amer. J. of Sociology,* 1962, 6, 682-689.

Schein, E. H. *Organizational psychology.* Englewood Cliffs, N. J.: Lrentice-Hall, 1965.

Schein, E. H. & Lippitt, G. L. Supervisory attitudes toward the legitimacy of influencing subordinates. *J. Appl. Behavioral Science,* 1966, 2, 199-209.

Schein, E. H. Organizational socialization. *Industrial Management Review* (M.I.T.), 1968.

Smith, M. B., Bruner, J. S., and White, R. W. *Opinions and personality.* New York: Wiley, 1956.

Strauss, A. *Mirrors and masks.* Glencoe, Ill.: Free Press, 1959.

17

Today's Problems with Tomorrow's Organizations

by Chris Argyris

There is a revolution brewing in the introduction of new organizational forms to complement or to replace the more traditional pyramidal form. I believe, on the basis of some recent research, that the new forms are basically sound. However, because of the methods used to introduce them and because of those used to maintain them, many of the unintended self-defeating consequences of the older structures are re-appearing.

Two major causes for this revolution are the new requirements for organizational survival in an increasingly competitive environment and the new administrative and information technology available to deal with complexity. Wallace (1963) summarizes these requirements as:

1. the technological revolution (complexity and variety of products, new materials and processes, and the effects of massive research),
2. competition and the profit squeeze (saturated markets, inflation of wage and material costs, production efficiency),
3. the high cost of marketing, and
4. the unpredictability of consumer demands (due to high discretionary income, wide range of choices available, and shifting tastes).

To make matters more difficult, the costs of new products are increasing while their life expectancy is decreasing.

Chris Argyris is James Bryant Conant Professor of Education and Organization Behavior, Harvard University.

From *The Journal of Management Studies*, 4(1), 1967, 31-55. Reprinted by permission.

Requirements of Tomorrow's Organizations

In order to meet these challenges, modern organizations need:

1. much more creative planning,
2. the development of valid and useful knowledge about new products and new processes,
3. increased concerted and cooperative action with internalized long-range commitment by all involved, and
4. increased understanding of criteria for effectiveness that meet the challenges of complexity.

These requirements, in turn, depend upon:

1. continuous and open access between individuals and groups,
2. free, reliable communication, where
3. interdependence is the foundation for individual and departmental cohesiveness and
4. trust, risk-taking, and helping each other is prevalent, so that
5. conflict is identified and managed in such a way that the destructive win-lose stances with their accompanying polarization of views are minimized and effective problem-solving is maximized.

These conditions, in turn, require individuals who:

1. do not fear stating their complete views,
2. are capable of creating groups that maximize the unique contributions of each individual,
3. value and seek to integrate their contributions into a creative total, final contribution,
4. rather than needing to be individually rewarded for their contributions, thus
5. finding the search for valid knowledge and the development of the best possible solution intrinsically satisfying.

Unfortunately, these conditions are difficult to create. Elsewhere I have tried to show that the traditional pyramidal structure and managerial controls tend to place individuals and departments in constant interdepartmental warfare, where win-lose competition creates polarized stances, that tend to get resolved by the superior making the decisions, thereby creating a dependence upon him. Also, there is a tendency toward conformity, mistrust, and lack of risk-taking among the peers that results in focusing upon individual survival, requiring the seeking out of the scarce rewards, identifying with successful ventures (be a hero), and being careful to avoid being blamed for or identified with a failure, thereby becoming a bum. All these adaptive behaviors tend to induce low interpersonal competence and can lead the organization, over the long run, to become rigid, sticky, less innovative, resulting in less than effective decisions with even less internal commitment to the decisions on the part of those involved.

Some people have experimented by structuring the organization in such a way that people representing the major functions (marketing, engineering, manufacturing, and finance) are coerced to work together. Unfortunately, the pyramidal structure does not lend itself to such a strategy. As Wallace points out, the difficulty is that typically each function approaches the business problems inherent in the product from a somewhat different point of view: marketing wants a good product at a low price; production, a product that is easily produced; engineering, a product that outclasses—engineering wise—all other products, and so on. None of these stances tends to lead to the resolution of conflicting ideas into a decision that tends to integrate the best of each view.

THE MATRIX ORGANIZATION

One of the most promising strategies to induce co-operation and integration of effort on crucial business problems is the development of project teams and the matrix organization. These administrative innovations were created initially to solve the complex problems of coordination and scheduling of large defense projects. They have been adapted and used by many other organizations because of their potential promise. The future role of the team approach and matrix organization is, in my opinion, an important one for administration.

A project team is created to solve a particular problem. It is composed of people representing all the relevant managerial functions (e.g., marketing, manufacturing, engineering, and finance). Each member is given equal responsibility and power to solve the problem. The members are expected to work as a cohesive unit. Once the problem is solved, the team is given a new assignment or disbanded. If the problem is a recurring one, the team remains active. In many cases, especially in the defense programs, the project manager is given full authority and responsibility for the completion of the project including rewarding and penalizing the members of the team. An organization may have many teams. This results in an organization that looks like a matrix; hence the title of matrix organization.

How effective are the project teams and the matrix organizations? In order to begin to answer that question, I have been conducting some research in nine large organizations utilizing a matrix organization structure. In preliminary interviews the executives reported that the matrix organization and team approach made sense, but that they found them

Representatives of	Project 1	Project 2	Project 3
Manufacturing			
Engineering			
Marketing			
Finance			
	Team 1	Team 2	Team 3

very difficult to put into actual practice. People still seemed to polarize issues, resisted exploring ideas thoroughly, mistrusted each other's behavior, focused on trying to protect one's own function, overemphasized simplified criteria of success (e.g., figures on sales), worked too much on day-to-day operations and short-term planning, engaged in the routine decisions rather than focus more on the long-range risky decisions, and emphasized survival more than the integration of effort into a truly accepted decision.

Others found fault with the team approach for not providing individuals enough opportunity to get recognition in their own functional departments for their performance on the team. Still others insisted that individuals sought to be personally identified with a particular accomplishment; that it wasn't satisfying for them to know that their group (and not they) obtained the reward. Finally, some said that during their meetings the teams got bogged down in focusing on the negative, i.e., what had not been accomplished.

Why are these new administrative structures and strategies having this trouble? I do *not* believe the concept of the matrix organization is inherently invalid. I believe the answer lies in the everyday *behavior styles that the managers have developed, in the past, to survive and to succeed within the traditional pyramidal organization.* The behavior styles needed for the effective use of the matrix organization are, I believe, very different. Also, the group dynamics that are effective in the pyramidal structure are different from those that will be effective in the matrix organization. Thus I do not agree that the comments above are 'natural' for all people. They are 'natural' for people living under the pyramidal concept. For example, groups *can* be created where individuals gain success from seeing integrated decision; where recognition *does* come more from success and less from compliments from others, where overcoming barriers and correcting faults and failures are not perceived as negative.

A second important cause for the ineffectiveness of the matrix type organization lies in the very processes that have given it birth. Again, the difficulty has been that the birth processes used were more applicable to the pyramidal than to the matrix organization. In short, I am suggesting that a basic problem has been that a new form of organization has been introduced in such a way as to make difficulties inevitable and that the leadership styles that the executives use to administer the matrix organization, on the whole, compound the felony. In order to illustrate my point I should like to take one of these nine studies and discuss it in some detail. The case that I have selected to discuss approximates the other eight. The variance among the cases was not high. More importantly, the establishment of a project and program approach had the most careful thought and analytical competence brought to bear on it by the top management. It is a study of a multi-million-dollar organization that decided to reorganize its *product planning* and *program review* activities into a team approach which resulted in a matrix organization. These two activities have been the ones most frequently organized into a matrix organization. The study lasted about one year. I interviewed all the top executives involved (25), asked them to complete questionnaires, and observed, taped, and analyzed nearly 35 meetings of the teams, ranging from 45 minutes to 2½ hours in length.

PRODUCT PLANNING AND PROGRAM REVIEWS

The responsibility of product planning program reviews was to collect and integrate, and maintain up to date information of the progress of any given activity in the organization. Under this concept, the top men could go to one source to get complete information on the organization's present plans, progress against plans, and so on. The staff group had no authority to order any of the line executives. It was their task to analyze what the problems were and to get from the line executives their plans as to how they were to be solved. If the line executives were unable to agree then the problem was taken to the chief executive for his decision. In the manual of the company there existed a sentence which stated, "... the president retains the authority for final decisions and can ordinarily expect that his product planning staff will achieve the agreement of all other departments before plans are presented." Still later, "Product planning provides team leadership to a team made up of appropriate, fully responsibly representatives of the (line) departments. The Product Planner as team leader encourages, challenges, and insists upon mature, complete and competent coverage by these representatives. Encouragement of better communication between departments is necessary and vital."

The assumption behind this theory was that if objectives and critical paths to these objectives were defined clearly, people would tend to cooperate to achieve these objectives according to the best schedule that they could devise. However, in practice, the theory was difficult to apply. Why? Let us first take a look at the processes by which these new concepts were introduced.

The management strategy for implementing this new program was primarily one of pushing, persuading, and ordering. The objective was to overcome the forces in the organization that were resisting change thereby pushing the level of effectiveness upward. However, the way this was done added, unintentionally, to the resisting forces. For example, 76 percent of the subordinates interpreted the processes of a small elite group planning the changes and then management unilaterally installing the activities by persuading the people to accept them, as implying that they (subordinates) had not been competent in the past and that they could not be trusted in making changes. These feelings were strengthened by the fact that the new activities required greater control over subordinates, more detailed planning, and more concrete commitments which could get the subordinate in trouble if they did not fulfill them. These activities of fear and mistrust still exist. For example:

> Sometimes I wonder if the real impact of program reviews isn't to teach people that we don't trust them. I think that the top people have got to have faith in the people, and eliminate some of these constant and repetitive type of meetings, just to check being checked. I think we can get management to get themselves pretty well informed just through a nominal report type of thing, rather than all this paper work that we have.

The increasing lack of cooperation, hostility, resistance to meeting program plans, were recognized by the people responsible for the activities. They responded by making the controls even tighter. They asked for more detailed reports, for a wider distribution of minutes, and they used the minutes as evidence that agreements were arrived at that were binding. But again the impact was not completely what was expected. For example:

> 'Do we need these complete minutes? We still have a number of people in the organization who feel that they have to document everything in terms of a letter or memo. To me this is an indication of fear.'
> 'The more trouble the programs got into the more paper work that we had to complete.'

It was not long before the completion of the paper work became an end in itself. Seventy-one percent of the middle managers reported that the maintenance of the product planning and program review paper flow became as crucial as accomplishing the line responsibility assigned to each group. For example:

> 'I'm afraid that we program the most minute things and the more we program, the less work we get done. I have tried to get this across to the president, but have not been very successful.'
>
> 'One problem I find is the amount of paper work that this system generates. I dare say out of the five-day week it would take you three quarters of a day or a day of your week to just keep up with the paper work. All of the paper work you get does not affect you, but you have to go through it to find out what does and what does not.'
>
> 'In all honesty I think we waste too damn much time around here. These program reviews are especially costly in time. Why one of the fellows the other day said that he received and sends out approximately 50 thousand pieces of paper a month.'

The final quotation illustrates the next problem that arose. Since each individual had his regular job to accomplish in addition to his role as product planning and program reviews, the load became very heavy. *The executives increasingly felt overworked and overloaded with activities that were not leading to increased effectiveness (83 percent).* For example:

> 'I believe —— held a scheduling type meeting, and they do call ordinary meetings, and then all the vice presidents call their people together for a meeting, so that one little meeting at a divisional level has a heck of a lot of man hours tied up into it for the background.'
>
> 'The number of jobs to be done. The sheer volume that has to be turned out. Sometimes you feel as though you are on a treadmill and you can't get off it because no matter what jobs you can see getting accomplished, there are so many more ahead of you that you know you are behind schedule, and it seems to drive you crazy at times. Everyone has the same feelings.'

In spite of these difficulties the level of effectiveness eventually stabilized. But now the resisting forces became much stronger. Also the level of organizational pressure rose.

Most of the lower level managers reported that they did *not* like to be associated with the restraining activities, because they saw such alliance as an indication of disloyalty. I believe that one way to resolve these dissonant feelings about themselves was to strengthen their personal opinions about the negativeness of the program by finding faults with it and by knowingly (and unknowingly) acting so as to make it less effective.

Another mode of adaptation was to withdraw and let the upper levels become responsible for the successful administration of the program. (This is their baby—let them make it work.) At the same time much hostility could be released safely by constant joking about 'everything is programmed.' For example, girls were asked had they programmed their sex life; men were asked if they had defined the critical path to the men's toilet; etc.

These attitudes threatened the upper levels. They saw them as suggesting that the managers were not as loyal and committed as they should be. The executives reacted by involving the potential wrath of the president. (He really means business—let's climb on board.) Soon the president found himself in the position of being cited as the reason why the programs may not be questioned. Also, his immediate subordinates encouraged him to speak out forcefully on the importance of these functions. The president began to feel that he must defend the programs because if he did not, the restraining forces may begin to overcome the management pressure for change. For example:

> 'Make no mistake about it, this is the president's baby. Have you ever tried to talk to him about it? He listens for a few minutes and then soon lets you know that he isn't going to tolerate much question.'
>
> 'No, we have pretty much consoled ourselves to the fact that the president is really behind this, and you might just as well forget it. You are entitled to a personal opinion, of course, but beyond that, you better not take any action.'

The increasing number of control activities and the increasing feelings of pressure led the subordinates to feel that product planning and program reviews had become dominant in the organization. They unknowingly or knowingly placed less attention upon their original line function activities. This reaction increased the probability that failures would occur, which increased the pressures from the president and in turn his staff people, which infuriated the line managers, and the loop was closed. The top management forces tended to increase, the middle and lower management resistance also tended to increase (even though such action may have made them feel a sense of disloyalty), the tension and pressures increased, and the effectiveness of the program was at a lower level than was potentially possible.

To make the situation more difficult, the majority of the participants reported that, in addition to the process of introduction being a dissatisfying one, they also reported overall dissatisfaction with the way the programs were being carried out. For example, the meetings tended: to suppress individuality, polarize issues into win-lose stances, censor bad news to the top and immobilize the groups with unimportant issues.

Overall Dissatisfaction with Small Group Meetings

Dissatisfaction was found to exist with the product planning and program review meetings. The dissatisfactions increased as one went down the chain of command. Thus 64 percent of the top executives and 83 percent of the middle managers expressed dissatisfaction with the group meetings.

'These committees are not the best way to administer an organization. We tend to make little problems into big ones and ignore the nasty ones. We also eat up a lot of time. People don't come in to really listen; they come in to win and fight not to lose.'

'I think the simple fact is even now there is probably less true acceptance of the product planning function than there was. And I think in truth there is quite fundamental and sincere nonacceptance of the role of planning in the function, not the general idea of ———; I've talked to people about this quite a bit.'

Why is that?

'Because the fact remains that we do have a schedule, and someone is after them for their answer at that point. And I guess that's tough for most of us to accept. Maybe this game of having an objective and planning their work accordingly and say what you are going to do. Management is flexible, you're so right. They know we run a high risk here, and the top management never beat them over the back for this kind of stuff.'

Suppressing Individuality

The members reported that in practice, the groups functioned so that individuality was not optimized; conformity and non-risktaking predominated (71 percent). Playing it relatively safe seemed to be a common activity. For example:

During a heated session about program reviews A accused B of being a coward for not standing up for his view. A replied 'Listen mister, when you have to live with these people as I do, then you can talk. If I really stuck to my views I'd be hated by everyone—and I'd come to hate myself.'

'Yes, I think the choice that we have been asked to make between no decision and one not so good is a negative choice. Most of the time it is an 11th-hour thing that they arrive at. You either can take it this way or you won't have it for another six months.'

What prevents a person from sort of digging in and saying no, I don't want anything else?

'Well, there is a lot of pressure. We've got commitments made to the management where we charge a certain amount of dollars for the dollars they have allowed us to invest in this business.'

Polarizing Issues

At the lower levels, there was a good deal more heated argument which caused the issues to be polarized and people felt that they were not being heard. This tended to lead to a decrease in the faith in the group's processes and, at the same time, increased the probability that people would tend to come to the meetings with prepared positions (83 percent). For example:

'We have a great deal of jockeying for position.'

'There are certain things that people are not willing to stick their necks out about. Particularly when it comes to a new program. When it comes to a new program everyone has preconceived positions, and they adhere to them.'

'I think at times people will take an extreme position one time, and another time be very compromising. To take the —— committee as an example, there are occasions where they do not agree and they say, "Too bad we couldn't agree, we'll set up a meeting at the next level." '

Censoring Bad News to the Top

Another major problem was that some of the more difficult issues developed at the lower levels were watered down by the time they were transmitted to the top. People had learned not to describe to their superiors the complete differences in views and the difficulties in discussing the issues in as strong terms as they experience them. (71 percent).

'By the way, there is an awful lot of time spent at the lower level and people getting information ready to beat the people at the upper level. And I would say in all honesty that we don't give all the information to the people on top. If we do present them with all the problems it would probably bring this place to a screeching halt.'

'When you have an overly protected meeting the people upstairs don't really get the facts. For example, you soon learn that in a review you take all the things out that might be arbitrary or that might raise difficulties with somebody else.'

Immobilizing the Group with Unimportant Details

Still another frequently reported problem was the immobilization of the group with countless small decisions. (63 percent). Some department representatives brought everything to the meetings partially to make certain that the program review group took the responsibility for all activities. Other department representatives raised many issues when they were upset with the direction a particular decision was taking or when they wished to delay the making of a decision until further data could be obtained. For example:

'Some people also don't mind flooding the committee with agenda items. And once there is an item on the agenda the board is committed to study it, whether it is important or not. I think it can be an awful expense of money and time.'

'If you looked at the minutes of our meetings, and you haven't attended any yet, of course, the number of topics we take up is fantastic, and to the point where we feel that too many people aren't deciding at lower levels, and bucking it is up to us.'

The members of a review group could postpone action or prevent themselves (and their department) from being held responsible for a decision by asking the group to make it. This was guaranteed to take time since those in the group who did not specialize in that particular technical area had to be briefed.

To summarize, the product planning and program review committees were viewed as plagued with ineffectiveness and win-lose dynamics. An executive who kept a count of how people described these committees concluded that the two most frequent categorizations were 'Committee management at its worse' and 'Moscow delegates' (i.e. delegates who couldn't make a contribution without checking with their department).

The same managers freely admitted that they could not see any resolution, 'any time you run a company by a committee, you'll always have trouble,' or 'it's human nature for people to lie and fight when they believe they are being exposed.' Such pessimistic diagnoses will not lead to action for correcting the situation. On the contrary, such diagnoses probably provide ideal rationalization why 'things cannot be changed' and why they can go on feeling and behaving as they do.

As in the problems presented in the previous section, management's reaction was not to deal with the issues openly. More subtle and covertly controlling actions were typically taken. Meetings were scheduled with greater precision, presentations were made both with viewgraph and written script, and even more detailed minutes were taken. The hope was that with tighter outside controls, the groups would tend to operate more effectively. If we may judge from the comments reported above as well as from the observations, the group dynamics have not been altered— indeed, one could argue with some justification that the group defenses are becoming stronger. Thus we conclude again that although the members are aware that the relative ineffectiveness of the group is a crucial problem, they are not able to solve the problems. Moreover, most of the action taken actually helps to increase the members feeling of being unduly controlled and mistrusted.

WHY DID THE PROBLEMS ARISE?

The explanations for problems like these are multiple and complicated. One way to begin to organize our thoughts is to view the problems as arising from a long causal chain of actions where one action causes several others, which in turn, breeds further actions, etc. I believe that at the beginning of this complicated causal chain lie the basic values or assumptions that executives have learned to hold about how to organize human effort effectively. These values, once internalized, act as commands to coerce the executives to behave in specific ways when they meet to solve problems.

Elsewhere I have shown that executives tend to hold three basic values about effective human relationships within organizations They are:

1. Get the job done. We are here to manufacture shoes, that is our business, those are the important human relationships; if you have anything that can influence those human relationships, fine.

2. Be rational and logical and communicate clearly. Effectiveness *decreases* as behavior becomes more emotional. 'Gentlemen, let's get back to the facts,' is the classic conference table phrase, or in other words, if you want to be effective, be rational, be clear. If you want to be ineffective, focus on the emotional and interpersonal.

3. People work best under carefully defined direction, authority and control, governed by appropriate rewards and penalties that emphasize rational behavior and achievement of the objective.

In Figure 1, I should like to illustrate what I believe may be one underlying causal chain causing the problems described above. Let us assume that an organization, at any given point in time, may be described as having a particular level of effectiveness; that there are forces pushing upward to increase the effectiveness (e.g. top management); and that, since the level is somewhat stable, there are forces pushing downward resisting or restraining the level from going higher.[1] A balance of forces exists.

Now, let us assume that management wants to increase the level of effectiveness (by developing a new product planning and program review activities as in this case, or by any other change the reader wants to imagine). I am suggesting that the underlying *strategy* for and the *processes of change* will tend to be greatly influenced by values the executives hold. For example:

1. Because of the emphasis on objectives and rationality, the executives will tend to assume that the way to get a new organizational activity accepted by the members of the organization is to show them clearly how it fits with the objectives of the organization and to explain rationally the advantages of the new activity over the old one. For example, 'We need tighter controls,' 'effectiveness must be increased,' 'I'm sure all of us want to manage in the best way available,' 'we must always remain alert for new management innovations.' As seen by the subordinates this means that management feels compelled to sell them a bill of goods; an implication that they resent. They see little need (if they are effective managers) for

---

1. The model is taken from Kurt Lewin's concept of quasi-stationary equilibria; 'Frontiers in Group Dynamics', *Human Relations*, Vol 1, No. 1 and No. 2, 1947, pp. 2-38. For the readers interested in organization theory, I mean to imply that people holding the three values above will always tend to create the problems originally depicted in Lewin's model. I am suggesting an explanation to Lewin's question as to why he found change activities in our society tended to take one form.

someone to tell them effectiveness should be increased, new concepts should be tried, etc. Indeed, many resent the implication that they are not doing this already.

In terms of our diagram, the strategy for change is to overcome the restraining forces by strengthening the pushing forces. This is done by management selling, pushing, and ordering. As we can see, at the second set of forces in our diagram, the level of effectiveness does increase.

2. But the resisting forces are also increased. The resistance increases because of (a) the negative interpersonal impact the necessity to sell the program had upon the managers, (b) the mistrust and condemnation of the subordinates implied by the new program, (c) the inhibition of the questions and fears the subordinates wished to express *before* they were 'sold', (d) the feeling of being manipulated by the fact that the changes were kept a secret while they were being planned, and (e) the dependence and submissiveness caused by the unilateral management strategy.

3. As can be predicted from knowing that management is uncomfortable in discussing negative feelings openly, the restraining forces are not dealt with directly. The result so far, is an increase in the level of effectiveness, an increase in resisting forces, and an increase in what we might call the gross organizational tension level.

4. Remaining true to their values the top executives respond by creating new rational forces (a new sales pitch on the values of the program); bringing to bear new controls, and issuing new orders to overcome the resistance. This tends to coerce the subordinates to suppress their confusion, feelings of distrust, and tension related to the new program, especially when interacting with the superiors. However, these feelings and tensions cannot be suppressed forever. They may erupt during the meetings that are part of the new change activities, thereby guaranteeing the ineffectiveness of these meetings.

5. The increased management pressure, the increase in controls through paper work, the overload of work, all act to increase the forces pushing the level of effectiveness upward. The mistrust, tension, ineffective meetings (in our case of product planning and program reviews), the willingness on the part of lower level management to make the top responsible for the change (this is their baby) become examples of how the restraining forces are increased. The organizational tension also increases. This, in turn, stimulates management to develop new controls, check points, new courses to explain the importance of the program. These actions further increase the upward forces, which, in turn, increase the resisting forces, which in turn increases the organizational tension. The loop is now closed.

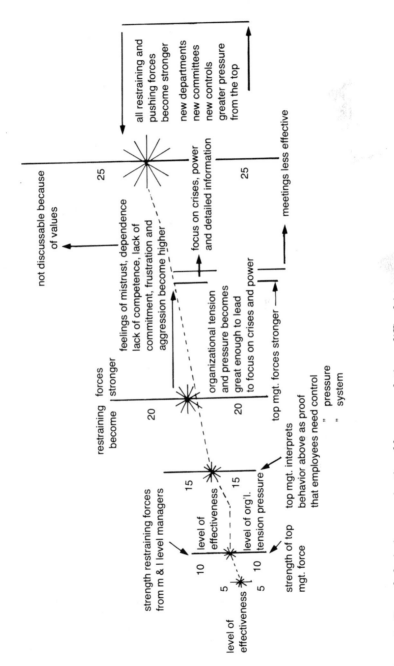

Figure 1. Causal chain in organizational human relations difficulties

At some point the difficulties and tensions reach a breaking point among the members. The top executives usually sense this and typically call for a one or two day meeting away from home base 'to take out the kinks in the program.' In my experience most of these meetings were not very effective because the subordinates feared bringing out their real feelings and the true difficulties. One interesting sign that the true problems did not come out in these meetings was the degree to which the participants assigned the causes of their problems to conditions that were typical under the pyramidal organizational structure. For example, people may spend time trying to find out who was the *one* person responsible for decision making; they craved identification of their individual contribution; they competed in win-lose battles.

The difficulties with these meetings is illustrated in the example below. Three years after the reorganizing plan went into effect developing a team approach, marketing and manufacturing were still having difficulties defining their roles and responsibilities. Manufacturing doubted that it needed marketing and *vice versa.* (If I included all the data we would see that engineering also had its doubts.) In reading the example, it is useful to note how many of the problems raised and the solutions suggested are typical of the traditional organizational climate and not those endemic of the matrix organization. Each group worried more about trying to show that it was truly 'the' most responsible. There was little attempt by the participants to help each other and to try to build a cohesive team where the whole was more important than any one part. Also when personality issues were ever so gently brought out (toward the end), the leader changed the subject.

A. Just the same way that the R and D department resents it and marketing man says 'my technology manager' and he says 'my manufacturing team.'

D. You know I don't resent that at all because I talk about my marketing manager.

C. Some of us do. We're all getting over it, but at the beginning we all tended to be rather sensitive.

A. Rather than the marketing managers' decisions, isn't the direction of the company contingent upon the company's decisions for these market opportunities determine the direction in which our future lies?

B. I'd like to reply to that because strategy is knowing the customer. The big part of it is knowing what the hell your competition's in. If you don't know your competition, you don't really know what the hell to do and who helps you play the strategy defense. It's got to be manufacturing. They've got to know their competing existing technology. They're the people that tell you what dollars ... they give you a good share of the judgments that you can apply to strategy.

D. An example to support your point is product X. This is a real good example because this is where the manufacturing team set, looked at all competitive economics, all known producers, all possible methods by which X could be produced, and came up with what we might call an equilibrium sales price. This is a price at which somebody could over the next ten years afford so this came out as an average sales price. Now that really established the basic strategy level, so we then compared all the methods by which we could apply ourselves to producing our requirements on this product and looked at the comparative economics of these and their performance in the in-use areas for all of the uses of the product. So all the market technology teams contributed to this area. But the prime mover in the whole thing and really the one who was developing the whole base for the decision was a manufacturing team who were drawing together all of these inputs on competitive products and competitive economics, long range planning, but the decision as it was arrived at was a completely composite decision in the different marketing areas where the products were going to be sold.

C. I don't have very much experience the way the other guys do, but I don't see how you can. There is no separation between our groups.

E. You fellows may not like this, but I really think that basically the company still sets the price beyond which profit can be made and it's the agents who are selling the goods from this company who still are responsible to maximize profit.

D. Well, what do you think this is? I can't see where we're in any conflict with manufacturing.

B. Like hell!

A. I think this is probably right and maybe this is because we don't agree with manufacturing's mandate. The whole group down there on the boondocks don't really understand what marketing's function is. That's why we're gathered around this table, to try to understand that. It's obvious that there are a lot of people that don't understand what marketing's function is because that's why we've got it on the agenda.

B. Well, maybe if we understand your point of view, maybe we can help you to understand us.

A. Manufacturing has to understand what every marketing group, how every marketing group understands their own job. If you're not going to be the same, then the manufacturing group has to understand how you understand your job and how everyone understands their job.

C. Let me ask this—maybe you can help clarify it. Suppose marketing technology's out of this thing and then just have the manufacturing team and the sales department. Could you operate on that basis? Do you need this marketing group?

A. It is a good question. The answer is probably no. We were almost doing this once before, before the reorganization, and obviously it wasn't working successfully. The thing we've got now is a good bit more successful.

B. This terminology really leaves me cold. What do you mean 'more successful'?

E. It's semantics, that's all.

B. The guys down at the boondocks now think that marketing should look at the sales department as a bunch of peddlers. These are the terms that are being thrown around.

D. I think this all helped. We understand each better, so what's the next topic? This is the thing that I want to avoid, that we bring personalities into this. It was nothing personal. It was simply a statement that you made that I was having trouble understanding.

B. Everybody's getting involved and yet the problem's not being solved. We talked about this last week. The manufacturing managers talked about this. All of us are talking and that's about all.

Some readers may wonder how typical is this situation. In my experience the confusion and conflict is quite typical. The meeting was more open than usual which permitted us to get a rich specimen of the conflict. By the way, I do hope that these observations will help top managements pause and question their belief that the best way to plan a reorganization is to appoint a top committee (with all the appropriate help) to develop a reorganization plan and then 'sell' it to the organization. The lower level managers soon hear about the meetings and see them as the first sign of mistrust. The reasons usually given for this strategy are that to get wider participation may upset people and make it more difficult to sell the new plan. In my experience people become doubly upset with the secrecy and the anxiety built up around the rumors related to the reorganization. The time necessary for getting the program truly accepted is easily doubled. (In some recent research with government bureaux the time is extended until the next reorganization.)

I also hope that these data will raise question with the advice that some recent theorists suggest that people's behavior can be changed by changing the organizational structure. If the data from these nine examples are valid, then we may conclude that their view is oversimplified. I would agree with them that changes in organizational structure do bring about intended changes in people's behavior. (In our figure the effectiveness level was increased.) However, they also bring about unintended behavioral changes; the restraining forces are strengthened and the organizational tension level is greatly increased. To my knowledge the proponents of this approach have never shown an example where by changing the organizational structure the restraining forces and tension levels were also not increased.

These results suggest that, in addition to organizational structural changes, one should also focus on altering the basic values of the executives so that they can develop change strategies that may minimize the unintended consequences. (One example will be discussed below.) Our approach is not to be viewed as taking sides in an argument of change in structure vs. changes in people: our view is changes in structure *through* changes in people's values. Nor does the approach imply a blanket condemnation of the change strategy illustrated in Figure 1. Such a strategy may be necessary where (for whatever reason) people refuse to alter their values, to become fully involved in the change, to take on their share of creating the change. If there is a lack of time for the more involving change process then one may use the more unilateral one depicted but may consider being quite open about the possible negative consequences and asking the people to help to reduce them.

A NEW PHILOSOPHY OF ORGANIZING AND MANAGING PEOPLE

I should like, at the outset, to repeat my view that project teams and matrix organizations are fundamentally valid. I believe that they are the most effective organizational structures for decisions that are complex and risky, that require the integration of many different inputs, and that depend on the continuing, long-range commitment of everyone involved without the organization's being saddled with excess and unneeded structures. (Once the project is complete, the team can be disbanded or a new project be assigned to it.)

One of the most important first steps is to communicate to the people that the matrix organization is not a simple extension of the traditional pyramidal structure. The pyramidal structure acquires its form from the fact that as one goes up the administrative ladder (1) power and control increase, (2) the availability of information increases, (3) the degree of flexibility to act increases, (4) the scope of the decisions made and the responsibilities involved increase. Implicit in the matrix organization are almost opposite tendencies. For example, power and control are given to the individual and/or to the groups who have the technical skill to accomplish the task, no matter what their organizational level. Thus a team could be composed of five people representing all different levels of authority (on the traditional chart), who are equal. The group could be chaired by the individual with the least organizational authority. The individual or groups are given responsibility and authority to make decisions of the widest necessary scope.

If we may extrapolate to the probable matrix organization of the future, Forrester suggests that the organization will eventually eliminate the superior-subordinate relationship and substitute for it the individual self-discipline arising from self-interest created by a competitive market mechanism within the system. The individual would negotiate continuously changing relationships. Each individual would be a profit center whose objective would be to produce the most value for the least activity; who would have the freedom to terminate as well as to create new activity, who would have access to all the necessary information. The organization of the future would be rid of internal monopolies which is the usual status of most traditional departments.

Although I would agree with Forrester, I belive that the organizations of the future will be a combination of the old and the new forms of organization. I believe that the old forms are going to be more effective for the routine, non-innovative activity that requires little, if any, internal commitment by the participants. However, as the decisions become less routine, more innovative and require more commitment, the newer forms such as the matrix organizations will be more effective.

LEADERSHIP STYLE AND MATRIX ORGANIZATION

In addition to being able to differentiate clearly between the old and the new forms, the future executive must also be able to know the conditions under which he will use the different organizational forms. Moreover, he will need to become skillful in several different kinds of leadership styles, each of which is consistent with a particular form. For example, an authoritarian leadership style is more consistent with the traditional structure; a participative style with the link pin organization defined by Likert and a style that develops risk-taking and trust for the matrix organization.

If recent research is valid, then the majority of executive leadership styles conform to the traditional pyramidal style. This is not surprising since leadership styles and organizational design would naturally go together. The findings that did surprise us were (1) the degree to which the executives believed in leadership styles that were consonant with the matrix organization, and (2) the degree to which they were *unaware* that they were *not* behaving according to their ideals.

Another important first step therefore is to help executives become more aware of their actual leadership style. Unless they develop such awareness, they are not going to be able to unfreeze their old styles, develop new ones, and most importantly, switch from one style to another as the administrative situations and the organization structure used is changed. Unless the switching from one style to another can be clearly identified by the person and the receivers, confusion will result.

Another finding that surprised us about executive decision-making was how many executives focused on keeping people 'happy'. Indeed, the most frequently cited reason for not being open with another was the fear that it might upset the receiver (and thus upset the sender). The most frequently cited reason for not bringing two groups together who are locked in interdepartmental warfare was that it would simply 'involve personalities and nothing but harm could come of it.' Although the executives that we studied were happiness-oriented in their behavior, they were not in their attitudes. They believed in strong leadership that could call a spade a spade and let the chips fall where they may. Again according to the observations, the spades were called spades and the chips placed on the line, but in private settings where few could be witnesses, or by such deft and diplomatic processes that few people, including the targets, were aware of what was happening. I cannot refrain from adding that there seemed to be a strong correlation between those executives who were critical of the field of 'human relations' as one whose objective was to make people happy and the degree of their blindness to the fact that they tended to do the very same thing when they were actually leading.

THE MANAGEMENT OF TENSION

Executives in the matrix organization will also need to learn, if I may be permitted to oversimplify, that there is productive and unproductive or crippling tension. The unproductive or crippling tension is tension that a person experiences but which he cannot control. The reason he cannot control the tension may be external (pressure from his superior) or internal (inability to control his own demands on himself, plus the accompanying feelings of impatience and guilt aimed at himself).

Productive tension is that tension that the individual can control and which comes from accepting new challenges, taking risks, expanding one's competencies, etc. These are the very qualities that are central to the matrix organization. Thus the executive of the future will have to learn how to define internal environments that challenge people, stretch their aspirations realistically, and help them face interpersonal reality. Some examples are financial controls that reward people for risk-taking; organizational situations that are optimally undermanned; incentive systems that reward excellence (not average performance), work that is designed to use people's complex abilities. To put this another way, we need to develop competence in manipulating the environment but not the people. (They should have the freedom and responsibility to choose if they will enter the new environment).

THE MANAGEMENT OF INTERGROUP CONFLICT

The matrix organization is composed of teams which in turn are populated by representatives of the traditional line functions. As we have seen, this leads to much intergroup conflict within the team as well as between teams.

Instead of trying to stamp out intergroup conflict as bad and disloyal, the executives need to learn how to manage it so that the constructive aspects are emphasized and the destructive aspects are de-emphasized.

This means that the organization needs to put on the table for diagnosis the interdepartmental fires, the incidents of throwing the dead cat over into the other department's yard, the polarized competitive warfare where success is defined by the participants in terms of which side won rather than the contribution to the whole. The executives will have to learn how (1) to bring the groups together, (2) where each discusses and seeks, in private, to agree on its views and attitudes toward the other and toward self, (3) then the representatives of both groups talk together in the presence of the other group members, followed by (4) private discussion to establish the way they are perceived by others in order (5) to develop (through representatives) an understanding of the discrepancy between their and others' views.

THE EXECUTIVE EDUCATIONAL ACTIVITIES

Most organizations send their executives to university executive programs or to internal executive programs usually designed following the concept of the university. I do not want to get into philosophical discussions about the nature of university education at this point. I would like to point out, however, that *there may be a discrepancy between the characteristics of university education and the needs of the matrix organiation.*

The university has typically assumed that learning (1) is for the individual, (2) occurs when it is given, (3) is tested by contrived examinations of the knowledge acquired, (4) need not be relevant to any immediate problem, (5) should be designed and controlled by the educator; it is the task of the educator to define the problems, develop ways to solve them and define the criteria for evaluation who passes and who does not. The matrix organizations require education that (1) focuses on individuals in team systems and (2) it occurs where the problem is located, (3) is learned by the use of actual problems, and (4) is tested by the effectiveness of the actual results, and (5) is controlled by those participating in the problem (aided by the educator as a consultant).

Executive education in the matrix organization will focus on system effectiveness. This means that the central educational department will now become an organizational development activity. It will have systems as its clients. A small team of consultants will enter the system and develop a diagnosis of its human and technical effectiveness. These data will then be fed back to representatives at all levels of the system to generate, at the grass-roots level, action recommendations. A steering committee composed of representatives of the client system and the organizational development will then prepare a long-range educational program designed to increase the immediate as well as the long-range effectiveness of the system.

Classes may then be held at the plant location or at a central facility, depending upon the resources needed, the time available, the availability of the 'students,' as well as the faculty. Teams and not disconnected individuals will study together for the majority of technical and management subjects. These teams will be actual working teams. This will place pressure on the faculty to develop learning that is valid for the real problems of the team and motivate the students to learn, since it is their problems upon which the education is focusing.

To put this another way, education will be for organizational and system diagnosis, renewal and effectiveness. It will be held with groups, subject material, and faculty that are organic to the organization's problem. One of the dangers of this education is the possibility that it will focus on the trivial, short-range problems. The quality control in this area will depend partially on the diagnostic competence of the faculty. In defining the problem they can help the organization to get to the underlying and basic causes. The students can also help by being alert to the validity of the education that is being offered to them.

Some critics wonder if teams of people working together can be pulled away from work. The answer, in my experience, is affirmative. The fear, for example, that the company will be in trouble if the top team leaves for a week, has been quietly exploded in several cases. The explosions have been quiet lest, as one president put it, 'it was learned how well things ran while the top management was away.'

More importantly, this new type of education is central to the work of the system. Thus, the team is not being pulled away from work. Indeed, in many cases, it is pulled away *in order to work.* Systems, like cars, need to have their organizational hoods opened and the motor checked and tuned. Unless this maintenance work is done, the system will deteriorate as certainly as does an automobile.

Finally, the concern of being away physically from the location should be matched with the concern about the number of hours being consumed needlessly while at work. In the studies listed previously, I have found that as many as half the meetings and as much as three quarters of the time spent at meetings are not productive and worse than unnecessary.

ORGANIZATIONAL CHANGE

Anyone who has planned major organizational change knows (1) how difficult it is to foresee accurately all the major problems involved, (2) the enormous amount of time needed to iron out the kinks and get people to accept the change, (3) the apparent lack of internal commitment on the part of many to help make the plan work, manifested partly (4) by people at all levels resisting taking the initiative to make modifications that they see are necessary so that the new plan can work. In preparing this article, I reviewed my notes from thirty-two major re-organizations in large organizations in which I played some consulting and research role. I did not find one that could be labeled as fully completed and integrated three years after the change had been announced (and in many cases had gone through several revisions). That is, after three years there were still many people fighting, ignoring, questioning, resisting, blaming the re-organization without feeling a strong obligation personally to correct the situation.

As I mentioned above, I believe the reasons for this long delay are embedded in the change strategy typically used by management. To refer to the diagram, the basic strategy has been for the top management to take the responsibility to overcome and outguess the resistance to change. This strategy does tend to succeed because management works very hard, applies pressure, and if necessary knocks a few heads together (or eliminates some). However, as we have seen, the strategy creates resisting forces that are costly to the organization's effectiveness, to its long run viability and flexibility, as well as to the people at all levels.

Reducing the Resisting Forces

What would happen if management experimented with the strategy of reducing the restraining forces by involving, at least, the management employees at all levels in the diagnosis, design, and execution of the change program? For example, in one organization a plan of reorganization was begun by getting all levels involved in diagnosing the present problems of the organizations. Groups were formed (which met only twice for several hours each time) to diagnose the effectiveness of the present organization. These groups were initially composed of people from various functions but holding positions of about equal level. Each group brain-stormed as much as it desired to get out the problems. They were not asked to suggest solutions at this time because no one group would have a total picture of the organization, and therefore its recommendations could be incomplete and misleading, with the added danger of each group becoming attached to their suggestions. Finally, people tend to be hesitant about enumerating a problem if they are asked for solutions and do not have any.

The results of these diagnostic sessions were fed to a top level steering committee which contained representatives of all the major managerial levels. This committee had the diagnoses collated, analyzed, and developed into an integrated picture. Wherever they found holes and inconsistencies in the diagnoses they made a note of them. Eventually they had compiled a lengthy list of major questions to be answered before the overall diagnosis could be accepted as valid. These questions were fed to small task forces whose composition was specifically designed to be able to answer the questions. Thus, in this phase, the groups were composed of managerial personnel from many functions and levels who were relevant to the questions being asked. These task forces were disbanded as soon as they provided the answers to the questions.

In the third phase the steering committee tried to develop a new organizational structure. In achieving this objective the steering committee began, for the first time, to suggest arrangements of individuals and groups tasks that could be threatening to various interests. This led to the members becoming more involved, cautious, and at times, defensive. Members who, up to this point, had felt free to be objective were beginning to feel themselves slipping into the role of protecting the groups toward which they had the closest attachment.

At this point, the task force went to the education group and asked for a course in such subjects as how to deal with intergroup rivalries and issues; with emotionality in groups, and with hidden agendas. This course was quickly but carefully planned. The steering committee members reported that it was a great help to them. It was especially helpful in welding them into a more fully functioning, open confronting of issues and risk taking. They also reported that as the members' confidence and trust in their group increased, the more willing they were to invite, at the appropriate time, members of departments whose future roles were being discussed so that the problems could be discussed and solved jointly.

The fourth phase was the preparation of a final plan. It was fully discussed with the top executives, then discussed systematically with key representatives of all the departments. Alterations were invited and carefully considered. Two members of the steering commmittee were members of top management who had authority to represent the top in approving most changes.

During the fifth phase two kinds of data were collected. First a questionnaire was sent to all who had participated, asking them for any individual comments about the plan as well as any comments about the effectiveness of the process of change to date. This diagnosis uncovered, in several cases, new ideas to be considered as well as several suggestions to be re-examined because individuals felt that they had been pushed through by a small but powerful clique.

The final plan was then drawn up with a specific time table (which had been discussed and accepted by people below). The top management, with the help of the steering committee, then put the new organizational plan into action. These phases took nearly seventeen months.

However, once the plan became policy (1) the resisting forces and the tensions were much lower than expected on the basis of previous experience, (2) wherever they existed there were organizational mechanisms already established and working to resolve them, (3) the internal commitment to the new policy was high (It is ours, not theirs.) and thus (4) changes were made as they became necessary without much fanfare or difficulty.

One of the most important outcomes of this type of change strategy was that it provided a living educational experience for individuals and groups on how to work together; on how to develop internal commitment among the members of the organization, and how to reduce the unnecessary and destructive win-lose rivalries. Thus the change program became an opportunity for education at all levels. The result was that a new system had been created which could be used for future changes and to increase the capacity of the organization to learn.

Even with these results, I have encountered some managers who wonder if an organization can take this much time for changing organizational structure. In my experience, although time is a critical factor, it is a false issue. Time will be taken, whether management is aware of it or not, by people to ask all the questions, make all the politically necessary moves, develop all the protective devices, and create all the organizational escape hatches that they feel are necessary. The real issue is whether the time will be used constructively and effectively so that the organization can learn from its experiences, thereby increasing its competence in becoming a problem-solving systems.

Reference

Wallace, W. L., 'The Winchester-Western Division Concept of Product Planning,' Olin Mathieson Chemical Corporation, January 1963.

Part 5. Organization Design and Change

It has probably been said by someone that the only other thing that is as sure as death and taxes is change. Although managers deal with change practically every day, the change that occurs is rarely planned. Many managers complain that all their time is reactive in nature; they never seem to have the time to anticipate change, to plan for it, to manage it.

The change that is most likely to occur in organizations, especially in large ones, is modifying the organization chart. When organizational problems occur, one of the first culprits fixed upon is the structure of the organization. Some managers joke about the "annual reorganization."

Planned change and the design of jobs and organizational structures are the subjects presented here. Part 5 begins with a consideration of organization development as it relates to, but is different from, training. The next three chapters deal with more specific approaches and methods, namely, quality-of-working-life interventions, management by objectives (MBO), and sociotechnical-system interventions. The final chapter in this section offers a case example, describing an overall approach to change in a single organization over a period of some years.

The lead chapter, "Training to Organization Change," by William B. Eddy, provides general background for understanding the major principles and problems of organization change. Eddy also facilitates an understanding of organization development, a relatively new intervention in the life of organizations, by relating it to a more established form of organization intervention—training.

With respect to method or technique, the Eddy chapter builds on the previous one by Argyris, who briefly covered the subject of organizational change. Argyris wrote about "reducing the restraining forces" as a method for implementing change. This method comes from the broader model of change, Force-Field Analysis, developed by Kurt Lewin. Eddy's broader coverage of organization development is based on the identical model and theoretical principles of change originally conceived by Lewin.

A recent development, akin to OD, is quality of working life (QWL), described by Eric Trist in "Adapting to a Changing World." Quality of working life, largely a product of the 1970s, has evolved as a response to worker complaints regarding, in particular, boredom on the job, especially in assembly-line types of activities and, in general, job dissatisfaction. In other words, QWL has served as an organizational intervention responding to the so-called "blue-collar blues." Doubtlessly, it has also been a response to the pervasive concern expressed by many top-level managers in the United States because of the gradual drops in productivity over the past decade.

Consequently, QWL is an attempt to improve the quality of life for people on the job. Like OD, it has strong underlying humanistic values, but unlike OD, quality of working life has been limited to activities at the "shop-floor" level of the organization, rather than dealing with "white-collar blues" or the quality of working life for managers. However, recent usage of QWL in organizations such as General Motors has begun to change this limitation. For example, GM considers QWL to be a corporate-wide process from the assembly worker to the chairman.

Management by objectives (MBO) is another intervention for organizational change that has evolved from the behavioral sciences. Of course, in the strict sense of the word, it is difficult to conceive of any organized effort being managed according to anything but objectives. It is illogical to think otherwise. But MBO is a particular process developed within the context of espousing greater participation by subordinates in setting objectives in the first place. The underlying principle of MBO is "involvement leads to commitment." In other words, the more people are involved in making those decisions they will be required to carry out, the more they will be committed to implementing them. As a consequence, MBO became popular as a way of obtaining better performance.

Even though MBO may have evolved as a form of participative management, French and Hollman are quick to point out in "Management by Objectives: The Team Approach" that "MBO efforts vary from being highly autocratic to highly participative among organizations and even within some organizations." As their title indicates, they make the case for a participative, team-centered approach to MBO. Apparently, no quantitative data exist to indicate one way or the other, but it is safe to assume that most MBO processes occur in a boss-to-subordinate, one-to-one manner. French and Hollman delineate a number of deficiencies inherent in this way of conducting MBO, and they argue for a team approach. They make their case well because the strength of their argument rests on sound, empirical evidence.

French and Hollman relate task—accomplishing some objective—with a particular aspect of organizational process, i.e., a team approach. This relationship of the more technical part of the organization with the human side is the fundamental feature of designing jobs and organizational structures and procedures according to sociotechnical principles—the subject of the chapter by Albert Cherns, "The Principles of Sociotechnical Design." The *sociotechnical* way of understanding an organization originated from members of the Tavistock Institute in England shortly after the Second World War.

If the reader notices similarities between the Cherns and the Trist chapters, this overlap is not accidental. Both men write from a common heritage—a sociotechnical-system perspective as conceived in the late 1940s and early 1950s by members of the Tavistock Institute in London.

Sociotechnical means that an organization consists primarily of two subsystems, the social system and the technical system—the techniques, equipments, tasks, type of service rendered or product manufactured, and money required for organizational operations. For organizational effectiveness, both of these systems must be treated jointly. The term typically used when the technological system and the social and psychological needs of the workers are jointly met is *joint optimization*.

Cherns also delineates some of the major principles in making an intervention according to sociotechnical principles. He emphasizes involving the people directly affected by the intervention in the planning and implementing of it. Moreover, he shows how a social and technological change can be both productive for the organization and rewarding for the individuals involved.

Concluding part 5 is an article retained from the first edition, "An Organic Problem-Solving Method of Organizational Change." Sheldon Davis provides a comprehensive summary of one organization's experience over a period of years with most of the elements covered in this section. TRW Systems, an aerospace business and Davis's employer at that time, the decade of the 1960s, was one of the first organizations to move to a matrix form of structure and to utilize sensitivity training as a method for change. As Davis points out, the use of sensitivity training quickly evolved to team building and, therefore, the dimensions for change and improvement became more closely tied to the tasks of work teams.

Davis makes McGregor's Theory X and Theory Y come alive by showing the relationships between theory and behavior, i.e., behavior as experienced by Davis and his colleagues in the actual world of TRW Systems. This is one of the few cases on record that thoroughly describes and accounts for a significant and longitudinal organizational change effort that employed the principles and practices of organization development.

The chapters in this section represent much, if not most, of the relatively new applications of behavioral science to organizations, especially with respect to change and the concurrent development of human resources. Although labels such as OD, QWL, and MBO may not be around forever, the contributions of applied behavioral science toward organizational improvement have proven themselves and therefore will continue to develop and evolve.

From Training to
Organization Change

by William B. Eddy

The concepts of management and organization have begun to change—and consequently the concept of training. It is clear that for purposes of understanding and dealing with the behavior of employees, it is more useful and valid to view the organization as a "social system" than as a mechanical system of technical skills directed by rational rules. The factors which frequently make the difference in the total performance and effectiveness of the organization include not only individual skills or work methods, but also the overall functioning of the organization as a system of interdependent parts. Some characteristics which often influence employees' performance include the quality of communication in all directions, clarity and acceptance of individual and organizational objectives and goals, cooperation among laterally-related units, trust level, distribution and use of power, effectiveness in resolving intraorganizational conflict, and adaptability to change. These findings have influenced organizations to shift their training focus to the skill areas that have to do with effective human relationships and team conditions.

Another impetus for the search for more effective organization training has been a series of new, or at least newly recognized, conditions confronting organizations. These have been described in detail by Bennis[1] and others. Technology is advancing so rapidly that older, more rigid organizational forms are sorely taxed. New management methods, such as project management and matrix structures, place a premium on rapid adaptation to change, teamwork, and temporary system (committee and task force) formation. Emerging societal values and the rise of professionalism influence employees to be less willing to be excluded

Dr. William B. Eddy is Kemper Professor of Administration, School of Administration, University of Missouri at Kansas City.

Adapted from *Personal Administration,* January, February, 1971, 37-43. Reprinted by permission.

from participation in goal setting and decision-making. Complex products or functions require the pooling of varied technical resources into workable units. These and other developments have spurred the search for techniques useful in changing not only individual skill levels, but also the process of the organization.

As the need to devise new ways of improving human effectiveness in organizations has become pressing, training directors, consultants and social scientists have looked for educational approaches which are capable of intervening at the system level. Ideas from the social psychology of attitude and social system change, group dynamics techniques, consulting and change agent skills, counseling, and personality theory currently form the nucleus of the *organization change process*. At its present stage, organization change refers both to a general point of view and to a variety of techniques which have been utilized to implement change. The terms organization development (OD), action research and planned change are often used to denote specific organization change efforts. The point of view and general characteristics of the approach can be summarized as follows:

1. Focus is on the total system of interdependent sub-organizational groupings (work units, teams, management levels) rather than upon individual employees as the object of training. Team development is frequently a major component of the change process.

2. The approach to change is "organic." It seeks to establish a climate in which growth, development and renewal are brought about as a natural part of the organization's daily operation, rather than superimposed unilaterally.

3. Experiential learning techniques in addition to the more traditional methods of consultation are utilized. Subject matter includes real problems and events that exist in the organization. Typically, there is gathering and analysis of organization data—either formally or informally.

4. As much emphasis is placed on competence in interpersonal relationships as on task skills. Much of the content and method is based on the behavioral sciences rather than on management theory, operations research, or personnel techniques—although these may be included in part of the change effort.

5. Goals frequently have to do with developing behavioral competence in areas such as communication, decision-making, and problem-solving, in addition to understanding and retention of principles and theories. The trainer often sees her- or himself more as consultant or change agent than expert-teacher.

6. The value system is humanistic. It is committed to integrating individual needs and management goals, maximizing opportunity for

human growth and development, and encouraging more open, authentic human relationships.

7. There is less intention to refute the traditional structural-functional conception of the organization than to augment this conception with newer data and help remedy some of its major dysfunctions.

Exhibit A compares the organization change process with the more traditional training approach.

Case descriptions of organization change efforts and their rationale and methodology are beginning to appear. Events at Union Carbide,[2] TRW Systems[3,4], Harwood Manufacturing Company,[5] and Esso Standard,[6] along with organizations studied by Argyris,[7] Mann,[8] Barnes and

Dimension	Traditional Training	The Organization Change Process
Unit of Focus	The individual	Interpersonal relationships—teams, work units, intergroup relations, superior-subordinate relations
Content of Training	Technical and administrative skills	Interpersonal and group membership skills—communication, problem-solving, conflict management, helping
Target Subjects	Primarily first line employees and supervisors. Managers trained outside organization.	All levels. Usually initial intervention with upper management in-house.
Conception of Learning Process	Cognitive and rational	Cognitive, rational, emotional-motivational
Learning Approach	Subject matter and teacher centered	Participant, immediate experience, problem-solving, and subject matter centered.
Learning Goals	Rationality and efficiency	Awareness, adaptation and change
View of Organization	Discrete functional skill units	Social system

Exhibit A. A comparison of traditional training and the organization change process

Greiner[9] and others have been documented. Warren Bennis,[10] Gordon Lippitt,[11] Floyd Mann,[12] Chris Argyris,[13] Edgar Shein,[14] and Robert Blake and Jane Mouton[15] are among those who have contributed to the literature in this field.

Major Thrusts

There is no clear-cut typology of the techniques associated with the change process. It is, however, possible to identify some of the major thrusts. Richard Beckhard advocates a "systematic information collection, feedback, and joint action planning" model in which a consultant assists working groups of management personnel in learning how to identify, understand and solve operational and interpersonal problems.[16] Blake and Mouton's Grid Organizational Development approach begins with a pre-established model of what effective managerial behavior should consist of, and through a systematic training procedure seeks to implement this model at both personal and organizational levels. Davis[17] and others assert that T-Group learnings pay off best in the organization when they are followed up with team building sessions in which groups of co-workers engage in group process discussions to explore and work through interpersonal and operational problems. Still another model is the survey-feedback design in which questionnaire data from employees at several levels are compiled. Meetings of employee groups are then held for the purpose of mutually analyzing and intepreting the results as an aid in solving organization problems.[18] Change projects may also include specific organizational programs such as work re-designing, job posting systems, and skill training sessions. The methods mentioned above do not constitute an exhaustive list, and there is a good deal of overlap.

It is not the purpose of this chapter to define and evaluate the various change methodologies. However, the need for evaluative research on the alternative methodologies, as well as on the overall approach should be emphasized.

It may be useful to compare the foregoing description of organization change with management development, as the term is currently used. Management development, as described by House, refers to "any attempt to improve current or future managerial performance by imparting information, conditioning attitudes, or increasing skills. Hence management development includes such efforts as on-the-job coaching, counseling, classroom training, job rotation, selected readings, planned experience, and assignment to understudy positions."[19] The focus is primarily on the manager and her or his behavior. The major contribution of current books and programs related to management development is that of presenting a more sophisticated and complete approach to training in the skill areas related to management. Such efforts may be a component of an organizational change effort.

Many training directors, human resource managers and managers in general are aware of the increasing interest in organization change programs and would like to try them. However, they frequently run into significant difficulty in convincing top management of the value of this approach and in developing financial and policy support. Thus, many change efforts never get off the ground, while others get watered down to impotent proportions. A part of this circumstance is doubtless due to unfamiliarity or lack of appreciation of the problem by managers—as is often asserted. But another significant part is probably due to more subtle forces. While traditional training was assumed to deal primarily with such relatively "safe" areas as technical job skills, change efforts deal not only with *how* a particular individual does a job, but puts that job in its context in the organizational system and claims as its legitimate domain the confrontation of such questions as *why* the job is structured as it is, organization policy that relates to that job, and the behavior of other people who relate to that job—including managers. In other words, it brings organization members at all levels in on issues that heretofore were considered to be the exclusive province of top management. Furthermore, it legitimizes the opportunity for employees to react openly to aspects of the social system which impinge upon them, and to attempt counter-influence in order to change organizational forces surrounding their roles.

Organizations considering embarking on change efforts should seriously review their development needs, the possible impacts of such programs on the organization, their readiness for self-examination and change, and the willingness of management to open up organizational issues which may be affecting employee performance. Below are listed some points worthy of consideration by organizations contemplating a broad gauged change effort.

a. Significant change efforts are rarely successful without continued *active* support and involvement from top management. Total responsibility cannot be vested in a middle staff person. Upper managers must be involved in formulating training goals, must participate in the training themselves, and must reinforce the behaviors sought after in training in their everyday managerial philosophy and behavior. They should also be involved in the evaluation of training.

b. The goal and impact of such an effort is *change*—to change the thoughts and feelings of members of the organization will likely result in changes in their behavior, relationships, and attitudes about the organization. Outcomes may challenge and call into question existing policies, structures, and managerial performance.

c. Training cannot realistically be expected to solve all the "people problems" of an organization, and attempts to raise morale, develop loyalty, or "sell the company" through training may be risky at best.

d. The outcomes of training will be influenced by the total organizational system. The "climate" of the organization may encourage and reinforce changes aimed at in the training, or it may make these changes impossible and frustrate the trainees. The organization must be willing to look at its climate to see if it fosters development, growth and change.

e. The organization must be willing to accept the fact that some of the people in whom it invests training resources may leave the organization and utilize their learning elsewhere. This possibility has kept more than one organization from instituting a significant change effort.

f. There is evidence to suggest that underlying the substance of many discussions that take place in training sessions are basic employee concerns about such factors as interpersonal relationships, status, and career potential. Many consultants who are involved in development programs try to build into the programs the possibility for these basic concerns to be legitimized and dealt with in the training situation. It is not realistic to expect to "keep feelings out of it," or to deal only with abstract principles.

g. The relatively early state of development of management theory leaves us with differing opinions about successful management approaches and with few clearly right or wrong answers or keys to success. No training or development program can provide quick and easy solutions which can be easily implemented.

h. Some organizations confuse change programs with show business. For example, the training director may become saddled with the responsibility for attracting and holding employee audiences on a volunteer basis by making programs entertaining. While participant feedback is an important aspect of a change program, the organization has no more responsibility to entertain its employees in training sessions than it does in budget conferences or planning meetings. The participants share with the trainer a responsibility to create conditions for productive learning. The criterion for measuring results is more effective managerial behavior—not enjoyment.

Vital Considerations

If a decision is made to pursue an organizational change effort, its success can be enhanced by building it into the management process. It may be useful to establish a permanent advisory group made up of management personnel from various parts of the organization. This group can work with the designated staff person or department in formulating, implementing and evaluating the program. And the advisory group can participate in the development of a comprehensive long-range plan for the effort and can periodically review and revise the program, if necessary.

A second difficult aspect of implementing such an effort—after getting the organization to accept and integrate the concept—is to locate training resources. If the training department is to effectively assist in implementation, some readjustments may be necessary. One area of readjustment may be the attitudes and skills of the training staff itself. Staff members whose experience and attitudes indicate a role of teacher, audio-visual expert, or administrator of skill training classes may need a considerable amount of re-training themselves in order to perform roles more akin to change agents in the management process.[20]

Another area of readjustment relates to the way the trainer is perceived by other members of the organization. The present roles of many trainers are viewed as roles of relatively low power whose legitimate domain does not include managerial behavior and organizational operation. As long as these perceptions exist, whether they be valid or invalid, the incumbent will have difficulty administering a change program.

A well-reasoned training and development effort can often utilize a combination of internal and external resources. Few companies can accumulate a large and well-qualified staff of trainers to meet all needs. Yet a willy-nilly mix of visiting speakers, professional meetings, and canned programs will probably not be effective. Depending on the size and characteristics of the organizations, some programs that are recurrent and specific to the organization, such as supervisory training, can often be best handled inhouse. Other programs can be developed out of regular visits by consultants, planned attendance at conferences and management seminars, and with regular reinforcement on the job through meetings, and reports. The distinguishing characteristic of most change efforts is a series of sessions for teams of employees in which consultants (either internally or externally based) assist participants in combining training with problem-solving and planning. No available program can realistically expect to meet all training needs. Most packages are based on certain premises and aimed at certain problem areas. They should be used to deal with specific organization problems in tandem with other development approaches.

In summary, moving from traditional skills training to an organization change effort may well mean that the organization has to deal with issues which are easy to ignore or avoid but crucial to the success of the effort. These issues have to do with the emphasis to be placed on development and the resources to be devoted to it, with implications regarding basic and sometimes uncomfortable issues such as influence, with change in behavior and attitude, and with the role and competencies of the staff available. Unless these issues are confronted and dealt with, the organization is likely to find that it is extremely difficult to sustain a meaningful change effort.[21]

Footnotes

[1]W. G. Bennis, *Changing Organizations*, (New York: McGraw-Hill, 1966).

[2]G. Burck, "Union Carbide's Patient Schemers," *Fortune Magazine*, (December, 1965).

[3]John Poppy, "New Era in Industry: It's O.K. to Cry in the Office," *Look*, (July 9, 1968), pp. 64-76.

[4]S. A. Davis, "An Organic Problem-Solving Method of Organizational Change," *Journal of Applied Behavioral Science*, Vol 3, (Jan-March, 1967), pp.3-21.

[5]A. J. Marrow, D. G. Bowers and Stanley Seashore, *Management by Participation*, (New York: Harper, 1967).

[6]P. C. Buchanan, "Training Laboratories in Organization Development" in *Issues in Human Relations Training*, I. R. Weschler & E. H. Schein (eds.) (Washington, D.C., National Training Laboratories—National Education Association, 1962), pp.86-92.

[7]C. Argyris, *Interpersonal Competence and Organizational Effectiveness*, (Homewood, Illinois: Dorsey-Irwin, 1962).

[8]F. C. Mann, "Studying and Creating Change: A Means to Understanding Social Organization," in D. M. Arensberg, *et al.*, *Research in Industrial Human Relations*, (New York: Harper, 1957), pp. 146-167.

[9]L. B. Barnes & L. E. Greiner, "Breakthrough in Organization Development, Part II." *Harvard Business Review*, (Nov.-Dec., 1964), pp. 139-155.

[10]W. G. Bennis, *op. cit.*

[11]G. L. Lippitt, "Emerging Criteria for Organization Development" *Personnel Administration*, (May-June, 1966), pp. 6-11.

[12]F. C. Mann, *op. cit.*

[13]C. Argyris, *op. cit.*

[14]E. H. Schein, "Management Development as a Process of Influence" *Industrial Management Review*, Vol. II, (May, 1961).

[15]R. R. Blake and Jane S. Mouton, *Corporate Excellence Through Grid Organization Development: A Systems Approach* (Houston, Texas: Gulf Publishing Co., 1968).

[16]*What's Wrong With Work?*, New York: National Association of Manufacturers, 1967, p. 13.

[17]Davis, *op. cit.*

[18]Mann, *op. cit.*

[19]R. J. House, *Management Development: Design Evaluation & Implementation*, (Ann Arbor: University of Michigan, 1967), p. 13.

[20]See the following for descriptions of the change agent role, R. Lippitt, Jeane Watson & B. Westley, *The Dynamics of Planned Change*, (New York: Harcourt, Brace and World, 1958) and W. G. Bennis, K. Benne and R. Chin, (eds.), *The Planning of Change*, (New York:Holt, Rinehart and Winston, 1961). Training programs in organization development and change agentry are currently being offered by the National Training Laboratories and several universities.

[21]The author is indebted to Seymour Levy, James Crabtree and Thomas Lukens for their helpful suggestions.

19

Adapting to a Changing World

by Eric Trist

People and the organizations they build are having to learn to cope with a quality in the environment that has become increasingly salient in recent years. This quality, which may usefully be referred to as *turbulence*, arises from the growing interdependence and complexity and the resulting higher level of uncertainty that exist in the world today. Among other factors, this turbulence is being induced by the accelerating rate of technological change. To put it succinctly, we have lost the *stable state*, and in order to regain it and reduce environmental turbulence, we can less and less depend on our inherited organizational values and forms. We have to seek new ones. Improving the quality of working life (QWL) is an essential part of the search for alternative organizational patterns.

As a consequence, in advanced industrial countries people are increasingly becoming concerned with the substitution of new ways for old in the world of work. These ways include collaborative rather than competitive values, participant management styles, transbureaucratic organizational forms, systems of shared power and control, and new principles of job design. Together these are aimed at creating work which is worth doing for its own sake by everyone in an organization. In short, a new work ethic is beginning to emerge, concerned with the quality of life in the workplace as a central part of the quality of life as a whole.

In the face of these developments, we have two broad choices. The first is to leave the vast bulk of jobs that must still be done in the manufacturing and service industries in the dull and monotonous state

Eric Trist is professor of Social Systems Sciences, University of Pennsylvania, and visiting professor, Faculty of Environmental Studies, York University, Toronto.

From George Sanderson (Ed.), *A New Role for Labour: Industrial Democracy Today*. Toronto: McGraw-Hill Ryerson, 1978. Copyright 1978 by Eric Trist. Reprinted by permission of the author.

in which they exist at present, while maintaining a scale of pay that enables satisfaction to be sought elsewhere. Unfortunately, this position still reflects a majority view, which accepts a low QWL for the many.

The second choice is to redesign jobs and organizational forms so that the majority rather than merely the privileged few can do work which is meaningful and fulfilling, while at the same time maintaining a high level of performance. This position reflects the minority but emerging view. It does not accept a low QWL for the many.

Alienation, a sort of non-work ethic, has been increasingly in the postwar period, especially among the younger generation whose expectations and experiences are different from those that arose under the conditions of scarcity that characterized the Depression years. Attitude surveys in several countries indicate that only the older worker continues to be willing to trade off dehumanizing work simply for good wages and employment security.

The problem is not simply that of either 'adjusting' people to technology or technology to people; it consists of organizing the man-machine interface so that the best match can be obtained between both. Rather it is essential that the whole socio-technical system—of which both technologies and humans are parts—be effectively 'optimized.' This is necessary at all levels and in all types of technology: the 'mediating' technologies with which the service industries are concerned, the intensive technologies with which professional and R&D organizations are concerned, as well as the 'long linked' technologies which form the basis of manufacturing. The task, in essence, is one of *joint optimization*.

The human individual has work-related needs other than those specified in a contract of employment (such as wages, hours, safety, security of tenure, and so on.) These *extrinsic* requirements, shown on the left of Table 1 form the legacy of the old work ethic. In addition, a variety of psychological requirements or *intrinsic* factors must also be met if the new work ethic is to develop. These intrinsic factors, which are shown on the right side of Table 1, include:

1. The need for the job to be reasonably demanding in terms other than sheer endurance and to provide a minimum of variety (not necessarily novelty, which is too much for some people though the spice of life for others). This is to recognize enfranchisement in problem-solving as a human right.

2. The need to be able to learn on the job on a continuing basis. Again, this is a question of neither too much nor too little, but of matching solutions to personal requirements. This is to recognize personal growth as a human right.

Table 1
Properties of Jobs

Extrinsic	**Intrinsic**
Fair and adequate pay	Variety and challenge
Job security	Continuous learning
Benefits	Discretion, autonomy
Safety	Recognition and support
Health	Meaningful social contribution
Due Process	Desirable future
—	—
Conditions of Employment	The Job Itself
Socio-economic	Psycho-social

3. The need for some area of decision-making that the individual can call his own. This recognizes the opportunity to use one's own judgment as a human right.

4. The need for some degree of social support and recognition in the workplace, from both fellow workers and bosses. This recognizes 'group belongingness' as a human right.

5. The need to be able to relate what one does and what one produces to one's social life. That is, to have a meaningful occupational identity which gives a man or woman dignity. This recognizes the opportunity to contribute to society as a human right.

6. The need to feel that the job leads to some sort of desirable future (not necessarily promotion). It may involve training or redeployment—a career at shop floor level leading to the development of greater skill. This recognizes hope as a human right.

These psychological needs and associated human rights are not confined to any one level of employment. Managers also need a high QWL. However, it must be recognized that it is not always possible to meet these needs to the same extent in all work settings; nor, indeed, do all kinds of people need them to the same degree—individual differences are considerable. Furthermore, these needs cannot always be judged from conscious expression such as that given in responses to attitude surveys about job satisfaction. Where there is no expectation that any of the jobs open will offer much chance of learning, a person will soon learn to 'forget' such a requirement. It is difficult to accept as real something one has not yet experienced. Nevertheless, a high QWL may still be built in terms of these factors—so long as the factors on the extrinsic list are also satisfied. Together they constitute the necessary and sufficient conditions for a high QWL—at the job or task level.

One popular approach to QWL has been through job enrichment, which is concerned with altering the boundaries of jobs so that the tasks included make a more complete whole, giving the worker more variety, more information, more decision-making and more autonomy than he or she previously enjoyed. Job enrichment entails considerably more than job enlargement and job rotation, though it may include both. All these activities, however, have centered on the individual rather than the group. Moreover, they have not in their orthodox form embraced participation but avoided it—the "enriching" has been devised solely by the experts hired by management.

When job enrichment projects include participation they become congruent with autonomous work groups. The project that brought together in a fully participative context the various findings concerning autonomous work groups and job enrichment in order to develop a first comprehensive model of work-linked democracy has become known as the Norwegian Industrial Democracy Project.

The project, which began in 1962 and is still proceeding, grew out of a crisis between the Norwegian Confederation of Employers and the Norwegian Confederation of Labour over a sudden increase in the demands for workers' representation on boards of management, initially proposed as a way of reducing alienation and increasing productivity. The two confederations (later joined by the government) requested the assistance of social scientists in order to gain a better understanding of what ordinarily would have been treated as a political problem. Research plans were drawn up in conjunction with representatives of the two confederations. Their participation in every step was crucial as the project entailed securing a very full understanding by the leadership of both sides of Norwegian industry of the findings as they became available. Effectively, the ownership of the project became theirs, a situation that is "a must" in the strategy of QWL.

The first phase consisted of a field study of what actually happened in the five major concerns where workers were represented on the boards. These were government-owned or part-owned enterprises obliged by law to have workers' representatives. The findings suggested that though such representation was positively valued for its own sake, there was nevertheless no increase in participation by the rank and file, no decrease in work alienation, and no increase in productivity, all results that have since been confirmed by other studies.

The widespread public discussion of the results opened the way for the second phase of the project:

> to search for ways of securing improved conditions for personal participation in a man's immediate setting as constituting a different and perhaps

more important basis for the democratization of the work place than the formal systems of representation which seemed to have reached their limit at least for the time being.

This led to the idea of field experiments in selected plants in key industries, which could serve as demonstration models for diffusion purposes. This method has since been widely followed in QWL projects in other countries; though it has recently been found to have serious drawbacks in that the high profile sites tend to become encapsulated.

One experiment of interest took place in the pulp and paper industry. A sophisticated chemical plant was selected where the basic work to be considered was information handling—the core task in the technologies of the post industrial revolution based on information and automation. Under these technologies, the requisite skills are perceptual and conceptual, while the requisite work organization is one capable of handling the complex information flows on which controlling the process depends. This requires immense flexibility as well as a high capacity for self-regulation. In the experimental plant a number of the key process uncertainties or variances were not being effectively controlled by the social system—that is by the men and their managers—nor indeed had some of the most important of them even been identified. The research team therefore had to engage those concerned in evolving a form of organization that would bring as many of these variances as possible under the control of the primary work groups.

The model was developed of a joint management-labour 'action committee.' This appointed a task force consisting of operators, supervisors and two specialists as collaborating interdependent resources to fashion an optimum work organization for a new technology while they were learning the know-how of its operation. This demonstration of the problem-solving capability of a self-regulating work group was a major advance on what had so far been shown. Indeed, this model has become the basis of much that has happened since in several countries, including much of what is at present being done in the U.S.

The next step was taken at Norskhydro, the largest enterprise in Norway, which manufactures fertilizers and other chemicals. Here a whole plant rather than just a department was taken as the system to be changed. The work practices of an old plant were refashioned and the entire range of organization and operating procedures were developed for a new one. The first of these tasks proved more difficult than the second, a fact that has since been found in a number of other plants. Indeed, to change values, attitudes, work customs and organizational arrangements in established plants, as total systems, appears to be one of the most difficult tasks in QWL. In some circumstances it does not work out at all, despite sedulous efforts, while in others it is painfully slow.

An additional innovation of the experiment was the fact that in the new plant a radically new principle of wage payment was tried out, namely paying people for what they know rather than for what they do. This idea opened up a new concept of pay, which has since been tried out in several countries, including the U.S., where it has been used in General Foods' Topeka plant. Under the system, it was recognized that as a man learned to perform more tasks he became more valuable, and hence was worth more money. The aim was to build up an all-around capability in the task force which would not only allow its members to be flexibly deployed according to the needs of a changing technological and economic environment, but would also enable them to contribute to the continuous improvement of the operation. This project demonstrated what might be achieved when an industrial organization is deliberately developed as a 'continuous adaptive learning system' in which the planning process takes on a 'transactive' character involving all concerned. This mode, again, has become the basis of much that has happened since in work and organizational design, in many countries.

Still another experiment is the more recent work in the shipping industry concerned with the design and experimental trial of sophisticated bulk carriers. This has led to a further innovative step, for in this case many technological alternatives were available, but the chosen design was that which met most fully the needs of the small shipboard community which had to live together under isolated conditions 24 hours a day for considerable periods of time, while simultaneously undertaking all the work tasks. Their needs were shown by preliminary studies to be of overriding concern. A common recreation room—as well as mess—was established, where all ranks could socialize (and drink together rather than be isolated with a bottle in the cabin). Deck and engine room crews were thus integrated, and status differences between officers and men were reduced, or even eliminated through the development of open career lines on one or two "all officer" ships. Serial career structures also have been accepted, and training for a future job on shore can now be begun at sea.

This project shows how the properties of the required social system may become the starting point for technical design. We can actually start with QWL, for we now have the technologies to do it. This model is likely to influence plant design more and more in the future. Volvo and Saab-Scania for example, were led to seek alternatives to the assembly line because Swedes would not work on the lines. Their job turnover and absenteeism were much too high, while foreign workers caused too much "re-work" and created social problems. So the engineers were asked to think again—not alone, either, but in composite design teams.

One finding of all the Norwegian experiments was the strong resistance encountered amongst middle management, and particularly by those who perceived themselves as likely to be adversely affected. Thus a positive reorganization of roles and career prospects at this level had to be worked out. The problem is still not completely resolved, however. It has haunted QWL endeavors everywhere, for supervisors and specialist staff are generally employed in traditional bureaucratic and technocratic organizations in numbers that are surplus to the requirements of innovative democratic organizations. Very often the manning level in the work force is also lower—sometimes much lower. This is one consequence of participation with which we must learn to deal, at least if we are determined to secure a high QWL for the many rather than the few. It means removing feather bedding, while facing up to the issue of job security. It also means working out desirable futures for those who may otherwise be adversely affected—or resistance will very soon put a stop to innovative schemes.

Thus, how to sustain innovation, when the wider organizational context is not as supportive as it might be, is another of the critical areas that the QWL enterprise needs to learn far more about than it does at present.

More than enough experience and research evidence is available to suggest that small isolated QWL projects in component parts of an organization do not survive in an alien organizational context. For example, some 70 such projects, most of which were doing quite well, and some very well, have faded away in the last three years in one large organization that I have recently studied. In this case, individual managers began to initiate small QWL projects some ten years ago without much support hhiger up or even from colleagues. The organizational context was not changed. However, this is essential. It means undertaking systemic transformation and that entails abandoning the philosophy on which the old organizational paradigm is based and working towards a new philosophy that will guide the operational realization of the new paradigm of QWL. To this task the support of top management is essential.

What have we learned about diffusing a higher quality of working life into the organization as a whole? And what lies ahead?

Table 2 sets out the key features of the new organizational paradigm, which can potentially lead to a high QWL for all members of the enterprise. They contrast strongly with those of the old organizational paradigm, set out on the left, and which has been instrumental in constraining most employees to a low QWL.

Our traditional organizations follow the technological imperative, which regards man simply as an extension of the machine and therefore as an expendable spare part. By contrast, the emergent paradigm is founded on the principle of joint-optimization, which regards man as complementary to the machine and values his unique capabilities for appreciative and evaluative judgment. He is a resource to be developed for his own sake rather than to be degraded and cast aside, for as my former Tavistock colleague Phil Herbst has aptly observed, "the product of work is people" and a society is no better than the quality of the people it produces.

Table 2

OLD PARADIGM	NEW PARADIGM
The technological imperative	Joint optimization
Man as an extension of the machine	Man as complementary to the machine
An expendable spare part	A resource to be developed
Maximum task breakdown, single, narrow skills	Optimum task grouping, multiple, broad skills
External controls (supervisors, specialist staffs, procedures)	Internal controls (self-regulating subsystems)
Tall organization chart, autocratic style	Flat organization chart, participative style
Competition, gamesmanship	Collaboration, collegiality
Organization's purposes only	Members' and society's purposes also
Alienation	Commitment
Low risk taking	Innovation

Traditional organizations are also characterized by maximum work-breakdown, which leads to circumscribed job descriptions and single skills—the narrower the better. Workers in such roles are often unable to manage the uncertainty or the variance that characterizes their immediate environment and they therefore require strict external controls. Layer upon layer of supervision comes into existence, supported by a wide variety of specialist staffs and formal procedures. A tall pyramidic organization results, which is autocratically managed throughout, even if the paternalism is benign. By contrast the new paradigm is based on an optimum task grouping, which encourages multiple broad-ranking skills. Workers in such a role system become capable of a much higher degree of internal control, having flexible group resources to meet a greater degree of environmental variance. This leads to a flat organization characterized by as much lateral as vertical communication. Moreover a participative management style emerges, with the various levels mutually articulated rather than arranged in a simple hierarchy.

In the traditional organization each member has first of all to compete with and defend himself against everyone else, whether as an individual or as the member of a functional group—maintenance versus production, staff versus line, and so on. Rewards of promotion and privilege go most of all to those who, in the metaphor of Michael Maccoby's recent book, are 'gamesmen.' They excel in playing the political game of the organization. Co-operation, though formally required wherever tasks are interdependent, takes second place as a value. The new paradigm, by contrast, gives first place to coping with the manifold interdependencies that arise in complex organizations. It therefore values collaboration between groups as well as collegiality within groups. It encourages the establishment of a negotiated order in which multiple and mutually agreed tradeoffs are continuously arrived at.

Traditional organizations serve only their own ends. They are, and indeed are supposed to be, selfish. However, the new paradigm imposes the additional task on them of aligning their own purposes with those of the wider society as well as with those of their members. By so doing they become both 'environmentalized' and 'humanized,' and thus become more truly purposeful, rather than merely remaining the impersonal and mindless forces that are increasing environmental turbulence.

A change in all these regards from the old paradigm to the new brings into being conditions that allow commitment to grow and alienation to decrease. Equally important is the replacement of a climate of low risk-taking with one of innovation. This implies high trust and openness in relations. All these qualities are mandatory if we are to transform traditional technocratic bureaucracies into a continuous adaptive learning system. And this *is* the central task.

This transformation is imperative for survival in a fast-changing environment. It involves nothing less than the working out of a new organizational philosophy.

I use the term philosophy advisedly to indicate that far more is involved than methods or techniques. These of course have their place, but a philosophy involves questions of basic values and assumptions. Those of the new paradigm are radically different from those of the old. The old is based on technocratic and bureaucratic principles, the new on socio-ecological and participative principles. Each sub-system has a wide repertoire of response capability. It can thus better meet uncertainty and contain turbulence. This is one of the most important features of self-regulating systems of autonomous work groups and of open mutually articulated levels. The old is geared to the requirements and characteristics of industrial societies as these have been fashioned historically. The new is geared to the requirements and characteristics of the emerging post-industrial order. At present we are in a transition channel between the two. A transition channel is always an uncomfortable place to be, full, as it is, of incompatibilities on the one hand and mirages on the other. It is no wonder that we have lost the stable state.

But I do not believe that the move towards a higher QWL as a central part of a broader quest for a higher quality of life is a mirage. It is a main way of absorbing environmental turbulence and so of regaining a more stable state.

In Norway the trend has been persistent and growing in strength for more than 15 years; in Sweden and one or two other countries for 10 years; in several others, including the U.S., for five years. Moreover, this trend does not appear to be reversible.

Nevertheless, it will be some considerable time before the new paradigm fully establishes itself as the dominant force in any country, even in Scandinavia. To change from the old to the new way involves a long and arduous process with many setbacks and disappointments, especially in transforming established organizations. A number of rear-guard actions will be doggedly fought by those among both management and labour who want to have nothing to do with the new way at any price, including the price of not doing very well as regards productivity.

The danger is that the required changes will come about too slowly to avert a degree of organizational dysfunction which will have serious consequences, economic and social, for the wider society. We have learned a great deal in the last two decades about facilitating organizational change. Much progress has been made in the field of organizational development; but we do not know very much yet about bringing about in large organizational populations the type of paradigm shift with which this paper has been concerned.

Let me mention two portents of hope. First, the QWL movement has weathered the recent recession. There have been setbacks here and delays there but the movement has been far stronger in 1976-77 than it was in 1973-74. The prime importance of improving job security, if the support of organized labour is to be won, has been learned.

Finally, we are passing into the era of a conserver society. This makes it more necessary than ever to develop to the full our human resources and so to learn to do more with less.

I believe this message about the enhanced importance of human resources is beginning to get through to an increasing number of people. Moreover as it does, a higher QWL will more easily become the goal for the many rather than the few, and as this happens, a critical enabling condition will be brought into existence that will help us to achieve a future more desirable than some that would otherwise be in store for us.

For myself, I am willing to be patient and modestly hopeful as regards the future of the new paradigm. In any case it is better to try to improve rather than simply bemoan the human condition, however much man may fall short of perfectability. That short fall need not prevent us from achieving a higher QWL for all in a work-a-day world, and thereby making life in the work-place more pleasant and more relevant to human purposes.

Accounts of the Norwegian Industrial Democracy Project are available in English in the following publications: F. E. Emery and E. Thorsrud, *Democracy at Work: The Report of the Norwegian Industrial Democracy Program (International Ser. on the Quality of Working Life: 2)*, 1977; and P. G. Herbst, *Alternatives to Hierarchies: International Ser. on the Quality of Working Life.* (No. 1), 1977. Both reports are published by Humanities Press, Atlantic Highlands, New Jersey, and by Martinus Nijihoff, Leiden, Netherlands.

Management by Objectives:
The Team Approach

by Wendell L. French and Robert W. Hollmann

Study of the many books, articles, case studies, speeches, and discussions about management by objectives (MBO) indicate that most forms of this approach tend to reinforce a one-to-one leadership style. It is also apparent that MBO efforts vary from being highly autocratic to highly participative among organizations and even within some organizations. In this article we present a case and strategy for *collaborative* management by objectives (CMBO), a participative, team-centered approach. This approach has a number of unique features that will minimize some of the deficiencies in more traditional versions, but as we shall see, the skills involved and the organizational climate required for its optimal effectiveness may not come easily.

One-to-One MBO

Let us first compare the autocratic and participative characteristics of one-to-one versions of MBO. Examples 1a through 1d in Table 1 illustrate how this form can differ along the autocratic-participative continuum. In one contemporary version of MBO, the superior prepares a list of objectives and simply passes them down to the subordinate. In a second version, the superior prepares the subordinate's list of objectives and allows him or her ample opportunity for questions and clarification. In a third version, the subordinate prepares his own list of objectives and submits this list to his superior for discussion and subsequent editing and modification by the superior. And in a fourth version, the superior and subordinate independently prepare lists of the subordinate's objec-

[1] Wendell L. French is professor of management and associate dean, Graduate School of Business Administration, University of Washington. Robert W. Hollmann is assistant professor of management, College of Business and Public Administration, University of Arizona.

Table 1
Objective Setting in Different Versions of MBO

Degree of Subordinate Influence on Objectives	Very Little	Some	Moderate	Considerable
Individual Orientation	**1a** Superior prepares list of subordinate's objectives and gives it to subordinate	**1b** Superior prepares list of subordinate's objectives; allows opportunity for clarification and suggestions.	**1c** Subordinate prepares list of his objectives; superior-subordinate discussion of tentative list is followed by editing, modification, and finalization by superior.	**1d** Superior and subordinate independently prepare list of subordinate's objectives; mutual agreement reached after extensive dialogue.
Team Orientation	**2a** Superior prepares individual lists of various subordinates objectives; hands out lists in group meeting and explains objectives.	**2b** Superior prepares unit and individual objectives allows opportunity for questions and suggestions in group meeting.	**2c** Superior prepares list of unit objectives which are discussed in group meeting; superior decides. Subordinates then prepare lists of their objectives, discuss with superior; individuals' objectives discussed in team meeting with modifications made by superior after extensive dialogue.	**2d** Unit objectives, including team effectiveness goals, are developed among superior, subordinates, and peers in a group meeting, usually by consensus; superior and subordinates later independently prepare lists of subordinates' objectives; reach temporary agreement; subordinates' objectives finalized after extensive discussion in team meeting.

tives and then meet to agree upon the final list. Similar degrees of subordinate participation also can occur at other steps in the MBO process (in determination of objective measures of performance and in the end-of-the-period evaluation, for example). Obviously many variations are possible, but the point is that the different versions of one-to-one MBO can fall anywhere along the traditional autocratic-participative continuum.

Deficiencies in One-to-One MBO

Disregarding the likely long-range inadequacies of any autocratic form of MBO, we believe that the one-to-one mode has a number of critical deficiencies. First, one-to-one MBO does not adequately account for the interdependent nature of most jobs, particularly at the managerial and supervisory levels. Second, it does not assure optimal coordination of objectives. And third, it does not always improve superior-subordinate relationships, as is widely claimed by MBO proponents (we do not know whether a team approach always will improve relations either, but we are much more optimistic about the latter). These deficiencies pertain to all versions of one-to-one MBO, regardless of how autocratic or participative, although we believe that the deficiencies would be more salient under autocratic supervisory behavior. Let us examine these limitations more closely.

Managerial interdependence. A number of writers have pointed out that one-to-one, superior-subordinate MBO does not recognize the interdependent or complementary nature of managerial jobs.[1] We concur with this criticism and believe that effective implementation of MBO requires a "systems view" of the organization. Each manager functions in a complex network of vertical, horizontal, and diagonal relationships, and his success in achieving his objectives is often (if not always) dependent upon the communication, cooperation, and support of other managers in this network.

The relevance of managerial interdependence is particularly evident when MBO is used with staff managers. A number of authors have described the difficulties in applying MBO to staff positions.[2] We need not reiterate their ideas here, except to stress the point that the advisory and supportive nature of staff work dictates that a staff manager's objectives be highly interrelated with the activities and objectives of other managers, both line and staff. Furthermore, staff objectives are often more qualitative than quantitative, and therefore more difficult to set and measure. Asking the staff manager to set either qualitative or quantitative objectives in isolation from those upon whom his attainment of these objectives is largely dependent does not make good sense.

An indication of the lack of attention to the interdependent nature of managerial jobs can be found in two recent works, one including descriptions of MBO programs in four British firms,[3] the other including five American companies.[4] Eight of the nine companies require that forms be filled out in the MBO programs, but in only one company's form is there any space for the manager to specify the extent to which his objectives require involvement of other managers.

Coordination of objectives. Another deficiency is associated with this interdependency. One of the highly touted advantages of MBO is that it results in effective coordination of objectives; that is, there is better integration (including minimization of gaps and duplication) of the objectives of all managers in the work unit. While this is certainly a desirable benefit, it must be recognized that one-to-one MBO places the responsibility for such coordination entirely upon the superior, since he is the only person in the MBO process to have formal contact with all subordinate managers. In effect, the superior is required to function as a "central processing center of objectives."

We believe that one-to-one MBO simply does not provide the opportunity for maximum coordination of objectives. The superior may be able to marginally, or even adequately, coordinate the objectives of his immediate subordinates on a one-to-one basis, but this procedure does not really do justice to the subtleties of interdependent relationships. Under such circumstances, except for information transmitted informally and sporadically between peers in on-the-job interaction, subordinate managers have little knowledge or understanding of each other's knowledge. On the other hand, if these subordinates were provided with the opportunity for dynamic interactive processes in which their objectives are systematically communicated and adjusted, final objectives probably would be more effectively coordinated.

The deficiency in the coordination of objectives is magnified in cases of managers performing highly interrelated tasks but working in different departments. For example, a sales manager in a marketing division organized along product lines needs to coordinate his objectives with those of the appropriate production manager responsible for manufacturing the product. The sales manager may meet his objective of a 5-percent increase in the sales of product X, but the organization is likely to suffer a loss of future sales and customers if the manufacturing output of product X, which is based upon the production manager's objectives, is inadequate to meet these sales commitments. One-to-one MBO between the sales and production managers and their respective superiors provides no systematic method for integrating their objectives, and accordingly, these two managers must rely entirely upon their own initiative for the development of integrative mechanisms. Quite frankly, we doubt that this haphazard approach results in optimal coordination.

Improved superior-subordinate relationships. The participative, or mutual involvement, form of one-to-one MBO is extolled largely for the improvement in superior-subordinate relationships it is expected to bring about. Not all research supports this claim, however. For example, Tosi and Carroll found that even after an intensive and carefully planned MBO program that stressed subordinate participation, subordinate managers did not feel that the superior-subordinate relationship had improved significantly in terms of helpfulness on the part of the superior.[5] While the researchers offered no specific empirical reasons for this finding, other authors have suggested factors that might provide some explanation.

Kerr believes that the typical organization hierarchy creates a superior-subordinate status differential that acts as a deterrent to the expected improvement in relationships.[6] For instance, when MBO is conducted in a somewhat autocratic manner the status differential inhibits the subordinate from challenging the decisions of his boss or the objectives he has established. Even in cases of greater subordinate involvement, status differences may hinder attainment of the desired ideal mutuality in the MBO process. A similar note is struck by Levinson, who believes that rivalry between a boss and his subordinate can easily impede the creation or maintenance of a positive relationship.[7] It is important to point out that Tosi and Carroll also found that the same MBO program stressing increased subordinate participation resulted in no significant increase in subordinates' perceived influence in the goal-setting process.[8] Perhaps superior-subordinate status differentials or rivalry were operating in this organization.

Incompatibility between the superior's role as a coach and his role as a judge may also hamper the superior-subordinate relationship. Researchers at The General Electric Company concluded that the two primary purposes of performance appraisal (performance improvement and salary adjustment) are in conflict.[9] They suggested that these two purposes could be better accomplished in two separate interviews—a proposal with which we agree. Yet even in this approach, it is easy to see the difficult position in which the superior is placed: prior to and during one interview he is expected to *constructively* evaluate the subordinate's performance and help him formulate plans for improvement, while in the second interview he is expected to *judiciously* evaluate the subordinate's performance in order to make crucial salary recommendations and to inform the subordinate of his decision. Only an exceptionally talented person could shift adroitly between these two roles (especially with the same subordinate), and it is our opinion that most managers have great difficulty doing so. Thus, an MBO program that requires the superior to have complete responsibility in performing these incompatible roles, even in separate interviews, could easily strain rather than improve superior-subordinate relationships.

Team Collaboration in MBO

We believe that MBO could be strengthened considerably by increasing the opportunities for systematic collaboration among managers. Furthermore, MBO programs based on cooperative teamwork and group problem solving would represent a positive step toward rectifying some of the deficiencies found in one-to-one MBO. Ironically, in his original description of MBO, Drucker said, "Right from the start ... emphasis should be on team-work and team results,"[10] but it doesn't look to us as if the MBO movement has gone this way. A number of other authors have called for group or peer goal setting and evaluation in MBO,[11] but with few exceptions,[12] suggestions for a group approach to MBO generally have not been augmented with systematic guidelines or frameworks for implementation.

MBO programs described in the literature and in operation that *do* acknowledge the collaborative dimension can be classified in three categories. First, there are programs that superficially refer to the need for some sort of collaborative effort during the MBO process. For example, the MBO instruction manual may include a statement such as: "Each manager should exert maximum effort to ensure that his objectives are effectively coordinated with those of other managers in his work group." Under this unsystematic approach, then, collaboration is left entirely to each manager's own initiative.

Second, there are programs that provide some formal means for collaboration (see examples 2b and 2c in Table 1). For instance, Wikstrom describes one company program that includes "cross-checking meetings" in which managers present their tentative goals, check the impact of these goals on one another, and make adjustments before finalizing the goals.[13] In a similar vein, Raia suggests team reviews between the superior and his subordinates.[14] Based upon a joint problem-solving approach, these regular review sessions are intended to measure the team's progress toward its goals and to improve team relationships. Raia also encourages the use of a "responsibility matrix" to identify the degree to which various other management positions are related to the major activities a manager performs to accomplish his specific objectives.[15] In essence, then, programs in this second category include collaboration as a tangential aspect of an essentially one-to-one approach.

Third, there are MBO programs that include systematic collaboration as an integral part of the entire process (see example 2d in Table 1). The three-day team objectives meeting described by Reddin illustrates this approach.[16] In this program each team (superior and his immediate subordinates) concentrates on such matters as team-effectiveness areas, team-improvement objectives, team decision making, optimal team organization, team meeting improvements, team-effectiveness evaluation, and team-member effectiveness. Such collaborative approaches appear to have many features congruent with contemporary organization development (OD) and are qualitatively quite different from one-to-one approaches.

MBO and OD Contrasted

One way to describe how CMBO differs qualitatively from a one-to-one approach is to contrast the one-to-one version with the emerging field of OD, which has a strong emphasis on team collaboration. Organization development, in the behavioral-science meaning of the term,[17] is a broader strategy for organizational improvement than is MBO, but it can include the collaborative version as we shall describe it. For instance, Blake and Mouton's six-phase grid OD program includes teamwork development (phase 2) and intergroup development (phase 3), both of which include collaborative goal setting.[18] In fact, they suggest that MBO can be "introduced as the culminating action of Teamwork Development."[19]

Some of the differences, as we see them, between the traditional one-to-one MBO and OD are shown in Table 2. Traditional MBO concentrates on the individual, on goal setting for the individual, on rationality, and on end results. In contrast, OD focuses on how individuals see the functioning of their teams and the organization, on nonrationality, as well as rationality, and on means as well as ends. In addition, OD has a recurring component of system diagnosis that seems to be minimal or absent from the traditional forms of MBO. Further, OD efforts usually move toward legitimizing open discussion of individual career and life goals, which most MBO programs largely ignore.

A Strategy for Collaborative MBO

Contemporary organization-development efforts can provide insights and some of the technology for more widespread emergence of collaborative forms of MBO. We would like to propose a nine-phase strategy for Collaborative MBO. Basically, the essential process is one of overlapping work units interacting with "higher" and "lower" units on overall organizational goals and objectives, unit goals and objectives, and individuals interacting with peers and superiors on role definition and individual goals and objectives.

Table 2

Traditional MBO Compared with OD

What Traditional (One-to-One) MBO Seems to Do	**What OD Seems to Do**
1. Assumes there is a need for more goal emphasis and/or control.	1. Assumes there may be a variety of problems: a need for more goal emphasis and/or control may or may not be a central problem.
2. Has no broad diagnostic strategy.	
3. Central target of change is the individual.	2. Uses an "action-research" model in which system diagnosis and rediagnosis are major features.
4. Asks organization members to develop objectives for key aspects of their jobs in terms of quantitative and qualitative statements that can be measured.	3. Central target of change is team functioning.
	4. Asks organization members to provide data regarding their perceptions of functional/dysfunctional aspects of their units and/or the total organization.
5. Emphasizes avoidance of overlap and incongruity of goals. Assumes things will be better if people understand who has what territory.	5. Emphasizes mutual support and help. Assumes that some problems can stem from confusion about who has what responsibilities, but also looks at opportunities for mutual help in the many interdependent components across jobs.
6. Focuses on the "formal" aspects of the organization (goals, planning, control, appraisal).	
7. Focuses on individual performance and emphasizes individual accountability.	
8. Stresses rationality ("logical" problem solving, man's economic motives).	6. Initially taps into "informal" aspects of the organization (attitudes, feelings, perceptions about both the formal and informal aspects—the total climate of the unit or organization).
9. Focuses on organizational end results of the human-social system (particularly as measured by "hard data") such as sales figures, maintenance costs, and so forth.	7. Focuses on system dynamics that are facilitating or handicapping individual, team, and organizational performance: emphasizes joint accountability.
10. Has little interpersonal-relations "technology" to assist superior and subordinate in the goal-setting and review processes.	8. Legitimizes for discussion nonrational aspects (feelings, attitudes, group phenomena) of organization life as well as rationality; frequently legitimizes open exploration of career and life goals.
	9. Focuses on both ends and means of the human-social system (leadership style, peer relationships, and decision processes, as well as goals and "hard data").
	10. Has extensive interpersonal relations, group dynamics, and intergroup "technology" for decision making, communications, and group task and maintenance processes.

Phase I: Diagnosis of Organizational Problems. A collaborative organizational diagnosis, by discussions or questionnaires involving a cross-section of organization members, suggests the usefulness of a CMBO effort in solving *identified problems.* It appears to us that MBO, as frequently practiced, is a solution in search of a problem. For a variety of reasons, including the existence of a strong goal emphasis under some other name, overwork of many key people in the organization, or problems requiring other solutions, MBO may not be timely or appropriate.

Phase II: Information and Dialogue. Workshops on the basic purposes and techniques of CMBO are held with top management personnel, followed by workshops at the middle- and lower-management levels. These workshops can be conducted by qualified members of the personnel or training departments, by line managers trained in the approach, or if the organization prefers, by a qualified consultant. Having top-level managers conduct the workshops with middle and lower managers may speed up the process of shifting toward the more supportive climate necessary for CMBO.

Phase III: Diagnosis of Organizational Readiness. This diagnosis, based upon interviews and group meetings, must indicate an interest in and a willingness to use the process on the part of several organizational units, especially those at the top of the organization. Ideally, a number of overlapping units should express a desire to implement CMBO; for example, in addition to the president of a manufacturing firm and his immediate subordinates expressing interest, the manufacturing director and his immediate subordinates may want to be involved, and two of these subordinate managers may wish to start the process with their subordinate teams, and so forth. Favorable interest in CMBO from a few units randomly scattered throughout the organization would probably be inadequate to create enough interaction and momentum to give the approach a fair try. A good deal of diagnosis of organizational readiness will have already occurred in the information-and-dialogue phase. Similarly, diagnosis of organizational readiness may reveal the need for supplemental CMBO workshops for some units or for suspending the CMBO effort.

Phase IV: Goal Setting—Overall Organization Level. Overall organization goals and specific objectives to be achieved within a given time period are defined in team meetings among top executives, largely on the basis of consensus. It is important that this phase be an interactive process with middle and lower levels of the organization; inputs about organization goals and objectives from subordinate managerial and supervisory levels must be obtained during (or before) this phase.

Phase V: Goal Setting—Unit Level. Unit goals and objectives essential to achieving overall organization goals and objectives are defined in team situations, largely by consensus. Again, this is an interactive process between higher units and their respective subordinate units.

Phase VI: Goal Setting—Individual Level. This phase begins with individual managers developing their specific objectives in terms of results to be achieved and appropriate time periods. Personal career and development goals are part of this "package." If desired, the manager's superior may simultaneously develop a list of objectives for the subordinate. The superior and subordinate discuss, modify, and tentatively agree on the subordinate's objectives. These discussions are followed by group meetings in which team members discuss each other's objectives, make suggestions for modification, and agree upon each manager's final list of objectives.

Phase VI assumes that there is agreement on the major responsibilities and parameters of the team members' roles. If major responsibilities need to be reviewed or redefined, the following sequence is used as the preliminary stage of phase VI: (1) individual team members list their major responsibilities; (2) individual team members meet with their superior to discuss, modify, and tentatively agree upon their major responsibilities; and (3) team members discuss and work toward consensus on their major responsibilities in group meetings.

Phase VII: Performance Review. On a continuing basis, either the subordinate or the superior initiates discussion whenever progress toward objectives should be reviewed; matters of team concern are discussed in regularly scheduled team meetings. Particularly relevant at this stage are occasions when internal or external factors suggest the need for revision in the original set of goals and objectives; if appropriate, these revisions should be made in collaborative team meetings.

At the end of the agreed-upon time period, each manager prepares a report on the extent to which his objectives have been achieved and discusses this report in a preliminary meeting with his superior. These reports then are presented by each individual in a group meeting, with the discussion including an analysis of the forces helping and hindering attainment of objectives. This review process occurs at all levels (organization, unit, and individual) and ordinarily would start at the lower levels as a convenient way to collate information.

Phase VIII: Rediagnosis. Diagnosis needs to reoccur, but at this phase it is the CMBO process itself that needs examining, as well as the readiness of additional units to use CMBO. Is the CMBO process helping? hindering? in what way? What is the process doing to the relationships between superiors and subordinates and within teams? Something has gone awry if goal setting and performance review are perfunctory or avoided, if the process seems unattached to the basic processes of getting the work of the organization done, or if relationships are becoming strained. On the other hand, if superiors and subordinates and teams find that the process is challenging and stretches and develops their capabilities, and if they feel good about it, the CMBO process is probably on the right track toward increased organizational effectiveness. Ideally such diagnosis should be ongoing as the CMBO process evolves.

Phase IX: Recycle. Assuming that rediagnosis has resulted in the decision to continue the CMBO effort, the cycle of phases IV through VIII is repeated, probably once a year at the overall organization level. Ongoing individual and team progress reviews may result in modification of unit- or individual-level goals more often than once a year. Through periodic problem sensing and rediagnosis, the details of the process will undoubtedly be modified to more adequately meet the needs of teams and individuals. The nine-phase strategy for implementing CMBO is presented in Figure 1.

Some Contingencies

CMBO is not likely to be an easy process for many organizations. Initial successes depend upon a strong desire on the part of the top-management team to cooperate with and help each other. In addition, the process requires some modicum of skill in interpersonal relations and group dynamics. Training in these skills can accompany the CMBO effort, or if an OD effort is under way, such skills will be emerging as part of this broader process.

Proper timing in the introduction of CMBO is also very important. CMBO is by no means a managerial panacea; it should be introduced only when diagnosis suggests its applicability and usefulness as well as organizational readiness. A CMBO effort can be time-consuming, and strong resistance can occur if the process is thoughtlessly superimposed at the wrong time—for example, during a period when people are preoccupied and harried with the annual budgeting process or faced with a major external threat to the organization. It is equally important to recognize that the utility of diagnosing organizational readiness is contingent upon the adequacy of information presented to managers in the CMBO workshops (phase II).

Successful expansion of the process to lower levels of the organization requires commitment to and skills in participative management, as well as a willingness and ability to diagnose the impact of the goal-setting and

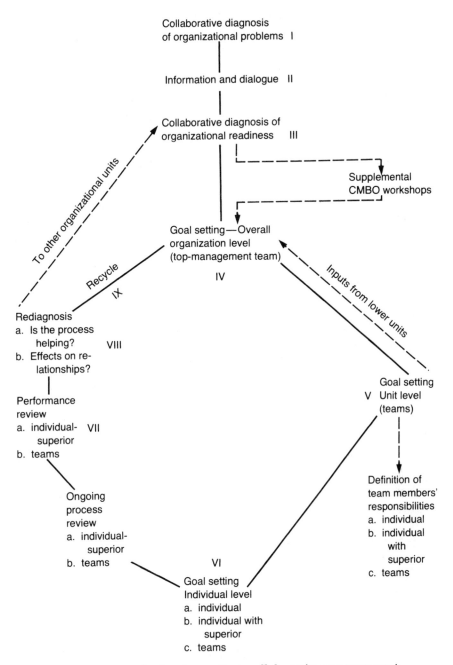

Figure 1. A strategy for implementing collaborative management
by objectives

review processes on organization members and organizational functioning. Such a diagnosis of how things are going might result, for instance, in temporarily postponing phase VI. Successful completion of phases I through V and the appropriate team aspects of phases VII through IX might in itself be a major achievement and a move forward in organizational effectiveness. Developing effective group dynamics takes time and an organization should proceed with caution in this area. A major shift to a collaborative mode cannot be made overnight.

The Merits of CMBO: Research and Practice Clues

There are a number of clues to the merits of a Collaborative MBO approach (that is, the kind that has a team emphasis, is truly collaborative, and exists in a climate of mutual support and help) in research reports and in practice. Likert cites a study of a sales organization in which salesmen held group meetings at regular intervals to set goals, discuss procedures, and identify results to be achieved before the next group meeting.[20] During these meetings the superior acted as a chairman; he stressed a constructive, problem-solving approach, encouraged high performance, and provided technical advice when necessary. The results of the study showed that salesmen using group meetings had more positive attitudes toward their jobs and sold more on the average than salesmen not using group meetings. According to Likert:

> Appreciably poorer results are achieved whenever the manager, himself, analyzes each man's performance and results and sets goals for him. Such man-to-man interactions in the meetings, dominated by the manager, do not create group loyalty and have far less favorable impact upon the salesmen's motivation than do group interaction and decision meetings. Moreover, in the man-to-man interaction little use is made of the sales knowledge and skills of the group.[21]

Another recent study found that managers' perceptions of the supportiveness of the organizational climate and their attitudes toward MBO were significantly related.[22] A supportive climate was viewed in terms of such features as high levels of trust and confidence between superiors and subordinates, multidirectional communication aimed at achieving objectives, cooperative teamwork, subordinate participation in decision making and goal setting, and control conducted close to the point of performance (self-control). Essentially, this climate was seen as comparable to Likert's Participative Group (System 4) management system.[23] The results of the study showed significant ($p < 0.01$) positive correlations between the supportiveness of the climate and how effective managers believed the MBO process to be. Managers' evaluations of MBO effectiveness were assessed in six areas: (1) planning and organizing work, (2) objective evaluation of performance, (3) motivation of the best job performance, (4) coordination of individual and work-group objectives, (5) superior-subordinate communication, and (6) superior-subordinate cooperation. Even more important was the significant (p < 0.01) positive correlation between supportiveness of the climate and managers' overall satisfaction with MBO as it related to their jobs.[24]

Holder describes how consensus decision making has been used at Yellow Freight System, Inc. since the early 1950s.[25] Work groups in the firm are organized according to the "linking-pin concept"[26] and decisions, including those dealing with managers' objectives, are made on a consensus basis within each work group. The writer's account is unclear as to whether consensus MBO operates throughout the management hierarchy; however, his description indicates that it extends to at least the regional-manager level. Although Holder provides no objective measure of effectiveness, he suggests that the length of time for which the program has been used attests to its success.

Finally, in explaining a job-enrichment program in a European chemical company, Myers reports: "In 1970, more than 40,000 additional employees conferred in work teams and functional groups to define criteria against which their performance could be measured and to set tangible goals."[27] According to Myers, the program has (a) moved decision making down to the levels where the work is performed, (b) resulted in better integration of individual and organizational goals, (c) required managers to rely upon interpersonal competence rather than official authority to get results, and (d) reduced the traditional barrier between management and nonmanagement. We think this experience is particularly significant; if operative work groups can effectively set objectives in a collaborative environment, it seems reasonable to expect that managers would also be able to do so.

Conclusions

The findings of these studies and organizational programs help confirm our belief that Collaborative Management by Objectives can work. We feel that CMBO, as we have described it, is congruent with a participative, team-leadership style and can avoid many of the dysfunctional spin-offs of the prevailing one-to-one versions of MBO. We do not wish to imply, however, that CMBO will work in all organizations and under any circumstances. Care must be taken to ensure that appropriate conditions are present before and that necessary skills emerge during the implementation of CMBO.

Successful application of CMBO requires that managers be motivated to shift the climate of the organization, or at least the climate of those units using CMBO, in the direction of more teamwork, more cooperation, more joint problem solving, and more support. While a team approach per se would tend to diminish the dysfunctional consequences of status differentials and could shift the locus of commitments among people away from the one-to-one arena toward the lateral or interdependent team arena, a team approach void of mutual support and group skills could create more problems than it would solve. Training of work teams in skills of communication, group processes, and joint problem solving is vital to this shift toward a more supportive climate.

Equally vital to the success of CMBO are skills in diagnosis—both the original diagnosis that identifies the need and readiness for CMBO and the subsequent diagnoses that tune into managers' perceptions of the functional and dysfunctional aspects of the CMBO process and their assessment of the emerging climate. Such continuous "tracking" will be hard work, but the resulting opportunities for modification and other corrective action should make the CMBO process that much more relevant to the needs of the organization and its members.

The nine-phase strategy we have proposed is one way of introducing more systematic collaboration into the MBO process. While it will undoubtedly take considerable effort and attention to make the CMBO strategy work well, this approach can help people, teams, and units become more goal-directed without undermining efforts to maintain or create a participative, responsive team climate in the organization.

References

1. See, for example, Gerald F. Carvalho, "Installing Management by Objectives: A New Perspective on Organization Change," *Human Resource Management* (Spring 1972), pp. 23-30; Robert A. Howell, "A Fresh Look at Management by Objectives," *Business Horizons* (Fall 1967), pp. 51-58; Charles L. Hughes, "Assessing the Performance of Key Managers," *Personnel* (January-February 1968), pp. 38-43; Bruce D. Jamieson, "Behavioral Problems with Management by Objectives," *Academy of Management Journal* (September 1973), pp. 496-505; Harold Koontz, "Making Managerial Appraisal Effective," *California Management Review* (Winter 1972), pp. 46-55; and Harry Levinson, "Management by Whose Objectives?" *Harvard Business Review* (July-August 1970), pp. 125-134.

2. See, for example, Thomas P. Kleber, "The Six Hardest Areas to Manage by Objectives," *Personnel Journal* (August 1972), pp. 571-575; Dale D. McConkey, "Staff Objectives Are Different," *Personnel Journal* (July 1972), p. 477ff.; and Burt K. Scanlan, "Quantifying the Qualifiable, or Can Results Management Be Applied to the Staff Man's Job?" *Personnel Journal* (March 1968), p. 162ff.

3. John W. Humble, ed., *Management by Objectives in Action* (New York: McGraw-Hill, 1970).

4. Walter S. Wikstrom, *Managing by- and with-Objectives* (New York: National Industrial Conference Board, 1968).

5. Henry Tosi and Stephen J. Carroll, Jr., "Improving Management by Objectives: A Diagnostic Change Program," *California Management Review* (Fall 1973), pp. 57-66.

6. Steven Kerr, "Some Modifications in MBO as an OD Strategy," *Proceedings, 1972 Annual Meeting*, Academy of Management, 1973, pp. 39-42.

7. Harry Levinson, "Management by Objectives: A Critique," *Training and Development Journal* (April 1972), pp. 3-8; see also Levinson, op. cit.

8. Tosi and Carroll, op. cit.

9. Herbert H. Meyer, Emanual Kay, and John R. P. French, Jr., "Split Roles in Performance Appraisal," *Harvard Business Review* (January-February 1965), pp. 123-129.

10. Peter F. Drucker, *The Practice of Management* (New York: Harper & Bros., 1954), p. 126.

11. See, for example, Carvalho, op cit.; Wendell French, *The Personnel Management Process: Human Resources Administration*, 3d ed. (Boston: Houghton Mifflin, 1974); Howell, op cit.; Charles L. Hughes, *Goal Setting* (New York: American Management Association, 1965), p. 123; Jamieson, op. cit.; Kerr, op. cit.; and Levinson, "Management by Whose Objectives?" op cit.

12. A notable exception is W. J. Reddin, *Effective Management by Objectives: The 3-D Method of MBO* (New York: McGraw-Hill, 1971), chapter 14. Also see Wendell French and Cecil H. Bell, Jr., *Organization Development: Behavioral Science Interventions for Organization Improvement* (Englewood Cliffs, N.J.: Prentice-Hall, 1973), pp. 167-168; and Anthony P. Raia, *Managing by Objectives* (Glenview, Ill.: Scott, Foresman, 1974).

13. Wikstrom, op. cit., pp. 22-23.

14. Raia, op. cit., p. 110.

15. Ibid., pp. 75-78.

16. Reddin, op. cit.

17. French and Bell, op. cit., p. 15.

18. Robert R. Blake and Jane S. Mouton, *Corporate Excellence Through Grid Organization Development* (Houston: Gulf Publishing, 1968); and Robert R. Blake and Jane S. Mouton, *Building a Dynamic Corporation Through Grid Organization Development* (Reading, Mass.: Addison-Wesley, 1969).

19. Blake and Mouton, *Corporate Excellence*, p. 110.

20. Rensis Likert, *The Human Organization* (New York: McGraw-Hill, 1967), pp. 55-59.

21. Ibid., p. 57.

22. Robert W. Hollmann, "A Study of the Relationships Between Organizational Climate and Managerial Assessment of Management by Objectives," unpublished Ph.D. dissertation, University of Washington, 1973.

23. Likert, op. cit.; and Rensis Likert, *New Patterns of Management* (New York: McGraw-Hill, 1961).

24. Hollmann, op. cit.

25. Jack J. Holder, Jr., "Decision Making by Consensus," *Business Horizons* (April 1972), pp. 47-54.

26. Likert, *New Patterns of Management* and *The Human Organization*.

27. M. Scott Myers, "Overcoming Union Opposition to Job Enrichment," *Harvard Business Review* (May-June, 1971), pp. 37-49.

The Principles of Sociotechnical Design

by Albert Cherns

The art of organization design is simultaneously esoteric and poorly developed. Most existing organizations were not born but "just growed." Many bear the recognizable stigmata of the operations of various well-known consultancy groups. There is, of course, no lack of available models and no one seeking to set up an organization need invent the wheel. But organization design is generally an outcome not an input. The input in manufacturing organizations is provided by the engineers, both those who design machines and equipment and those who design work methods and layout—the industrial engineers. Increasingly, operations researchers, systems analysts, the designers of computerized information systems, and the providers of "management services" of all kinds are having their say. In nonmanufacturing work organizations, it is the latter who are most influential. And all of them, whether they recognize it or not, bring assumptions about people into their operations and their design. Most simply put, these assumptions can generally be described as Taylorist or System X. People are unpredictable. If they are not stopped by the system design, they will screw things up. It would be best to eliminate them completely; but since this is not possible, we must anticipate all the eventualities and then program them into the machines. The outcome is the familiar pattern of hierarchies of supervision and control to make sure that people do what is required of them, and departments of specialists to inject the "expert" knowledge that may be required by

I am indebted to Louis E. Davis, on whose work in designing new organizations I have drawn heavily in this article, which arises out of the courses we have given together at UCLA and elsewhere.

Albert Cherns is professor of social sciences and chairman, department of social sciences, University of Loughborough, Leicestershire, England.

Reprinted from Albert Cherns, "The Principles of Sociotechnical Design," HUMAN RELATIONS, 1976, 29 (8), 783-792. Used with permission of Plenum Publishing Corporation.

the complexities of manufacturing, marketing, and allied processes, but is equally often required to make the elaborate control, measurement, and information systems work.

We have found in our own work, both teaching and consulting, that engineers readily perceive that they are involved in organization design and that what they are designing is a sociotechnical system built around much knowledge and thought on the technical and little on the social side of the system. There is, of course, the danger that the term *sociotechnical system* very rapidly becomes a shibboleth, the mere pronouncing of which distinguishes the *cognoscenti* from the ignorant and uninitiated. But recognizing that a production system requires a social system to integrate the activities of the people who operate, maintain, and renew it; account for it; and keep it fed with the resources it requires and dispose of the products does nothing by itself to improve the design. And while discussion of the characteristics of social systems is helpful, that still leaves us with the problem that there are many ways of achieving their essential objectives.

We teach engineers that any social system must, if it is to survive, perform the function of Parson's (1951) four subsystems. As we present them, these functions are attainment of the goals of the organization; adaptation to the environment; integration of the activities of the people in the organization, including the resolution of conflict whether task-based, organization-based, or interpersonally based; and providing for the continued occupation of the essential roles through recruitment and socialization. The advantage of this analysis is that it tells the designer that if he doesn't take these absolute requirements of a social system into account, he will find that they will be met in some way or other, quite probably in ways that will do as much to thwart as to facilitate the functions for which he does plan. But it still leaves wide open the question of how to design a social system or, more fundamentally, how much a social system should be designed. That there is a choice in such matters can be as much a revelation to the engineer as the fact that there is a choice of technology to achieve production objectives is to the social scientists.

How, then, do you design a sociotechnical system? Can we communicate any principles of sociotechnical design? The first thing to be said is that a lot depends upon your objectives. As we have said, all organizations are sociotechnical systems; that is no more than a definition, a tautology. But the phrase was first used with, and has acquired, the connotation that organizational objectives are best met not by the optimization of the technical system and the adaptation of a social system to it, but by the joint optimization of the technical and the social aspects, thus exploiting the adaptability and innovativeness of people in attaining goals instead of overdetermining technically the manner in which these goals should be attained.

It is an obvious corollary that such design requires knowledge of the way machines and technical systems behave and of the way people and groups behave. Unless a designer is himself an engineer and a social scientist, both are required, which means engineers discussing alternative technical ways of attaining objectives with social scientists. This is not easy unless social scientists will take the trouble to learn enough about technology to understand the kinds of options that are open to engineers. The design team has indeed to be a multifunctional one as we have describe elsewhere (Cherns, 1972.).

In the process of designing ideas, no doubt the constant interchange among engineer, manager, social scientist, financial controller, personnel specialist, and so on can do much to ensure that all aspects are considered, but the sociotechnical concepts involved need not be hammered out afresh every time. They can be collected and presented in such a way as to ensure that they are taken account of, yet not straitjacketing the designer. To this end, we have described nine principles, which we offer as a checklist, not a blueprint. They represent a distillation of experience and owe more to the writings of others (Emery & Trist, 1972; Herbst, 1974) than to our own originality. They have not, however, previously been systematized. These principles are:

Principle 1: Compatibility

The process of design must be compatible with its objectives. A camel has been defined as a horse designed by a committee, and that joke unkindly incorporates negative evaluations of camels and committees. Camels certainly have minds of their own, but perhaps any attempt to draw more parallels between a camel and a social system would be unduly fanciful. Would a horse be more acceptable to a despot and a camel to a democrat? The point to be made, however, is that a participative social system cannot be created by fiat.

If the objective of design is a system capable of self-modification, of adapting to change, and of making the most use of the creative capacities of the individual, then a constructively participative organization is needed. A necessary condition for this to occur is that people are given the opportunity to participate in the design of the jobs they are to perform. In a redesign of an existing organization, the people are already there; a new design has, however, to be undertaken before most of the people are hired. To some extent their jobs will have been designed for them in advance, but this extent can be kept to a minimum. In one case (Davis & Cherns, in press) the design team took the view that they would not design other people's lives. Having defined what were to be the objectives to be met and the competencies required to meet them, they deferred until the individual was appointed any discussion of how the job was to be performed. And, as in most cases, "job" was not defined, this meant involving the people appointed as a team. Clearly some decisions had and have to be taken in advance; there has to be a pretty firm notion of how many people will be required and of what kinds of competence must be sought, but this is governed by the second principle.

Principle 2: Minimal Critical Specification

This principle has two aspects, negative and positive. The negative simply states that no more should be specified than is absolutely essential; the positive requires that we identify what is essential. It is of wide application and implies the minimal critical specification of tasks, the minimal critical allocation of tasks to jobs or of jobs to roles, and the specification of objectives with minimal critical specification of methods of obtaining them. While it may be necessary to be quite precise about what has to be done, it is rarely necessary to be precise about how it is to be done. In most organizations there is far too much specificity about how and indeed about what. Any careful observer of people in their work situation will learn how people contrive to get the job done in despite of the rules. As the railway men in Britain have demonstrated, the whole system can be brought to a grinding halt by "working to rule." Many of the rules are there to provide protection when things go wrong for the man who imposed them; strictly applied, they totally inhibit adaptation or even effective action.

In any case, it is a mistake to specify more than is needed because by doing so options are closed that could be kept open. This premature closing of options is a pervasive fault in design; it arises, not only because of the desire to reduce uncertainty, but also because it helps the designer to get his own way. We measure our success and effectiveness less by the quality of the ultimate design than by the quantity of our ideas and preferences that have been incorporated into it.

One way of dealing with the cavalier treatment of options is to challenge each design decision and demand that alternatives always be offered. This may result in claims that the design process is being expensively delayed. Design proposals may also be defended on the ground that any other choice will run up against some obstacle, such as a company practice, or a trade union agreement, or a manning problem. These obstacles can then be regarded and logged as constraints upon a better sociotechnical solution. When they have all been logged, each can be examined to estimate the cost of removing it. The cost may sometimes be prohibitive, but frequently turns out to be less formidable than supposed or than the engineer has presented it to be.

Principle 3: The Sociotechnical Criterion

This principle states that variances, if they cannot be eliminated, must be controlled as near to their point of origin as possible. We need here to define *variance*, a word much used in sociotechnical literature. Variance is any unprogrammed event; a key variance is one which critically affects outcome. This might be a deviation in quality of raw material, the failure to take action at a critical time, a machine failure, and so on. Much of the elaboration of supervision, inspection, and management is the effort to control variance, typically by action which does less to prevent variance than to try to correct its consequences. The most obvious example is the inspection function. Inspecting a product, the outcome of any activity, does not make right what is wrong. And if this inspection is carried out in a separate department some time after the event, the correction of the variance becomes a long loop which is a poor design for learning. The sociotechnical criterion requires that inspection be incorporated with production where possible, thus allowing people to inspect their own work and learn from their mistakes. This also reduces the number of communication links across departmental boundaries (see also Principle 5). The fewer the variances that are exported from the place where they arise, the fewer the levels of supervision and control that are required and the more "complete" the jobs of the people concerned, to whom it now becomes possible to allocate an objective and the resources necessary to attain it. Frequently what is required to attain this objective turns out to be the supply of the appropriate information as discussed (see Principle 6).

Identifying variances and determining the key variances is a process often requiring lengthy analysis, and from time to time efforts have been made to codify it. One version, known as the nine-step analysis, has been developed by Davis and Cherns (in press). It has been used in enough organizations to give us some assurance that it can be adapted to use with any type of work organization, not just with manufacturing industry.

Principle 4: The Multifunctional Principle—Organism vs. Mechanism

The traditional form of organization relies very heavily on the redundancy of parts. It requires people to perform highly specialized, fractionated tasks. There is often a rapid turnover of such people but they are comparatively easily replaced. Each is treated as a replacement part. Simple mechanisms are constructed on the same principle. Disadvantages arise when a range of responses is required, that is, when a large repertoire of performances is required from the mechanism or the organization. This usually occurs if the environmental demands vary. It then becomes more adaptive and less wasteful for each element to possess more than one function. The same function can be performed in different ways by using different combinations of elements. There are several routes to the same goal — the principle sometimes described as equifinality. Complex organisms have all gone this route of development. The computer, for example, is a typically multifunctional mechanism. The principle of minimal critical specification permits the organization to adopt this principle also.

Principle 5: Boundary Location

In any organization, departmental boundaries have to be drawn somewhere. Miller (1959) has shown that such boundaries are usually drawn so as to group people and activities on the basis of one or more of three criteria: technology, territory, time. Grouping by technology is typically seen in machine shops, where all the grinding machines are in one room, the Grinding Department, the milling machines in another, the Milling Department, and so on, with each department under the supervision of a specialist, a foreman grinder, etc. The consequences of this for the scheduling of work has been well described by Williamson (1972). A part in construction may spend months shuffling between departments, spending 1% of that time actually in contact with the machines. The consequent excessive cost of such work has been one of the stimuli to "group technology," the establishment of departments which each contain a variety of machines so that a part can be completed within one department. This corresponds to a grouping on the basis of time — the contiguity in time of operations indicates that they may well be organized together. Group technology also has consequences for the operation of the department as a team with its members taking responsibility for the scheduling of operations and possibly the rotation of jobs.

Other examples of grouping on the basis of technology, but not of course group technology, are the typing pool and the telephone switchboard.

The switchboard may also be an example of the criterion of territory. Switchboard operators are bound together by the design of the machine. But the territorial principle can operate on the basis of little other than spatial contiguity. If the engineers have for convenience located different activities in the same area, the maintenance of control over the people working there suggests that they be made answerable to the same supervision. Retail trade organization is often of this kind with a floor supervisor. Organizations of this kind give rise to "dotted-line" relationships of functional responsibility.

All these criteria are pragmatic and defensible up to a point. But they possess notable disadvantages. They tend to erect boundaries which interfere with the desirable sharing of knowledge and experience. A simple example may suffice. In an organization concerned with the distribution of petroleum products studied by Cherns and Taylor (unpublished data), the clerks who collected customers' orders were organized in a department separate from that of the drivers for whom schedules were worked out. A driver would pick up a schedule allocating him a vehicle and a route. Frequently the receipt of the routing would stimulate a string of expletives from the driver, "If I do what this *** has told me to, I should not be able to do half the job. I would arrive at customer B just after 12 o'clock when the only man with the key to the pumps has gone off to his lunch break. And it's no use my turning up to customer P until I have discharged enough of my load for his short pipe to reach my tank. And finally I would end up on the *** road just in the middle of the rush hour. It would serve him right if I followed these instructions; I would run out of time [exceed the permitted number of consecutive driving hours] right in the middle of the throughway." There was no doubt pardonable exaggeration in all this; the point is that the drivers had acquired a great deal of knowledge about customers, routes, etc., but being organized into a separate department they shared very little of this knowledge with the routing clerks who, however, received the customers' complaints before the drivers.

The principle has certain corollaries. One very important one concerns the management of the boundaries between department and department, between department and the organization as a whole, and between the organization and the outside world. The more the control of activities within the department becomes the responsibility of the members, the more the role of the supervisor/foreman/manager is concentrated on the boundary activities—ensuring that the team has adequate resources to carry out its functions, coordinating activities with those of other departments, and foreseeing the changes likely to impinge upon them. This boundary maintenance role is precisely the requirement of the supervisor in a well-designed system.

Under favorable circumstances, working groups can acquire and handle a greater degree of autonomy and learn to manage their own boundaries. This implies locating responsibility for coordination clearly and firmly with those whose efforts require coordination if the common objectives are to be achieved. The role of supervisor now becomes that of a "resource" to the working group.

Principle 6: Information Flow

This principle states that information systems should be designed to provide information *in the first place* to the point where action on the basis of it will be needed. Information systems are not typically so designed. The capacity of computer-controlled systems to provide information about the state of the system both totally and in great detail to any organizational point has been used to supply to the top echelons of the organization information which is really useful only at lower levels and which acts as an incitement to the top management to intervene in the conduct of operations for which their subordinates are and should be responsible. The designer of the information system is naturally concerned to demonstrate its potentialities and is hard to convince that certain kinds of information can be potentially harmful when presented to high organizational levels. Properly directed, sophisticated information systems can, however, supply a work team with exactly the right type and amount of feedback to enable them to learn to control the variances which occur within the scope of their spheres of responsibility and competence and to anticipate events which are likely to have a bearing on their performance.

Principle 7: Support Congruence

This principle states that the systems of social support should be designed so as to reinforce the behaviors which the organization structure is designed to elicit. If, for example, the organization is designed on the basis of group or team operation with team responsibility, a payment system incorporating individual members would be incongruent with these objectives. Not only payment systems, but systems of selection, training, conflict resolution, work measurement, performance assessment, timekeeping, leave allocation, promotion, and separation can all reinforce or contradict the behaviors which are desired. This is to say that the management philosophy should be consistent and that management's actions should be consistent with its expressed philosophy. Not infrequently a management committed to philosophies of participation simultaneously adopts systems of work measurement, for example, which are in gross contradiction. Even management as progressive and committed to the humanization of work as that of Volvo's Kalmar plant has retained a commitment to a system of payment based on MTM, a technique of work measurement utilizing time and method study. Until replaced, this may, in fact, pose an obstacle to the further humanization of work at Kalmar to which the management is committed.

Principle 8: Design and Human Values

This principle states that an objective of organizational design should be to provide a high quality of work. We recognize that quality is a subjective phenomenon, and that not everyone wants to have responsibility, variety, involvement, growth, etc. The objective is to provide these for those who do want them without subjecting those who don't to the tyranny of peer control. In this regard we are obliged to recognize that all desirable objectives may not be achievable simultaneously.

What constitutes human work is a matter again of subjective judgment based on certain psychological assumptions. Thorsrud (1972) has identified six characteristics of a good job which can be striven for in the design of organizations and jobs. They are as follows: (1) the need for the content of a job to be reasonably demanding of the worker in terms other than sheer endurance, and yet to provide a minimum of variety (not necessarily novelty); (2) the need to be able to learn on the job and to go on learning (again it is a question of neither too much nor too little); (3) the need for some minimal area of decision-making that the individual can call his own; (4) the need for some minimal degree of social support and recognition in the workplace; (5) the need for the individual to be able to relate what he does and what he produces to his social life; and (6) the need to feel that the job leads to some sort of desirable future (not necessarily promotion).

Principle 9: Incompletion

Design is a reiterative process. The closure of options opens new ones. At the end we are back at the beginning. The Forth Bridge, in its day an outstanding example of iron technology, required painting to fend off rust. Starting at the Midlothian end, a posse of painters no sooner reached the Fife end than the Midlothian end required painting again. Varying the image, Jewish tradition prescribes that one brick be omitted in the construction of a dwelling lest the jealousy of God's angels be excited. Disregarding the superstition, the message is acceptable. As soon as design is implemented, its consequences indicate the need for redesign. The multifunctional, multilevel, multidisciplinary team required for design is needed for its evaluation and review.

Concluding Remarks

Who is the sociotechnical designer to whom this paper is especially addressed? The analysis, preparation, and implementation of a sociotechnical design is, as we have indicated, the property of no individual or set of individuals; it belongs to the members of the organization whose working lives are being designed. Special skills and knowledge may well be and often are required and these are provided as a resource by sociotechnical consultants or action researchers.

But participation by employees in the design of their organizations may imply that they accept or show readiness to accept work roles which go beyond the agreements and constraints evolved by negotiation between manager and union on their behalf. Unions are thus inevitably involved in the process, whether in a collaborative, neutral, or antagonistic role. Can they be partners in design? This is a role which has seldom been offered to, and even more rarely accepted by, unions. It is not a role for which they have prepared themselves, and it is one which could easily blur their primary responsibilities to their members. Yet without them the viability of the design must be in some doubt. And the design of a social support system implies designing the functions of the shop steward if not the union official. Our first principle, compatibility, requires that the unions be brought into the design if that is at all possible. But if they are to come in, they, too, will need to acquire new competencies. Unions are organizations, but the first is yet to be the client of a sociotechnical design.

References

Cherns, A. B. Helping managers: What the social scientist needs to know. *Organizational Dynamics*, Winter 1973, 51-67.

David, L. E., & Cherns, A. B. *Designing organizations around human values* (2 vols.). New York: Free Press (in press).

Emery, F. E., & Trist, E. L. *Towards a social ecology*. London: Plenum Press, 1972.

Herbst, P. G. *Sociotechnical design*. London: Tavistock, 1974.

Miller, E. J. Technology, territory and time: The internal differentiation of complex production systems. *Human Relations*, 1959, *12*, 243-272.

Parsons, T. *The social system*. London: Routledge and Kegan Paul, 1951.

Thorsrud, E. Policy making as a learning process. In A. B. Cherns, R. Sinclair, & W. I. Jenkins, (Eds.), *Social science and government: Policies and problems*. London: Tavistock, 1972.

Williamson, D. T. N. *The anachronistic factory*. Proceedings of the Royal Society, A331, 1972, 139-160.

An Organic Problem-Solving Method
of Organizational Change

by Sheldon A. Davis

In my opinion, behavioral science literature does not give proper emphasis to the principle of confrontation as it relates to the improvement and
development of organizations. Furthermore, sensitivity training is not
effectively put into a larger context as a means to an end. This paper
describes an extensive organizational development effort within TRW
Systems which places a heavy emphasis on confrontation and the use of
sensitivity training as part of an effort to improve the culture of an
organization. The improvement focuses on the quality of working relationships between interdependent individuals and groups.

A few months ago, I learned from a vice-president of a large national
corporation that two of the three top executives in his company had recently
participated in a Presidents' Conference on Human Behavior conducted by
the National Training Laboratories. I learned further that, both before and
after attending the conference, these two persons were highly committed to
Theory Y notions, as described by Douglas McGregor in *The Human Side of
Enterprise*. My acquaintance expressed concern, however, with the form this
commitment was taking. One of these men had chaired a meeting during
which he expressed his commitment to those assumptions stated by
McGregor. As a concrete example of this commitment, he said that a few days
earlier a key subordinate had presented some work for approval. The "boss"
did not like the quality of the work and said so. The subordinate pointed out

When he wrote this article, Sheldon A. Davis was vice president and director of industrial relations, TRW Systems. Presently, he is vice president, personnel, of Digital Equipment
Corporation, Maynard, Massachusetts.

Reprinted by permission of the author and NTL Institute for Applied Behavioral Science,
associated with the National Education Association, from "An Organic Problem-Solving
Method of Organizational Change," by Sheldon A. Davis in the *Journal of Applied Behavioral
Science*, Volume 3, Number 1 (January/February/March 1967), pp. 3-21.

that his people had worked very hard in producing the work and were highly committed to it. The top executive said, "OK. In that case, let's go ahead."

To me, this is *not* an example of what McGregor meant. It is an example of very soft human relationships that are not task-oriented and therefore, in my opinion, are irrational. It does represent, however, a problem presented in laboratory training. How can we eliminate some of the soft, mushy, "sweetness and light" impressions that some people feel are implicit in sensitivity training?

A different approach was recently illustrated within TRW Systems.

> A section head, the lowest managerial level in the organization, discovered that a certain quality control procedure for Manufacturing hampered his effectiveness. He sought to get the procedure modified, only to be told that this was impossible because it covered all of the divisions and therefore could not be modified. He was further told that a change would raise the ire of at least one general manager of another division. The section head refused to accept the explanation and personally called a meeting of the general manager identified, the manager of Manufacturing—both vice-presidents of the company, and four levels above the section head—and the director of Product Assurance. Within an hour the procedure was modified in the direction desired by the section head.

The foregoing vignettes dramatize the differences which can occur because of markedly different applications of behavioral science theories within an organization. In both instances, the individuals involved were convinced that they were using the best of behavioral science techniques. The consequence of their interpretation and application had decidedly different payoffs.

The Missing Element in Behavioral Science Literature

The values that McGregor stood for and articulated regarding organizational development have a toughness: In dealing with one another, we will be open, direct, explicit. Our feelings will be available to one another, and we will try to problem-solve rather than be defensive. These values have within them a very tough way of living—not a soft way. But, unfortunately, in much of the behavioral science literature, the messages come out sounding soft and easy, as if what we are trying to do is build happy teams of employees who feel "good" about things, rather than saying we are trying to build effective organizations with groups who function well and can zero in quickly on their problems and deal with them rationally, in the real sense of the word. As an example of this kind of softness, I do not remember reading in any book in the field that one of the alternatives in dealing with a problem person is the possibility of discharging him.

There is no real growth—there is no real development—in the organization or in the individuals within it if they do not confront and deal directly with their problems. They can get together and share feelings, but if that is all they do, it is merely a catharsis. While this is useful, it has relatively minimal usefulness compared with what can happen if they start to relate differently within the organizational setting around task issues.

Laboratories Are Not Enough

I think one important theme of the nearly four-year organizational change effort at TRW Systems is that of using laboratory training (sensitivity training, T Grouping) clearly as a means to an end—that of putting most of our energy into on-the-job situations, real-life inter-group problems, real-life job-family situations, and dealing with them in the here-and-now. This effort has reached a point where sensitivity training, per se, represents only 10 to 15 percent of the effort in our own program. The rest of the effort, 85 to 90 percent, is in on-the-job situations, working real problems with the people who are really involved in them. This has led to some very important, profound, and positive changes in the organization and the way it does many things, including decision making, problem solving, and supervisory coaching of subordinates.

One generalization I would draw from this and similar experiences is that laboratory training in and of itself is not enough to really make the difference in an organization forcefully trying to become more rational in its processes of freeing up the untapped potential of its people and of dealing more sensibly with its own realities. Attending a strangers' laboratory or, in our case, a cousins' laboratory (that is, being in a T Group with people who are not necessarily from the same job family but are from the same company) is a very useful, important experience. Most people learn much in laboratory training, as has been well documented and discussed. However, this is not enough.

We have felt that the laboratory experience (the sensitivity training experience itself) should not be just three days or a week or whatever is spent in the off-site laboratory. As a result, we have undertaken important laboratory prework as well as postwork. The prework typically consists of an orientation session where the staff very briefly presents some of the theoretical aspects of the program and an explanation of why we do laboratories. During this time, participants in the coming laboratory can ask any kind of questions, such as: Is this therapy? Is the company going to evaluate my performance? and so on.

Also, we typically hand out a questionnaire to the participants for their own use (they are not asked to turn it in). It presents questions such as: "What are the three most pressing problems you feel you pose for those who have to work with you?" It is an attempt to get the person to become introspective about his own particular work situation, to begin his articulation process within himself.

Then there is the laboratory itself. This is followed up by on-site sessions several weeks apart, perhaps one evening every other week for three or four sessions. At this time, a variety of actions are taken in an attempt to help people phase into their work situation. There is continued working in the small training groups; there can be exercises such as intergroup competition.

The laboratory is a highly intensive experience. Attitudes toward it can be extremely euphoric, and people can experience tremendous let-downs when they return to the ongoing culture—even a highly supportive one. Therefore, there is major emphasis on working in the ongoing situation in real-life job families as well as in intergroup situations and mergers, for example.

Recently, we have added to the follow-on work an opportunity for the wives of the participants to experience a micro-laboratory. This might be a 1:00 to 5:00 p.m. session on a Saturday, with a staff available, to give the wives some feel for the laboratory experience.

One of the problems many people have as a result of laboratory training is returning to their continuing organizational culture and finding it quite hostile to the values learned and to the approaches they would like to try. The notion very early in the TRW Systems effort was to focus on changes in the ongoing culture itself: the norms, values, rewards, systems, and processes. If all we did was to have a lot of people attend sensitivity training, this might indeed be useful to them as individuals, but its usefulness would be quite limited with respect to the total organization.

We have had other kinds of concerns with laboratory training. We have tried hard not to *send* people to a laboratory but to make it as voluntary as possible. People who are *sent* usually spend much of their time wondering why they were sent instead of working on relevant issues.

If we look at the processes of change itself, it is quite clear that it is not enough for an individual to gain enormous insight into his own situation, his own dynamics, and his own functioning. Granted, this will help him develop a better understanding of how groups work and of the complexity of communication processes. However, if he cannot take this understanding and turn it into action in the on-the-job situation, if he cannot find other people who are interested in trying some of the same ideas, if he cannot bring about a difference in his real life, the value of the laboratory is very severely minimized. In real life, what do we find? Typically, highly traditional methods of management and unrealistic assumptions about people (the kind of Theory X assumptions that McGregor stated). There has to be an emphasis on changing the ongoing organization. The direction has to be toward working in the organization on a day-to-day basis.

Organizational Setting and Development of Program

I should like to describe the program under way at TRW Systems as an example of this kind of effort—of a nonmechanical, organic approach to career development—the development of the careers of the individuals in the organization and the career of the organization itself, both inextricably tied.

TRW Systems currently employs about 13,300 persons. About one third are professional engineers, and half of these have advanced degrees. It is an organization with products of tremendous innovation and change. It is an organization that is highly interdependent. We have a matrix organization: there are project offices and functional areas of technical capabilities such as structures, dynamics, guidance, and control. A project office, to perform its task, must call upon capabilities and people throughout the organization. This is a highly complicated matrix of interdependencies. No one can really get his job done in this kind of system without working with others. As a result, problems of relationships, of communication, of people being effectively able to problem-solve with one another are extremely critical.

The program started at a time when the company was going through a significant change in its role—from an organization with essentially one Air Force contract for systems engineering on ballistic missile programs (Thor, Atlas, Titan, and Minuteman) to a company that would be fully competitive in the aerospace market. This has indeed happened over the past six years. We now have many contracts, many customers. Most of our work is done under fixed-price and incentive contracts; we produce hardware such as unmanned scientific satellites, propulsion engines for the Apollo mission, as well as other types of hardware. The company has become exceedingly more complex in its product lines and its mix of business.

All through this growth and diversification there has been a concern about the careers of the people in the organization, about trying to maintain certain qualities within the organization. Exhibit I was prepared in September of 1965 and is an attempt to list qualities which seem to have a direct bearing on the kind of success we have been having over the past six years. That success has been quite striking: a tremendous increase in sales, and in the number of contracts, a good record in competitions for programs in our industry, and a large increase in the number of employees.

1. The individual employee is important, and focus is on providing him the tools and other things that he needs to carry out his assignments.

2. The policies and procedures have been designed to be a platform *from which* the individual operates rather than a set of ground rules *within which* he must confine himself.

3. The work we do ought to be fun (personally rewarding, meaningful, enjoyable), and this has had a direct effect on assignments, among other things.

4. There is a great deal of trust displayed in the individual, a minimum of rules, controls, and forces telling him what to do and how to do it.

5. There is a relative lack of social distance between employees and managers and among the various echelons of management. The accoutrements of rank are not used as barriers between managers and others at lower levels of the organization.

6. A heavy emphasis on quality: Attract the best people, give them excellent working conditions, provide them with challenging assignments, demonstrate that paramount importance is placed on professional and technical excellence.

7. Although there has been continuous and rapid change, the organization as a whole has been relatively stable, providing long-term career opportunities for a high percentage of our key people.

8. In giving responsibility to individuals, we have had a bias toward giving "too much" responsibility rather than being conservative. This has "stretched" the individual and, for those who are capable, it has led to rapid growth and outstanding performance.

9. There is, in a relative sense, less organization "politics" (people ruthlessly working at getting ahead, back-stabbing) and more focus on task. Part of the language is "working the problem."

10. On task issues there is a great deal of direct confrontation rather than "passing the buck," maneuvering, and so on.

11. There is a great deal of delegation downward, so that a large number of persons find themselves assigned to tasks with relatively high responsibility.

12. The management group has been quite experimental in its approach to its task rather than generally traditional.

13. The individual employee enjoys relative freedom to be personally responsible for himself and his job. The job is generally seen as an important one and as making a significant contribution to the technological advances in our society.

14. People who will be markedly affected by decisions feel that they will have the opportunity, to a greater degree than is customary elsewhere, to participate in the decision-making process.

Exhibit I. Qualities of TRW Systems which have a direct bearing on its
success

In the middle of 1961, TRW Systems, then called Space Technology Laboratories, began to think about organizational development. At that time, Herbert Shepard, then on the faculty at Case Institute of Technology, spent a portion of the summer at TRW, including some time with key executives. The following summer he spent a month with the organization. Just prior to this visit, the director of Industrial Relations and his associate attended a laboratory conducted by the University of California at Los Angeles.

Shepard's visit and discussions centering around it led to a growing articulation of what we might want to do with respect to career development. A number of things happened in the next several months.

One was the preparation of a white paper on career development—a statement of how we might approach the subject. The paper discussed why a program was needed, assumptions to be made about employees (Theory Y), the type of organizational climate and training needed, as well as some general indications of how we might proceed.

An assumption we made was that most of the people in the organization were highly competent, very intelligent, and certainly experimental. If they could be freed up enough to look at some of their behavior, to question some of their assumptions, to look at assumptions other people were making, to try new approaches, they could, within limits, develop their own specific management theory.

The white paper was circulated to a number of key persons. Interviews were then conducted to determine possible next steps. A series of events led from this point.

One event was the first of many team development laboratories. (By team development laboratory, I mean an activity which might, for example, be a three-day off-site meeting involving a supervisor and the people who immediately report to him. The agenda for the meeting would be "How can we improve our own effectiveness?") The first team meeting involved one of the program offices in the company. It turned out to be quite successful. With this experience under our belts, we had further discussions to formulate what we wanted to do as an organization with respect to the careers of the people comprising it.

Employees within the personnel organization began attending sensitivity training laboratories such as the Arden House Management Work Conferences, conducted by National Training Laboratories.

A very significant event in the total development of this change effort occurred in May of 1963 when a group of 12 key executives attended a laboratory. Their co-trainers were Herbert Shepard, an outside consultant, and myself, a member of the TRW Systems organization.

The participants in this first laboratory were quite positive in their feedback to the director of Industrial Relations and to the president of the company, who himself was very much interested in how people were reacting to the training. The president had given support for us to be experimental: "Let's try things. If they work, continue them. If they don't, modify them, improve them, or drop them."

A consulting team evolved over time. The consultants were not used in any one-shot way but were asked to make a significant commitment of time. They have become involved with us. They have learned our culture and our problems. While our consultants are all qualified T Group trainers, most of their time is spent in on-the-job situations. There is a need to function as a team, since we are all dealing with one organization, one culture, one social system. The kind of cohesiveness that takes place during consulting team meetings has been a critical part of the program at TRW Systems.

In one sense we started at the top of the organization, and in another we did not. In the beginning, there was a shared general understanding between the president and the key people in Industrial Relations about the type of program we wanted. There were some shared values about the organization we had and wanted to maintain, build, and develop. So this was not Theory X management and Theory Y training effort. Both had a Theory Y quality.

The president and others of the top management team were relatively late in becoming involved in laboratory training and in applying this training to their own job families. The president of the company attended an NTL Presidents' Conference on Human Behavior early in 1965. Directly after that experience, his top team had an off-site team development meeting in March of 1965. In April 1966, they had a follow-up meeting.

Prior to this top team activity many other things had happened with a number of other people in other job families. In fact, this other activity helped us get to the point where the top management team became interested in trying to apply some of these techniques.

Since the program started, more than 500 key persons in the organization have attended sensitivity training laboratories, primarily laboratories conducted by the company. The staff of these laboratories is drawn from our consultants, the personnel organization, and, more recently, from skilled and interested employees in line management positions.

We have also conducted more than 85 team development efforts. These vary in format, but a typical one involves interviews with each of the members of the team (a job family consisting of a supervisor and his immediate subordinates) and then perhaps a three-day off-site meeting where the interview data are fed back for the groups to work with. The team ends the meeting with explicit action items. Follow-on to the off-site meeting involves implementing the many action items.

We have been devoting much effort to intergroup problems: relationships between Manufacturing and Engineering, between Product Assurance and other parts of the organization, between various interfacing elements in the engineering organizations. We have found that these efforts have a great deal of leverage. We have done some work on facilitating mergers and with key people on approaching satellite launches. The latter become very tense, tight operations where people can become extremely competitive and behave in ways which clearly get in the way of having an effective launch.

Characteristics of the Process

We "wound up" with a number of notions. We did not want to have a program that was canned but one that was experimental. We wanted participation to be voluntary rather than something that the company forced upon employees. We did not want it to be a crash program. (In our industry there are many crash programs.) We wanted the training to be highly task oriented. (If it were not relevant to making a difference on today's problems, it would not be a successful program.) We wanted to have the emphasis on experience-based learning, which implies, in a very general sense, the use of laboratory methods, of people really looking at how they are doing, examining the assumptions behind their management style, identifying alternate ways of problem solving, and making choices based on a wider range of possibilities. We wanted to be concerned with the careers of all employees, not those of key people only. We wanted to be concerned about company goals and the actual, on-the-job work environment, since this has a profound effect on the careers of people. We wanted to place the emphasis on measuring ourselves against our potential, on being quite introspective on how we were doing. So, for example, if there were an either/or situation (and there usually is not), we would rather not have someone come in and lecture on how to conduct staff meetings, but would ourselves look introspectively at the conduct of our own staff meetings. And we wanted to do continuous research on how we were faring so that it could be fed back into the program for further development.

I should like to describe what I think we have come to mean by an organic approach to organizational change within TRW Systems. There are a number of points which, at least for me, tend to describe what is meant by organic methods.

1. There is the notion that if you are interested in improving a particular culture—a particular social system—you must be able to step out of it in the sense of being very analytical about it, of understanding what is going on, by not being trapped within the culture and its own particular values. If you look at a culture from the viewpoint of its own values, you are not going to come up with anything very startling and different for it to do. You have got to be able to step out of it and say,"What really would make sense here?" This ability to step out of the culture and yet not leave it, not become alienated from it, is a very important one.

2. Optimism regarding the chances for meaningful organizational development to take place increases the psychological freedom for those trying to introduce the change. There is certainly a tremendous amount of evidence at this point that significant, even profound, changes can occur in the behavior of individuals and organizations.

3. Taking a systems engineering approach to the effort (i.e., looking at the totality of the system, dealing with fundamentals within it, considering how a change in one part affects parts elsewhere) provides an analytical approach which increases the conceptual freedom.

4. The extensive use of third-party facilitation is made with respect to interpersonal and organizational problems. A consultant who is not directly involved in an emotional sense in a situation can be useful just by that fact.

5. Direct confrontation of relevant situations in an organization is essential. If we do not confront one another, we keep the trouble within ourselves and we stay in trouble. With respect to confrontation, the whole notion of feedback is crucial. Giving persons feedback on how they are doing gives them a choice to do better. Caring plays an important part. Confronting without caring can be a rather destructive process. (See Albee's *Who's Afraid of Virginia Woolf?*) It does turn out that people in general can be very caring of one another.

6. Becoming the "other" is an important part of the organic method. This is the empathic notion that Carl Rogers and others developed. To have a really meaningful exchange, one somehow has to look at the situation as the other sees it. For a consultant to work effectively with an organization, he has to be perceptive and understanding about the organization and its people from *their* point of view.

7. Dealing with the here-and-now and increasing the ability of people within the organization to do the same have a great deal of leverage. It is important in an organizational development effort to start with what is going on now within the organization and to deal with those things effectively. One of our objectives is to help the organization build its own capability, to deal with its problems as they emerge. Problems are constantly emerging in any live organization, and so our objective is *not* to end up with an organization that has no problems: that would be a very fat, dumb, and happy kind of place.

8. Multiplier planning is rather crucial in the early stages of introducing organizational change. What can we next do that will have the largest effect? There is always a wide range of alternatives and possibilities; there is never enough time, money, or energy to do all the things we might do, so we are constantly picking and choosing.

9. Fanning out is coupled with the multiplier planning aspect. It is important in an effort of this kind—if it is not to be subversive, sub rosa, hidden, squashed out—to be something that does fan out: someone does something that leads to others doing something that leads to still others doing something.

10. A person can act, then act again and then act again; or he can act,

critique what he just did, then act, then critique, then act. And that is the whole notion of going back and forth between content and process, between doing the job and then looking at how we are doing it. Building that into the day-to-day culture is a major objective.

11. Finally, there is the notion of testing of choices. One always has choices within any particular situation. However, it is typically true that we do not test the choices we have. So someone might say, "Well, I really can't do that because these fellows won't let me," or "Yes, I would very much like to do the following, but I can't because of so and so." Given these limits, some choices do not get tested. One of the efforts is to get people to be aware of the various possibilities they have and to test them—not to accept the stereotypes in the situation, the sacred cows, that exist in any kind of organization, but to say, "OK, this is what makes sense to me in working that problem. This is what I want to try to do."

Next Steps

In TRW Systems, we are now moving in a number of directions, some of which I should like to describe. We are moving more toward day-to-day coaching—on-the-job feedback, if you will—with or without consultants and without calling special meetings, but just as we work together. We are paying continuing attention to process as a way of doing business. We are moving more and more toward using third-party facilitation as a standard operating procedure.

So far there has not been a heavy involvement of the rank and file. The first several years in the effort were specifically biased toward working with key people. These are the ones who have a large effect upon the culture, upon the processes of the organization, upon the tone of the climate. But we are now at a point where we want to get more and more involvement of all the employees within the organization.

I think that the experience of the past several years within TRW Systems has rather clearly demonstrated the potential high leverage of applying some of the behavioral science formulations of people like McGregor, Lewin, and Likert. I think it has also demonstrated that there needs to be much more organizational theory development based upon experience, not upon someone's sitting in a room by himself and thinking about the topic. Some of the statements written about organizational development are to me naive, impractical, unrealistic, and unrelated to organizational problems as they actually exist. Through experiences gained at TRW Systems and many other places, we should be able to develop a more sophisticated understanding of organizational development.

Part 6. Issues in Modern Management

In the original 1969 edition of this book, the article on "Values, Man, and Organizations" by Tannenbaum and Davis was the lead chapter and the only one that addressed values directly. Many, if not all, of the other chapters dealt with values, at least implicitly, but the Tannenbaum and Davis chapter was the one that highlighted value issues in general, and depicted organizational values, in particular, as being in a state of transition. In general, the organizational value shifts they saw occurring over a decade ago were shifts from Theory X to Theory Y, associated with McGregor's assumptions about human behavior in organizations (see chapter 14 in this volume). In other words, Tannenbaum and Davis displayed their personal values and argued that organizational trends regarding the treatment of people were moving, at that time, toward a more humanistic and holistic view of people.

When asked if they wished to update their chapter for this revised edition, Tannenbaum and Davis discussed the matter and decided against revision. The editors accepted this decision and also agreed with it, primarily for two reasons. First, the statements they made at the end of the 1960s still seem to hold today. Second, the transitions they depicted are anything but complete; the trends still are occurring rather than having already accomplished a "new state" of organizational behavior. What is perhaps more obvious is that shifts in human values, especially as complex as those Tannenbaum and Davis delineated, require more than a mere decade to take effect.

Not only are these trends still in effect, but they are currently more pervasive than before. That is, these shifts in behavior, and particularly in the managerial treatment of people, are occurring in a broader array of organizations. Federal regulations are no doubt abetting this greater spread. In any case, a broader treatment of the subject of values in this revised edition is in order and is timely.

One value shift listed by Tannenbaum and Davis concerns the fear of individual differences, namely, "away from resisting and fearing individual differences toward accepting and utilizing them." In her chapter on "Managing Integration," Eileen Morley examines in detail a particular version of this transition. Her coverage addresses those "strangers" in organizations who happen to be women and people of color. The primary value statement, at least implied, is that, as subparts or extensions of our society, organizations have the responsibility of redressing societal inequities, especially those in the domain of nondiscriminatory practices regarding hiring, promoting, rewarding, etc. That is, in general, organizations should provide equal opportunity for all.

Although recent years have reflected beneficial changes in organizations for women and people of color, there is considerable distance yet to be traveled to reach completely nondiscriminatory practices. Morley helps us to understand the issues more thoroughly. First, she outlines the process that typically occurs when nontraditional people, "strangers," enter organizations. If this process moves finally to integration of these individually different persons into their organizations, four previous phases will have successively occurred: resistance, isolation, assimilation, acculturation—and then, if completed, integration. Morley examines the implications of all these dynamics for managers and provides recommendations for managers to deal more effectively with the integration of strangers into an organization.

The chapters by Tannenbaum and Davis and by Morley are concerned largely with individual values in the organizational and managerial frame of reference. In "The Organizational Imperative," Hart and Scott deal more with organizations per se. Although they do start with a consideration of individual values, it is within the context of how American society has shifted from the individual and "pluralistic forces that shaped our national character" to "the organizational imperative," the more current and appropriate way of describing what has been a major change in societal values. Hart and Scott contend that we have become so dependent on organizations that "the needs of organization overwhelm all other considerations, whether those of family, religion, art, science, law, or the individual."

Thus, this book ends with statements that rugged individualism is a thing of the past and that not only is this a highly organized society but, more importantly, its members are almost totally dependent on organizations for their well-being. It is an understatement to say that we need to take up the banner of organizational improvement so that individuals of all types can survive as the most important elements of organizations and be treated humanely in the process. It is the editors' hope that with this volume we have contributed to such a cause by bringing together the latest in behavioral science knowledge that can be applied to the improvement of organizations and the effectiveness of those people who run and manage them.

Values, Man, and Organizations

by Robert Tannenbaum and Sheldon A. Davis

We are today in a period when the development of theory within the social sciences will permit innovations which are at present inconceivable. Among these will be dramatic changes in the organization and management of economic enterprise. The capacities of the average human being for creativity, for growth, for collaboration, for productivity (in the full sense of the term) are far greater than we have recognized ... it is possible that the next half century will bring the most dramatic social changes in human history.[1]

For those concerned with organization theory and with organizational development work, this is an exciting and challenging time. Probably never before have the issues at the interface between changing organizations and maturing man been so apparent, so compelling, and of such potentially critical relevance to both. And to a considerable extent, the sparks at the interface reflect differences in values both within organizations and within man—human values which are coming loose from their moorings, whose functional relevance is being re-examined and tested, and which are without question in transition.

Many organizations today, particularly those at the leading edge of technology, are faced with ferment and flux. In increasing instances, the bureaucratic model—with its emphasis on relatively rigid structure, well-defined functional specialization, direction and control exercised

1. McGregor, D. M., *The Professional Manager*. New York, McGraw-Hill, 1967, p. 244.

Robert Tannenbaum is retired professor of behavioral science, Graduate School of Business Administration, University of California, Los Angeles. Sheldon A. Davis is vice president, personnel, of Digital Equipment Corporation.

From *Industrial Management Review*, Vol. 10, No. 2, pp. 67-83. Copyright 1969 by the Alfred P. Sloan School of Management, Massachusetts Institute of Technology. Reprinted by permission.

through a formal hierarchy of authority, fixed systems of rights, duties, and procedures, and relative impersonality of human relationships—is responding inadequately to the demands placed upon it from the outside and from within the organization. There is increasing need for experimentation, for learning from experience, for flexibility and adaptability, and for growth. There is a need for greater inventiveness and creativity, and a need for collaboration among individuals and groups. Greater job mobility and the effective use of temporary systems seem essential. An environment must be created in which people will be more fully utilized and challenged and in which people can grow as human beings.

In his recent book, *Changing Organizations*, Warren Bennis has pointed out that the bureaucratic form of organization "is becoming less and less effective, that it is hopelessly out of joint with contemporary realities, and that new shapes, patterns, and models ... are emerging which promise drastic changes in the conduct of the corporation and in managerial practices in general."[2] At least one of the newer models, the one with which our recent experience is most closely connected, is organic and systems-oriented. We feel that, for the present at least, this model is one which can suggest highly useful responses to the newer demands facing organizations.

At this historical juncture, it is not just organizations which are in flux. Man, perhaps to an extent greater than ever before, is coming alive; he is ceasing to be an object to be used, and is increasingly asserting himself, his complexity, and his importance. Not quite understanding why or how, he is moving slowly but ever closer to the center of the universe.

The factors underlying man's emergence are complex and interrelated. They include higher levels of educational attainment, an increased availability of technology which both frees man from the burdens of physical and routine labor and makes him more dependent on society, an increasing rate of change affecting his environment which both threatens and challenges him, and higher levels of affluence which open up opportunities for a variety and depth of experiences never before so generally available.

The evidences of this trend are many. They are to be found, for example, in the gropings within many religions for more viable modes and values. They are to be found in the potent thrusts for independence of minorities everywhere, and in the challenges of our youth who find our values phony and often materialistically centered. They are to be found in the involvement of so many people in psychotherapy, in sensitivity train-

---

2. Bennis, W. G., *Changing Organizations*, New York, McGraw-Hill, 1966, p. 4.

ing, and in self-expression activities in the arts and elsewhere. They are also to be found in the continuing and growing interest in writings and ideas in the general direction of the humanistic-existential orientation to man.

Organizations are questioning and moving away from the bureaucratic model, in part because man is asserting his individuality and his centrality, in part because of growing dissatisfaction with the personally constraining impact of bureaucracies. In this flux, organizations and man must find a way with each other. In our view, this way will be found through changing values—values which can hopefully serve the needs for effectiveness and survival of organizations and the needs for individuality and growth of emergent man. Those concerned with organization theory and with organizational development have, in our judgment, a most important role to play in this quest.

Values in Transition

Deeply impressed with the managerial and organizational implications of the increasing accumulation of knowledge about human behavior, Professor Douglas McGregor formulated his assumptions of Theory Y.[3] According to him, these assumptions were essentially his interpretations, based upon the newer knowledge and on his extensive experience, of the nature of man and of man's motivation. In our view, McGregor was overly cautious and tentative in calling the Theory Y tenets "assumptions" and in limiting them to being his "interpretations." In trying to be "scientific," he seemed reluctant in his writing to assert explicitly as *values* those elements (including the Theory Y assumptions) which so much affected his organizational theory and practice. He was not alone in his reluctance. Perhaps the most pervasive common characteristic among people in laboratory training and in organizational development work is their values, and yet, while organizational development academicians and practitioners are generally aware of their shared values and while these values implicitly guide much of what they do, they too have usually been reluctant to make them explicit.

We want here not only to own our values but also to state them openly. These values are consistent with McGregor's assumptions and in some instances go beyond his. They are not scientifically derived nor are they new, but they are compatible with relevant "findings" emerging in the behavioral sciences. They are deeply rooted in the nature of man and are therefore basically humanistic. As previously suggested, many of the values underlying the bureaucratic model and its typical implementation

---

3. See p. 157.

have been inconsistent with the nature of man, with the result that he has not been fully utilized, his motivation has been reduced, his growth as a person stunted, and his spirit deadened. These outcomes sorely trouble us, for we believe organizations can in the fullest sense serve man as well as themselves.

Growing evidence strongly suggests that humanistic values not only resonate with an increasing number of people in today's world, but also are highly consistent with the effective functioning of organizations built on the newer organic model. As we discuss a number of these values, we will provide some face validity for their viability by illustrating them with cases or experiences taken from our involvements with or knowledge of a number of organizations which recently have been experimenting with the interface between the organizational and humanistic frontiers described above. The illustrations come primarily from TRW Systems, with which we have had a continuing collaboration for more than four years. Other organizations with which one or both of us have been involved include Aluminum Company of Canada, Ltd., U.S. Department of State, and the Organizational Behavior Group of Case Institute of Technology.

We clearly recognize that the values to which we hold are not absolutes, that they represent directions rather than final goals. We also recognize that the degree of their short-run application often depends upon the people and other variables involved. We feel that we are now in a period of transition, sometimes slow and sometimes rapid, involving a movement away from older, less personally meaningful and organizationally relevant values toward these newer values.

Away from a View of Man as Essentially Bad Toward a View of Him as Basically Good—At his core, man is not inherently evil, lazy, destructive, hurtful, irresponsible, narrowly self-centered, and the like. The life experiences which he has, including his relationships with other people and the impact on him of the organizations with which he associates, can and often do move him in these directions. On the other hand, his more central inclination toward the good is reflected in his behavior as an infant, in his centuries-long evolution of ethical and religious precepts, and in the directions of his strivings and growth as a result of experiences such as those in psychotherapy and sensitivity training. Essentially man is internally motivated toward positive personal and social ends; the extent to which he is not motivated results from a process of demotivation generated by his relationships and/or environment.

We have been impressed with the degree to which the fairly pervasive cultural assumption of man's badness has led to organizational forms and practices designed to control, limit, push, check upon, inhibit, and punish. We are also increasingly challenged by the changes in behavior resulting from a growing number of experiments with organizational forms and practices rooted in the view of man as basically good.

Within an organization it is readily apparent to both members and perceptive visitors whether or not there is, in general, an atmosphere of respect for the individual as a person. Are people treated arbitrarily? Are there sinister coups taking place? How much of the time and energy of the members of the organization is devoted to constructive problem solving rather than to playing games with each other, back-biting, politicking, destructive competition, and other dysfunctional behavior? How does management handle problems such as the keeping of time records? (Some organizations do not have time clocks and yet report that employees generally do not abuse this kind of a system.) One of the authors can remember a chain of retail stores which fired a stock clerk because he had shifty eyes, although he was one of the best stock boys in that chain. There are all kinds of negative assumptions about man behind such an incredible action.

> For a long period of time, two senior engineers, Taylor and Durant, had real difficulty in working together. Each had a negative view of the other; mutual respect was lacking. Such attitudes resulted in their avoiding each other even though their technical disciplines were closely related. A point in time was reached when Taylor sorely needed help from Durant. Caught up in his own negative feelings, however, he clearly was not about to ask Durant for help. Fortunately, two of Taylor's colleagues who did not share his feelings prodded him into asking Durant to work with him on the problem. Durant responded most positively, and brought along two of his colleagues the next day to study the problem in detail. He then continued to remain involved with Taylor until the latter's problem was solved. Only a stereotype had kept these men apart; Taylor's eventual willingness to approach Durant opened the door to constructive problem solving.

Away from Avoidance of Negative Evaluation of Individuals Toward Confirming Them as Human Beings —One desire frequently expressed by people with whom we consult is: "I wish I knew where I stand with my boss (with this organization) (with my colleagues) (with my subordinates). I'd really like to know what they think of me personally." We are not referring to the excessively neurotic needs of some persons for attention and response, but rather to the much more pervasive and basic need to know that one's existence makes a difference to others.

Feedback that is given is generally negative in character and often destructive of the individual instead of being focused on the perceived shortcomings of a given performance. It seems to be exceedingly difficult for most of us to give positive feedback to others—and, more specifically, to express genuine feelings of affection and caring.

When people are seen as bad, they need to be disciplined and corrected on the issue only; when they are seen as good, they need to be confirmed. Avoidance and negative evaluation can lead individuals to be cautious, guarded, defensive. Confirmation can lead to personal release, confidence, and enhancement.

A senior executive reported to one of us that he did not get nearly as much feedback as he wanted about how people thought about him as a person and whether or not they cared for him. He reported that one of the most meaningful things that had happened to him in this regard occurred when the person he reported to put his arm around him briefly at the end of a working session, patted him on the shoulder, and said, "Keep up the good work," communicating a great deal of warmth and positive feelings towards the person through this behavior. This event had taken place two years ago and lasted about five seconds, yet it was still fresh in the senior executive's memory and obviously has had a great deal of personal meaning for him. In our culture, most of us are grossly undernourished and have strong need for the personal caring of others.

Away from a View of Individuals as Fixed, Toward Seeing Them as Being in Process —The traditional view of individuals is that they can be defined in terms of given interests, knowledge, skills, and personality characteristics: they can gain new knowledge, acquire additional skills, and even at times change their interests, but it is rare that people really change. This view, when buttressed by related organizational attitudes and modes, insures a relative fixity of individuals, with crippling effects. The value to which we hold is that people can constantly be in flux, groping, questing, testing, experimenting, and growing. We are struck by the tremendous untapped potential in most individuals yearning for discovery and release. Individuals may rarely change in core attributes, but the range of alternatives for choice can be widened, and the ability to learn how to learn more about self can be enhanced.

Organizations at times question whether it is their responsibility to foster individual growth. Whether or not it is, we believe that for most organizations, especially those desiring long-term survival through adaptability, innovation, and change, it is an increasing necessity. Further, evidence suggests that to have people in process requires a growth-enhancing environment. Personal growth requires healthy organizations. This value, then, carries with it great implications for work in organizational development. In organizations, people continuously experience interpersonal difficulties in relating to the other people with whom they must work. Some reasons for the difficulties are that people listen very badly to each other, attribute things of a negative nature to another person, and make all kinds of paranoid assumptions, with the result that communication breaks down rather severely.

There have been many instances within TRW Systems of people, who, in the eyes of others around them, produce some fairly significant changes in their own behavior. Most of these changes have been reported quite positively. In some cases there have been rather dramatic changes with respect to how a person faces certain kinds of problems—how he handles conflicts, how he conducts staff meetings. In those cases an individual who is perceived as having changed quite often reports that these changes are personally rewarding, that he feels better about himself and more optimistic and expansive about life.

TRW Systems is committed to a continuation and improvement of its Career Development program, which places considerable emphasis on the personal and professional growth of its members. Although the original commitment was perhaps largely based on faith, experience gained in recent years strongly suggests that one of the most productive investments the organization can make is in the continuing growth of its members and in the health of the environment in which they work.

Away from Resisting and Fearing Individual Differences Toward Accepting and Utilizing Them —The pervasive and long-standing view of man as bad takes on even more serious implications when individual differences among men appear—differences in race, religion, personality (including personal style), specialties, and personal perceptions (definitions of truth or reality). A bad man poses sufficient problems but a strange bad man often becomes impossible.

Organizations and individuals are frequently threatened by what they consider questioning of or challenge to their existing values and modes, represented by the presence of alternative possibilities. And they choose to avoid the challenge and the related and expected conflicts, discomforts, and the like, which might follow. As a result, they achieve drabness, a lack of creativity, and a false sense of peace and security. We firmly believe that the existence of differences can be highly functional. There is no single truth, no one right way, no chosen people. It is at the interface of differences that ferment occurs and that the potential for creativity exists. Furthermore, for an organization to deny to itself (in the name of "harmony" or some similar shibboleth) the availability of productive resources simply because they do not conform to an irrelevant criterion is nothing short of madness. To utilize differences creatively is rarely easy, but our experience tells us that the gains far outweigh the costs.

In the play "Right You Are," Pirandello makes the point that truth in a particular human situation is a collection of what each individual in the situation sees. Each person will see different facets of the same event. In a positive sense, this would lead us to value seeing all the various facets of an issue or problem as they unfold in the eyes of all the beholders and to place a positive value on our interdependence with others, particularly in situations where each of us can have only part of the answer or see part of the reality.

> An organization recently faced the problem of filling a key position. The man whose responsibility it was to fill the position sat down with five or six people who, due to their various functional roles, would have a great deal of interaction with the person in that position and with his organization. The man asked them to help him identify logical candidates. The group very quickly identified a number of people who ought to be considered and the two or three who were the most logical candidates. Then the group went beyond the stated agenda and came up with a rather creative new organizational notion, which was subsequently implemented and proved to be very desirable. After this took place, the executive, who had called the meeting in order to get the help for the decision he had to make, reported that it was very clear to him that doing the job became much easier by getting everyone together to share their varying perceptions. This meant that he had more relevant data available to him in making his decision. Furthermore, the creative organizational concept only came about as a result of the meeting's having taken place.

In most organizations persons and groups with markedly different training, experience, points of view, and modes of operating frequently bump into each other. Project managers face functional performers, mechanical engineers face electrical engineers, designers face hardware specialists, basic researchers face action-oriented engineers, financial specialists face starry-eyed innovators. Each needs to understand and respect the world of the other, and organizations should place a high value upon and do much to facilitate the working through of the differences which come into sharp focus at interfaces such as these.

Away from Utilizing an Individual Primarily with Reference to His Job Description Toward Viewing Him as a Whole Person — People get pigeon-holed very easily, with job description (or expectations of job performance) typically becoming the pigeon hole. A cost accountant is hired, and from then on he is seen and dealt with as a cost accountant. Our view is that people generally have much more to contribute and to develop than just what is expected of them in their specific positions. Whole persons, not parts of persons, are hired and available for contribution. The organizational challenge is to recognize this fact and discover ways to provide outlets for the rich, varied, and often untapped resources available to them.

One of many personal examples that could be cited within TRW Systems is that of a person trained as a theoretical physicist. Having pursued this profession for many years, he is now effectively serving also as a part-time behavioral science consultant (a third-party process facilitator) to the personnel organization within the company. This is an activity for which he had no previous formal training until a new-found interest began asserting itself. The organization has supported him in this interest, has made a relevant learning opportunity available to him, and has opened the door to his performing an additional function within the organization.

An organizational example involves the question of charters that are defined for particular sub-elements of the organization: divisions, staffs, labs, etc. What are their functions? What are they supposed to do? To state the extreme, an organizational unit can have very sharply defined charters so that each person in it knows exactly what he is supposed to do and not do. This can lead to very clean functional relationships. Another approach, however, is to say that the *core* of the charter will be very clear with discrete responsibilities identified, but the outer edges (where one charter interacts with others) will not be sharply defined and will deliberately overlap and interweave with other charters. The latter approach assumes that there is a potential synergy within an organization which people can move toward fully actualizing if they can be constructive and creative in their interpersonal and intergroup relations. Very different charters are produced in this case, with very different outcomes. Such charters must, by definition, not be clean and sharply described, or the innovative and coordinated outcomes that might come about by having people working across charter boundaries will not occur.

Away from Walling-Off the Expression of Feelings Toward Making Possible Both Appropriate Expression and Effective Use —In our culture, there is a pervasive fear of feelings. From early childhood, children are taught to hide, repress, or deny the existence of their feelings, and their learnings are reinforced as they grow older. People are concerned about "losing control," and organizations seek rational, proper, task-oriented behavior, which emphasizes head-level as opposed to gut-level behavior. But organizations also seek high motivation, high morale, loyalty, team work, commitment, and creativity, all of which, if they are more than words, stem from personal feelings. Further, an individual cannot be a whole person if he is prevented from using or divorced from his feelings. And the energy dissipated in repression of feelings is lost to more productive endeavors.

We appreciate and are not afraid of feelings, and strongly believe that organizations will increasingly discover that they have a reservoir of untapped resources available to them in the feelings of their members, that the repression of feelings in the past has been more costly, both to them and to their members, than they ever thought possible.

One of the relevant questions to ask within an organization is how well problems stay solved once they are apparently solved. If the feelings involved in such problems are not directly dealt with and worked through, the problem usually does not remain solved for very long. For example, if two subordinates are fighting about something, their supervisor can either intervene and make the decision for them or arbitrate. Both methods can solve the immediate difficulty, but the fundamental problem will most likely again occur in some other situation or at some other time. The supervisor has dealt only with the symptoms of the real problem.

The direct expression of feelings, no matter what they are, does typically take place somewhere along the line, but usually not in the relevant face-to-face relationship. A person will attend a staff meeting and experience a great deal of frustration with the meeting as a whole or with the behavior of one or more persons in it. He will then talk about his feelings with another colleague outside the meeting or bring them home and discuss them with or displace them on his wife or children, rather than talking about them in the meeting where such behavior might make an important difference. To aid communication of feelings, participants at a given staff meeting could decide that one of the agenda items will be: "How do we feel about this meeting; how is it going; how can it be improved?" They could then talk face-to-face with each other while the feeling is immediately relevant to the effective functioning of the staff group. The outcomes of the face-to-face confrontation can be far more constructive than the "dealing-with symptoms" approach.

Away from Maskmanship and Game-Playing Toward Authentic Behavior — Deeply rooted in existing organizational lore is a belief in the necessity or efficacy of being what one is not, both as an individual and as a group. Strategy and out-maneuvering are valued. Using diplomacy, wearing masks, not saying what one thinks or expressing what one feels, creating an image — these and other deceptive modes are widely utilized. As a result, in many interpersonal and intergroup relations, mask faces mask, image faces image, and much energy is employed in dealing with the other person's game. That which is much more basically relevant to the given relationship is often completely avoided in the transaction.

To be that which one (individual or group) truly is — to be authentic — is a central value to us. Honesty, directness, and congruence, if widely practiced, create an organizational atmosphere in which energies get focused on the real problems rather than on game-playing and in which individuals and groups can genuinely and meaningfully encounter each other.

Recently, two supervisors of separate units within an organization got together to resolve a problem that affected both of them. At one point in their discussion, which had gone on for some time and was proving not to be very fruitful, one of them happened to mention that he had recently attended a sensitivity training laboratory conducted by the company. At that point, the other one mentioned that sometime back he had also attended a laboratory. They both quickly decided "to cut out the crap," stop the game they were playing, and really try to solve the problem they had come to face. Within a very short period of time, they dramatically went from a very typical organizational mode of being very closed, wearing masks, and trying to outmaneuver each other, to a mode of being open and direct. They found that the second mode took less energy and that they solved the problem in much less time and were able to keep it solved. But, somehow, at least one of them had not felt safe in taking off his mask until he learned that the other one had also gone through a T Group.

When people experience difficulty with others in organizations, they quite often attribute the difficulty to the fact that the other person or group is not trustworthy. This attitude, of course, justifies their behavior in dealing with the other. On numerous occasions within TRW Systems, groups or individuals who are experiencing distrust are brought together and helped to articulate how they feel about each other. When the fact that "I do not trust you" is out on the table, and only then, can it be dealt with. Interestingly, it turns out that when the feeling is exposed and worked through, there are not really very many fundamentally untrustworthy people. There certainly are all kinds of people continuously doing things that create feelings of mistrust in others. But these feelings and the behavior that triggers them are rarely explored in an effort to work them through. Instead, the mistrust escalates, continues to influence the behavior of both parties, and becomes self-fulfilling. Once the locked-in situation is broken through and the people involved really start talking to each other authentically, however, trust issues, about which people can be very pessimistic, become quite workable. This has happened many, many times in organizational development efforts at TRW Systems.

Away from Use of Status for Maintaining Power and Personal Prestige Toward Use of Status for Organizationally Relevant Purposes —In organizations, particularly large ones, status and symbols of status can play an important role. In too many instances, however, they are used for narrowly personal ends, both to hide behind and to maintain the aura of power and prestige. One result is that dysfunctional walls are built and communication flow suffers.

We believe that status must always be organizationally (functionally) relevant. Some people know more than others, some can do things others cannot do, some carry more responsbility than others. It is often useful for status to be attached to these differences, but such status must be used by its holder to further rather than to wall off the performance of the function out of which the status arises. An organization must be constantly alert to the role that status plays in its functioning.

It is relatively easy to perceive how status symbols are used within an organization, how relatively functional or dysfunctional they are. In some organizations, name-dropping is one of the primary weapons for accomplishing something. A person can go to a colleague with whom he is having a quarrel about what should be done and mention that he had a chat with the president of the organization yesterday. He then gets agreement. He may or may not have talked with the president, he may or may not have quoted him correctly; but he is begging the question by using a power figure in order to convince the other person to do it his way. In other organizations, we have observed that people very rarely work a problem by invoking the name of a senior executive, and that, in fact, those who do name-drop are quickly and openly called to task.

At TRW Systems, with only minor exceptions, middle- and top-level executives, as well as key scientists and engineers, are typically available for consultation with anyone in the organization on matters of functional relevance to the organization. There is no need to use titles, to "follow the organization chart," to obtain permission for the consultation from one's boss or to report the results to him afterwards. As a result, those who can really help are sought out, and problems tend to get worked at the point of interface between need on the one hand and knowledge, experience, and expertise on the other.

Away from Distrusting People Toward Trusting Them—A corollary of the view that man is basically bad is the view that he cannot be trusted. And if he cannot be trusted, he must be carefully watched. In our judgment, many traditional organizational forms exist, at least in part, because of distrust. Close supervision, managerial controls, guarding, security, sign-outs, carry with them to some extent the implication of distrust.

The increasing evidence available to us strongly suggests that distrusting people often becomes a self-confirming hypothesis—distrusting another leads to behavior consciously or unconsciously designed by the person or group not trusted to "prove" the validity of the distrust. Distrust begets distrust. On the other hand, the evidence also suggests that trust begets trust; when people are trusted, they often respond in ways to merit or justify that trust.

Where distrust exists, people are usually seen as having to be motivated "from the outside in," as being responsive only to outside pressure. But when trust exists, people are seen as being motivated "from the inside out," as being at least potentially self-directing entities. One motivational device often used in the outside-in approach involves the inculcation of guilt. Rooted in the Protestant ethic, this device confronts the individual with "shoulds," "oughts," or "musts" as reasons for behaving in a given way. Failure to comply means some external standard has not been met. The individual has thus done wrong, and he is made to feel guilty. The more trustful, inside-out approach makes it possible for the individual to do things because they make sense to him, because they have functional relevance. If the behavior does not succeed, the experience is viewed in positive terms as an opportunity to learn rather than negatively as a reason for punishment and guilt.

Organizations which trust go far to provide individuals and groups with considerable freedom for self-directed action backed up by the experience-based belief that this managerial value will generate the assumption of responsibility for the exercise of that freedom.

> In California, going back about 27 years, a forward-looking director of one of our state prisons got the idea of a "prison without walls." He developed and received support for an experiment that involved bringing prisoners to the institution where correctional officers, at that time called guards, carried no guns or billy clubs. There were no guards in the towers or on the walls. The incoming prisoners were shown that the gate was not locked. Under this newer organizational behavior, escape rates decreased, and the experiment has become a model for many prisons in this country and abroad.

> An organizational family embarked upon a two-day team-development lab shortly after the conclusion was reached from assessment data that the partial failure of a space vehicle had resulted from the non-functioning of a subsystem developed by this team. At the outset of the lab, an aura of depression was present but there was no evidence that the team had been chastised by higher management for the failure. Further, in strong contrast with what most likely would have been the case if they had faced a load of guilt generated from the outside, there was no evidence of mutual destructive criticism and recriminations. Instead, the team was able in time to turn its attention to a diagnosis of possible reasons for the failure and to action steps which might be taken to avoid a similar outcome in the future.

> During a discussion which took place between the head of an organization and one of his subordinates (relating to goals and objectives for that subordinate for the coming year), the supervisor said that one of the things he felt very positive about with respect to that particular subordinate was the way he seemed to be defining his own set of responsibilities. This comment demonstrated the large degree of trust that was placed in the subordinates of this particular supervisor. While the supervisor certainly made it clear to this individual that there were some specific things expected of him, he consciously created a large degree of freedom within which the subordinate would be able to determine for himself how he should spend his time, what priorities he ought to have, what his functions should be. This is in great contrast to other organizations which define very clearly and elaborately what they expect from people. Two very different sets of assumptions about people underlie these two approaches.

Away from Avoiding Facing Others with Relevant Data Toward Making Appropriate Confrontation — This value trend is closely related to the one of "from maskmanship toward authenticity," and its implementation is often tied to moving "from distrust toward trust."

In many organizations today there is an unwillingness to "level" with people, particularly with respect to matters which have personal implications. In merit reviews, the "touchy" matters are avoided. Often, incompetent or unneeded employees are retained much longer than is justified either from the organization's or their own point of view. Feelings toward another accumulate and at times fester, but they remain unexpressed. "Even one's best friends won't tell him."

Confrontation fails to take place because "I don't want to hurt Joe," although in fact the non-conformer may be concerned about being hurt himself. We feel that a real absurdity is involved here. While it is widely believed that to "level" is to hurt and, at times, destroy the other, the opposite may often be the case. Being left to live in a "fool's paradise" or being permitted to continue with false illusions about self is often highly hurtful and even destructive. Being honestly confronted in a context of mutual trust and caring is an essential requirement for personal growth. In an organizational setting, it is also an important aspect of "working the problem."

A quite dramatic example of confrontation and its impact occurred in a sensitivity training laboratory when one executive giving feedback to a colleague said to him that he and others within the organization perceived him as being ruthless. This came as a tremendous jolt to the person receiving the feedback. He had absolutely no perception of himself as ruthless and no idea that he was doing things which would cause others to feel that way about him. The confrontation was an upending experience for him. As a result, he later began to explore with many people in the organization what their relationship with him was like and made some quite marked changes in his behavior after getting additional data which tended to confirm what he had recently heard. In the absence of these data (previously withheld because people might not want to hurt him), he was indeed living in a fool's paradise. A great deal of energy was expended by other people in dealing with his "ruthlessness," and a considerable amount of avoidance took place, greatly influencing the productivity of everyone. Once this problem was exposed and worked through, this energy became available for more productive purposes.

Away from Avoidance of Risk-Taking Toward Willingness to Risk —A widely discernible attribute of large numbers of individuals and groups in organizations today is the unwillingness to risk, to put one's self or the group on the line. Much of this reluctance stems from not being trusted, with the resulting fear of the consequences expected to follow close upon the making of an error. It often seems that only a reasonable guarantee of success will free an individual or group to take a chance. Such a stance leads to conformity, to a repetition of the past, to excessive caution and defensiveness. We feel that risk-taking is an essential quality in adaptable, growthful organizations; taking a chance is necessary for creativity and change. Also, individuals and groups do learn by making mistakes. Risk-taking involves being willing "to take the monkey on my back," and it takes courage to do so. It also takes courage and ingenuity on the part of the organization to foster such behavior.

At TRW Systems, the president and many of the senior executives were until recently located on the fifth floor of one of the organization's buildings, and part of the language of the organization was "the fifth floor," meaning that place where many of the power figures resided. This phrase was used quite often in discussion: "The fifth floor feels that we should —." In working with groups one or two levels below the top executives to explore what they might do about some of the frustrations they were experiencing in getting their jobs done, one of the things that dominated the early discussions was the wish that somehow "the fifth floor" would straighten things out. For example, a group of engineers of one division was having problems with a group of engineers of another division, and they stated that "the fifth floor" (or at least one of its executives) ought to go over to the people in the other division and somehow "give them the word." After a while, however, they began to realize that it really was not very fruitful or productive to talk about what they wished someone else would do, and they began to face the problem of what they could do about the situation directly.

The discussion then became quite constructive and creative, and a number of new action items were developed and later successfully implemented — even though there was no assurance of successful outcomes at the time the action items were decided upon.

Away from a View of Process Work as Being Unproductive Effort Toward Seeing it as Essential to Effective Task Accomplishment —In the past and often in the present, productive effort has been seen as that which focused directly on the production of goods and services. Little attention has been paid to the processes by which such effort takes place; to do so has often been viewed as a waste of time. Increasingly, however, the relevance to task accomplishment of such activities as team maintenance and development, diagnosis and working through of interpersonal and intergroup communication barriers, confrontation efforts for resolution of organizationally dysfunctional personal and interpersonal hang-ups, and assessment and improvement of existing modes of decision making is being recognized. And, in fact, we harbor growing doubts with respect to the continued usefulness of the notion of a task-process dichotomy. It seems to us that there are many activities which can make contributions to task accomplishment and that the choice from among these is essentially an economic one.

Within TRW Systems, proposals are constantly being written in the hope of obtaining new projects from the Department of Defense, NASA, and others. These proposals are done under very tight time constraints. What quite often happens is that the request for the proposal is received from the customer and read very quickly by the principals involved. Everybody then charges off and starts working on the proposal because of the keenly felt time pressure. Recently, on a very major proposal, the proposal manager decided that the first thing he should do was spend a couple of days (out of a three-month period of available time) meeting with the principals involved. In this meeting, they would not do any writing of the proposal but would talk about how they were going to proceed, make sure they were all making the same assumptions about who would be working on which subsystem, how they would handle critical interfaces, how they would handle critical choice points during the proposal period, and so on. Many of the principals went to the meeting with a great deal of skepticism, if not impatience. They wanted to get "on with the job," which to them meant writing the proposal. Spending a couple of days talking about "how we're going to do things" was not defined by them as productive work. After the meeting, and after the proposal had been written and delivered to the customer, a critique was held on the process used. Those involved in general reported very favorably on the efforts of the meeting which took place at the beginning of the proposal-writing cycle. They reported things such as: "The effect of having spent a couple of days as we did meant that at that point when we then charged off and started actually writing the proposal, we were able to function as if we had already been working together for perhaps two months. We were much more effective with each other and much more efficient, so that in the final analysis, it was time well spent." By giving attention to their ways of getting work done, they clearly had facilitated their ability to function well as a team.

Away from a Primary Emphasis on Competition Toward a Much Greater Emphasis on Collaboration —A pervasive value in the organizational milieu is competition. Competition is based on the assumption that desirable resources are limited in quantity and that individuals or groups can be effectively motivated through competing against one another for the possession of these resources. But competition can often set man against man and group against group in dysfunctional behavior, including a shift of objectives from obtaining the limited resource to blocking or destroying the competitor. Competition inevitably results in winners and losers, and at least some of the hidden costs of losing can be rather high in systemic terms.

Collaboration, on the other hand, is based on the assumption that the desirable limited resources can be shared among the participants in a mutually satisfactory manner and, even more important, that it is possible to increase the quality of the resources themselves.

As organizational work becomes more highly specialized and complex, with its accomplishment depending more and more on the effective interaction of individuals and groups, and as the organic or systems views of organizational functioning become more widely understood, the viability of collaboration as an organizational mode becomes ever clearer.

Individuals and groups are often highly interdependent, and such interdependency needs to be facilitated through collaborative behavior rather than walled off through competition. At the same time, collaborative behavior must come to be viewed as reflecting strength rather than weakness.

In organizations which have a high degree of interdependency, one of the problems people run into regarding the handling of this interdependency is that they look for simple solutions to complex problems. Simple solutions do not produce very good results because they deal with the symptoms rather than with the real problems.

> A major reorganization recently took place within TRW Systems. The president of the organization sketched out the broad, general directions of the reorganization, specifying details only in one or two instances. He assigned to a large number of working committees the development of the details of the new organization. The initial reaction of some people was that these were things that the president himself should be deciding. The president, however, did not feel he had enough detailed understanding and knowledge to come up with many of the appropriate answers. He felt strongly that those who had the knowledge should develop the answers. This was an explicit, conscious recognition on his part of the fact that he did indeed need very important inputs from other people in order to effect the changes he was interested in making. These working committees turned out to be very effective. As a result of the president's approach, the reorganization proceeded with far less disruption and resistance than is typically the case in major reorganizations.
>
> Another example involved a major staff function which was experiencing a great deal of difficulty with other parts of the organization. The unit having the trouble made the initial decision to conduct briefings throughout the organization to explain what they were really trying to accomplish, how they were organized, what requirements they had to meet for outside customers, and so on. They felt that their job would be easier if they could solicit better understanding. What actually took place was quite different. Instead of conducting briefings to convince the "heathen," the people in this unit revised their plan and met with some key people from other parts of the company who had to deal with them to ask what the unit was doing that was creating problems at the interface. After receiving a great deal of fairly specific data, the unit and the people with whom they consulted developed joint collaborative action items for dealing with the problems. This way of approaching the problem quickly turned interfaces that had been very negative and very hostile into ones that were relatively cooperative. The change in attitude on both sides of the interface provided a positive base for working toward satisfactory solutions to the problems.

Some Implications of These Values in Transition

Many people would agree with the value trends stated in this paper and indeed claim that they use these guidelines in running their own organizations. However, there is often quite a gap between saying that you believe in these values and actually practicing them in meaningful, important ways. In many organizations, for example, there is a management-by-objectives process which has been installed and used for several years — an approach which can involve the implementation of some of the values stated earlier in this paper. If, however, one closely examines how this process takes place in many organizations, it is in fact a very mechanical one, one which is used very defensively in some cases. What emerges is a statement of objectives which has obtained for the boss what he really wants, and, at the the end of the year, protects the subordinate if he does not do everything that his boss thought he might do. It becomes a "Pearl Harbor file." The point that needs emphasis is that the payoff in implementing these values by techniques is not in the techniques themselves but in how they are applied and in what meaning their use has for the people involved.

To us, the implementation of these values clearly involves a bias regarding organizational development efforts. Believing that people have vast amounts of untapped potential and the capability and desire to grow, to engage in meaningful collaborative relationships, to be creative in organizational contexts, and to be more authentic, we feel that the most effective change interventions are therapeutic in nature. Such interventions focus directly on the hangups, both personal and organizational, that block a person from realizing his potential. We are referring to interventions which assist a person in breaking through the neurotic barriers in himself, in others around him, and in the ongoing culture.

We place a strong emphasis on increasing the sanity of the individuals in the organization and of the organization itself. By this we mean putting the individuals and the organization more in touch with the realities existing within themselves and around them. With respect to the individual, this involves his understanding the consequences of his behavior. How do people feel about him? How do they react to him? Do they trust him? With respect to the organization, it involves a critical examination of its culture and what that culture produces: the norms, the values, the decision-making processes, the general environment that it has created and maintained over a period of time.

There are obviously other biases and alternatives available to someone approaching organizational development work. One could concentrate on structural interventions: How should we organize? What kind of charters should people in various functional units have? The bias we are stating does not mean that structure, function, and charters are irrelevant, but that they are less important and have considerably less leverage in the early stages of organizational development efforts than working with the individuals and groups in a therapeutic manner. Furthermore, as an individual becomes more authentic and interpersonally competent, he becomes far more capable of creative problem-solving. He and his associates have within them more resources for dealing with questions of structure, charters, and operating procedures, in more relevant and creative ways, than does someone from outside their system. Such therapeutic devices include the full range of laboratory methods usually identified with the NTL Institute: sensitivity training, team building, intergroup relationship building, and so on. They also include individual and group counseling within the organization, and the voluntary involvement of individuals in various forms of psychotherapy outside the organization.

In order to achieve a movement towards authenticity, focus must be placed on developing the whole person and in doing this in an organic way. The program cannot be something you crank people through; it must be tailored in a variety of ways to individual needs as they are expressed and identified. In time, therapy and individual growth (becoming more in touch with your own realities) become values in and of themselves. And as people become less demotivated and move toward authenticity, they clearly demonstrate that they have the ability to be creative about organization matters, and this too becomes a value shared within the organization. Once these values are introduced and people move towards them, the movement in and of itself will contain many forces that make for change and open up new possibilities in an organization. For example, as relationships become more trustworthy, as people are given more responsibility, as competition gives way to collaboration, people experience a freeing up. They are more apt to challenge all the given surroundings, to test the limits, to try new solutions, and to rock the boat. This can be an exciting and productive change, but it can also be troublesome, and a variety of responses to it must be expected.

Therapeutic efforts are long-term efforts. Movement towards greater authenticity, which leads to an organization's culture becoming more positive, creative, and growthful, is something that takes a great deal of time and a great deal of energy. In this kind of approach to organizational development, there is more ambiguity and less stability than in other approaches that might be taken. Patience, persistence, and confidence are essential through time if significant change is to occur and be maintained.

For the organizational development effort to have some kind of permanency, it is very important that it becomes an integral part of the line organization and its mode of operating. Many of the people involved in introducing change in organizations are in staff positions, typically in personnel. If, over time, the effort continues to be mainly one carried out by staff people, it is that much more tenuous. Somehow the total organization must be involved, particularly those people with line responsibility for the organization's success and for its future. They must assimilate the effort and make it a part of their own behavior within the organization. In other words, those people who have the greatest direct impact on and responsibility for creating, maintaining, and changing the culture of an organization must assume direct ownership of the change effort.

In the transition and beyond it, these changes can produce problems for the organization in confronting the outside world with its traditional values. For example, do you tell the truth to your customers when you are experiencing problems building a product for them, or do you continue to tell them that everything is going along fine? For the individual, there can be problems in other relationships around him, such as within his family at home. We do not as yet have good methods developed for dealing with these conflicts, but we can certainly say that they will take place and will have to be worked out.

As previously stated, the Career Development program at TRW Systems, now in its fifth year of operation, is an effort in which both authors have been deeply involved. We feel it is one of the more promising examples of large-scale, long-term, systematic efforts to help people move toward values we have outlined.

One question that is constantly raised about efforts such as the Career Development program at TRW Systems relates to assessing their impact. How does one know there has been a real payoff for the organization and its members? Some behavioral scientists have devised rather elaborate, mechanical tools in order to answer this question. We feel that the values themselves suggest the most relevant kind of measurement. The people involved have the capacity to determine the relevance and significance to them and to their organizational units of what they are doing. Within TRW Systems, a very pragmatic approach is taken. Questions are asked such as: Do we feel this has been useful? Are these kinds of problems easier to resolve? Are there less hidden agenda now? Do we deal more quickly and effectively with troublesome intergroup problems? The payoff is primarily discussed in qualitative terms, and we feel this is appropriate. It does not mean that quantitative judgments are not possible, but to insist on reducing the human condition to numbers, or to believe that it can be done, is madness.

The role of the person introducing change (whether he is staff or in the line) is a very tough, difficult, and, at times, lonely one. He personally must be as congruent as he can with the values we have discussed. If people perceive him to be outside the system of change, they should and will reject him. He must be willing and able to become involved as a person, not merely as the expert who will fix everybody else up. He, too, must be in process. This is rewarding, but also very difficult.

Introducing change into a social system almost always involves some level of resistance to that change. Accepting the values we have described means that one will not be fully satisfied with the here and now because the limits of man's potential have certainly not been reached. All we know for sure is that the potential is vast. Never accepting the status quo is a rather lonely position to take. In effect, as one of our colleagues has put it, you are constantly saying to yourself, "Fifty million Frenchmen are wrong!" From our own experience we know that this attitude can produce moments when one doubts one's sanity: "How come nobody else seems to feel the way I do, or to care about making things better, or to believe that it is possible to seek improvements?" Somehow, these moments must be worked through, courage must be drawn upon, and new actions must follow.

We are struck with and saddened by the large amounts of frustration, feelings of inadequacy, insecurity, and fear that seem to permeate groups of behavioral science practitioners when they meet for seminars or workshops. Belief in these values must lead to a bias towards optimism about the human condition. "Man does have the potential to create a better world, and I have the potential to contribute to that effort." But in addition to this bias towards optimism, there has to be a recognition of the fundamental fact that we will continuously have to deal with resistance to change, including resistances within ourselves. People are not standing in line outside our doors asking to be freed up, liberated, and upended. Cultures are not saying: "Change us, we can no longer cope, we are unstable." Commitment to trying to implement these values as well as we can is not commitment to an easy, safe existence. At times, we can be bone weary of confrontation, questioning, probing, and devil's-advocating. We can have delightful fantasies of copping out on the whole mess and living on some island. We can be fed up with and frightened by facing someone's anger when we are confronting him with what is going on around him. We can be worn out from the continuous effort to stretch ourselves as we try to move towards living these values to the fullest.

On the other hand, the rewards we experience can be precious, real, and profound. They can have important meaning for us individually, for those with whom we work, and for our organizations. Ultimately, what we stand for can make for a better world—and we deeply know that this is what keeps us going.

This paper was prepared for the McGregor Conference on Organizational Development, sponsored by the Organizational Studies Group, Sloan School of Management, MIT, October 1967.

Managing Integration

by Eileen Morley

Organizations are changing today in ways that were undreamed of twenty or thirty years ago. One extensive change involves the process of integration—the dynamics that occur when people attempt to become members of groups composed of others who differ from them. Until relatively recently, few people realized that there were any "dynamics" involved at all. Few understood that the approach of a stranger to a group of different others would evoke certain predictable responses. Few realized that the behaviors that tend to occur in such a situation have more to do with dominance and subordinacy, with high power and low power, with being highly valued and being little valued, with being an insider and being an outsider, than they have to do with biological skin color or gender.

Once we realize that the mixing or separation of groups is a social and cultural process, we can look to sociology, psychology, and anthropology to help us predict, understand, and manage that process. We can predict, for instance, that a particular national or cultural group is likely to respond to the approach of a foreigner in much the same way as a group of white American men typically responds to the approach of a black American—that is, unless the foreigner is for some reason viewed as unusually powerful by the native group. Indeed, foreign nationals working for American multinational corporations are frequently discounted, undervalued, and in other ways treated by the U. S. nationals just as they would treat women and people of color.

In other words, the processes of segregation are predictable human phenomena likely to be encountered anywhere. However, they run

I am indebted to my friend and colleague, Professor Asa Davis, for introducing me to "stranger" theory.

Eileen Morley is a private consultant. She resides in Cambridge, Massachusetts.

counter to the principle of equal opportunity and, therefore, to the central democratic value system of our society. The processes of equal employment and affirmative action are designed to move the behavior of Americans closer to this core value for integration. This paper will examine the dynamics and management of integration.

THE DYNAMICS OF INTEGRATION

A system-based set of concepts enables us to describe the process that occurs when nontraditional people (*strangers*) enter organizations or groups composed of people with markedly different characteristics. The process falls into five stages that occur in a consistent way in all kinds of different situations. The stages are resistance, isolation, assimilation, acculturation, and integration.

1. Resistance and Rejection

All living systems, from a cell to a planet, have a natural tendency to resist intrusion from possibly harmful outsiders. Cells resist intrusive bacteria; the body resists alien organs such as a replacement heart or kidney; urban gangs resist suburban intruders and vice versa. Not least, the traditional white male power system resists intrusion by lower-valued subordinate people, such as women or people of color. The stage of *resistance* is one in which women or people of color approach a white male group and are prevented from entering. The group may reject them vigorously or out-maneuver them more subtly, but it does not let them in.

The group resists outsiders because they threaten its "culture," its shared values, its accepted ways of behaving, its sense of identity and security, its power and influence. Fear of the approaching stranger is a fear that the stranger with different norms will change or destroy the existing system or take it over. For example, men have resisted the access of women to professional and lunch clubs because, they say, they are afraid that women will "turn it into a coffee klatch."

A second fear centers on the fact that the strangers come from a less valued, less powerful sector of society, so that no matter how properly they behave, the dominants will lose face and influence in the eyes of the outside world by associating with them.

In a situation when a group is threatened by direct hostile attack, these resistant behaviors are extremely obvious. When the values of the group insist that it is "right" to resist the outsider, the group can close ranks to keep the stranger out with whole-hearted single-minded energy. The situation is more complex when the core values of society begin to change in ways that conflict with tradition. Then the dominant group is under dual pressures. Its internal values demand that the stranger be resisted, while external demands press for the stranger's acceptance.

This is the position in which many white male managers find themselves today. Most were traditionally raised to assume that women and people of color would take on subordinate support roles and that white men would direct them. When social values began to require managers to accept as peers some of the people whom they had traditionally been taught that they should keep subordinate, and who should support them, they naturally experienced considerable conflict.

One part of this conflict is caused by tension between the traditional manager's internal values and the new external pressures for acceptance of nontraditional people. For if he does respond to external pressures and admit women or black people, the white male manager is likely to be rejected or censured by white male peers for this "disloyal" behavior. He may find himself outside the group. Another part of the conflict stems from the manager's preception that if he does accept subordinate strangers as equals, he and his white male peers stand to lose a great deal to this new source of competition.

2. Isolation

The second stage, *isolation*, occurs after initial resistance has died down or been stopped. In this stage, the nontraditional stranger is admitted to the system but is isolated within it. Again there are analogies at other system levels. Our bodies isolate an intrusive splinter or fragment of shrapnel by building a protective layer around it. National governments have frequently isolated intrusive or undesirable ethnic groups, walling them off in ghettos (European Jews), in concentration camps (American Japanese in World War II), or other special territories (black people in South Africa).

However, although isolation decreases the strangers' chance of infiltrating the dominant white culture, it has one important side effect. Segregation increases the subordinates' internal solidarity, reinforces their sense of identity, and ensures the perpetuation of their culture within the ghetto boundaries, even if that culture is discounted and devalued outside. Unfortunately, this process in turn can strengthen the resistance of the dominant system towards the subordinates, prolonging and hardening their stereotypes, and in extreme cases can lead to the extinction of the stranger group.

In work systems, this isolation consists of spatial and psychological distance between members and strangers. System members do not talk to the strangers, do not help them, do not give them work—at least not worthwhile work. Strangers are excluded from important activities and alliances. And while the overt hostility of the resistance stage is no longer present, passive hostility can continue.

If isolation is successful, the strangers become invisible. White men may work with them all day, but never invite them to lunch or home to dinner. White men can be in the same room with them, but never ask them to join a conversation or introduce them to other white men or respond if they speak. White men can talk in front of the strangers as if they were not present, making remarks that any impartial observer would judge to be unquestionably offensive. White men attribute the comments of nontraditional strangers to other white men, denying the stranger's presence and contributions. White men discount and devalue what strangers have to say, sometimes by a minute gesture or the subtlest change in facial expression, which nevertheless communicates that "I'll wait politely until this person of no account has finished talking." In the stage of isolation, nontraditional people live continuously in a state of being left out.

It is crucial to understand that, in the vast majority of cases, white American men do not do this maliciously, deliberately, or for the most part consciously. Discounting of the less valued people by the more valued people (and by the less valued people themselves) is a usual process in any society. The present change efforts stem from the fact that what is usual is no longer acceptable in terms of American values.

Isolation is increased by the fact that many subordinate people in the system share the perception of women or people of color as less worthy, less powerful, less deserving. This creates particular problems for women or persons of color who are managers: subordinates resist or avoid their requests and discount their instructions; their work may be done last of all; their telephone messages lost or delayed, their role subverted in a host of small ways. Again, some of this is an unconscious response by people who report to a nontraditional manager, based on their perception of him or her as powerless and unimportant compared with white male managers.

There are two forms of isolation. One occurs when the strangers are isolated from involvement in the dominant group; the other occurs when they are cut off from others of their own kind. By far the most common way of introducing strangers into any white male group is one at a time. The practice is widespread, and affects the movement of individual women and black men into groups as diverse as unions, professional partnerships, university sections, service academies, and Coast Guard ships. This dispersion is undertaken in the name of heterogenity. "We only have a small number of women/black people and we must make sure there is one in every group/section/platoon/ship." This policy of "divide and control" is so pervasive that it is difficult to believe that it is as unconscious a process as most white men claim, given its effectiveness in reducing the chance that the strangers will join forces and thereby increase their power to enter the dominant group.

When a stranger is allowed to enter a group, the assumption is usually made that it is up to that person to make things work—that whatever problems occur are "theirs" to solve. This is a more intense form of isolation that is called *victimization*. Victimization is a process in which the victim of discrimination or abuse from members of a more powerful group is seen as someone who brought it on him- or herself. Victimization occurs in many situations, a not uncommon example being that of rape.

By assigning responsibility for correcting an injustice or solving a problem to the relatively powerless victim of that injustice or problem, the members of the dominant group avoid responsibility for the injustice. This projection of responsibility enables the members of the dominant group to escape feelings of guilt because problems can then be viewed as belonging to the strangers. And since the victims are members of the relatively powerless subordinate group, there is a comparatively low chance that the dominants will have to change their behavior or give up an advantage.

Carried to the extreme, the stranger buys into this scenario, turning it into *self*-victimization, accepting this projection of responsibility instead of resisting it or demanding at least a collaborative partnership with the white male power group in addressing the problems.

Support and educational group activities are obviously of great benefit to women and people of color in reducing isolation. But since most of them have no formal place in, or interaction with, the management power structure, these groups can constitute another form of isolation. It is unrealistic to think that any substantial change can occur in organizational practices without the active involvement of some members of the dominant management group. This does not mean that support groups cannot provide a stepping stone to change. But if this is to happen, they must have access to the managerial structure, and management action must result.

3. Assimilation

In the assimilation stage, the group "takes over" the intruder and subordinates him or her in various ways. As long ago as 1949, sociologists in the Western world observed that although a minority people may be drawn into the top-management sponsorship circle, in the process they lose all ties with the ethnic group from which they have come. They take on symbols of identification of the receiving group, which in the case of skin color and other racial features, is not so easy to do. The same is true of gender characteristics.

Sometimes the characteristics of the original group are at odds with the characteristics of the entrant, so that assimilation makes the entrant appear ridiculous in the eyes of fellow strangers. In the early stages, the entrant may learn to live with this image. Later he or she changes it. The present experimentation with professional styles of dress for women and styles of hair for black people reflects this kind of incongruity. The tradition of the business world has been for men to dress in low-key colors and formal apparel, with short, flat hair styles. Presently, women are in the process of evolving a modified version of the business suit and black people are evolving Afro-hair-styles appropriate to the business world.

The requirements for assimilation tend to generate a reciprocal resistance on the part of the stranger to the discounters and loss of important personal characteristics. There is a sense of resentment and hostility at the demand to become "white" or "male." The extremely masculine style adopted by women in managerial roles some years ago ensured that they were more or less accepted at work, but prevented them from being viewed as attractive women in social and domestic settings. Similarly, black people who adopted the three-piece suit and the repressed unemotional behavior characteristic of Anglo-Saxon American men were often viewed as "selling out" their own cultural origins, their spontaneity, and their expressiveness for the sake of acceptance by the establishment. But, in fact, this willingness to "act white male" is a necessary step in the process of "paying one's dues" and becoming accepted.

The requirement to make oneself over in the image of the white man creates an ambivalence in the stranger that is often expressed in rebellious verbal or nonverbal behavior without apparent cause or a cause that is so minor that it is out of keeping with the intensity of the stranger's reaction. For a little while, the reaction reduces the tensions experienced by the stranger. In the long run, however, defiant or angry outbursts are not in the stranger's long-term interest because members of the existing system are likely to perceive this behavior, not as a necessary way of letting off steam, but as evidence that the person will never be able to adapt sufficiently to existing norms.

A different kind of reaction occurs among the less powerful members of the ruling caste when they see nontraditional entrants willingly adopting the behaviors of system members and becoming assimilated. Those who feel less secure become anxious about their own positions, increased competition, and possible loss of advantage. Commonly, this reaction is known as the white-male backlash.

4. Acculturation or Parallel Systems

Acculturation is a process and state in which the members of the subordinate group learn the culture of the dominant group and find ways to interact with it—but without being taken over by it. Or, if they have been taken over, they find ways to recreate their own system, either within or parallel to the dominants' organization.

Berelson and Steiner (1964) have usefully compared assimilation and acculturation processes by contrasting Northern Negroes and the Amish. Northern Negroes have been more often assimilated. That is, they have been obliged to adopt the behaviors and values of the Northern white community and to accept a place for themselves within it as one of its least valued elements. On the other hand, the Amish have maintained their identity and ways of living as a separate cultural entity, valuing and taking pride in themselves.

The independent existence of the Amish has continued without interruption. This has been possible because they found ways to interact economically as a group with the larger American society, in order to ensure their basic survival. Once this economic survival is reasonably assured, the Amish can place limits on other forms of interaction (such as participation in non-Amish schools) that would dilute their culture.

Today, the reaffirmation of the black identity is for many black people a process of withdrawing from the state of assimilation in which they previously existed and re-establishing a base of black culture that is not merged with white culture, even though it is connected in very complex ways by economic, social, and other ties.

In the working world, some parallel systems have always existed, staffed at all levels by members of the subordinate group. This trend is growing. Black businesses exist side by side with white businesses; women's banks along with men's banks; women's tennis with men's tennis; black magazines alongside white magazines; a black plant within a predominantly white manufacturing company. Small women's entrepreneurships (carpentry, painting) grow up alongside male craft businesses; women's professional organizations and lunch clubs alongside men's.

External parallel systems tend to be set up because nontraditional people inside organizations begin to understand the structure and working of that system as a whole. They want part of the rewards. They find themselves denied access to higher levels of responsibility and reward or find the level of pain intolerable. Consequently, they choose to leave and start their own organizations instead. In other words, parallel systems often emerge as an expression of entrepreneurial spirit and desire for leadership on the part of nontraditional people. They take the risk of breaking out of the traditional system so as to function at a level of opportunity, risk, and potential power and reward that would be foreclosed to them if they stayed inside.

5. Integration

One difficulty with integration is the variance of definitions of what it means. Some black people mean *acculturation* when they talk about integration. Many white people mean *assimilation*. In this paper integration is defined as:

> Recognition and respect for each other's specific characteristics; a sense of pride in one's own culture and characteristics; a willingness to share them with others; and an equal willingness to be open to the culture of others; and when tasks are involved, the identification of behaviors that are most relevant to task accomplishments, independent of gender or ethnic identity.

One example is provided by the families in which the men are choosing to take a more lively part in child-rearing and are deliberately learning certain behaviors previously thought of as "feminine." To the extent that the wife may also choose to take on nontraditional ("masculine") behaviors, this could be defined as an integrated family.

The sharing of behavior has important implications for the business world. A recent informal study revealed that in a retail organization, certain store managers described the importance of "listening to someone who is upset;" of "sensing what that person is disturbed about, even if he or she is not very articulate;" of "being responsive to her point of view," whether or not they agreed with it; and of "taking care of him and his problem." In contrast, a woman manager who managed a warehouse and therefore had low customer exposure talked about her need "to be firm and assertive" and the expectations of her truck drivers that she would behave that way.

Clearly, the integration of masculine and feminine behavior in this situation was related more closely to role than to gender. A store manager had to take care of customers and a warehouse manager had to direct truck drivers. This suggests that as more women move into formerly "masculine" jobs and some men begin to move into "feminine" occupations (such as secretarial work or nursing), each sex will develop a set of task-related behaviors independent of gender; although, to the casual glance, it will look as though the process of sex stereotyping is being reversed. In such cases, however, the person's overall behavioral repertoire will simply be expanding to cover a wider variety of demands. Away from work, the assertive female manager will not necessarily become less tender and caring towards husband or children; nor will the male nurse compete any less energetically with his buddies at pool or touch football.

Examples of the differences in black and white behavior and their relevance to task are harder to find. It is clearly going to be a long time before white America looks to black America as a source of valuable forms of task behavior that are not indigenous to white culture, adopts the behaviors on the job, and values them accordingly.

MANAGING INTEGRATION: THE ROLE OF THE WHITE-MALE MANAGER

The separation of people into more or less powerful, more or less dominant, more or less central groups, is a characteristic of almost all human
societies, and one that has existed for thousands of years. When we
attempt to eliminate the inequities of discrimination and shape our
society in terms of more democratic values, we are engaging in a very
complex, difficult, and long-term form of cultural change.

All white American men born before about 1950 grew up in a culture
in which the subordination of women and people of color was part of the
natural order of things—the way things "should be." Such men learned a
set of traditional attitudes and expectations about their place in the world,
both in relation to women and people of color and in relation to other
white men. Although these expectations included responsibilities and
obligations, such as "head of the household" and "breadwinner," they also
included advantages, not the least of which was preferential access to
power. White men learned that they were members of a white male
subculture (or supraculture) with its own expectations and norms for
mutual support, allegiance, and loyalty. For most traditional white men,
their place in the world was not a matter for conscious thought and choice.
It was as much a part of the way things were supposed to be as eating with
a knife and fork, or using a toothbrush instead of a twig to clean one's teeth.

In the years since 1960, assumptions about the place of white men in
society and about the structure of their world have altered substantially.
Now white men are told that the inferior position of people of color and
of women is no longer a given, but is a major flaw in a social structure
that must be changed.

This situation imposes a variety of stresses on white men. First,
because white men control so much power, they are being called on to
change this flawed structure. This introduces a new dimension of responsibility and complexity into their lives. Second, they stand to lose a
great deal in the process of upgrading opportunities for subordinate
people. This brings with it a fear of loss of power. Third, white men have
traditionally been raised to experience certain obligations from and to
each other. New demands for integration are in direct conflict with these
mutual expectations. Fourth, white men who are in any way sensitive
human beings are likely to experience some sense of personal or collective regret, or even guilt, at the injustices imposed on people of color and
women. And not the least kind of stress results from the need to interact
more freely and frequently with subordinate women and with people of
color as peers and colleagues, which creates uneasiness about how to
behave appropriately towards formerly subordinate people.

In the work setting, these stresses are likely to come into more intense focus around job performance, especially if the man is a manager. *Effective management of integration is not presently a well-understood managerial competence.* The chance of running into a difficult grievance or class-action suit is a new and ever-present occupational hazard. White-male managers are likely to experience anxiety or anger as a reaction to these general stresses. In addition, they perceive that demands for integration are making their jobs much harder, and they are aware that lack of knowledge about how to integrate and about how to evaluate and reward effective management of integration is placing new hazards in the path of their career success.

Guidelines for Managing Integration

If white men are to manage integration processes effectively, they need to be aware of the following effective ways of coping with integration:

- *Be aware of the problem or issue*: collect information about it; keep it in mind; identify possible courses of action.
- *Be aware of and express personal feelings*: find appropriate ways to talk about them so as to reduce tension and avoid inappropriate impulsive action.
- *Seek and use help*: in collecting information, exploring feelings, and in planning and taking action.

The last section of the chapter examines the implications of these principles for the white man who is a manager.

1. Be Aware of the Problem or Issue

The Particular Case

Most managers can become aware of and collect information about a particular problem, grievance, or allegedly discriminatory action in a very simple way—by listening to the accounts of the people involved. However, for many white men, listening is very difficult, especially if they are attempting to listen to a woman. Traditionally, men have been taught to treat women as listeners, but the ability to listen is crucial when a manager is collecting information about problems involving women or people of color. White men are accustomed to talking with some fluency and confidence. Women and people of color are not—at least in the presence of a relatively powerful white man. If he is going to be able to gather the information he needs, the white manager must learn to listen without interruption, to suspend judgment until he has heard the whole story, to refrain from analyzing, lecturing, or giving advice or instructions, and to communicate nonverbal encouragement that will enable the woman or person of color to explain the situation in full. The process of listening may sound easy, but in fact it is extremely difficult and requires special skills that many white men do not learn as part of their upbringing.

The General Case

In addition to collecting data about a particular discriminatory problem, managers also should understand the following different aspects of the general problem that integration presents to them.

a. Technical (regulatory) information. This means understanding both the specific requirements of the law and the way that the law affects a particular organization.

b. Knowledge of the dynamics of entry. The entry process falls into the five stages already described that occur when a stranger seeks entry to a group of dominants.

c. Knowledge about sexism and racism. This includes knowledge of: traditional socialization and its effects on adult attitudes and behavior, the forms those traditional behaviors are likely to take (stereotyping), and the ways in which they will impede integration.

The traditional male-female styles of verbal interaction are just one small example of such traditional behaviors. Information about these dynamics is available in articles and books (see the bibliography at the end of this chapter), and is increasingly available in seminars and workshops. The manager needs to understand his own attitudes and behavior because, whether he knows it or not, these are apparent in his treatment of women and people of color in day-to-day relationships. Self-knowledge of this kind is best acquired in workshops or training programs that include women and people of color as participants.

d. Knowledge of the processes of development. These are the processes that women and people of color go through as they develop a more mature sense of their own identity, confidence in their capabilities, and an expanding sense of entitlement to opportunity.

Palmer (1979) has described the stages that women go through: curiosity, anger, and a growing sense of personal powerfulness. Anger is an important element in women's development because it releases energy and confidence. Yet a woman's anger can create real problems for those around her. Since anger is the most difficult stage for any manager to deal with, knowledge about what is happening in the overall pattern of women's development can provide an extremely valuable perspective. It can enable the manager to avoid taking such aggressive feelings personally, even if they do seem to be directed at him. Similar understanding of the different stages in the emergence of black people's awareness can be equally valuable.

e. Knowledge of the relation between discrimination and organization structure.

Kanter (1977) has described the ways in which attitudes and behavior are related to the position of individuals in the organizational structure, to the amount of opportunity and power they have, and to their relative numbers in any given setting. Few white male managers have had an opportunity to learn what enabled their careers to prosper and how their opportunities differ from those of subordinate people. Knowledge of these dynamics helps managers and organizations begin to institutionalize some of the advantages that were informally available to white men. This means introducing major changes in human resource management, particularly in the areas of career development and career management, and managers need to be knowledgeable about them.

2. Be Aware of and Express Personal Feelings

To become aware of and to express personal feelings is a difficult process for many white men who have been traditionally trained to keep a "stiff upper lip," to avoid personal introspection and concentrate on the external and instrumental, and to restrain the expression of feelings. In contrast, women have been traditionally trained to be aware of feelings and to express them. This leads to the paradox that when a woman is asked what she thinks, she will often respond with what she feels, but when a man is asked what he feels, he will usually talk about what he thinks.

Many men are able to talk fluently about technical subjects, business and sports, but lack a vocabulary with which to express feelings. Because their traditional socialization patterns have not developed expressive verbal skills, many men literally lack the words in which to talk about their personal experience with depth or shading. An even stronger taboo exists against the expression of any negative feelings, such as anxiety, conflict, personal inadequacy, pain, or weakness. Many men do not allow these feelings to surface in their own awareness, let alone express them to others.

On the occasions when a man does express feelings, the person with whom he is most likely to share them is a woman. This is because emotional support has traditionally been provided by women to men (in exchange for economic support in the reverse direction). Consequently, men's communication is split: some topics they talk about mainly to other men; other topics, including feelings, they talk about mainly to women. According to this traditional system, the person a man would normally talk to when he is feeling anxious, upset, angry, or inadequate, is not another man, but a woman. However, if he is feeling upset about integration, the fact of the woman's gender is likely to inhibit or complicate the conversation, no matter how close or how trustworthy a relationship he has with her.

For all these reasons, white men often respond to integration-related stresses in ways that prevent their feelings from coming into awareness or being expressed. They deny these feelings, or they avoid thinking and talking about them. Only one feeling—anger—is sometimes exempt. This is because anger is the feeling that it is most legitimate for a white man to show.

The feelings considered the least legitimate for white American men to express are those of inadequacy, guilt, and human tenderness. But, in fact, the recognition of such feelings is critical to the effective management of integration for several reasons. First, the process of integration is so new and so complex that even the most effective manager is likely to experience some feeling of disorientation and inadequacy as he struggles with it. Second, many of the historical injustices imposed on subordinate people have been so serious that it is natural for more sensitive and responsible white people to feel some pain and guilt as they reflect on this. Third, the desire to help others learn and grow is so fundamental that it is natural for adult managers to experience feelings of nurturance and tenderness from time to time.

Few of these feelings are openly admissible among white men. But unless they can share with each other the fact that they do sometimes feel inadequate, they cannot start to look for ways to collaborate in creating the society that our changing cultural norms call for. Unless men can confront their sense of guilt, they cannot develop a more realistic perspective that will make them accountable, not for all the evils of past history, but simply for that piece of the world in which they live and which they can influence. Unless they can share their sense of concern for others, they cannot make it an explicit part of their agenda for creating effective organizations and seek collaboration with others who share that value.

Being aware of feelings has two critical aspects for white men:

- Being able to express what they feel to *someone* else—anyone—and
- Being able to express what they feel to another white man.

3. Seek and Use Help

Most larger employers in the United States have accepted demands for integration as a fact of contemporary organizational life, although the extent to which they embrace or resist it varies according to internal attitudes and pressures from both inside and outside the organization. The ability to manage integration, at whatever level is required in his particular job, has thus become a permanent feature of a manager's life. However, it is a skill that is relatively difficult to acquire, compared with others such as planning, budgeting, or supervising. There are no texts, no college or correspondence courses, and few management-development programs that address these issues.

Consequently, the manager has to find his own resources. These may include articles, books, lectures and workshops, other managers in the organization, and internal or external consultants. Some resources also exist outside the work setting, such as the programs on sexism or racism that are provided from time to time by professional associations, churches, and other interest groups.

In attempting to understand his own socialization, attitudes, and behavior, the manager has additional sources of help. One is the other white men in his organization who are interested in increasing their own self-awareness. The numbers of men in any given organization who are concerned about these issues presently tends to be small, but there are usually some, even if they are not very visible. The second source of help in increasing knowledge and personal insight are the women and people of color whom the manager trusts sufficiently to seek and use their help.

SUMMARY

In summary then, for white men as for women and people of color, the effective management of integration depends on being able to find appropriate help in the following processes:

- Understanding the general issues;
- Understanding their own feelings, personal attitudes, and behavior;
- Being effective in identifying and analyzing the issues involved in any particular case;
- Planning and taking actions that on a small scale will lead to the solution of individual problems and on the large scale will create more equitable career and opportunity structures; and
- Developing ways of assessing and rewarding effective management of integration.

Movement towards an integrated society is a long slow process, and its success is not easily discernible in any organization's bottom line. In recent research, Taylor (1979) has described affirmative-action change as an *inching process* that proceeds situation by situation and case by case. It is a process that requires a certain minimum level of readiness in the organization before it can acquire any momentum. As more is said and written about integration as one major aspect of organization development, then the state of readiness, the pace of the inching process, the evolution of new opportunity structures, and the interpersonal dynamics described in this chapter will all come to be seen as issues that require effective management.

References

Ackerman, R. W. How companies respond to social demands. *Harvard Business Review*, 1978, July-August, *56* (4).

Athos, A., & Gabarro, J. J. *Interpersonal behavior*. Englewood Cliffs, NJ: Prentice-Hall, 1978.

Miller, J. B. *Towards a new psychology of women*. Boston: Beacon Press, 1977.

Bardwick, J. M. *The psychology of women*. New York: Harper & Row, 1971.

Berelson, B., & Sreiner, G. A. *Human behavior: An inventory of scientific findings*. New York: Harcourt Brace Jovanovich, 1964.

Eakins, B. W., & Eakins, R. G. *Sex differences in human communication*. Boston: Houghton Mifflin, 1978.

Fasteau, M. F. *The male machine*. New York: Delta, 1975.

Kanter, R. M. *Men and women of the corporation*. New York: Basic Books, 1977.

Lyon, H. C., Jr. *Tenderness is strength*. New York: Harper & Row, 1977.

Morley, E. *Women's thinking and talking* (Case Clearing House, Graduate School of Business Administration) Cambridge, MA: Harvard University, 1977.

Palmer, J. Stages of women's awareness. *Social Change*, 1979 9(1).

Sargent, A. G. *Beyond the sex roles*. New York: West, 1977.

Taylor, M. *The role of the staff specialist in the policy implementation process*. Unpublished doctoral dissertation, Harvard University, 1979.

One proviso remains. In writing this chapter, I have tried to outline some of the issues that will be critical to good management in the future. In addition to writing from my identity as an academic and as a practitioner-consultant, I also write out of my identity as a white Angle-Saxon woman. However hard I may try to understand the viewpoint of the man or woman of color, I can never write from *inside* their experience. Consequently, I am bound by the limits of my own unconscious racism. The limitations of this chapter in expressing the viewpoint, the difficulties, and the needs of people of color are therefore all mine. I can only say to my minority colleagues: please think and write in your own behalf, so that when we think and talk about managing integration, we can define the process in terms of the needs and experience of every disadvantaged group.

The Organizational Imperative

by David K. Hart and William G. Scott

American values have undergone a massive change. The pluralistic forces that shaped our national character have withered away and the collective strivings of our society have been consolidated into a single social invention: modern organizations. They are *vast, complex, technologically based administrative systems which synthesize clusters of resources into rationally functioning wholes*. In contemporary America, the needs of organization overwhelm all other considerations, whether those of family, religion, art, science, law, or the individual. This has had a shattering impact on us, for it has caused us to become a different people than we thought we would be. However, that value change is by now a fait accompli, and the dominant force behind that change has been "the organizational imperative." Why has this happened?

Basically, it has been because modern organizations have been so immensely successful. They seemed to advance the material welfare of both individuals and the nation quite automatically. Such organizations, under the guidance of administrative elites, turned our enormous potentials—physical and human—into an unprecedented material abundance. This job was done so well and so unobtrusively that the automatism of material progress became an article of faith for Americans. We accepted what we had gained neither gratefully nor ungratefully, but as a simple and just inevitability.

However, in order to accomplish such material miracles, we had to become a different people from what we had historically hoped and dreamed for ourselves. The abundance created by modern organizations required a shift away from the values of the American tradition, even though we have continued to profess a pathetic loyalty to the lost values

David K. Hart is professor of government and William G. Scott is professor of management and organization. Both are on the faculty of the Graduate School of Business, University of Washington.

"The Organizational Imperative," by David K. Hart and William G. Scott is reprinted from *Administration & Society*, Vol. 7, No. 3 (Nov. 1975), pp. 259-284 by permission of the Publisher, Sage Publications, Inc.

of our national youth. Thus, no small part of our present national malaise is the result of an increasingly obvious disparity between what we had idealized and what we have become. When we look closely at what we made for ourselves, we recoil, for we see American values that are suitable for the efficient performance of organizations, but painfully inadequate for man himself.

However, the situation is even more complicated. There is a dawning realization that the earth cannot sustain our automatic progress into that good future. Even worse, we are beginning to comprehend that affluence has not brought a marked increase in personal happiness. The question now being asked is how we have managed to drift into this appalling situation. We have written this essay in partial response to that question. Our main contention is that a new value *paradigm* (Kuhn, 1970) has displaced the old paradigm, and that the organizational imperative is both the cause and the center of the new order.

THE ORGANIZATIONAL IMPERATIVE

The organizational imperative consists of two a priori propositions and three rules for behavior. The imperative is founded on a primary proposition, which is absolute: *whatever is good for man can only be achieved through modern organization*. The question of what is "good" for man is left open; what must be beyond question is the conviction that the only way to achieve that good is through modern organization. The secondary proposition derives from the first: *therefore, all behavior must enhance the health of such modern organizations*.

From the primary and secondary propositions come three rules for organizationally healthy behavior, which define, guide, and evaluate all administrative performance. They apply to every administrator in every organization in modern society. The behavioral rules require that the administrator be rational, a good steward, and pragmatic. Since the concepts of rationality, stewardship, and pragmatism carry heavy burdens of numerous interpretations, it is necessary to specify their exact meaning as part of the organizational imperative.

Rationality. The rule of rationality provides the common denominator for all scientifically conditioned, technologically oriented organizations in advanced industrial nations: administrators must be rational. This does not refer to the philosophic tradition of rationalism, but to that form of rationality central to scientific method, which requires the economizing of means to achieve ends.

Drawing on its heritage of science, engineering, and economics, administration has made rationality indistinguishable from efficiency—the ratio of $E = O/I$. The task of administration, guided by this operational formula, is to increase the value of E by adjusting the relative values of outputs over inputs. While we may argue over definitional refinements, this formulation must be accepted, along with its behavioral implications, because there is no other way to account for what managers do in modern organizations.

Stewardship. The organizational imperative requires stewardship behavior from administrators. Ultimately, an administrator is a steward of the a priori propositions, but practically he must manage the more immediate affairs of the organization in the interest of "others." It does not make a particle of difference who the others are: the public at large, stockholders of corporations, members of consumer cooperatives, members of labor unions, and the like. The rule of stewardship applies with equal force in all cases. For one thing, it legitimizes a necessary hierarchy. If the administrator as a steward is to fulfill this behavioral commitment, those who work for him must be obedient to his commands and he becomes steward for the combined destinies of his subordinates.

Additionally, stewardship requires the administrator to husband organizational resources. Thus administrators are socially and legally responsible to their clients outside the organization for their behavior as stewards; if the stewardship rule is successfully executed, the health and wealth of the organization is protected and increased, the welfare of the people dependent on the organization is improved, and the fortunes of its administrators are advanced. Just as with rationality, contrary ideas about the nature of stewardship are unthinkable within the framework of administrative theory and practice that has developed during the last 75 years.

Pragmatism. Pragmatic behavior enables the organization to survive in good health in changing environments, since practical circumstances continually impose different necessities on administrators. The rule of administrative pragmatism simply requires expedient behavior, guided by the a priori propositions. Beyond this, the rule for pragmatic behavior has *no other moral content*.

The organizational world of administration is one where complex problems of short-term duration must be dealt with expediently. Pragmatism demands that administrators direct their energies and talents to finding solutions for practical, existing problems within an immediate time frame. The language, reward systems, and activities of administration demonstrate this concern for the present and indicate the devotion that administrators have to securing an orderly, purposeful world composed of endlessly fascinating, narrow puzzles to be solved. This pragmatic puzzle world unburdens administrators of the need for moralistic reflection. Successful, expedient solutions to administrative puzzles are rewarded, and little honor goes to those whose efforts do not have immediate payoffs in terms of organizational performance (Scott and Hart, 1973).

Each of these behavioral rules entails the others. They exist in a web of interrelationships within the imperative, with the primary purpose of strengthening the a priori propositions of the imperative.

Thus, the organizational imperative is the sine qua non of administrative theory and practice. It cuts across all jurisdictional boundaries and applies to all organizations: public, private, educational, religious, or whatever. It changes slowly, if at all. It is not affected tangibly by political and social turmoil, or even war—in fact, the imperative might even be strengthened by them. The imperative is, so to speak, the metaphysic of administration: absolute, immutable, and unchanging. It is *persuasive* (it alters values in order to alter behavior), it is *universal* (it governs through the a priori propositions all collective efforts for achieving major social and individual objectives), and it is *durable* (it is the one source of stability and continuity in a turbulent world). For these and other reasons, the organizational imperative has become the dominant moral force in our society.

ADMINISTRATIVE NORMS

Administrative does the vital job of linking organizations (which are the most elaborate of abstractions) with the institutional infrastructure of society at large. Organizations are run by administrators who must make decisions about goals, policies, and strategies of action that influence human values and behaviors, both within and outside the organizations. Administrators respond with varying sensitivity and accuracy to the needs and interests of the different groups affected by their decisions. But their loyalties are seldom given to those they touch most profoundly, and certainly they are neither trained nor encouraged to speculate about the moral worth and moral impact of their decisions.

Conventional wisdom has it that an administrator's primary loyalty should be to those who own his organization: the stockholders (if it is a private company) or the citizens (if it is a public organization). While this wisdom may have been correct once, it is certainly not now. The overriding concern of the administrator is to keep the organization healthy. This mission of organizational health is best accomplished by the administrator's total allegiance to the organizational imperative. To advance this mission, the values of *all* people who influence the organization—whether from within or from without—must be modified so that they are supportive of the organizational imperative. The administrator, therefore, must discipline himself, his subordinates, and his relevent clients to arrange their values, expectations, and practical affairs so that the organizational imperative is served.

The result of such modification has been the conversion of almost all social values into administrative norms. Administrative norms serve as the guidelines for organizationally useful behavior and are the links between the organizational imperative and social values—partaking of both, but with the advantage going to the organizational imperative. It is important to understand why these norms came to be in this central location, and how they influence the direction of value change.

Traditional American values have always been rooted in the dream that a good life was available to everyone, and no small part of that dream has been the possibility of a relatively high degree of material well-being. Americans believed that this dream could be realized through individual efforts, working directly on the natural environment. Historically optimistic, blessed by the natural advantages of a geographically and geologically favored land, and fired by a work ethic, Americans saw material affluence as a realizable goal—if not for themselves, then at least for their children.

Out of this dream grew the belief that material *growth* was absolutely essential to the vitality of national life and that the material *abundance* obtained from such growth was limitless. These were the necessary preconditions for the good life. Whatever else Americans sought could be found by them, as individuals, in the consumption of products and services. Material well-being was, to an appreciable extent, the basis of a major consensus in the social order.

There has not been much difference between how Americans defined their individual aims and what administrators tried to accomplish within organizations. *Administrative norms generally have been consistent with the expectations of Americans at large, since successful administrative practices were thought to be translatable into individual welfare.* As technology was carried by modern organization into nearly every corner of society, a new—and extremely important—premise was added to the concept for a good life. This premise did not eradicate customary assumptions about individual happiness. Rather, it converted them into organizational terms. The most important change it wrought was to create popular acceptance of the thesis that the dream of individual welfare could be realized *only* by the preeminence of modern organization and its administrative apparatus.

The traditional social values survived, but their connotation changed. Thus, growth was a good, but the most important growth was organizational. Abundance was a good, but it was an organizationally produced abundance. Consensus was a good, but the crucial consensus was among potentially conflicting interest groups within organizations. For the most part these organizationally derived goods did benefit individuals. By managing organizational resources efficiently, growth resulted in material abundance that, when distributed in a reasonably equitable way, promoted positive attitudes about the utility of organization, the legitimacy of administration, and the general community of interest in expanding productivity. Thus the norms of growth, abundance, and consensus were the "guidelines of administrative practice"—administrative norms that resulted from the reconciliation of the organizational imperative with extant social values.

But, as we said in the introduction, we have had to become a different people from what we idealized for ourselves in order to accomplish the great achievements made possible by the modern organization. Traditional American values had been significantly battered about in the process of our industrial maturation, creating major social and psychological displacements—value lags separating what we thought we were from what we were forced to be as citizens within an organizational society. As technology, organization, and administration penetrated the social order, collisions of increasing severity could hardly be avoided between the values of our past and the new value requirements of the organizational imperative.

The major American value change, nearly completed at present, was largely unanticipated even a decade ago. However, warnings were sounded by perceptive observers such as William H. Whyte, Jr. His book *The Organization Man* enjoyed great success in the 1950s because it was a sensitive, accurate, and timely appraisal of some extraordinarily important events. Whyte argued that America was shifting from an individualistic ethic to a social ethic—but that the latter was not then articulated. His contention was that organizations, through their administrative systems, had imposed their imperative on all they contacted, in nearly every human situation imaginable.

> People grow restive with a mythology that is too distant from the way things actually are, and as more and more lives have been encompassed by the organization way of life, the pressures for an accompanying ideological shift have been mounting. The pressures of the group, the frustrations of individual creativity, the anonymity of achievement: are these defects to struggle against—or are they virtues in disguise? The organization man seeks a redefinition of his place on earth—a faith that will satisfy him that what he must endure has a deeper meaning than appears on the surface. He needs, in short, something that will do for him what the Protestant Ethic did once. And slowly, almost imperceptibly, a body of thought has been coalescing that does that [Whyte, 1956: 6].

Unfortunately, most people misunderstood that message and read the book simply as a nonfiction version of the popular novel *The Man in the Gray Flannel Suit*, which had appeared a year earlier in 1955. The theme of conformity was blown all out of proportion, and the essential meaning of Whyte's book, pertaining to the organizational imperative behind the value change, was almost completely overlooked.

Somewhere in the turmoil of the last decade, Whyte's warnings were forgotten. But in spite of campus riots, civil rights demonstrations, militant peace movements, and all of the other distractions of that era, the organizational imperative continued to work, and to work well indeed. As America drifted inexorably into an organization-dominated society, the contemptible organization man of the 1950s turned into a laudable model of administrative obedience. Further, in order to bring coherence and security into his life, he constantly exerted pressures to bring social values into a harmonious and reinforcing relationship with the organizational imperative, to which he had given total allegiance.

So, contrary to popular assumptions, the "ideal" man of the 1960s was *not* the "with-it" hippie, the peace activist, the committed and articulate university student, or the humanist psychologist. Rather, he was the superbly trained, functionally amoral administrator—the "best and the brightest" among us. They were we, and most of us became they—if not in actuality, then at least in spirit. The irony of it all was that we presumed we were following another path: John F. Kennedy set a style and proclaimed the doctrine of an accelerated national performance in 1960. But we did not become like him—we became like those he hired. Whyte's prophecy was fulfilled with barely the slightest public acknowledgement of what was happening.

The new faith of which Whyte wrote emerged as a public acceptance of the organizational imperative—that large-scale, technologically based administrative systems are the optimal mode of social organization. From commitment to this belief, all else follows, including the fact that the organizational imperative must go on unremittingly even if American values change. Administrators can serve the imperative regardless of whether society is faced with scarcity or an abundance of resources; whether the economy is expanding or contracting; or whether conservation or exploitation of the environment is the order of the day. The point is that through the intermediating process of administration, social values have become either actually or potentially reinforcing to the organizational imperative. In defense of this contention, in the next few pages we compare some of the displaced values of our past with some of the present, organizationally determined values that serve as administrative norms.

CULTURAL VALUES AND ADMINISTRATIVE NORMS

The new order of organizational dominion fired by the human instrumentality of administration requires specific cultural value commitments if it is to survive. To illustrate, we discuss five sets of paired values: the first indicating a value of our tradition, the second indicating the value now dominant. The pairings are: from individuality to obedience; from indispensability to dispensability; from community to specialization; from spontaneity to planning; from voluntarism to paternalism. The pairings are not exhaustive—they do not describe "either-or" situations, nor are they complete. However, they do delineate the major changes in the fundamental American value paradigm.

From Individuality to Obedience

De Tocqueville, among others, correctly observed that Americans have ranged, with marvelous inconsistence, from individuality to conformity. Nevertheless, individuality held a unique and dominant place in our tradition, no matter how badly we abused it. It has been interpreted many ways, but central to them all was the confidence the individual knew (or could know) what was best for himself. As Mill (1950: 178) wrote: "with respect to his own feelings and circumstances, the ordinary man or woman has means of knowledge immeasurable surpassing those that can be possessed by any one else." Thus, legitimacy was conferred on social, economic, and political values to the extent that they conformed with the individual's perception of the right. Granted, this was an ideal, but nonetheless it was an ideal we tried to practice. The most significant justifications for action came from the individual, and the satisfactions derived from such personal actions were infinitely superior to those that came from obedience to collectivities. All of that has now changed.

Poignantly, we still proclaim the importance of individuality on public occasions—knowing all along that very little of importance gets done without modern organization. Given that reality, we have shifted our allegiance from individuality to obedience to the organizational imperative and that obedience must be total. The belief is now that superior satisfactions are to be obtained from such obedience. In short, it is good to be obedient.

There are many things that should be said about obedience, for it is the cornerstone of the organizational edifice. However, it would take a book to develop these and related ideas in the detail they deserve (Milgram, 1974; Janis, 1972). We will limit the discussion herein to some observations about two features of obedience that are particularly important.

First, we have become an obedient people, as distinguished from a conformist people. Milgram (1974: 113) distinguishes between the two as follows:

> *Conformity* ... [is] ... the action of a subject when he goes along with his peers, people of his own status, who have no special right to direct his behavior. *Obedience* ... [is] the action of the subject who complies with authority.

To say that Americans have become an obedient people is to say that we have accepted the premise of the organizational imperative. In that way, we have become all the same, not because we are conformists—looking to significant others in search of security—but because we have *individually* committed ourselves to a single ultimate value. By all accepting (most often implicitly) the organizational imperative and by agreeing to abide by the administrative norms derived therefrom, we become, de facto, homogenous. This is different from conformity—we have not become a herd. The traditional value of individuality was NOT abolished—rather it was converted into an individual commitment to obedience to the demands of the organizational imperative. This makes us homogenous.

Second, a widely accepted administrative truism for modern organizations is the disruptiveness of individual goals that are not congruent with organizations' goals. Obviously, individual idiosyncrasies cannot be allowed to impede the effective functioning of the organization. Hence, the desired moral stance for individuals vis-à-vis the organization is functional amorality—the willingness to substitute organizational valuations for personal valuations. In order to be maximally useful to a modern organization, an individual must be personally amoral and organizationally moral. That is, he must willingly internalize the goals of the organization as his goals, without qualm. Notice, we do not say that the individual must be immoral—just that he must be ethically malleable. If the goals of his organization are socially approved, then he will be adjudged a worthy man by his society. The reverse is also true. However, the comparative goodness or badness of organizational goals, in and of themselves, is not the central issue. The key issue is the nearly unanimous acceptance, in administrative theory and practice, of the ethical superiority of the organizational imperative over individual ethical commitments. The reader may argue that he is not required to do such things, nor would he, even if management insisted. Perhaps. But obedience to authority is so deeply ingrained by now that it takes a formidable personality to be disobedient.

We are not talking about a new phenomenon altogether. Human history is filled with accounts of "true believers"—individuals who obtained meaning for their lives by committing themselves totally to mass movements. What is new is that the organizational imperative does not require the fanaticism so common to mass movements. Indeed, the organizational way of life is scarcely a mass movement at all. But the central feature of mass movements is present: the substitution of the collective absolute for personal values.

Certainly, this is *not* the age of the individual; heroes are in short supply, the individual moral virtue, while often extolled, is seldom separated from organizational needs. Thus, individual values are usually implicit, not clearly understood and, hence, weakly defined. When confronted with the clarity and force of the organizational imperative, conflicting individual values are easily converted into organizationally relevant values. By adopting the organizational imperative as the foundation of personal values, the individual articulating his moral commitments removes his agonies, and purpose is returned to private lives.

This situation is strongly reinforced by the fact that the conversion is usually painless, materially rewarding, and brings with it the distinction of being "a professional." The hallmark of professional administrative education is the emphasis it places on loyalty to the organizational imperative and the resultant administrative norms. The moral rule that emerges from this—which is nearly universal throughout our institutions—is that efficiency in the service of organizational goals equals morality. Thus, we condition ourselves for functional amorality.

To summarize, because of the successes of modern organizations, organizational values are given precedence over individual values. The individual is invariably rewarded for such value substitution. This necessitates a belief in man's moral malleability—that he can make value substitutions whenever and as often as required. Once that malleability is accepted, there is no "reason" why people should hold values other than those that are organizationally useful (Scott and Hart, 1971; Hart and Scott, 1972). Thus the burden of individual responsibility for identifying a personal value system is removed. The organizational imperative is now sufficient.

From Indispensability to Dispensability

An important value in the American tradition has been the right of individuals to feel indispensable to the groups, organizations, and communities of which they are a part. An honorable man could feel confident that his loss would have a profound effect on those who surrounded him. For beyond sorrow was the fact that their world would be less without him. The reader may protest, arguing that throughout history—including our own—men have dispensed with one another in callous and brutal ways. It is also safe to assume that most people have never really felt indispensable. Be that as it may, the *ideal* of personal indispensability has been central to our tradition as one of the important rewards earned through good effort. Simply, it was the sense of being necessary to one's world.

Presently, the organizational imperative demands that nothing be indispensable and that, indeed, dispensability is a prized commodity. The modern American economy is built on the dispensability of things. Obsolescense serves the major purpose in enriching organizations. Our lives are spent in surroundings of constant material replacement, because our technology and our economy have made it more efficient to dispose of things rather than to reuse them.

All of this is well known. What is less well understood is how an individual within a society that exalts dispensability might eventually come to view himself. Alternatively, how does a society which demands that nothing be indispensable come to value the individual? The answer is obvious. The organizational imperative requires that each person understand he is dispensable and, further, that this is a good thing.

Modern organizations cannot allow individuals to become indispensable. If they did, the organization then would become dependent on those individuals. That prospect is anathema to administrative theory and practice. Allow us to illustrate with the metaphor of the organization as machine. It assumes that in the organization, as in the machine, each part is linked as efficiently as possible with all other parts. Each performs its specific tasks in a productive rhythm with all of the others. If there is an ample supply of spares, any part of the machine is dispensable, even though some parts are more expensive to replace than others. The primary mission of the engineer is not only to keep the machine running, but also to ensure an adequate supply of spare parts.

So it is with the people in an organization, *at all levels and in all capacities*. Personnel must be instantly replaceable by others with similar abilities, with a minimal loss of efficiency during the substitution. If there are enough human spares, then there need never be any major upheavals with the turnover of personnel. Like the engineer, one of the primary responsibilities of the administrator is to ensure that an adequate supply of spare parts is immediately available, including his own. Indeed, how often do we hear the incantation, "Train your own replacement!"? The difficulty, of course, is that while no machine part needs to be convinced of its dispensability, a human being does.

This educational task is central to all schools of administration. Books, articles, and teachers hammer away at the theme that the individual has no *right* to expect to become indispensable, nor should he attempt to. It is stressed (as a "fact of life" in the "real world") that the dream of personal indispensability is childish and, even worse, organizationally bad. The point was well made by one of our graduate students, who observed that he was like a sausage being prepared for consumption by a large organization. He argued that nothing should be stuffed into him that would give his prospective organization "indigestion." This may be a bit blunt, but some variant of this evaluation is drilled into our students as an essential part of the administrative "attitude" they will take with them onto the job.

But the process does not stop at the boundaries of the employing organization. As the organizational imperative has touched more and more social values, this attitude has been extended into all areas of our lives. Thus, there is a pervasive belief in our society that indispensability is an illusion, nowhere to be found. As a final defense, the reader might argue that he is indispensable to his family. Perhaps. But, given the condition of the American family, the unfortunate truth is that the economic role played by the father could be more efficiently performed by an organization. Certainly this theme is constantly stressed by the advertising of our large financial institutions. Thus, a lethal blow is thrown at the last area where personal indispensability might be found. If man has an innate need to be necessary in his world, then this particular value transition is quite destructive. People convinced of their personal dispensability suffer many consequences, from alienation to existential fear. To avoid these conditions, most of us flee more deeply into the organization, searching for security. Ironically, we find there that we are the most dispensable commodity of all.

From Community to Specialization

Part of the American's magnificent inconsistency has been a stubborn commitment to the seemingly contradictory values of individuality and community (Nisbet, 1969; McWilliams, 1973; Stein, 1972). However, the values of community and indispensability went hand in hand, for one who was valued for his personal qualities contributed something unique to the warm, supporting, and persisting nature of the community. When he was gone, the quality of the communal relationships could never be reexperienced in quite the same manner.

The organizational imperative has diminished and transformed the value of community. In this instance, the organizational imperative requires that the individual's dedication be primarily to a specialty that is harmonious with and contributory to the ultimate success of an organization. Clearly, specialization does not exist for its own sake. For specialization to have any meaning, it must have *utility* for the organization, whether one is a vice-president or a foreman. The stewardship of one's responsibility is measured by its contribution to the total organization. Loyalty must not be given, therefore, to the work group, to the place, or to some abstract ideals of honor, hospitality, or obligation; rather loyalty must be to the specialized function the successful performance of which adds to the whole organizational effort. In short, the organization has evolved as an inadequate surrogate for community.

It is important to note that the criteria on which individual worth is evaluated in a community are quite different from the criteria by which individual utility is assessed in an organization. An individual's worth, in organizational terms, is not measured affectively in the quality of his relationship with others. When has friendship ever been considered as a standard in wage and salary administration? Worth is measured quantitatively, wherever possible, by the level of one's specialized performance relative to the achievement of organizational goals.

Finally, specialization and dispensability are comfortable—even necessary—partners. Specialty has aways been treated as depersonalized in administrative theory and practice. The most efficient way to meet the obligations of stewardship is to objectify, as far as possible, what people do in organizations and to assign quantitative standards in order to judge performance. These standards allow little room for affective considerations, other than those that might have organizational utility. There is no room for community, in the best sense of the word, within modern organizations, since in order to thrive it must have stability and continuity of human relationships. The loss of meaning in one's life because of the absence of community cannot be replaced easily by the rewards that come from specialization.

From Spontaneity to Planning

Another value central to the American tradition has been spontaneity. It was interpreted in a number of ways. In its more dramatic form, it was believed that people should be willing to abandon the security of the known in order to venture into the unknown, taking risks for the sake of personal gain. But in its most significant form, it was believed that the really urgent problems most often would be solved by individuals through spontaneous, creative action. While such spontaneity was unanticipatable in detail, it was assumed that it would somehow occur, in mysterious ways and at appropriate times, to the benefit of society in general or to specific organizations in particular. The spontaneous, creative, enterprising individual would work wonders in all areas, from farming to industry, and even to the political system. The results of such actions would be more efficacious ways of doing things, producing more jobs, goods, and services.

Thus, spontaneity became an integral part of the American entrepreneurial ethic, defined as ingenuity or "Yankee know-how." The moral lesson in the Horatio Alger and Frank Meriwell stories was simply that a young man with "pluck and luck" could move inexorably ahead in business, finance, or whatever. The essence of the American value of spontaneity is found in this pluck-and-luck theme. Pluck meant the motivation to act creatively (even impulsively), in unforeseen circumstances, to solve problems. Luck pertained to the element of risk that a plucky person had to assume if he was to make his way successfully through life. The interesting twist in these stories was that if a person took action from an instinctive knowledge of what was right, Lady Luck would bend in his favor. So individual, spontaneous action was prized because it was believed that it brought favorable outcomes for all concerned, especially when guided by a sense of moral rectitude. This gave Americans an additional reason to be optimistic about the future. The uncertainties of the future were not to be feared, for they were the breeding ground of opportunity.

However, this has been changed by the administrative needs of modern organization. As we have said, the world of administration is concerned with complex, short-term problems. Nevertheless, the future must obviously be taken into account in order to set goals, to map strategies, to make budgets, to establish policies, to allocate resources, and so on. Administrators must plan, and there is no way they can plan for spontaneity. Thus, the organizational imperative not only reduces the premium formerly placed on spontaneity, the imperative makes spontaneity dysfunctional. Planning has replaced spontaneity as the primary means of handling the uncertainties of the future. It requires speculation about events that are anticipated but as yet unrealized. So planning is, in some ways, incompatible with the rule of pragmatism. But the needs of modern organizations have forced a reconciliation between the two, and this reconciliation has caused the change in the way spontaneity is perceived and valued.

As more investment capital is committed to plant and equipment, as the time span between the beginning and end of tasks or projects lengthens, as more specialized manpower is hired, and as the flexibility of an organization diminishes in relation to its increased fixed resources, long-range planning activities expand dramatically. The problem is how to adjust the planning function to the rule of pragmatism. Certain planning practices have evolved to this end. First, guesswork must be eliminated. This necessitates the development and application of a technology of forecasting. Second, as many external "variables" as possible must be controlled. They influence the future direction of the organization in uncertain ways. By controlling these variables, today's forecasts are made into tomorrow's self-fulfilling prophecies. Third, the possibilities that aberrant individual behavior will unpredictably alter the course of planned future events must be eradicated. This practice has two subconditions. Behavior in the planning *process* itself must be controlled. This means that planning ideally should be a collective process, because group performance is more visible and predictable than individual performance. Then, the implementation of plans must be controlled by means that are visible and understandable to all involved.

Control, therefore, is the way that planning and pragmatism are reconciled. That control and planning are conceptual counterparts is a frequently cited, but poorly understood, administrative adage. However, it is a certainty that as planning grows, controlling also grows, if for no other reason than to prevent random or aberrant events from confounding plans. This explains why spontaneity is by now a less valued, even dangerous behavior. It is unpredictable, and therefore uncontrollable. So, while the organization may lose some advantage from spontaneously creative acts, this loss is offset by the more easily controlled behavior that arises from collective planning processes.

From Voluntarism to Paternalism

In the past, when individuals desired concerted action to achieve common aims, it was assumed that they would combine in voluntary interest groups and that their resultant efforts would be sufficient to accomplish their goals. Associations of freely participating individuals were so much a part of the American way of doing things that the traditional political theory of pluralism and the economic theory of countervailing power rested in substantial degree on the efficacy of voluntarism. This principle molded the familiar American ideals of industrial democracy, collective self-determination, federalism, decentralization, government by consent, and so on.

We have traditionally believed that social phenomena are the result of deliberate decisions traceable to individual acts. This belief implied autonomy, free will, individual responsibility and accountability, and generalized social norms that guided the conduct of individuals in making choices. However, it is also true that we believed in the usefulness of collective action, especially when the leverage of power was required to advance one's own interests in the face of opposing collective interests. So voluntarism allowed a person to retain the rights and obligations of individualism, but it also permitted him to take advantage of the power of concerted action, within a self-governing organizational framework. The principle of voluntarism was accepted through American society. Laborers, farmers, accountants, consumers, doctors, professors, engineers, businessmen, lawyers, and many others have formed voluntary associations at different times in our history, with varying degrees of success. The point is that voluntarism reflected a compromise between individualism and collectivisms; presenting us with an ingenious amalgamation of these polarities.

Voluntarism was an effective but fragile compromise. It was always under assault—both from the side of individualism and from the side of collectivism. For example, even the most conservative—craft unions still are damned in some quarters because they allegedly curtail individual autonomy. Political lobbyists are portrayed as greedy power merchants whose interests are opposed to those of individual citizens. The argument used against the unionization of university professors is that individual freedom, for many the sine qua non of scholarly excellent, will be destroyed. Yet, at present, the most devastating attacks on voluntarism are not coming from those who advocate individualism. Rather, the strongest assault is coming from those who advocate collectivism, and it has taken form as organizational paternalism.

It is not as if paternalism—the benevolent concern of management for the welfare of their employee "children"—is something new on the organizational scene. The spirit of business welfarism has been prevalent in Great Britain and in the United States for a long time. This spirit initially grew out of the social doctrines of Calvinism, which imposed on the "elect" the responsibility for the collective spiritual welfare of their charges. Following the industrial revolution in England such responsibilities were reflected in the rules of work and worship that were widely circulated and applied in factory towns. Regardless of how primitive, convoluted, and cynical this early paternalistic thinking may seem to us now, it was justified as following Christian teachings.

As social change swept through Great Britain and America, it produced major transformations in paternalistic doctrines. First, society became secularized, so that the religious justification for paternalism became irrelevant. Second, organizational economic benefits became the dominant rationale. As Carnegie (1902: V) put it: "The employer who helps his workmen through education, recreation, and social uplift, helps himself." Third, responding to the challenge of unionism in the 1920s, management adopted the paternalistic "American plan" as a counterstrategy.

Paternalism was used by management for the practical purposes of either fighting unions or raising worker productivity. While the focus of paternalism shifted from the spiritual to the temporal, it remained basically a collective undertaking, ideologically justified as the means of promoting general employee welfare. In any event, there was nothing in paternalism that allowed for any tolerance of the voluntaristic principle of self-determination.

With the rise of sophisticated professional management in the 1930s another shift occurred in the doctrine of paternalism that can be traced directly to the rule of stewardship. This new aspect of the doctrine is, in some respects, the most effective attack on voluntarism yet mounted. It is the result of some fundamental value changes, directly attributable to the growing dominance of organizations in our society and to a concomitant influence of the behavioral sciences over social policy-making. While the first assault of paternalism on voluntarism was spiritual in origin and the second was clearly secular, the third and most recent assault is therapeutic.

As we explained earlier, professional administration from its inception has been guided by the rule of stewardship. The separation of corporate ownership from control gave managers virtual sovereign power to dispose of the resources of the organization in ways that would most satisfy the interests of its clientele. When stewardship and the separation of ownership and control were being examined analytically for the first time (Berle and Means, 1933), emphasis was on the management of material resources, particularly financial resources. However, it did not take long for the grasp of managerial stewardship to extend to the human resources of an organization as well. How were they to deal with them?

Managers of modern organizations quickly succumbed to the utility of behavioral science therapy values. The lessons of the various humanistic movements were learned and put into practice by administrators. These lessons contained the following premises. First, "normal" people behave dysfunctionally in organizations if they do not accept the imperatives of obedient behavior. Second, the administrative elite of the organization has sovereign power to impress the norms of the organization on the people in it, for their own welfare. Third, organizationally "deviant" behavior (and values) should be "cured" by applying behavioral science techniques rather than punishment.

Paternalism has traveled the entire route, starting with spiritual welfare, moving through physical welfare, and ending with the mental welfare of employees. The last is the most insidious, since in our age the best way to ensure obedience is to create a state of psychological dependency. This is exactly what the new form of paternalism does—it defines self-determination, autonomy, and the other conditions of individualism as illness. Clearly, voluntarism as well is a principle that therapeutic paternalism cannot abide. Thus we have completed the circle, returning to where we began this discussion of changing values—to Milgram's analysis of "obedience to authority." There is no more despotic authority than the "father" righteously legislating the terms of mental health for his children, and equipped with the means for enforcing these terms.

CONCLUSION

The organizational imperative is the core of our well-entrenched value paradigm, which has displaced the values of our tradition. The period of transition was marked by feelings of alienation and dislocation among large numbers of people as those traditional values were found inappropriate to the demands of the present. Regardless, the organizational imperative prevailed and has assumed its final shape. Not all people are committed to the organizational imperative. There are still some few who live in the ignored corners of our society who have little to do with it. Nonetheless, the organizational imperative is the dominant article of faith for all administrators of the innumerable, overlapping, and inescapable organizations that make up contemporary society. Theirs is the significant involvement. But this is also true of workers who must conform to the rules of modern organization and those others whose lives are inextricably involved as clients of modern organizations. In short, *all* must embrace the values of the organizational imperative if they want to obtain the great rewards promised by modern organization.

This promise seemed about to be fulfilled in the decade of the 1950s.

The unanticipated turmoil of the 1960s seemed but a temporary setback. During this time the deep-rooted sense of American optimism persisted. We believed that our leaders, public and private, would somehow assert themselves and get us successfully through the heavy weather. Our optimism has not been justified.

The 1970s have brought considerable national peril, exacerbated by the war in Vietnam, festering domestic inequalities, government venality, incivility in our major cities, shortages of basic commodities, serious economic inflation, and a major recession. The dreary list could be multiplied, but, what is even worse, we know that the future will be filled with even greater perils. Somehow, the promise of the leadership of the best and the brightest has turned sour, and the people are increasingly aware of it.

There is evidence of growing public doubt that our expectations for continuous growth and affluence are realizable. Conditions point toward a non-growth, stable-state economy. Yet politicians, public administrators, and business executives resist policies of economic stabilization, reduction of agency services, or the leveling of sales volume and corporate earnings. Even more, schools of administration will have nothing to do with such topics. Who, for instance, has ever taken a course in an administrative curriculum on "How to Shrink a Business"? Articles and books are seldom found in the professional literature of administration advocating models of nongrowth, although there are some notable exceptions. Such things do not happen, because they are *seemingly* foreign to the organizational imperative, and hence to the norms of administrative theory and practice.

But modern organizations can exist in such an environment. Further, public attitudes about these matters can be conveniently changed and with little disruption (Ellul, 1965). The organizational imperative will *easily* survive. It has the power and the flexibility to ride out these crises without having to change its essential features. In fact, the a priori propositions and their rules will be strengthened in the process of responding to those crises. The major casualty will be the individual. Is there any doubt that modern organizations, public or private, will arrive in that unprecedented future in much better shape than the individual?

Thus, we can anticipate the strengthening of the organizational imperative as large-scale organizations restructure themselves to meet the future challenges. This will require, of course, an intensification of mass loyalty to the organizational imperative. However, that can be accomplished once those in the significant positions in society understand what is needed.

Given this situation, we cannot just sit tight and "muddle through," on the anticipation that everything will turn out well. We are confronted with the problems right now, and administrators have begun to solve those problems. Now if this new paradigm is not harmful to man qua man, then these "soft" normative issues can be dismissed and we can get down to the "hard" work of making organizations more effective. But, if one believes that the paradigm is destructive to man, then corrections must be made immediately.

Thus, the most fundamental task of our time is to provide an answer to the ancient and persistent question, *What is man that these things should or should not be done to him?* Is there anything innate in man that is offended, and perhaps even destroyed, by the values of the new paradigm? Unless that question is answered first, there is really no reason to resist the organizational imperative. In fact, resistance is counterproductive, for it just slows down the fight for organizational survival in times of great peril.

Further, the question cannot be resolved by empirical means, for by its very nature, it transcends empiricism. It will require moral discourse of a high order and a *deliberate* selection of new values that enhance that which is morally innate in man, if indeed there is such a thing. To choose values deliberately is unprecedented in human history, but it must be done (Gorney, 1972: 8-9).

References

Berle, A. A., Jr., and G. S. Means (1933) *The Modern Corporation and Private Property*. New York: Macmillan.

Carnegie, A. (1902) *The Empire of Business*. New York: Doubleday, Page.

Ellul, J. (1965) *Propaganda*. New York: Alfred A. Knops.

Gorney, R. (1972) *The Human Agenda*. New York: Simon & Schuster.

Hart, D. K. and W. G. Scott (1972) "The optimal image of man for systems theory." *Academy of Management J.* 15 (December): 531-540.

Janis, I. L. (1972) *Victims of Groupthink*. Boston: Houghton Mifflin.

Kuhn, T. S. (1970) *The Structure of Scientific Revolutions*. Chicago: Univ. of Chicago Press.

McWilliams, W. C. (1973) *The Idea of Fraternity in America*. Berkeley: Univ. of California Press.

Milgram, S. (1974) *Obedience to Authority*. New York: Harper & Row.

Mill, J. S. (1950) *Utilitarianism, Liberty, and Representative Government*. New York: Dutton.

Nisbet, R. A. (1969) *The Quest for Community*. New York: Oxford Univ. Press.

Scott, W. G. and D. K. Hart (1971) "The moral nature of man in organizations," *Academy of Management J.* 14 (June): 241-255.

Scott, W. G. and D. K. Hart (1973) "Administrative crisis: the neglect of metaphysical speculation." *Public Administration Rev.* 33 (September/October): 415-422.

Stein, M. R. (1972) *The Eclipse of Community*. Princeton: Princeton Univ. Press.

Whyte, W. H., Jr. (1956) *The Organization Man*. Garden City, N.Y.: Anchor.